P9-AOB-181

The Other Nuremberg
The Untold Story of the Japanese War Crimes Trials

At the end of World War II, when the International Military Tribunal for the Far East convened in Tokyo, eleven judges representing *three quarters of the world's population* were faced with the awesome task of determining the guilt or innocence of those Japanese in the dock. The Tokyo trials lasted two and a half years. (The trials of the Nazi war criminals at Nuremberg lasted only ten months.) The charges against the accused included "murder, extermination, enslavement, deportment and other inhumane acts." How the trial was resolved is a chilling chapter chapter of history.

Critical Acclaim for
The Other Nuremburg

"Gripping and sometimes gory... According to Brackman the policy decision to protect Hirohito was so intense that the chief prosecutor contacted Toja secretly to make sure that he did not inadvertently implicate the Emperor... Rich material indeed."   *—Philadelphia Inquirer*

"As a harvest of facts, stories, and vignettes from the American occupation of Japan in general, and the Tokyo trial in particular, *The Other Nuremberg* is a remarkable work. As a sharp indictment of Japanese wartime behavior, it makes compelling reading."   *—Los Angeles Times*

"A smoothe chronological summation of the proceedings... and some especially lively insights concerning the famous issue of The Man Who Was Not There."   *—The Washington Post*

"Highly readable... A public service."   *—Baltimore Sun*

"A lesson for our times"   *—San Francisco Chronicle*

"A personal and insightful account"   *—Library Journal*

"A wealth of new material... A book that is long overdue."   *—Publishers Weekly*

"The author makes the wartime Japanese political scene come alive."   *—Kirkus Reviews*

"A valuable contribution to history"   —Kingsport *Times-News*

"A valuable service in reminding the world of unpleasant truths"   —Los Angeles *Daily News*

THE OTHER NUREMBERG

Other books by Arnold C. Brackman:

A DELICATE ARRANGEMENT
THE LUCK OF NINEVEH
THE SEARCH FOR THE GOLD OF TUTANKHAMEN
THE DREAM OF TROY
THE LAST EMPEROR
THE COMMUNIST COLLAPSE IN INDONESIA
SOUTHEAST ASIA'S SECOND FRONT
INDONESIAN COMMUNISM

THE OTHER NUREMBERG

THE UNTOLD STORY OF THE TOKYO WAR CRIMES TRIALS

Arnold C. Brackman

QUILL · WILLIAM MORROW
NEW YORK

H-Y LIB
(W)

JX
5438.8
.B72
1987
C.2

HARVARD-YENCHING LIBRARY
HARVARD UNIVERSITY
2 DIVINITY AVENUE

YANKEE

APR 12 1989

W 3544.84/144 (c.2)

Copyright © 1987 by Arnold C. Brackman

All rights reserved. No part of this book may be reproduced or utilized in
any form or by any means, electronic or mechanical, including
photocopying, recording or by any information storage and retrieval
system, without permission in writing from the Publisher. Inquiries should
be addressed to Permissions Department, William Morrow and Company,
Inc., 105 Madison Ave., New York, N.Y. 10016.

Library of Congress Cataloging-in-Publication Data

Brackman, Arnold C.
The other Nuremberg : the untold story of the Tokyo war trials /
Arnold C. Brackman.
p.   cm.
Bibliography: p.
Includes index.
ISBN 0-688-07957-1 (pbk.)
1. Tokyo Trial, Tokyo, Japan, 1946–1948.   I. Title.
[JX5438.8.B72   1988]
341.6′9′02685213—dc19   88-2712
CIP

Printed in the United States of America

2 3 4 5 6 7 8 9 10

BOOK DESIGN BY BERNARD SCHLEIFER

For Helen J. Beattie, F. Fraser Bond, Gregory Mason, C. Hayes Sprague, and Leon R. Whipple, friends and mentors

Foreword

The research for the book spanned more than a quarter of a century and over 100,000 miles. In the text and the notes I have identified many of the sources I have relied on. Written material on the Japanese war-crimes trial is thin, especially in comparison with that available on the Nuremberg trial. John R. Lewis's *Uncertain Judgment: A Bibliography of War Crimes Trials* (Santa Barbara, Calif., and Oxford: Clio Books, 1979) contains 1,290 entries relating to the tribunal at Nuremberg and a scant 231 on the International Military Tribunal for the Far East. This volume also contains 143 entries on the Vietnam War, chiefly on My Lai. At the IMTFE, a thousand My Lais emerged.

Even Lewis's list is misleading on the paucity of material on the Tokyo trial; as of this writing few books have appeared on the subject. Perforce, in my research I have been compelled to rely principally on the voluminous trial transcript (some 49,000 pages) and on other material in my own files covering the period 1946–48: notebooks, official and unofficial documents, typescripts, copies of my original United Press stories, and articles published in the Japanese, U.S., and foreign press. I have bridged the gaps in this material by using the U.S. National Archives and Records Service, which holds a selection of transcripts, court papers, court exhibits and rejected exhibits, and so forth, as well as using interviews conducted in person or by correspondence.

In the present era of fabricating quotes—phony "docudramas" on television, the Janet Cooke affair in the press, and "faction" in publishing—I must stress at the outset that every quote in this book is genuine. The only liberties I have taken are in spelling, tense, and grammar, especially in reproducing the English transcript of the trial, which is often uneven (for example, the interchangeable use of "fliers" and "flyers").

The exchange of ideas and the assistance in ferreting out information provided by hundreds of people have been invaluable in this work.

Aristides Lazarus, defense counsel for Field Marshal Shunroku Hata, was of great help, not only in several hours of interview but also through his voluminous letter writing and his zest in everything he does. Judge A. Frederick Mignone of Connecticut took time out of his busy schedule to be interviewed in his chambers. Leslie S. Nakashima, prewar and postwar staffer in the United Press Tokyo bureau, worked as my translator. His was the first Japanese house I entered on my arrival in Tokyo in 1946, and there I had the honor and pleasure of meeting his wife, Yachiyo, and their baby daughter, Kazue. In 1981 Les accompanied me on my visit to Sugamo Prison and the site of the courtroom at Ichigaya. Among others who helped were Timothy P. Mulligan of the NARS Military Archives Division; Shozo Nakano and K. Okamura of the National Diet Library, Tokyo; J. Pavey of the Imperial War Museum, London; Frederick W. Pernell of the General Archives Division, National Archives.

Judge B.V.A. Röling, now a professor at the Rijksuniversiteit, Groningen, the Netherlands, was generous in taking time to answer the many questions I put to him. He was also kind enough to send me an English-language version of a lecture he delivered in Haarlem in 1978, which was published the same year in *de Haarlemse Voordrachten,* No. XXXVIII (English title, "Some Aspects of the Tokyo Trial"). In it, he makes the point that Nuremberg has been paid more attention than Tokyo because the accused there were well known in the United States and Europe. Also see his contribution in *Buddhism and Culture* (Kyoto, 1960), "The Tokyo Trial in Retrospect." Röling also wrote the introduction to the unabridged edition of *Judgments of the International Military Tribunal for the Far East,* published in two volumes by the University of Amsterdam in 1977. (Astonishingly, this was the first time all six opinions of the justices were published together.)

To this day no Allied government has printed a complete transcript of the trial.

I am grateful to John Barton of the media service at Western Connecticut State University; Mary T. Brody, reference librarian at the New York Public library; Marilyn Bullock, my typist; Barbara Burger of the National Archives audiovisual division; George Chalou, director of the reference branch, Washington National Records, Suitland, Maryland; and Edwin R. Coffee of the Military Archives Division. Michael T. C. Chen of Taipei, Taiwan, was invaluable as aide, liaison, and interpreter and in managing to locate Justice Mei's brother, Professor Mei Ju-an of Cheng Chi University, Taiwan; S. T. Hsieh (Tjia) also provided help in this effort. I am also indebted to Beverly Coleman, Valentine Deale, and Robert Donihi, who were kind enough to be interviewed; to N. J. Flanagan and W. L. Fogarty of the Australian War Memorial in Canberra; to Robert Furlonger, to George A. Furness of Furness, Sato and Ishizawa, to G. Osmond Hyde, and to Charles C. Kohler of the U.S. Army; to Mary Kohn, former chief reference librarian at Western Connecticut State University, who always managed to come through on my requests, although at times the difficulties seemed insurmountable; and to my editor, Bruce Lee.

Further help was provided by Sol Sanders; Masaei Sato, Japanese curator at the University of Michigan's Asian Library; Frank Joseph Shulman, director of the East Asia Collection the McKeldin Library of the University of Maryland, where I made use of some of the papers of Gordon W. Prange, and George W. Ware, Jr., then a graduate student there; Takeshi Sumitani of the National Diet Library, Tokyo; Raymond R. M. Tai, deputy director, General Government Information office, Taipei; John E. Taylor of the Military Archives Division, who unfailingly answered my numerous letters and telephone calls; Ryochi Tobe of the National Defense Academy, Yokosuka, Japan; Kumao Toyada, who provided me with information regarding General Suzuki; and George Wagner of the Military Archives Division. I also made use of the archives at the Australian War Memorial, Canberra, especially Sir William Webb's papers.

Carrington Williams, defense counsel for Naoki Hoshino, sent a five-page answer to my inquiries that was most helpful and enlightening—worthy of publication in itself. I'm also grateful for the help of the late George Yamaoka, for many years associated with the law firm of Hill, Betts and Nash; Onuma Yasuaki, of the law faculty at the University of Tokyo, who tipped me off to an article he had written about the trial in the *Asahi* (December 18 and 19, 1980); and Major General Shih Mei-yu, chief justice of the war crimes court in China, who also consented to be interviewed. Where opinions and perspectives on the trial appeared to be lacking, it is not for lack of effort. Among those from whom I was unable to get a statement was Professor J. English, who replied, "As a matter of policy, I do not comment and have never commented on the trial." Also I wrote General Douglas MacArthur in 1963 for comments on the trial and did not receive a reply.

For those interested in further reading, a superb listing of U.S. government holdings, compiled by Jarritus Wolfinger, is contained in the booklet *Preliminary Inventory of the Record of the International Military Tribunal for the Far East* (Washington, D.C.: National Archives and Records Service, PI 180/RG 238, General Services Administration). Another excellent source for material on the Tokyo trial is *The Allied Occupation of Japan, 1945–1952* (Chicago: American Library Association, 1972) by Robert E. Ward and Frank Joseph Shulman.

An excellent source on links between prewar Germany and Japan is veteran foreign correspondent Nessell Tiltman's *Nightmares Must End* (London: Mayflower Press, 1940), which illustrates how Germany and Japan marched to the same drum. Russian-Japanese relations are detailed by Leonard Mosley in *Hirohito, Emperor of Japan* (Englewood Cliffs, N.J.: Prentice-Hall, 1966). Mosley's Hirohito comes out as a strong personality and a man of integrity. Otto D. Tolischus' *Tokyo Record* (New York: Reynal and Hitchcock, 1943) covers the period from February 1941 to August 1943, when Tolischus was in Tokyo as a correspondent for *The New York Times*. Soon after Pearl Harbor was attacked, he was sent to prison. (I disagree with Tolischus on one point: He writes that the geisha is romanticized in the West but considered a prostitute in Japan; I would not class a geisha as a prostitute unless she was specifically identified as one.)

Among sources in Japanese, particularly useful are *Hiroku Itagaki Seishiro,* by Seishiro Itagaki (Tokyo: Fuyo Shobo, 1972); *Sugamo nikki,* by Mamoru Shigemitsu (Tokyo: Bungei Shunju, 1953); *Heiwa no Hakken,* by Shinsho Hanayama (Tokyo: Asahi Shimbunsha, 1949); and *Kido Koichi nikki,* by Koichi Kido (Tokyo: Tokyo Daigaku Shuppankai, 1966).

* * *

In the Japanese language a person's family name precedes the given name, as Tojo Hideki. In this book I have followed the standard Anglo-American practice of placing the given name before the surname—Hideki Tojo. Also, the Chinese names in this book follow the pre-1978 Wade-Giles romanization system, which was used in standard histories of pre-Communist China and in which I was trained when I studied Chinese as a college student.

Contents

Introduction

In 1931, at the age of eight, I decided to become a foreign correspondent in Asia. My father was in the Chinese art field, and my boyish imagination was stirred by the Japanese invasion of China that year. I still retain my first news clippings of that war, when the names of such Japanese warlords as Itagaki and Doihara became familiar to me. By 1937 I had learned new names, such as Matsui, the Japanese commander during the Rape of Nanking, where no less than a quarter of a million men, women, and children were slaughtered over a six-week period. (By the time the war on the Chinese mainland ended in 1945, 6 million civilians had been killed by the Japanese—the forgotten holocaust.) After December 7, 1941, of course, I added still more names to memory, notably that of Hideki Tojo, who was premier and war minister from 1941 to 1944.

In 1946, at the age of twenty-three, I found myself in Tokyo as a United Press staff correspondent, covering the major Japanese war-crimes trial, the International Military Tribunal for the Far East (IMTFE). In the dock were the familiar names and faces of my childhood, among them Itagaki, Dohihara, Matsui, Tojo, and twenty-four others. These were the "Class A" war criminals, indicted on fifty-five counts of crimes against peace, outright murder, and other war crimes. The trial was the Japanese counterpart of the Nuremberg court, where the trial of twenty-four leading Nazis had begun in November 1945.

In Tokyo, the court was assembled at Ichigaya, which had been the hilltop headquarters for the Japanese military during the war. The occupation authorities, under General Douglas MacArthur, had transformed the building's huge old auditorium into an ultramodern courtroom setting, complete with wood paneling, klieg lights, and a glass-enclosed booth for the translators. The stage was indeed set for what the tribunal's chief judge called "the trial of the century."

My own seat for the spectacle was in the front row of the press section. The justices of the eleven Allied nations* sitting in judgment were perched on an elevated platform about fifty feet to my left; the accused were arrayed in the dock on my right. Between judges and accused, in the pit, were the legal gladiators: the prosecuting and defense attorneys, their legal aides, and their law clerks. The spectators sat in the balcony. Almost everyone in the courtroom wore earphones, since the official proceedings were conducted in both English and Japanese. The trial lasted two and a half years, including the seven months it took the justices to arrive at a judgment. More than 200,000 spectators attended the trial, 150,000 of them Japanese. No less than 419 witnesses—from buck privates to the last emperor of China—gave testimony. In addition, 779 affidavits and depositions were introduced in evidence. On any given day there were about 1,000 people in court—judges, accused, lawyers, legal staffs, MPs, stenographers, translators, cameramen, spectators, Japanese and foreign press. Seven news agencies had regular correspondents at the trial—Reuters, Agence France-Presse, the Chinese News Agency, Tass, and the three American news agencies: Associated Press, International News Service, and my own United Press.

Each morning in the press room the newsmen were handed a transcript of the previous day's testimony; I believe I was the only one who squirreled away these papers with the vague thought of writing a book after the trial was over. Each day I filed three or four stories, timed with the midmorning, lunch, midafternoon, or end-of-day recess. I did this five days a week, week after week, month after month. I sat through most of the prosecution's case and half of the defense's before being pulled out by UP and sent on another assignment in Southeast Asia. But even after I left,

*Australia, Canada, China, France, Great Britain, India, the Netherlands, New Zealand, the Philippines, the Soviet Union, and the United States of America.

the press section saw to it that I continued to receive the tribunal's daily transcript. No correspondent covered the trial in its entirety. In fact, as far as I have been able to determine, there was no one who attended every session. Every judge was periodically absent for one reason or another (the first American judge resigned early in the trial, and the president of the IMTFE, an Australian, was gone for more than two months during part of the defense presentation). The accused were also absent regularly. Two died of natural causes during the trial, one was committed to an insane asylum, and others were either hospitalized briefly or absent periodically to confer in prison with counsel. Prosecuting and defense attorneys came and went like waves at sea.

In the years since I sat in the courtroom, thinking about the trial, I have puzzled over the fact that hardly anyone today remembers it or attaches much importance to it. The names of the war criminals are for the most part forgotten. So are their deeds. Some people dimly recall a handful of Japan's atrocities during World War II: the Rape of Nanking, the Bataan Death March, the POWs and other slave laborers building the Siam-Burma Death Railway, including the bridge over the River Kwai. But who remembers the mass murder of 18,000 Filipino men, women, and children in the town of Lipa? Or the murder of 450 French and Vietnamese POWs at Langson, Vietnam, where the Japanese first machine-gunned them in the legs and then dispatched the squirming targets in a bayonet drill? At the trial we heard so many horrifying statistics that after a while they became meaningless. I can hardly remember all of them now, but I will never forget the words of those individuals who had suffered man's inhumanity to man, and somehow survived.

The testimony was punctuated with references to the beheading of prisoners—on the decks of hellships transporting prisoners, on remote South Pacific islets, in jungle clearings stretching from New Guinea to the Burma-India border. Incredibly, like Lazarus, there were survivors among the "beheaded" who came back from the dead to testify at the IMTFE, among them an Australian. He was Colin F. Brien, and I remember him clearly. The Japanese had captured Brien on February 26, 1942, during the fighting at Singapore. On March 1, his hands were bound and he was taken into a jungle clearing where a platoon of soldiers, a dozen officers, and a freshly dug, shallow grave awaited him. "I was told to sit down with my knees, legs, and feet projecting into the grave," the youthful Brien said hesitantly. "My hands were tied behind my back. A small towel was tied over my eyes, and then—"

He paused, groping for words as he relived the moment.

"Go ahead," Alan Mansfield, the Australian associate prosecutor, prompted.

"My shirt was unbuttoned and pulled back over my back, exposing the lower part of my neck," Brien continued. "My head was bent forward, and after a few seconds I felt a heavy, dull blow sensation on the back of my neck."

Brien stopped again, and Mansfield prompted, "Yes?"

"I realized I was still alive, but pretended to be dead and fell over on my right side; after that, I lost consciousness."

When he awoke, he found himself at the bottom of a shallow grave with wooden pilings and clods of fresh earth atop him, his hands still tied behind his back. He was drenched in sweet-smelling blood.

He lay there for about an hour, Brien testified, and then dislodged the debris above him with his feet. Emerging from the grave, he crawled into hiding in a nearby patch of *lalang,* a tall and thick grass. He was recaptured, and the amazed Japanese put him in a hospital and then a POW camp, where he survived the war as a novelty.

For every case of beheading at the trial, there were countless accounts of gang rape. Is gang rape worse than beheading? Given the evidence I listened to at the IMTFE, the answer would appear to be yes. One of the most harrowing tales was recounted by Esther Garcia Moras, a dark-eyed Manila woman in her mid-twenties who had been rounded up by the Japanese on February 9, 1945, with about 1,500 persons. She and two dozen other young women were segregated and confined to a room, unfurnished except for a few mattresses, in the Bay View Hotel.

The nightmare began when three Japanese soldiers entered and, swinging flashlights, selected two of the youngest women and dragged them out of the room. About an hour later it was Esther Moras's turn. She was taken to a bare room and forced to lie on the floor, then her dress was lifted and her panties torn off while the Japanese laughed. When she tried to resist, they slapped her repeatedly across the face. "While the marine held me pinned to the floor with one hand," she recounted, "he unbuttoned his trousers with the other hand and then forced his sexual organ into me.

"He stood up," she continued, "and one of the others got down on me. . . . When he had finished, he got up and the third one attacked me in the same manner."

She crawled back to the room where the other girls were confined. "I was in a mental haze all the rest of the night," she said. "The Japs kept coming in and out of the room, dragging out girls individually and in small groups of two or three. . . . I was raped between twelve and fifteen times during that night. I cannot remember exactly how many times. I was so tired and horror-stricken that it became a living nightmare. . . . Finally, at about four o'clock in the morning, I was raped by a marine whose organ was so large that it tore my insides and I bled from my private parts. Only then did they leave me alone, utterly exhausted, in great pain and bleeding badly."

On the afternoon of February 12 the hotel was hit by shellfire, and she escaped.

Another monstrosity exposed by the Allied evidence tendered at the Tokyo trial was vivisection. There were, of course, no survivors to testify either by affidavit or in person. Once again the Japanese indicted themselves, through their own words and observations in their own diaries and affidavits.

In one Japanese account placed in evidence, the deponent testified that live, healthy Allied prisoners had been used for medical demonstrations. "The man was tied to a tree outside the Hikari Kikan office," the affiant said of one occasion. "A Japanese doctor and four Japanese medical students stood around him. They first removed his fingernails, then cut open his chest, and removed his heart, on which the doctor gave a practical demonstration."

Often, when this kind of testimony was taken at the trial, some of those in the dock removed their headphones. With heads bowed, others with eyes closed, they were unwilling or unable to hear the worst. The tableau presented at the IMTFE resembled Hieronymus Bosch's frightening landscape *The Descent into Hell,* which I first viewed as a child at the Metropolitan Museum of Art, and which I have never forgotten.

The Allied prosecution eventually proved the chain of causation between the accused at Tokyo and the mass inhumanities that Japanese inflicted on POWs, on civilians, and on Asian forced laborers. These terrible events were not isolated incidents—*all* wars have isolated incidents, and war itself is an atrocity—but were part of the Japanese militarists' overall strategy of rule by terror. One of the most cultured and sensitive men in the dock, Foreign Minister Mamoru Shigemitsu, later wrote, "It is terrible to think that after the Second World War many wrongful acts involving inhumanity were brought to light, so that our good name was lost and the impression was created abroad that the Japanese people are cruel monsters."

In the light of these revelations, how does one account for the virtual disappearance of the IMTFE from history? Why have the swarms of journalists and scholars writing about World War Two virtually ignored the Tokyo trial? In truth, the IMTFE has simply been swallowed up by the biggest black hole in the history of the twentieth century. Out of the thousands of books about the war, only two have dealt with the Tokyo trial. The first of these books, a legal tract written in 1950 by the Allied chief prosecutor and an aide, centered on the legality of the trial. The other, written some twenty years later by an academic, was concerned with the trial's illegality. There have been more books on Steinbrenner and his New York Yankees. *No* book has ever appeared on the trial itself, its chronological development, the testimony, the characters who crowded the Tokyo stage. This stands in sharp contrast to the writing about Nuremberg, which has included dozens of books and thousands of magazine and newspaper articles.

When I wrote to a friend of my intention to write a book about the Tokyo trial, he dropped me a note and said that he had mentioned the project to Brigadier General Telford Taylor, the American chief prosecutor at Nuremberg. "Taylor told me the other day he thought it was a great idea on your part." But why has this "great idea," if that is what it is, been neglected for so long? For that matter, why have the Allied governments themselves shunned it? "Unhappily," the same Telford Taylor commented in a monograph published almost thirty years ago, "public indifference to the Tokyo trial has been matched by an apparent lack of interest on the part of the sponsoring governments themselves."

Admittedly, the dimensions of the trial are intimidating. For example, before embarking on this book, I reread the 10-million-word transcript and prepared an index of the contents of all 50,000-odd pages of the record. I also reworked the Asia-Pacific beat from Canberra to Tokyo, tracking down documents, interviewing participants in the trial, and revisiting the site of the tribunal.

The trial's length and its breadth of coverage were not the only obstacles to writing about it effectively. In addition, the cast of characters was (and is) large and, to most people, virtually unknown. It is doubtful if the average literate person today is familiar with the names of more than one or two of those involved, usually Emperor Hirohito (who was not tried) and Premier Tojo. Nuremberg was different in this respect as in others. At least in the West, the names of the accused Germans are easily remembered and can be found in every American metropolitan telephone directory—the Fricks, Franks, Görings, Rosenbergs, Bormanns, and so on. The atrocities hit closer to home, too. Few have forgotten the photographs of the concentration camp victims, the heaped-up corpses and the emaciated survivors.

Tokyo also had a language problem. The trial was conducted in English and Japanese simultaneously (and, as the occasion arose, in Chinese, Russian, and French). However, the Japanese language is one of the most difficult to translate, and there were often squabbles over the meaning of a single word or phrase. Attorneys soon learned to keep their questions as simple as possible, but even then some of the interchanges between witnesses, lawyers, and justices were laced with confusion.

It is generally agreed that the trial was poorly conducted and badly organized. Instead of grabbing the attention of the Japanese and Allied publics immediately with the compelling evidence of the link between the accused and the reign of barbarism they had conducted as state policy from 1931 to 1945, the prosecutors plunged into murky Japanese domestic politics of the 1920s and 1930s. Their intent was to show how the militarists had manipulated the government after 1928 to gain mastery of Japan. They presented evidence on the assassination of Japanese premiers, the imposition of censorship, the use of the dread Kempeitai (Japan's Gestapo) to snuff out opposition, and the wholesale violation of international treaties and covenants, including the Hague and Geneva conventions on the rules of war. Too often, the evidence bogged down in such arcane matters as interpretations of the Japanese Constitution. The drama inherent in the situation was often dissipated in a blur of legalistic maneuvers.

In the end, it seems to me virtually impossible to write a chronological history of the trial without having witnessed it. To observe the trial was as necessary as studying the picture on the box of a jigsaw puzzle before starting to put it together. For there were indeed many and varied pieces. Both the prosecution and defense, sometimes for reasons beyond their control, called witnesses out of turn, introduced evidence out of sequence, and went off on tangents unrelated to the testimony at hand. This scrambling of evidence and procedures was accompanied by overblown rhetoric on the part of several defense attorneys and the Allied chief prosecutor, Joseph Keenan.

The defense, which included both Japanese and American lawyers, was often deliberately obstructive. Some of the defense attorneys admitted to me years later that they had dragged out the trial with motions of one kind or another in the expectation that the Allies would fall out among themselves and that China, the United States, and Japan would align themselves in a common defense against the Soviet Union, thereby enhancing their clients' claims. Thus, much of the court's time—perhaps more than a third—was taken up by motions, briefs, and interminable arguments over what seemed to most of us rather fine points of law.

As a result of all these problems, the judicial flow was often reduced to a trickle. News coverage of the trial had started with éclat, but the stories soon slipped from the front pages to the back pages and ultimately slid from view. At the time and ever since, doubts have been raised over whether justice was indeed served at Ichigaya, but for the most part they have sunk in a sea of ignorance and apathy.

The role of critic is easy. The conditions under which the IMTFE was organized were manifestly difficult. In the normal course of a trial there are codified laws, a judiciary, a prosecutorial staff, a defense, a grand jury, and established procedures. At Tokyo not only were these elements missing when the IMTFE was organized, but in the bombed-out capital of the former Japanese empire there was not even a courthouse in which to hold the trial. When I arrived in Tokyo, I was handed a U.S. Army map of the city that bore the legend "War damage has wrought a tremendous change in Tokyo—more than meets the eye. . . . Certain streets are 'right off the map.' " But there were far more vexing problems. The law of the case at Tokyo (and Nuremberg) was under attack, and still is.

Not all jurists agree with the concept of criminal responsibility for war. Former Supreme Court justice Arthur Goldberg, whom I interviewed in 1980, felt that the defendants had been rightly tried on the grounds of crimes against humanity and violations of the Geneva accords, as part of the general movement of history toward a world of law. But, he said, "I find no ground for trying the accused for crimes of aggression or waging war. To wage war is not a crime, and there is no basis for it in international law." Tokyo and Nuremberg, he noted, represented a step in that direction.

Since recorded time there have been sporadic attempts at making belligerents legally responsible for their actions in wartime. Almost 500 years before Christ, for example, the Chinese philosopher Mo Ti wrote three essays that condemned aggressive war or, as he defined it, "offensive war." Western classical writers such as Homer, Herodotus, Thucydides, and Polybius explored the nature of war, and slowly, painfully, over the centuries, their concepts gave rise to "customs of war." In the fifth century Saint Augustine published his theory of "just war." Spain's Francisco de Vitoria—who lived in the age of Columbus and was a precursor to Holland's Hugo Grotius, the acknowledged father of international law—in his *Law of War* developed the notion that "aggressive" war was "illegal."

Despite all this work by individual scholars and philosophers, it was not until 1899 that the first international codification of the laws of war was attempted. Eight years later, most of the participating nations signed the Hague Conventions. Their stated purpose was to "diminish the evils of war, so far as military requirements permit." W. E. Hall, a British authority on international law, forecast that "if the next war is unscrupulously waged, it will be followed by a reaction towards increased stringency of law." Hall's assessment was confirmed in 1919 when a commission of the victorious Allies, including Japan, compiled a list of thirty-two war crimes committed by the Germans. In the end, however, Germany was permitted to try her own war criminals. Most were acquitted, though a few received light sentences.

In 1928, the movement to develop laws of war attained a new plateau when, largely as a by-product of U.S. agitation, the major powers—with the exception of the Soviet Union—ratified the Pact of Paris, more popularly known as the Kellogg-Briand Pact, which outlawed "wars of aggression." Japan was a signatory. This treaty was to become one of the legal bases for the Nuremberg and Tokyo trials.

By any objective standard, Japan and her Nazi partner during World War II engaged in many actions that were far more inhumane, far more contrary to natural and man-made law, than what had occurred during World War I. In Axis-occupied territories, and among the Allies, sentiment spread for the trial and punishment at the war's end of German and Japanese "war criminals." The consensus among the Allies, now called the United Nations, was expressed by Lord Wright, an Australian and the first chairman of the UN War Crimes Commission (UNWCC), which was formed in London in 1943 by seventeen nations, including such Asia-Pacific states as China, Australia, the United States, New Zealand, and India. "The Second World War was deliberately created by a number of very evil men," Wright said, "including Hitler and his clique and corresponding figures in the Far East. . . . The war was purely acquisitive and aggressive. Their motives were naked, blatant and unashamed."

Early in 1945 UNWCC produced a paper that spelled out the nature of war criminality. In their analysis of the war in the Pacific, the Allies held that Japan's outrageous actions did not consist alone of individual and isolated incidents but were "deliberately planned and systematically perpetrated throughout the Far East and Pacific." Tokyo, and not just its commanders in the field, was responsible for the atrocities committed by imperial forces.

The paper was not diplomatic. "Inhabitants of countries which [the Japanese] overran have been ruthlessly tortured, murdered and massacred in cold blood; rape, torture, pillage and other barbarities have occurred. . . . Despite the laws and customs of war, and their own assurances, prisoners-of-war and other nationals of the United Nations have been systematically subjected to brutal treatment and horrible outrages calculated to exterminate them."

The UN set out to prove that Japan had devised, put in motion, and/or directed criminal plans that resulted in waging aggressive war and oppressive occupation of various territories. "The persons to be charged should be determined by the rule that all who participate in the formulation or execution of a criminal plan involving multiple crimes are liable for each of the offenses committed and responsible for the acts of each other."

On balance, the Tokyo and Nuremberg trials may have been the only method of dealing with Japanese and Nazi actions toward the people of occupied countries and prisoners of war. When I interviewed one of the defense lawyers, George Furness, in Tokyo in 1981, he stated his firm opposition to both war crimes trials and capital punishment. But even he was stymied when I asked him what he would do in the case of Adolf Hitler. His only reply was "I don't know. That's a hard one."

* * *

This book is an attempt to set the record straight on what actually happened at the trials. For how can there be a sensible debate on the pros and cons of the IMTFE when hardly anyone knows anything about the trial and decidedly nothing about the testimony? As I came to see it, chance had placed me in a position to write the first chronological account of the proceedings and to make of "the other Nuremberg" what it truly is, a watershed in the histories of World War II, the Sino-Japanese War, and contemporary Asian affairs.

There have been times during my lengthy research when I have hesitated. Would a chronological reconstruction of the war crimes trial unnecessarily offend today's pro-Western Japanese? Why dredge up the past? In the end, I came to the conclusion that this account should not anger the Japanese any more than the burgeoning literature of Nuremberg has angered the Germans. After all, as the Allied prosecutors at Tokyo stressed repeatedly, it was not the Japanese people who were on trial, it was their leaders— in particular, the militarists who took over the government.

Moreover, the constant exposure of Germany's Nazi regime is now recognized as a major obstacle to the revival of Nazism in Germany. The Germans are aware of the unspeakable behavior of their former leaders. This is not the case in Japan, where, for example, the younger generation has little knowledge of the recent past. As a law professor at Tokyo Imperial University explained, "[We] Japanese tend to forget bad things quickly."

In 1977 Japan's Education Ministry published guidelines for new textbooks. In a basic history of Japan, several hundred pages in length, the account of World War II was reduced to six pages, mostly taken up by a photograph of Hiroshima's ruins, a tally of Japan's war dead, and pictures of the U.S. fire-bombing of Tokyo. "There is no mention in this text of the casualties of the other side, war crimes, of the forced evacuation of Chinese and Koreans to labour camps in Japan," the London *Economist* observed dryly.

The very next year the rehabilitation of the Class A war criminals received an unexpected boost. Fourteen militarists, including Tojo, were secretly enshrined as "martyrs" at the Yasukuni Shrine, which is dedicated to Japan's war dead and is Japan's most revered Shinto temple. When the story broke in the Japanese press, the high priests at the shrine claimed that their decision was justified because the war criminals had "devoted their lives to the Emperor and to Japan." Ultrapatriotic organizations characterized the enshrinement as "proper" because Japan had no alternative but to fight the Pacific War and the war was a "sacred mission."

Despite the furor, Premier Masayoshi Ohira, on the eve of his first journey to the United States for a meeting with President Carter, visited the Shinto shrine and paid his respects to those who had fallen in the war, including Japan's war criminals. Japan's parliament and press were shaken. Some legislators charged that the war criminals had been responsible for the great suffering of the Japanese and other peoples, and that their enshrinement in so sacred a place as Yasukuni was "impermissible." The *Yomiuri,* one of Japan's big three national dailies, solemnly warned in an editorial: "The attempt to turn the clock back to prewar days fills us with anxiety."

In 1982 the textbook controversy emerged in full flower. This time the Japanese Ministry of Education described the Japanese invasion of China as an "advance," and the Rape of Nanking was attributed to the resistance of the Chinese Army. "When they [Chinese Nationalist Forces] inflicted heavy losses on the Japanese army," the new textbooks averred, "the Japanese troops were enraged and, as a result, they killed many Chinese soldiers and civilians." The draft of slave laborers in Korea was rephrased as a "mobilization" of labor.

Now, throughout Asia, there was an uproar. Protests were lodged by the two Chinas—Peking and Taipei—and the two Koreas—Seoul and Pyongyang—along with Singapore and Malaysia, Indonesia, the Philippines, Hong Kong, and others. Peking accused the Japanese of "distorting the history of Japanese militarist aggression against China." The *China Daily* branded the Japanese rewrite of history "Absurd!" In Korea there were anti-Japanese demonstrations, and the *Korea Herald* accused Tokyo of trying to hoodwink a new generation, terming Japan's behavior "a matter of serious concern." Indonesia accused Japan of "attempting to justify its international crimes" but pointed out that since the memory of them was still fresh in Asian minds, "this attempt at obliteration is useless." The foreign minister of the Philippines said the textbook revisions "disturbed" Filipino thinking on the probable direction of Japan's future relations with its East Asian and Pacific neighbors. Only the Americans, ever sensitive to Japan's sensitivity, shied away from the debate. President Reagan, in a little-noticed precursor of his visit to the German military cemetery at Bitburg, told a news conference that he could see no point in raking up the ashes of the past.

The reaction of many Japanese officials to the protests of their fellow Asians was an echo of the positions taken by the Japanese defense at the IMTFE. "When Japan advanced into a foreign country, it did not use the word 'invade,' " the director-general of a Japanese government agency explained. "To change 'advance' into 'invasion' would be a distortion of facts. Children would say their forefathers should not be respected because they did a bad thing."

Critics shredded this argument. "According to the director-general's logic, because none of the aggressors, including Germany's Hitler and Italy's Mussolini, who were Japan's allies during World War II, had ever used the word aggression when they advanced into other countries, no aggression ever occurred," China's army journal said.

Not all Japanese proved insensitive to the issue. One of Tokyo's mass-circulation dailies, the *Asahi Shimbun,* observed curtly: "Japan sent a large army to China, killed ten million Chinese, and caused great damage. If this is not aggression, what is?" And although the *Asahi* did not refer directly to the IMTFE, it alluded to the trial record. "What happened in those countries which Japan invaded during World War II has been put on the record as historical facts, and it should never be abolished by a play on words," the Japanese paper said.

Senior Japanese officials realized that Tokyo had inadvertently opened Pandora's Box and announced in the aftermath of the uproar that Japan would amend the double-speak textbooks. Unfortunately, during the flap, a new Japanese film, *Dai Nippon Teikoku (The Great Japanese Empire),* was released in Tokyo and played to SRO houses. The film glorified Japan's aggression and implied that Hideki Tojo had been unjustly tried by the IMTFE. The *Japan Times* charged that the film turned Tojo from a "ruthless militarist into a benign, sensitive super-patriot." The film producer, a Japanese right-wing version of the leftist Costa-Gavras, said that he felt Tojo "should not be portrayed as warlike."

Clearly, the Japanese are divided on the causes and effects of World War II in the Pacific. It is my hope that the chronological reconstruction of the Tokyo trial in this book will help to clear up some of the misinformation and ignorance. My intentions here should not be misunderstood. The Japanese people are not being tried or retried in these pages any more than they were at the Tokyo trial. The late Joseph Grew, America's prewar ambassador to Japan, put the sorry tale that unfolds here in perspective. "For me," Grew wrote in his diary, "there are no finer people in the world than the best type of Japanese." The best type did not rule Japan between 1931 and 1945.

It is understandable that a great nation does not want to call to mind constantly the dark side in its history, whether the acts of Japanese and Nazi war criminals during World War II, the brutish colonialism of the European powers in Asia, or the existence of slavery in the Moslem world and in North and South America. But as Whitney R. Harris, a member of the Allied prosecution at Nuremberg, expressed it, "This is as it should be, provided that in shunning the evil of yesterday we do not forget the wrongs to which it led—and having forgotten them believe them never to have happened."

This is a book that is long overdue.

ARNOLD C. BRACKMAN

Tokyo, Japan
Brookfield Center, Connecticut

"I hasten to emphasize the fact that I am far from esteeming myself capable of reporting all that took place at the trial in full detail or even in the actual order of events. I imagine that to mention everything with full explanation would fill volumes. And so I trust I may not be reproached for confining myself to what struck me. . . . But I see I shall do better not to apologize. I will do my best and the reader will see for himself that I have done all I can."

—FYODOR MIKHAILOVICH DOSTOYEVSKI,
The Brothers Karamazov

1
War Criminals at Bay

On July 26, 1945, Japan was presented a choice: surrender or suicide. For on that day the three major Allies in the war against Japan—China, Great Britain, and the United States—issued the Potsdam Proclamation, warning Japan that she must surrender or face "utter destruction." The proclamation added: "Japan shall be given an opportunity to end the war." Thus, unknown to the Japanese, the U.S. decision on whether or not to explode the atomic bomb was to be based on Tokyo's actions.

With or without the existence of the bomb, the Japanese Empire was in a precarious position. The army had been defeated in the Philippines and Okinawa, the navy at the Battle of Leyte Gulf. Japanese industry, transportation, and agriculture had been crippled by U.S. bombers, and the country was slowly starving to death. The only hope offered by the military was the *kamikaze:* victory through suicide.

The Allied surrender terms came down to four basic demands: demobilization of the Japanese armed forces, Allied occupation of Japan, elimination "for all time [of] those who have deceived and misled the people of Japan," and the trial of Japanese war criminals by an Allied tribunal. "Stern justice shall be meted out to all war criminals," the tenth paragraph read, "including those who have visited cruelties upon our prisoners."

The reference to war criminality appeared to be the least important of the demands; it was the last on the list. But in the secret debate among the Japanese leaders in Tokyo, the war crimes issue was paramount. To them, the Potsdam Proclamation implied the trial not only of those who had committed "conventional" war crimes, such as the mass murder of POWs and civilians, but also the policy-makers at the highest levels of government. This was a direct threat to the leaders of Japan, perhaps even the emperor. Tokyo already had a vivid example of what the Allies had in mind. After Germany's collapse a few weeks earlier, those members of the Nazi ruling elite who were still alive or who had not disappeared had been summarily arrested as war criminals.

The Potsdam demand that Japan's war criminals face "stern justice" generated a tidal wave of anger, resentment, and fear among most Japanese leaders. There was also some measure of disagreement, as evidenced by the debate in the ruling council of the Japanese Empire—the Supreme Council for the Direction of the War. Foreign Minister Shigenori Togo concluded that Potsdam's call for the "unconditional surrender of the Japanese armed forces" represented a softening of the previous declaration, signed at Cairo two years earlier, which had specified the "unconditional surrender of Japan." Potsdam also referred to "our terms"; an unconditional surrender implies no terms. He gained some support for this view from two of his colleagues, Kantaro Suzuki, the vacillating, seventy-seven-year-old prime minister, who had been given that post after Hideki Tojo's removal from office in 1944, and Admiral Mitsumasa Yonai, the navy minister and former premier, who had originally opposed allying Japan with Hitler and who had opposed the war against the United States. These three wanted to proceed cautiously, hoping that Japan's plea to the Soviets to use their "good offices" to achieve peace would lead to an honorable way of ending the war.

The other three members of the council opposed any accommodation, declaring that the war had not yet been lost. This formidable trio was composed of General Korechika Anami, the obdurate war minister, whose hobbies were swordplay and archery; Yoshijiro Umezu, the army chief of staff, a humorless warlord, sometimes known as "the Ivory Mask"; and Admiral Soemu Toyoda, the flabby-faced, polished, xenophobic navy chief of staff, a member of the same family clan as Umezu.

From the viewpoint of the militarists, Japan still had 2.5 million troops ready for combat, over 1 million tons of shipping, and

9,000 military aircraft. In addition, there was no shortage of volunteers for the *kamikaze* missions that had sunk or damaged a number of U.S. Navy ships in the past year. Moreover, Japan's imperial legions still ruled over Korea and Manchuria, a large part of China, and almost all of Southeast Asia. To defend the home islands the military had plans to organize more than twenty million men into a suicide ground force, to be hurled in a human wave against any Allied invasion.

The warlords were inflexible in their attitudes. Shrewdly, they put forth their own terms to end the war. One condition was that the Allies acknowledge the emperor's inviolability. Second, there could be no more than a token Allied occupation of Japan, with Tokyo off limits. Third, Japan would disarm her own troops and try her own war criminals. The Supreme Council, deeply divided, did not communicate this or any other counteroffer to the Allies. The Japanese response to the Potsdam Proclamation was, in the word of Premier Suzuki, *mokusatsu*—to kill it with silence.

Even those in favor of accepting the Allied surrender terms were adamant that Hirohito must be declared inviolate. Their greatest fear was that their god-emperor would be placed in the dock as a common criminal. Even the most rational and worldly leader on the six-man council, Foreign Minister Togo, upheld the status of the emperor. If the Allies insisted on Hirohito's trial as a war criminal, Togo vowed that Japan must "be resigned" to a last-ditch suicidal stand.

Faced with no response to Potsdam and with the prospect of invading Japan in what would surely be the bloodiest battle in history, killing millions, President Harry Truman authorized dropping the atomic bomb.

The introduction of atomic weapons into the war at this point has been the subject of widespread controversy ever since. Many critics, including propagandists, unbiased historians, and all those in between, have charged that the war in the Pacific would have ended in 1945 with or without the bomb. But when one examines the events of the time, it is no surprise that to many people who lived through the war the bombing seemed the only way to end its devastation. Masuo Kato, a veteran Japanese correspondent who became postwar editor of Kyodo, the Japanese news agency, provided insight into this aspect of the conflict in *The Lost War*. He wrote that "the Japanese are a people of paradoxes. That is why they could cling to the idea of victory in the midst of the fact of defeat. Even though some had come to accept defeat as likely, a companion conclusion was that it would come only after Japan had gone down gloriously fighting to the last man." Laurens van der Post, an officer in the British Army who spent several years in a Japanese prison camp, wrote that when the bomb fell on Hiroshima, "it must have looked as if their Sun Goddess Ama-Terasu herself had hurled fragments of her sun at Japan to shatter it out of its suicidal course."

Shortly after 5 A.M. on August 6, 1945, the city of Hiroshima was destroyed by a nuclear explosion. Two days later, the Soviet Union, brushing aside Japanese pleas for mediation, declared war on Japan and invaded Manchuria. The confidence of the militarists was shaken, and the propeace group in Tokyo gained strength. The emperor himself sent a message to the prime minister saying that the war must end. Yet the cabinet remained reluctant to take action—there was still no sense of urgency. Then a second nuclear device was dropped over Nagasaki on August 9. By this time, and despite military censorship, all the Japanese leaders had become aware of the destructive power of the bomb. Yet again the Supreme Council met in long debate, and yet again there was no agreement.

This time Prime Minister Suzuki was unwilling to let events continue to drift. With Foreign Minister Togo he rushed to the Imperial Palace late on the night of August 9 to seek an immediate audience with the emperor. Hirohito was quick to sense the gravity of the situation and gave orders to reconvene the council in the imperial bunker within the hour. The conferees included the six members of the Supreme Council, the *jushin* or elder statesmen, and the president of the Privy Council. Again the arguments went round and round in familiar grooves; Hirohito, the master of the politics of silence, did not utter a word. Again the issue of a war crimes trial surged to the fore. Who are the war criminals? Who will try them? Where will they be tried? Although Japan faced "annihilation,"* the word threatened in the Potsdam Proclamation, the triumvirate of the war minister and the army and navy chiefs of staff remained adamant. Unless their four conditions were met, there must be a suicidal last battle.

Suddenly, shunting aside all established traditions and constitutional conventions, the forty-five-year-old emperor spoke. As

---

*Unknown to the imperial conference was the best-kept secret of the war after the bomb itself: The United States had exhausted its stockpile of two atomic bombs.

the leaders of his government sat in respectful, stunned silence, Hirohito called for the acceptance of the Potsdam Proclamation and thereby, in one fell swoop, agreed to the Allied demand to dispense "stern justice" to Japan's war criminals. "It goes without saying that it is unbearable for me to see the brave and loyal fighting men of Japan disarmed. It is equally unbearable that others who have rendered me devoted service should now be punished as instigators of the war. Nevertheless, the time has come when we must bear the unbearable. . . ." As everyone at the meeting rose to his feet, Hirohito slowly left the room. No one dared dispute the words of the god-emperor.

The conference ended immediately, and the Allies were notified that Japan was prepared to surrender "with the understanding that the said decision does not compromise any demand which prejudices the prerogatives of His Majesty as a Sovereign Ruler." The unyielding point of both the war and peace factions was that Hirohito himself could not be arraigned in the dock as a war criminal. The Japanese public was not informed of this action other than by a cryptic announcement in the media implying that "changes" were in the offing. On the other hand, War Minister Anami issued a bold statement: "We have but one choice; we must fight on. . . ." And a group of young officers began planning a coup that would remove from positions of power the "defeatists" who had been "misleading" the emperor. The Allies' reply artfully dodged Tokyo's delicately phrased condition, and this in turn set the stalemate within the Japanese camp back to square one. Of particular import in the reply was one sentence: "The ultimate form of government of Japan shall . . . be established by the freely expressed will of the Japanese people." Did this stricture include the emperor? On this point the leaders in Tokyo disagreed.

The militarists now pressed home their point: Mobilizing the nation for one last stand would force the Allies to soften their terms. At a meeting of the cabinet on August 13 the leaders once again failed to settle the issue; once again, Premier Suzuki was forced to ask for a meeting with the emperor. As he did so, the do-or-die firebrands in the War Minister rushed forward with their plans for a coup. Anami and the other military chiefs refused to join the plot, however, and struggled to maintain their control over the armed forces.

The second imperial conference met on the morning of August

14. Although a strong majority now favored acceptance of the Allied terms, the militarists argued against peace. Once again, Hirohito spoke. The twenty-four men, many with tears in their eyes, listened as the emperor summed up the situation. Japan was defeated and would be destroyed if the war continued. He would not permit that to happen no matter what his own fate might be. "As the people of Japan are unaware of the present situation, I know they will be deeply shocked when they hear of our decision. If it is thought appropriate that I explain the matter to them personally, I am willing to go before the microphone. . . . I desire the cabinet to prepare as soon as possible an Imperial Rescript announcing the termination of the war."

The emperor's words set in motion not only the machinery of surrender but also the engines of revolution. The war hawks were enraged at what they considered to be a betrayal of their honor, and they vowed to continue the fight. Japanese officialdom moved quickly to blunt their efforts, though many were afraid for their own lives. Directors of NHK, the Japanese Broadcasting Corporation, were immediately ordered to make preparations for the emperor's unprecedented broadcast. Hirohito himself had decided that only his voice—the Voice of the Crane, held sacred by the Japanese people—would be able to preserve the national calm and unity in the face of surrender.

Conservatives were horrified at the idea of the emperor speaking directly to the people, and so it was decided that his voice would be recorded the night of August 14, for broadcast to the nation at high noon the next day. When the time came, Hirohito had no hesitation in approaching the microphone and speaking frankly to his "Good and Loyal Subjects." In his distinctive, reedy voice the emperor told of the increasing defeats suffered by Japanese forces in the war and, finally, of the enemy's "new and most cruel bomb. . . . Should we continue to fight, not only would it result in an ultimate collapse and obliteration of the Japanese nation, but also it would lead to the total extinction of human civilization."

With his scientific background—he was a respected amateur marine biologist—and with the information from his more clear-eyed advisers, Hirohito had a better idea than most government leaders of the significance of nuclear weapons. There was nothing to do now but to give up, no matter what that might mean to him personally. In the end he encouraged his people, "Unite your total strength, to be devoted to construction for the future."

The recording made, checked, and securely stored to be ready for use the next day, the emperor returned to his quarters. All was quiet for a little while.

The young firebrands, reminiscent of the fanatical nationalists and the Kwantung Army clique who had pulled the strings of government in the 1930s, swiftly put into motion their plans for a coup. Not having heard the emperor's words, they were nevertheless convinced that he had been misled by devious, self-seeking courtiers and cowardly government functionaries. Above all, they wanted to find the recording and destroy it. Death to the traitors! was their cry. *Banzai!*

In the wee hours of the morning on August 15, General Takeshi Mori, commander of the Imperial Guard, was among those shot to death by rebels attempting to take over the palace. The alarm went up all over Tokyo, and senior army officers moved to contain the rebellion. The ultimate purpose of the invaders was to reach the emperor and liberate him from his defeatist advisers. But first they looked for the recording they knew had been made earlier that night. The imperial chamberlains stood up to the invasion with courage and cunning, though they feared for their own lives at every moment. The rebels were given different stories by different people in the palace, and soon found themselves in confusion. This state was complicated by the fact that no one among them knew who was in charge. They were, in reality, a mob, for there was no one leader of the revolution. Perhaps if there had been one, history would have written a different tale that night. As it was, just after the break of dawn, the supreme commander of the Eastern District Army, General Shizuichi Tanaka, arrived at the palace and ordered the officers and troops to end their acts of disloyalty and to obey the orders of the properly constituted authorities. Shocked by his presence and by word that the War Ministry and field commanders were not supporting them, the rebels gave up.

Broadcast of the emperor's speech announcing the end of the war went on as scheduled. The people were profoundly moved and disturbed, but there was no disorder, no questioning of the emperor's supreme authority. The following day, August 16, the Allies accepted Japan's surrender. Then, as if both sides were pausing for reflection, events moved more slowly. The advance party of Americans did not arrive in Tokyo until August 28, and five days later, on September 2, the surrender document was signed aboard the U.S.S. *Missouri* in Tokyo Bay.

The Japanese militarists took advantage of the hiatus to destroy evidence of war criminality by the warehouseful. At War Ministry offices on Ichigaya Hill, bonfires glowed day and night as tons of records were burned. Similar fires crackled in other government buildings, at army and navy installations throughout the Japanese Empire, and at the headquarters of the Kempeitai and other units of the secret police. Among the documents destroyed were the transcripts of *all* imperial conferences, *all* the records of the Supreme Council for the Direction of the War, *all* the deliberations of the Cabinet and Privy Council, *all* files on prisoners of war, *all* orders and plans relating to the attack on the Philippines and Southeast Asia, and *all* the documents relating to the Manchurian and Chinese campaigns.

Fortunately for history, not all incriminating documents were destroyed. Some files of the Kempeitai unit at Kagoshima, Japan, inadvertently escaped the flames, fell into Allied hands, and were later used in evidence by the war crimes prosecutors. Tokyo had ordered the unit to prepare for "disarmament," a euphemism for surrender, by putting the torch to evidence of war criminality. "Such documents as will be harmful when they fall into the hands of the enemy—for example, documents concerning foreign affairs, counterintelligence, thought control, peace preservation, etc., and materials by which national power may be estimated and secret histories such as the February 19 Incident [the assassination in 1932 of a Japanese premier who opposed war in China]—must be destroyed as soon as possible," the order read. "On the other hand, code-books, registers of *Kempeitai* personnel, documents concerning undisposed intendance and general affairs, etc., should not be destroyed until they are of no use."

On August 21 a new order was issued from Tokyo observing that some agencies had failed to destroy all incriminating evidence. "Since there are many examples of blunders having been committed inadvertently, careful examination should be made of such matters. . . . You are instructed to be certain that of secret documents that required destruction, not a single sheet be left behind."

What were these blunders? The order spelled them out: papers stuck in the rear of drawers, papers inserted under the legs of desks to stabilize them, papers behind filing cabinets and shelves.

Senior government and military personnel were also advised to scour their homes for incriminating letters and diaries.

A top-secret cable was also sent to Japanese field commanders stating that "personnel who mistreated prisoners of war and [civilian] internees . . . are permitted to take care of it by immediately transferring or by fleeing without a trace." The cable added that "documents which would be unfavorable for us in the hands of the enemy are to be treated in the same way as secret documents, and destroyed."

On August 27 another communiqué ordered that documents not yet destroyed were to be divided into three categories: those marked for destruction, those prepared for destruction but whose destruction was to be held in abeyance, and those to be preserved. Among the documents to be preserved, apparently as red herrings for Allied prosecutors, were filing cabinets filled with military assignment reports, lists of arms, service records, clothing receipts, and "ordinary books."

Allied prosecutors at the Tokyo trial later complained bitterly about this destruction of incriminating evidence. One of these lawyers, H. A. Hauxhurst, observed in explaining the dearth of documents that "as practically every city in Japan except Kyoto had been 80 percent destroyed by bombing, many records had been destroyed, and when surrender was inevitable and before the occupation . . . many of the remaining important records were burned."

Not only did the surrender interval leave time to destroy documents, it also provided an opportunity to falsify records. A classic fabrication occurred on Wake Island, where the Japanese naval garrison slaughtered ninety-six American prisoners in 1943. The Japanese commandant on Wake summoned his junior officers and told them of his intention to claim that the prisoners had died during an Allied sea bombardment. To this end, for the next two days the decomposed bodies of the prisoners were dug up and transferred to a stretch of beach that had been shelled by U.S. warships. When naval headquarters requested "official" information from the garrison on the disposition of prisoners, the fabricated yarn was transmitted to Tokyo.

Other examples of falsified reports abound. Captain John D. Murphy, the U.S. Navy director of war crimes investigations in the Pacific, complained that "all records concerning prisoners of war captured by the Japanese in the Pacific Ocean areas were destroyed by the Japanese authorities and in every instance investigators have been confronted with false information by the Japanese commanding officers as well as the deliberate intention on the part of the Japanese to conceal any and all information concerning persons who were known to have been captured alive."

Closer to Tokyo, the commandant of the notorious Fukuoka prisoner-of-war camp had begun butchering his prisoners on August 11, in anticipation of Japan's surrender. On August 16, the day after Hirohito's surrender broadcast, sixteen American prisoners were marched off to a nearby glade, stripped, and, with the girlfriends of the guards looking on in amusement, hacked to death. On their return to camp the guards falsified the prison records.

Attempts were also made to destroy the physical evidence of murdered prisoners. On July 18, 1945, for example, at Osaka, Japan, two American fliers were tortured by the Kempeitai and then executed (in the Kempeitai, there was a tradition that men on Death Row should be tortured mercilessly before their execution). A week after Hirohito's surrender broadcast, the Japanese guards at Osaka panicked; they exhumed the bodies and torched them. But the Japanese had difficulty burning the damp, decayed matter. The grisly cremation took twelve hours and required eighteen liters of gasoline.

Attempts at doctoring evidence were also made on a massive scale. At Pontianak, Borneo, about 1,000 Indonesian men, women, and children were tortured and murdered by the Japanese on the ground that they were "spies conspiring against Japan." When, immediately after the surrender, Allied interrogators asked the Japanese area commander if he could prove the existence of the conspiracy, he replied, "I have seen the official records of the interrogations on this matter." When asked to produce the records of the Pontianak incident, he said, "They were burned before the capitulation."

Similar mass-scale destruction of evidence occurred throughout the Japanese Empire. Ferdinand Gabrillagues, director of the French Indochinese Bureau of War Criminal Suspects, summarized the problem: "The number of war crimes is considerable, the documentation concerning them voluminous, but there is no question of making a complete exposé of them." Why? Evidence had been systematically destroyed, including witnesses, he said.

The Japanese militarists not only destroyed the records and the witnesses of their atrocities, they also engaged in an orgy of self-destruction. *Hara kiri,* or suicide in the face of defeat or dishonor, was an old Japanese tradition. It was employed to "save face," to protect one's honor or the honor of one's family or nation, to amend a wrong, as a demonstration of loyalty to a dead liege, out of frustration, or to defy reality.

During the war there were numerous examples of Japanese officers and men in the field committing *hara kiri* rather than surrendering to the Allies. In 1941 Premier Hideki Tojo promulgated his infamous "frontline code of honor," stating that death—even suicide—was preferable to being taken prisoner. Often, in the ghastly emotional heat of battle, with their positions overrun, Japanese soldiers committed suicide en masse rather than surrender.

After Hirohito's surrender broadcast, there were daily suicides "by those who felt responsibility for defeat, or for war guilt, or who merely could not face the future," according to Masuo Kato.

A few committed the act in the traditional, ritualistic fashion, among them the father of the *kamikaze* units, Vice Admiral Takijiro Onishi, who had sent thousands of young men on suicide missions. "I have suffered the supreme agony these past few days. . . . By disemboweling myself I cannot apologize sufficiently," Onishi said before he thrust a dagger into his stomach, twisted it, and drove it up and forcefully to the right. War Minister Anami, who had opposed surrender but who refused to join his junior officers in their attempt at a coup, ended his life in similar fashion.

General Shigeru Honjo, mastermind behind the Mukden Incident in 1931 which had touched off the Sino-Japanese War, and leader of the cabal known as the Kwantung Army clique, also thrust a knife into his abdomen and then, rather than prolong the suffering, slit his own throat.

Many others chose the same method as Field Marshal Hajime Sugiyama, the former army chief of staff who put a pistol to his temple and blew out his brains. Sugiyama's wife attempted to follow him in the traditional manner, but she hedged. She drank a cup of cyanide and then fell upon an unsheathed, upright dagger. General Shizuichi Tanaka, commander of the Eastern Army, which would have met the Allied invasion of Japan head-on, shot himself.

There was also a rash of suicides among officers of lower rank. Captain Ariizuma, a submarine commander who had enjoyed beheading Allied seamen taken prisoner after his sub had sent their ships to the bottom, killed himself in late August. A member of his crew later defended the captain's murder of POWs on the ground that "Ariizuma had orders from the naval general staff to execute all survivors from sunken enemy vessels." No copy of that criminal naval order was ever found by Allied investigators. It had been destroyed.

By the end of August, more than 1,000 officers and men of the imperial armed forces had committed suicide. In the weeks and months to come, others followed.

A relative handful went underground. For instance, Colonel Keijiro Otani, commander of a Tokyo Kempeitai unit, left two letters in his house indicating that he and his mistress planned suicide. In late 1946 a body that resembled Otani was found in Yamanashi Prefecture, and the Allies closed their case on him. But two years later, the Japanese police were tipped off that Otani was alive and well, flourishing as a green tea merchant in Nagasaki. When he was arrested, potassium cyanide crystals were found on him.

Former Premier Hideki Tojo shocked and disappointed many Japanese by not immediately following his own wartime orders to commit *hara kiri* rather than to surrender. But on September 11, 1945, as U.S. military police finally moved in to arrest him as a war criminal, Tojo shot himself. "I should like not to be judged before a conqueror's court," he said. He did not get his wish. The tough old warrior was rushed to a U.S. Army field hospital and given transfusions of American blood. He survived, having bungled his suicide as, in the eyes of many Japanese, he had bungled the war.

2

MacArthur in Tokyo

The Supreme Commander for the Allied Powers in Japan, the legendary Douglas MacArthur, arrived in Tokyo six days after the signing of the surrender aboard the battleship *Missouri*. As MacArthur set up his headquarters and began the day-to-day business of the occupation, Japanese leaders watched and waited for the other shoe to drop. Who would be taken into custody, and what would become of them?

Tojo and the other Japanese leaders, of course, had long been aware of the Allies' intention to arrest and prosecute those considered guilty of war crimes. The United Nations War Crimes Commission (UNWCC) had been set up in London in the summer of 1943. To prepare for the prosecution of those responsible for Axis war crimes, the commission coordinated the worldwide gathering of information and evidence. On August 25, 1945, the commission published a white paper recommending that Japanese war crimes suspects be "apprehended by the United Nations for trial before an international military tribunal," and that the accused include those in authority in the governmental, military, financial, and economic affairs of Japan.

The tribunal's job was to determine who among the Japanese leaders had promoted the waging of aggressive war and instituted oppressive occupation policies in various territories. "The persons to be charged should be determined by the rule that all who

participate in the formulation or execution of a criminal plan involving multiple crimes are liable for each of the offenses committed and responsible for the acts of each other.''

The appointment of an international military tribunal was placed
in the hands of the Supreme Commander for the Allied Powers
(known as SCAP—as was the administration under him). General
MacArthur had no sooner established his headquarters in Tokyo
than the Allied press began to cry loudly for the arrest and prosecution of war criminals. Yet, it would have been dangerous for
the Allies to publish a list of suspected Japanese war criminals
before their occupation forces in Japan were secure and before
the Japanese armed forces were disarmed.

"No one need have any doubt about the prompt, complete,
and entire fulfillment of the terms of surrender," MacArthur announced. "The process, however, takes time." Unknown to the
press, Washington was still working out American policies toward
the Japanese war criminals. Early in September the final policy
paper, which had been drawn up by the State-War-Navy Coordi-
nating Committee (SWNCC), was transmitted to MacArthur.

Captain James J. Robinson, a naval officer attached to SCAP's
legal section who later became a prosecutor at the Tokyo trial,
recalled in an interview MacArthur's announcement to his staff.
"I received today a radiogram from Washington which you have
seen," the general intoned. "It directs me to proceed to arrange
trials of war criminals. . . . The trials must be conducted in the
full light of publicity. They must be fair and free from vengeance
or politics. They must be examples to the world of law and justice." And Robinson—who jotted down notes as MacArthur
spoke—reported that the Supreme Commander ended on this
theme: "We shall be criticized, but we shall strive for the verdict
of history."

SWNCC advised MacArthur to keep the names of the suspects secret until the moment of their arrest and to divide suspects into three categories: Class A—those who allegedly had
planned, initiated, or waged war "in violation of international
treaties"; Class B—those who had violated "the laws and customs of war"; Class C—those who had carried out the tortures
and murders ordered by superiors. In line with an earlier suggestion by the Chinese, MacArthur was to detain all those suspected
of war crimes, starting from "the period immediately preceding
the Mukden Incident on September 18, 1931," the incident that

had touched off the war with China and in the end, the war in the Pacific. Those suspected of having perpetrated war crimes were to be held in close confinement and denied access to the press to plead their case, pending the creation of an international court. (MacArthur was gratified by this order, since it released him from direct responsibility for trial procedures.)

For the most part, the SWNCC directive followed expected lines of action. The kicker was buried in the seventeenth paragraph, however. "You will take no action against the Emperor as a war criminal," MacArthur was instructed, "pending receipt of a special directive concerning his treatment." Washington was opposed to any detention of Hirohito. There was some disagreement about this matter among the Allies. The Australians, in particular, had taken a strong stand during the deliberations of the UN War Crimes Commission in favor of indicting the emperor.

On September 11 MacArthur made his first move against the war criminals and ordered the detention of thirty-nine suspects. Among those accused were Hideki Tojo and most of his Pearl Harbor cabinet. As noted, the former premier failed in his *hara kiri* attempt, but Kumihiko Hashida, former minister of education, and Chikahiko Koizumi, former minister of welfare and army surgeon general, who had probably been privy to Japan's experiments on live POWs and Chinese civilians, committed suicide before they could be arrested. Shigenori Togo, the foreign minister at the start and at the end of the war, suffered a nonfatal heart attack. Also taken into custody were the commandants of several notorious POW camps, the head of the Kempeitai in the Philippines, other top military leaders, and several Allied nationals who had worked for the Japanese propaganda apparatus during the war.

The arrests jarred Japan, and the postsurrender cabinet of Prince Higashikuni moved to preempt SCAP by ordering the arrest of war crimes suspects by Japanese courts. Boldly, the influential English-language *Nippon Times,* whose editorials generally mirrored the view of the Japanese government, cautioned the Allies to "exercise the greatest circumspection in their demand for the punishment of so-called war criminals." The first question that must be answered, the editorial said, was: Who were the war criminals? Those who had been guilty of cruelty toward war prisoners should be severely punished, and "no one will plead for any leniency on their behalf," the paper said. But punishment for war criminality of a political character presented a different problem.

The *Times* rejected the notion developed by the Allies that the war had been the willful creation of a few evil-minded individuals. Instead, the Japanese newspaper argued, so colossal a phenomenon as a world war must be the result of a concourse of innumerable and complex social forces that sweep powerless individuals along in their irresistible wake.

The editorial suggested that any Japanese punished as war criminals by foreigners would emerge as patriots and martyrs. "A house-cleaning undertaken by the Japanese themselves . . . is likely to be far more lasting in its effects than any measures arbitrarily imposed from without," the *Nippon Times* concluded.

By now a split had developed between MacArthur's military and civilian advisers over the question of the war criminals. Except for the Soviet Union's stalling on the repatriation of Japanese war prisoners, the demobilization of Japanese military personnel was moving along smoothly. The occupation itself was proceeding without incident, and the inclination among MacArthur's military aides was "Don't rock the boat." But the pressure to arrest more war-criminal suspects had a momentum of its own. Several prominent Japanese civilians were hesitant to take an active part in the new postwar government for fear they might be suddenly arrested as war criminals. And the Allied press again complained that MacArthur was dragging his feet.

MacArthur's chief political adviser, Ambassador George Atcheson, Jr., a U.S. career Foreign Service officer, pressed the general to complete the roundup of suspects. "The Japanese people today *expect* the American authorities to make more arrests and, on the part of the great majority, they will not resent those arrests," he said.

MacArthur's acting chief of staff, Major General R. J. Marshall, argued that the central problem was "to determine just who are the war criminals." Marshall said he did not oppose arrests, but the Allied war crimes lists provided an inadequate guide because they were not accompanied by hard evidence. Marshall cautioned against taking into custody men against whom it would later turn out "we had no case."

On November 12 and 14, as the debate at headquarters heated up, MacArthur received two master lists of war criminal suspects from the United Nations War Crimes Commission. Among those cited were seven generals from the notorious Kwantung Army clique and Fusanosuke Kuhara, a former minister of communications and prominent member of the zaibatsu (Japan's powerful financial and industrial combines), along with twenty-two others, including three former premiers. The most noted among the latter was Prince Fumimaro Konoye, who had held the premiership three times and was widely regarded among Japanese and foreigners alike as a "man of three eyes"—intrigue, influence, and indecision.

The listing of someone as close to the emperor as Konoye jarred SCAP. The prince was already positioning himself for a postwar political comeback by ingratiating himself with MacArthur's staff. He had also given interviews to the Allied and Japanese press in which he portrayed himself as a prince of peace, and he had assumed the chairmanship of the committee to rewrite Japan's Constitution. Many Americans and Japanese in positions of power liked Konoye because he was an implacable foe of the Soviet Union and an avowed enemy of the Communists within Japan. Thus, his name on the war criminal list embarrassed MacArthur, who apparently was grooming Prince Konoye to play a major role in postwar Japan.

At this critical juncture, Stalin's agent of influence within MacArthur's high command strode to center stage. Herbert Norman, a Canadian, was now chief of the research and analysis section of SCAP's Counterintelligence Corps. He was also an employee of the KGB. (Norman later took his own life on the eve of an inquiry into his Soviet links. In 1979, Sir Anthony Blunt, an influential British art historian who was close to the royal family as Surveyor of the Queen's Pictures, was publicly unmasked in London as a long-time Soviet agent; in his confession he singled out Herbert Norman as "one of us.") The dossier Norman prepared on Konoye ended on this note: "The most valuable service which Konoye performed on behalf of the Japanese aggression was . . . the fusing of all the dominant sections of the ruling oligarchy, the court, army, *zaibatsu* and bureaucracy. His prestige with the army and his unassailable position at court uniquely equipped him to reconcile personal differences among the various leaders."

In another political analysis, Norman put forth a powerful case for arresting Marquis Koichi Kido, the emperor's principal agent and confidant, as a Class A war criminal. Norman described Kido as an energetic, bustling man with an excellent mind, orderly rather than brilliant, quick and perceptive and, "in contrast to his friend and former patron Konoye, once his mind is made up he acts quickly." Norman cited Kido's recommendation to the emperor that Tojo be appointed premier in 1941 as the decisive action that had brought about that fateful choice. "[This] makes his political responsibility for the events of this period exceedingly heavy." Clearly, Norman was out to remove the emperor's principal advisers, perhaps leading up to the arrest of Hirohito himself. There is no doubt that at this time there was strong pressure from the left to try the emperor as a war criminal.

After some hesitation, MacArthur and Atcheson came down in favor of Norman's recommendations. But MacArthur continued his cautious strategy of testing the waters by arresting those on the UNWCC lists in piecemeal fashion.

As a prelude to the arrest of Prince Konoye and Marquis Kido, MacArthur ordered the detention of another member of the royal house, Prince Nashimoto. The seventy-one-year-old Nashimoto was a popular figure, a prince of the blood who had taken part in the Russo-Japanese and China wars, held the rank of field marshal, and been a supreme war counselor during the Pacific War. Many Japanese were shaken by his detention. For the first time, the Japanese government intervened with MacArthur on the issue of war criminality, formally requesting a "postponement" of the prince's arrest. SCAP replied that no special dispensation would be shown a member of the imperial house. One Tokyo newspaper interpreted Nashimoto's arrest as "tantamount to an inquiry into the responsibility of the emperor himself." On the other hand, the Allied press was elated. One correspondent called it "a vast cancelling of debts."

On December 6, 1945, MacArthur finally ordered the arrest of Konoye and Kido. Each man was given ten days in which to put his personal affairs in order before reporting to Sugamo Prison in Tokyo, which had become the holding pen for Class A war-criminal suspects. "I expected it," Kido confided in his diary. "I heard the news with a calm heart." But Hirohito was shaken. Two days later, the emperor asked to see MacArthur. Against the judgment of his own advisers, Hirohito now offered himself up to SCAP and "to the judgment of the powers you represent as the one to bear the sole responsibility for every political and military decision made and action taken by my people in the conduct of the war." In effect, Hirohito's action was a masterstroke. If he was indicted or, at a minimum, called as a witness at the major war-crimes trial, he would simply shoulder responsibility for the war, and all the other defendants in the trial would have to be acquitted. His strategy failed. Unknown to the Emperor, MacArthur's hands were tied, since Washington had ordered the general to take no action against the emperor as a war criminal.

As scheduled, on December 16 Kido arrived at Sugamo Prison in a sleek, jet-black limousine bearing the imperial crest, the chrysanthemum. Konoye, however, did not appear. Early that morning the prince had taken potassium cyanide. "I have made many political blunders since the China Incident for which I feel deep responsibility," Konoye wrote in a suicide note, "but it is unbearable to me to be tried in an American court as a so-called war criminal."

The Soviet Union now took the lead among those angry at the growing number of suicides—Konoye, General Honjo of the Kwantung Army, War Minister Anami, Field Marshal Sugiyama, and many others. "The Japanese police who arrested the war criminals on the instructions of General MacArthur gave them many opportunities to commit suicide and thus avoid trial," Moscow's *New Times* argued. "These suicides also constitute an attempt to set up the martyr's halo over people whose names were connected with Japanese expansionism in the Far East." Moscow also took the opportunity to redirect attention to the emperor: "World opinion insists that Hirohito be brought to trial." SCAP brushed off the criticisms but tightened security at Sugamo, to the discomfort of the inmates.

As the Allied military continued the slow, deliberate roundup of Class A suspects in Tokyo, Allied trials of war criminals were already under way in other parts of the now-defunct Greater East Asia Co-prosperity Sphere. In Manila, General Tomoyuki Yamashita, the "Tiger of Malaya" who became supreme commander of all Japanese forces in the Philippines, was brought to trial on October 29, 1945, convicted, and on December 7 was sentenced to death. Yamashita's trial, conducted by a five-man U.S. military commission, was in fact the first major war crimes trial after World War II. Also in the Philippines, General Masaharu Homma, commander of the troops who forced U.S. and Filipino prisoners of war into the infamous Bataan Death March, was convicted in a U.S. military court, as were 193 other Japanese. In addition, the government of the Philippines tried 169 Japanese and convicted 133. Generals Yamashita and Homma and 90 others were sentenced to death by U.S. tribunals; of those convicted in Filipino courts, 17 were sentenced to be executed.

Other trials were conducted by the U.S. military in the Marianas and other Pacific island battlegrounds, resulting in a total of 113 convictions. U.S. allies in the Pacific War also held war crimes trials outside of Japan. During 1945 and 1946 Nationalist Chinese courts convicted 504 Japanese as war criminals. In this same period the French convicted 198, the Dutch 969, the British 811, and the Australians 644.

The Soviet Union had entered the war only a week before the Japanese surrender but had captured hundreds of thousands of prisoners of war in Manchuria and surrounding territory. Despite protests that continued into the 1950s, many of these captives never returned home; some estimates put the number of Japanese soldiers lost to the Soviets during this period at 370,000. There is no reliable record of any judicial proceedings against these prisoners.

The trials conducted by the Allies were in sharp contrast to the Soviet handling of Japanese prisoners. Allied trials were public, all the testimony was transcribed, and the accused were afforded the opportunity to defend themselves. Indeed, a number of those brought to trial were acquitted; for example, a Chinese court acquitted a Japanese general who ranked number four on China's war criminal list. In today's climate of opinion, where multiple murderers are given prison terms that are periodically reviewed by parole boards, the Allied trials, in retrospect, may discomfit some. Yet *all* the executions and sentences of convicted Japanese war criminals rolled into one would not equal a single day's murder of innocent civilians by the Japanese during one day at Nanking in 1937 or at the Rape of Manila eight years later, much less in the countless other atrocities that took place in Asia from 1931 until mid-1945.

Moreover, the overwhelming number of Japanese (and Nazi) war criminals were never indicted. As Lord Wright, the first chairman of the UN War Crimes Commission, confessed, "The majority of the [Axis] war criminals will find safety in their numbers. It is physically impossible to punish more than a fraction. All that can be done is to make examples." During a visit to the Tokyo trial, Wright reaffirmed his view that "less than 10 percent of the world's war criminals would face trial." The real figure is probably less than 1 percent, especially in Asia, where, as a noted bibliographer of Japanese materials said privately, "there are no Simon Wiesenthals." In point of fact, when the trials ended in the

Far East, Asians were content to let bygones be bygones, and most Japanese war criminals were able to elude justice.

In Japan, as the Class A war-criminal suspects awaited word on their fate, the Class B and C suspects were brought to trial before U.S. military tribunals in Yokohama, headquarters of the Eighth Army. The men* in the dock were mostly lower-level officers and some civilians accused of such offenses as abuse of POWs and atrocities against civilian populations. In all, 854 Japanese were convicted at Yokohama, and 51 were executed. Although these trials were conducted by U.S. military officers, they were officially Allied trials, since they had been held by order of Douglas MacArthur in his position as Supreme Commander for the Allied Powers. The day-to-day supervision was left to the Eighth Army, commanded by Lieutenant General Robert Eichelberger. MacArthur's principal concerns remained with those who had been arrested as Class A suspects and the effect their trial would have on the Allied occupation of Japan.

On November 30, 1945, President Truman announced the appointment of Joseph Berry Keenan as the chief prosecutor of Japanese war criminals. Within a week Keenan was in Tokyo and conferring with MacArthur about the forthcoming big trial, already in the shadow of Europe as people began referring to it as "Japan's Nuremberg."

*The one woman actively sought by U.S. officials was "Tokyo Rose," who had broadcast anti-American propaganda during the war. In fact, there had been a number of female commentators on Radio Tokyo, but only one, Iva Toguri d'Aquino, a U.S. citizen, was arrested. She was returned to the United States and convicted of treason.

3

The Allied Prosecutors

A good prosecutor is often thought of as tough in addition to having a strong sense of policy. It is the prosecutor who has primary responsibility for indictment and for setting the parameters of the subsequent trial. Joseph Keenan fit this role physically and temperamentally. He was a broad-shouldered, barrel-chested man with a large crimson nose, a florid face, and a penchant for polka-dot bow ties. He was a formidable, flamboyant attorney who had been one of the original American "gangbusters." As head of the U.S. Justice Department's criminal division, he had supervised the prosecution of numerous "public enemies," working in close collaboration with J. Edgar Hoover and the FBI during the 1930s.

Keenan was also a politician of the old school. He had become one of Franklin D. Roosevelt's cronies, a member of the White House inner circle. Known as "Joe the Key," he was said to have influenced many key appointments in Washington during FDR's later terms. Although Keenan avoided intellectual pretensions and played the role of "one of the boys," he was well schooled, a product of Brown University and Harvard Law School. His knowledge of Asian affairs, however, did not extend beyond chow mein.

Unlike Roosevelt, Truman was not attracted by Keenan's personality. Speculation was that the president had given him the Tokyo assignment simply to ease him out of the White House.

In almost any situation, the volatile Keenan was likely to be controversial. In Tokyo, where the role of Americans in every capacity was magnified, Keenan was often at the center of a storm. "Frankly, that's where we got off on the wrong foot," Frederick Mignone, a prosecutor on Keenan's staff, reminisced recently. "He did not measure up to the job." This assessment was echoed by many of the defense attorneys. Beverly Coleman, who was for a time chief of American defense counsel, said to me over lunch in 1980, "Keenan was a good lawyer, but he was not the man to handle a trial like this." Another leading defense attorney, a Japanese American named George Yamaoka, told me disgustedly, "Keenan was not a student of history, the Far East, or the war." One of Yamaoka's colleagues, Carrington Williams, considered Keenan "a questionable choice as chief prosecutor." And this grudgingly: "Despite his self-assurance and his clear ability on occasion to command the situation, his 'habit problems' became all too obvious." The "habit" was alcohol. The rumor—in some cases, assumption—around Tokyo was that Keenan was a drunk. But Robert Donihi, one of Keenan's youngest prosecutors, contradicted much of the talk. "I lived with Keenan and I had a high regard for him," Donihi said. "I saw qualities in him that others did not. He had high blood pressure, and his face was usually flushed. I never saw him take a drink." Yet Donihi also characterized Keenan as a "man of vision and a victim of drink."

Tales of Keenan's drinking abound in the scanty literature on the IMTFE, including stories of his uproarious behavior at the Foreign Correspondents Club in Shimbun Alley. In the period I lived at the club, however, I never once saw Keenan at the bar.

The qualities that Donihi referred to, and that even many of the prosecutor's critics admired, were Keenan's abilities as good listener, negotiator, and organizer. He delegated authority easily and freely. He liked to see his colleagues promoted in their jobs. He excelled in a gruff form of diplomacy and in putting together a team of diverse personalities. The prosecutorial staff in Tokyo, a cacophonous UN with lawyers from a dozen countries, was a ready-made challenge for a man like Keenan.

The first team of prosecutors, led by Keenan, landed at Tokyo's Atsugi Airport on December 6, 1945, the same day MacArthur ordered the arrests of Prince Konoye and Marquis Kido. The initial prosecutorial team consisted of 39 men and women, including 22 lawyers recruited by the U.S. Department of Justice.

Before the trial was over, Keenan was directing a staff of 50 attorneys, about half of them Americans, and a staff comprising 104 Allied nationals and 184 Japanese.

Keenan later admitted that he and his assistants landed in Japan "without a clear idea of the size of the court or the number of nations that would participate in the prosecution, or the exact nature of the charges." Nevertheless, in a nervous burst of energy, Keenan hit the deck running. He conferred at length the next day with MacArthur and found him "tremendously interested in the subject matter of the prosecution."

True to form, Keenan immediately made headlines in Tokyo, announcing that Japan's Class A war-crimes suspects would be tried for starting wars in China and the Pacific. He added that the trial would be under American criminal law "since the initial attack was against American territory at Pearl Harbor." Asian experts sighed. But Keenan, though ignorant, was no fool. He embarked on a cram course in Far Eastern affairs, and while he never mastered the subject, he soon concluded that "there seems to be no logical place to start, short of the [Japanese] invasion of Manchuria in 1931."

Like almost everyone else, Keenan thought the Tokyo trial would last six months or less, beginning in January, and that MacArthur would appoint an international tribunal to which the nine Allied powers signing the instrument of surrender would send judges and prosecutors. In discussing indictments with the Tokyo press corps, Keenan said, "The best way I can describe what we are trying to do in Japan is to say that what a man does to start a war must be his personal responsibility. He must pay the price for his acts."

Three days after his arrival, on December 9, Keenan appointed Lieutenant Colonel Ben Sackett, a former FBI man, as chief of investigations for the International Prosecution Section (IPS) and told him his first job was to find out how far SCAP had advanced in developing a case against the Class A suspects. Sackett's initial findings were disheartening. "To my knowledge no staff section or individual connected with this headquarters [SCAP] has made any detailed study or formed any concrete theory relative to the scope of the prosecution against major Japanese war criminals," Sackett reported in a secret memo now in the U.S. National Archives. "No evidence was collected or specifically searched for bearing on the case against major war criminals."

Worse was to follow. Keenan had named John A. Darsey, Jr., the Justice Department's liaison man on Japanese war-crimes prosecution in Tokyo, as his executive assistant and assigned him ten IPS lawyers to screen the Allies' war criminal files. Darsey soon reported back that "very little concrete evidence indicating the guilt of any of the suspects is presently readily accessible." Keenan was shaken to learn that Japanese government agencies—particularly the military—had continued to function after the surrender with their same wartime personnel, that the Japanese had burned or otherwise destroyed incriminating evidence, and that requests for information from the Japanese government had to be submitted to the Japanese Liaison Office in writing, a laborious procedure that lent itself to stonewalling. And Darsey topped everything with the disclosure that "there were practically no records in the possession or under the control of this headquarters which could be analyzed to determine who planned and initiated the wars of aggression."

Keenan's investigators also discovered that "the information relative to who was in [Sugamo] prison and why such people were arrested is very confused." Sugamo held about 1,200 inmates, including the 80 Class A suspects.

Keenan now cast in every direction for help, energetically issuing a stream of orders and attempting to bring order out of disorder. MacArthur was completely cooperative: The faster the distracting war-crimes trial was over, the quicker SCAP would get these civilian lawyers out of Tokyo.

As it developed, the IPS soon lucked into a rich haul of evidence. Shortly after his arrest, Marquis Kido had stunned the prosecution by voluntarily revealing the existence of his voluminous diaries. These detailed journals, which covered the period from January 1, 1930 to December 15, 1945, and contained 5,920 entries, caused a sensation. Solis Horwitz, a member of Keenan's staff who later wrote a monograph, *The Tokyo Trial,* described the diaries as "the working bible of the prosecution and the main key to all further investigations." Here was an authoritative record giving names, dates, and places for every important political development in contemporary Japanese history as viewed by the emperor's principal agent. The diaries were the IMTFE's Watergate tapes.

Kido's motivation for telling the prosecutors about the journals has been debated ever since. The consensus is that the marquis was convinced that a careful study of the record would demonstrate that the militarists had been in control of Japan and that they had acted independently of the emperor. It is interesting to speculate about what would have happened to the Allied case if the Canadian KGB man Herbert Norman had not insisted on Kido's arrest. In all probability the diaries would never have come to light. The Soviets had outfoxed themselves, since they wanted the emperor in the dock.

Next to the Kido diaries, the prosecution's richest sources of information were the interrogations of suspects. Keenan called for the questioning of "all individuals in prison or who have been ordered into custody on the theory that they are suspected Class 1-A war criminals." He arranged also for weekly staff conferences and set up an elaborate cross-filing system whereby all the evidence against an individual was collected under the suspect's name. Many of his procedures were patterned on the methods of the FBI.

The prosecutors also received evidence from Japanese who had opposed the war—"confidential informants," as they were termed. These included senior officials in the government and army who made secret arrangements with Keenan and his staff to turn over leads and hard evidence. On February 25, 1946, for example, one of Keenan's investigators reported to the IPS executive committee that a prominent member of the Japanese Foreign Office had turned over information "of a substantial nature concerning many of the key defendants," while another source reported to the IPS that "important as well as secret documents not destroyed by fire will be available upon request," including a copy of the secret clauses in the German-Japanese Axis Pact. The late Prince Konoye's private secretary provided the IPS with the original notes of a Konoye memoir written shortly before he committed suicide.

General Ryukichi Tanaka, who turned out to be one of the trial's most controversial witnesses, provided extraordinary leads, including evidence of the army's trafficking in narcotics in China. "Revenue derived from the opium and narcotics traffic was the chief source of income for the Manchukuo government [the Japanese puppet regime in Manchuria]," he secretly informed the IPS. Tanaka fingered General Kenji Doihara, then in Sugamo as a Class A suspect, as "undoubtedly knowing everything there is to know" about the Japanese Army's drug trafficking.

Keenan drove himself and his staff relentlessly, the Allied governments that had signed the instrument of surrender displayed only minimal interest in the trial. MacArthur's political adviser, George Atcheson, recommended that "if there is no prospect of establishing an International Tribunal within a very short time, the trials be conducted by a purely American tribunal." MacArthur concurred and let it be known to the press, through "sources close to the General," that he was "impatient" with the Allies' delay. Fortuitously, on December 27, 1945, the foreign ministers of the United States, Great Britain, China, and the Soviet Union agreed that "the Supreme Commander shall issue all orders for the implementation of the Terms of Surrender, the occupation and control of Japan and directives supplementary thereto." To advise and consult with MacArthur, they set up an eleven-nation Far Eastern Commission composed of the Allied signatories at Japan's formal surrender—Australia, New Zealand, Canada, the Netherlands, France, Britain, the United States, the Soviet Union, and China—plus the Philippines and India. They also established an Allied Council for Japan for "consulting and advising the Supreme Commander in regard to the implementation of the Terms of Surrender, which included the trial of Japanese war criminals." The council consisted only of Britain, China, the Soviet Union, and the United States.

As a follow-up, the State Department informed the Allies that MacArthur intended to appoint an international military tribunal to try the major Japanese war criminals and that an indictment would be handed down on February 1, 1946. Washington called on each of the Allies to nominate a judge and to appoint an associate prosecutor and staff by January 5.

On January 16, after no appointments had been made by any of the Allies, MacArthur issued a declaration: "I, Douglas MacArthur, as Supreme Commander for the Allied Powers, by virtue of the authority so conferred upon me, in order to implement the Terms of Surrender which requires the meting out of stern justice to war criminals, do order . . . there shall be established an International Military Tribunal for the Far East (IMTFE) for the trial of those persons charged individually, or as members of organizations, or in both capacities, with offenses which include crimes against peace."

The IMTFE's charter, drafted jointly by Keenan's staff and SCAP's legal section, followed the broad outline of the Big Four agreement in London that had established the Nuremberg tribunal. The difference, of course, was that while Nuremberg was the product of four-power negotiation, the Tokyo tribunal derived its authority from SCAP, who acted as an agent for the powers that had signed the instrument of surrender. (This would become a source of contention later.)

The charter contained seventeen briskly worded articles. It is a measure of the solid work done by MacArthur and Keenan and their staffs that after the arrival of Allied prosecutors, only a few changes were made. In the charter, MacArthur invested himself with the authority to appoint the judges nominated by the Allies and to select from among them the president of the tribunal. The charter also provided that decisions and judgments of the tribunal, including conviction and sentence, would be by majority vote. In the interests of a fair trial, all those accused would receive an indictment spelling out the charges against them, and they would be given the right to defense counsel. The trial would be conducted in English "and in the language of the accused." In an effort to avoid legal wrangles, and taking into consideration the fundamental differences among Anglo-Saxon, Roman, and other legal systems followed by the individual Allies, the charter held that "the tribunal shall not be bound by technical rules of evidence."

Since so much incriminating evidence was known to have been destroyed, the charter provided that evidence against the accused might include "a document, regardless of its security classification and without proof of its issuance or signature, which appears to the Tribunal to have been signed or issued." This was in addition to diaries, letters, and other papers, including sworn and unsworn statements relating to the charges in the indictment.

The heart of the charter was contained in Articles 5 and 6, which covered the tribunal's jurisdiction and the responsibility of the accused. "The Tribunal shall have the power to try and punish Far Eastern war criminals who as individuals or as members of organizations are charged with offenses which include Crimes against Peace." The latter was defined as "the planning, preparation, initiation, or waging of a declared or undeclared war of aggression or a war in violation of international law." As a professional soldier, MacArthur was careful to ensure that no member of the imperial Japanese armed forces was indicted simply for fighting the war. In addition to crimes against peace, two other crimes were included within the jurisdiction of the court—conventional war crimes, which were described as violations of the customs of war, and crimes against humanity, which were defined as inhumane acts committed against "any civilian population, before or during the war."

Article 6 dispensed with the notion that an accused could plead "superior orders" as a defense. "Neither the official position, at any time, of an accused, nor the fact that an accused acted pursuant to [an] order of his government or of a superior shall, of itself, be sufficient to free such accused from responsibility for any crimes with which he is charged, but such circumstances may be considered in mitigation of punishment if the Tribunal determines that justice so requires."

Finally, the tribunal was empowered to impose on those convicted "death or such other punishment as shall be determined by it to be just." Unlike the procedure at Nuremberg, where the court consisted of four justices (from France, the United Kingdom, the USSR, and the United States), the Tokyo charter provided for a bench of not less than five and not more than nine judges. At Nuremberg, each judge had an alternate; in Tokyo, none was provided for. At Nuremberg, too, each of the four sponsoring powers appointed its own chief prosecutor. At Tokyo, there was only one chief prosecutor, and each Allied prosecutor was designated "associate prosecutor" under his direction. This feature startled even Solis Horwitz, Keenan's aide. "For the first time [the Allied] nations had agreed in a matter other than actual military operations to subordinate their sovereignty and to permit a national of one of them to have final direction and control," Horwitz observed.

After MacArthur's action on the charter and Washington's threat to go it alone at Tokyo, the Allies scrambled to get to Tokyo.

Many of the American prosecutors ruefully admitted that the legal teams sent to Tokyo by the Allies were of generally higher caliber than the American staff. Among outstanding Allied prosecutors was Arthur S. Comyns-Carr, a former member of the British Parliament and a leading barrister. In one major respect, he was the obverse of Keenan, for Comyns-Carr shunned publicity. Others destined to play a prominent role in the trial were Hsiang Che-chun, chief prosecutor of the Shanghai High Court and former prosecutor before the Supreme Court of China, who was well versed in international law; W. G. Frederick Borgerhoff-Mulder, who had served as judge on the Special War Criminals Court set up in The Hague the previous year; and Robert L. Oneto of the

French Ministry of Justice, who had narrowly escaped being shot in 1944 as a member of the Resistance and who, after the liberation of France, had become the chief prosecutor of the Special Versailles Court that tried Nazi and Vichy war criminals and collaborators (in the course of the trial, Oneto met, pursued, and married an American WAC).

The prosecutorial teams from Australia, Canada, and New Zealand were also highly regarded. Justice Alan Mansfield of the Supreme Court of Queensland, who had investigated Japanese war criminality on New Guinea, was a brilliant cross-examiner and in both substance and style was greatly admired by the defense. Brigadier Henry Nolan, the Canadian Army's vice judge advocate, was widely considered among the top legal minds in the IPS. New Zealand also sent a brigadier, Ronald Quilliam, a former examiner in criminal law at the University of New Zealand and deputy adjutant general of the New Zealand Army.

For some inexplicable reason, after announcing the appointment of Minister S. A. Golunsky as the Soviet associate prosecutor on February 2, Moscow failed to clear his departure until the eve of the trial, two and a half months later. Golunsky had taught at the Moscow Institute of Law and the Red Army Military Academy of Law and was fluent in English. As a high functionary of the Foreign Ministry, he had attended the San Francisco conference in 1945 that had established the United Nations. (He was the best contact I had in the Soviet delegation.)

The prosecution was off to a rocky start.

4

The Judges

With the tribunal's charter in place, the Class A suspects under arrest, and the Allied prosecution building its case, attention in Tokyo shifted to the arrival of the judges. By February 15, 1946, nine of the signatories to the instrument of surrender had each nominated a judge to sit on the IMTFE, and on that day Mac-Arthur formally appointed all of them. No nominee to the bench was ever rejected by SCAP.

Keenan sought to add luster to the tribunal by obtaining the appointment of a man of stature as the U.S. justice. On January 18, two days after MacArthur promulgated the charter, Keenan recommended Willis Smith, president of the American Bar Association. Keenan argued that the international importance of the appointment "cannot be over-estimated [since] the appointments and nominations received from other nations comprise a panel of jurists of world-wide reputation and distinction." If Smith was not available, the next best choice, Keenan cabled Washington, was Roscoe Pound, dean of Harvard Law School. Keenan went on to suggest that if the nominee came from the federal judiciary, he should sit on a court no lower than the U.S. Circuit Court of Appeals, or, if he was a military man, should hold at least rank of major general, which was the rank of the U.S. Army's judge advocate general, Myron C. Cramer.

For reasons lost in the murky Democratic politics of the era, the Truman administration named John P. Higgins, chief justice of the Massachusetts state Superior Court, to the IMTFE. Keenan was aghast. In one of his notoriously frank cables to Washington Keenan described himself as "disturbed" by the selection and declared that "with all due respect for Judge Higgins, he is . . . known only locally in his state [and] would not constitute an appointment comparable to the foreign members who have been nominated." Lest there be a misunderstanding, Keenan reiterated that "the Superior Court of Massachusetts being local in its jurisdiction and intermediate in rank does not in the eyes of others reach the dignity of the U.S. District Court."

Keenan's strident objections notwithstanding, Higgins's nomination was sent to MacArthur. The general's reaction to the Higgins appointment is not known, but Keenan's lightly concealed outrage upset their joint plans to appoint the American judge as the president of the tribunal.

Keenan had been correct in describing the other Allied appointees as judges of "reputation and distinction." For the most part they were.

As expected, Australia nominated her expert on Japanese war crimes, Sir William Webb, then chief justice of the Supreme Court of Queensland. When MacArthur, on February 20, named Webb the president of IMTFE, Canberra reacted by elevating Webb to the Australian High Court Bench, or Supreme Court. Although Webb had the reputation of a roaring lion, he was actually a pussycat. In all his years on the bench, Webb had never passed a death sentence. In truth, he opposed capital punishment, and it was one of the stranger aspects of the Tokyo trial that to this day, as in my original notebooks on the trial, Webb is referred to as "the Hanging Judge."

No sooner had Webb been nominated and appointed to the tribunal than the question arose whether or not he should disqualify himself. Before he was appointed to the Tokyo position, he had been chief of the Australian group investigating Japanese atrocities against Australian troops. In fact, Webb raised the issue himself, telling the IPS that he did not want to take up his duties without MacArthur being aware of his background. SCAP was informed and concluded, in Keenan's words, that Webb's role as a war crimes investigator "would not of itself disqualify the Justice from sitting on the IMT." Nevertheless, at the outset of the trial the defense protested the presence of Webb and the Filipino judge, Delfin Jaranilla, who had been a prisoner of the Japanese. The protest was disallowed.

The Soviet nominee was I. M. Zarayanov, who had served as commissar of justice during the bloody days of Lenin's Bolshevik Revolution and had taken part in the Stalin's stage-managed Moscow purge trials in 1935–38. Zarayanov, a Red Army major general and a member of the Military Collegium of the Supreme Court, had served as chief of the Red Army Military Academy of Law, where Minister Golunsky, the Soviet associate prosecutor, taught. Like Webb, Zarayanov was linked to Japanese affairs; in 1935 he had sat in judgment of three White Russians whom the Japanese had recruited in Manchuria and sent into the Soviet Union as secret agents. The three had been captured, tried, and condemned to death as "counterrevolutionaries." A Stalinist judge on the bench was clearly the most embarrassing element in the bench's composition. Russia had earned a seat on the IMTFE by her declaration of war on Japan shortly before the Japanese surrender and, as Lord Hankey, Britain's most caustic critic of the Tokyo proceedings, pointed out, "in breach of her nonaggression pact with Japan."

I remember Zarayanov as a jovial man, as big and burly—and as dangerous—as a Kodiak bear. He always smiled, displaying elaborate gold bridgework. At Russian parties he loved to teach his IMTFE colleagues and journalists how to drink vodka out of a shot glass in one gulp. "Bottoms up!" he commanded—in the only two English words he knew. (All the judges except Zarayanov were fluent in English.) Zarayanov's chauffeur was an American GI. "I don't agree with his politics," the driver said, "but he sure is a nice boss."

Like the Russians, the Chinese selected a major general as their judicial representative. Shih Mei-yu was a man of iron integrity, the chief justice of the Chinese War Crimes Court, which the Republic of China (ROC) had set up after the Japanese surrender. But he never got to Tokyo. Shih was still needed at home, where the Chinese held more than 2,000 Japanese war criminal suspects. The man sent in his place was Mei Ju-ao, the eldest son in a family of nine, a member of the Democratic League—China's "third force" between the Nationalists and Communists—a prominent attorney, and a member of the legislative Yuan, where he served as acting chairman of the foreign affairs committee. I remember him as friendly and outgoing. A brilliant lawyer, Mei had graduated from Stanford and the University of Chicago *magna cum laude*. He was a prolific writer and the author of *Constitutional Government in China* and *China's Wartime Legislation*. When the trial concluded in 1948, the Chinese Civil War was moving rapidly toward a climax, and Mei flew to Hong Kong instead of returning to China. Ultimately, he joined the newly established Communist regime and subsequently served in the People's Consultative Congress. During the Tokyo trial, Mei and Sir William Webb became fast friends. "The Chinese judge sits alongside me in court," Webb wrote a friend October 23, 1947. "He is a very pleasant chap. We are good friends. He has told me quite a lot about conditions in China."

Another high-caliber appointee was the Dutch judge, the youngest member of the bench, a forty-year-old professor of law at Utrecht who brought his violin along with him to Tokyo. B.V.A. Röling also dabbled in Buddhism and, like Comyns-Carr, was an enthusiastic mountain climber. Röling was the first member of the IMTFE to scale Mount Fuji, which rises 12,365 feet not far from Tokyo and holds mystical charm for many Japanese.

Like the judges sent by the Soviet Union and Australia, New Zealand's appointee was a representative of his country's Supreme Court. Harvey Northcroft had established a distinguished military record in World Wars I and II and served as judge advocate general of the New Zealand armed forces during the war against Japan. Northcroft was white-haired, had a penchant for striped suits and black homburgs, and was an ardent angler. Whenever court duties would permit, which was infrequently, he would sneak off to Hakone for trout fishing. When Webb was unavailable to preside in chambers, Northcroft generally filled in for him.

The seventh appointee to the IMTFE was Canada's Edward Stuart McDougall, a man of small build, ruddy outdoor complexion, and bushy eyebrows, who possessed a relatively undistinguished record as a jurist. His most important posting had been in 1942 as puisne judge, Court of King's Bench, Appeal Side. For most of the war he had been a member of the royal commission inquiring into labor unrest. Although McDougall was a political appointee, his complete lack of background for the job raised eyebrows in both Japan and Canada. Yet, as the trial progressed his stature grew. Frederick Mignone, one of Keenan's American assistants, recalled him "as one of the better judges at Tokyo," as did American defense attorney Carrington Williams.

The British and French appointments to the tribunal were the last to be made by the signatories of the instrument of surrender. Britain settled on Lord Patrick, a king's counsel and dean of the Faculty of Advocates who was a judge on Scotland's College of Justice, or Supreme Court. I remember him as a remote, aloof figure who seemed to have come directly from central casting. In his black robes, he looked like and acted as a judge—tall, somber, gray-haired, crisp, and authoritative. Although the judges isolated themselves from the prosecutors and defense lawyers, in the close foreign community in occupied Tokyo it was inevitable that they socialize to some extent. At Allied diplomatic receptions or in the confines of the Imperial Hotel, Lord Patrick was exceptionally reserved. As one of the attorneys at the trial later observed, "He never permitted anyone to get close to him." He also detested the press and on one occasion described news photographers as "dogs." Patrick was widely considered a dignified representative of the English court system and one of the tribunal's better legal minds. He and Webb got along well.

The first French nominee never got to Tokyo. Henri Reimburger, a former legal adviser to the Ministry of Overseas Affairs, resigned abruptly on April 5, apparently for personal reasons, and was replaced by Henri Bernard. "Well," the quip went, "at least we still have an Henri." Bernard had fought at the Somme and Ardennes in World War I—where he learned English among the Tommies and doughboys—and had spent the years between the two great wars in the colonial service in West Africa. After the fall of France he joined de Gaulle's Free French forces, serving first as chief prosecutor on various courts in Brazzaville and then with the First Military Tribunal of Paris after the liberation, trying Nazi war criminals and collaborators. His face was unremarkable, and even black robes failed to give him a distinguished appearance. But he quickly earned a reputation on the bench, as one source put it, as "a plus."

With the exception of Mei, all the judges were of European ancestry, reflecting the preeminent position of the white man in colonized prewar Asia. Yet, in addition to China, both India and the Philippines were members of the Far East Commission established by the Big Four foreign ministers' conference at the end of 1945. The IPS, in addition to a Chinese legal staff, also had Indian and Filipino associate prosecutors and an Indian, Filipino, and

Burmese staff. The Philippines had suffered grievously as a result of the Japanese invasion and occupation, and MacArthur was inclined to have Filipino representation on the IMTFE bench. India, which had suffered thousands of casualties defending such British real estate holdings as Hong Kong, Malaya, Singapore, and Burma, as well as in protecting the Indian border from a token Japanese invasion, also had troops in southern Japan as part of the British Commonwealth Occupation Force (BCOF). India was miffed by its lack of representation on the IMTFE bench, and London "strongly" supported New Delhi's desire to be represented at the proceedings, the British informed Washington in an aide-mémoire. Matters came to a head on February 4, when Keenan reported to Washington, in a dispatch classified secret, "We have been confidentially informed that India has been especially sensitive to the fact that France, whose participation in the Pacific theatre in defensive and offensive warfare has been limited, should receive recognition in the appointment of a judge and prosecutor and India omitted with reference to an appointment to the judiciary."

How limited was not spelled out in Keenan's memo. France had been a participant in the Pacific or Great East Asia War, as the Japanese called it, for four and a half months. When the Japanese struck south in 1941, France's three colonies in the Far East—Vietnam, Cambodia, and Laos—had been governed from Vichy, the seat of Hitler's collaborationist French regime. As a result of Japanese and German pressure on Vichy, the French permitted Japanese troops to use French Indochina as a base of operations against the rest of Southeast Asia. It was not until March 1945 that the Japanese, alarmed by the collapse of Vichy and the imminent collapse of Germany, carried out a coup d'état and occupied the whole of Indochina. As usual, the Japanese immediately unleashed a reign of terror against the local population. By comparison, the Philippines, already self-governing and scheduled to acquire complete independence July 4, 1946, were invaded, overrun, occupied, and ravaged by the Japanese over a three-and-a-half-year period. Yet the Filipinos were unrepresented on the bench. Clearly, the Philippines had a greater right to a place on the bench then France or, for that matter, India.

Power politics, of course, was the explanation. France was a member of the Big Four in Europe and the Big Five in the Security Council of the United Nations. At that time the Philippines and India carried relatively little weight in international affairs.

The issue of broader Asian representation on the bench at Tokyo also boiled over at the first meeting of the eleven-nation Far Eastern Commission. The FEC's Fifth Committee, which dealt with war criminality, agreed to draw up a policy paper on the "apprehension, trial and punishment of war criminals in the Far East." The chairman of the committee represented China; his deputy, the Philippines. India was a member. On April 3, 1946, the committee's report was issued, stating that every member of the FEC had the right to appoint a judge to the IMTFE.

MacArthur acted promptly and three days later promulgated an amended charter that raised the number of judges on the IMTFE to "not less than six members nor more than eleven members, appointed by the Supreme Commander for the Allied Powers from the names submitted by the Signatories to the Instrument of Surrender, India and the Commonwealth of the Philippines." Thus, the IMTFE bench was expanded to eleven, and thereafter a majority of six judges constituted a quorum.

Since the basic legal system of seven members of the bench was Anglo-Saxon (Australia, Canada, India, the Philippines, New Zealand, the United States, and, of course, Britain), the IMTFE was inescapably an Anglo-Saxon court. If critics of the bench's makeup looked askance at the presence of a Stalinist judge on the tribunal, then perforce the Russians looked askance on the Anglo-Saxon composition of the court. As the co-founder of communism, Friedrich Engels, put it, in Anglo-Saxon courts "the clever lawyer can always find a loophole in favor of the accused." After the completion of the trial, one of the Soviet assistant prosecutors, General A. N. Vasiliev, wrote angrily, "The chief justice [Webb] in the Tokyo trial demonstrated that the English and American court system has not changed since Engels and 'clever lawyers' can obtain at least prolongation of the case even though they may not be able to exonerate the accused."

Another wrinkle in the amended charter suggested that MacArthur (and Keenan) had abandoned their optimism that the trial would be over in "four or five months." The amended charter held that if a judge was at any time absent and afterward was able to be present, he would be permitted to take part in subsequent proceedings, "unless he declares in open court that he is disqualified by reason of insufficient familiarity with the proceedings which took place in his absence." Thus, in effect, the charter permitted the judges to come and go as they pleased. By contrast, each of the four judges at Nuremberg was backed by an alternate. In Tokyo this was impractical. With eleven judges on the bench and eleven alternates in court, the already cluttered bench would have become a mob. "A bench of twenty-two judges would have been so unwieldly as to hamper the progress of a trial already faced with many obstacles militating against expeditious proceeding," Solis Horwitz explained in his monograph. As it was, when the trial got underway, each spectator received a three-by-five-inch printed "scorecard" that identified the eleven judges and twenty-eight defendants. The only thing missing in Tokyo was a number on the back of each man's clothing.

Immediately after the amended charter was promulgated, India nominated as its judge Radhabinod Pal, who joined the IMTFE on May 17. Delfin Jaranilla of the Philippines took his seat on the bench on June 13. Both were strong appointments.

A graduate of the University of Calcutta, Pal was a former math professor who had turned to law. Before the war he had been elected one of the joint presidents of the International Law Association, and in 1940 he was appointed to the High Court of Calcutta. Pal was also a lecturer at the University Law College and author of *The Hindu Philosophy of Law* and *The Law of Limitation in British India*. During the trial his wife took seriously ill, and he shuttled between Japan and India on frequent trips to be at her bedside.

Jaranilla's credentials were equally impressive. He had served as attorney general of the Philippines and as a member of the Supreme Court. In 1940, as the Japanese war in China deepened and tension heightened in the Pacific, Jaranilla was commissioned a colonel in the Philippine Scouts and named judge advocate general. The Japanese soon took him prisoner, and he was in the Bataan Death March. In February 1945, after the Japanese had been cleared from Luzon, Jaranilla was named secretary of justice, and six months later he was appointed to the Supreme Court. Like so many of the other judges on the tribunal, Jaranilla also taught law. Between 1926 and 1940 he had been associated with the University of the Philippines and the University of Manila.

The U.S. appointment to the IMTFE was so weak by comparison that the impression was created, rightly or not, that the paramount power in Japan considered the tribunal of secondary importance. This conclusion was unavoidable when the Americans at Nuremberg were compared with those at Tokyo, particularly with the presence of a U.S. Supreme Court justice, Robert Jackson, as a prosecutor at Nuremberg. As defense counsel George Yamaoka saw it, "For most of the Allies, perhaps, Germany was the principal enemy; Japan was a collateral enemy." A tribunal judge also believed that the Americans did not treat the IMTFE fairly. "They treated it as a second-rate court," Röling, the Dutch judge, wrote me recently.

In the early days of the court, before the arrival of the Soviet, Indian, and Filipino appointees, the eight judges in Tokyo agreed unanimously that their deliberations in chambers would be kept *in camera* and that there would be no separate or dissenting opinions at the conclusion of the trial. The tribunal's judgment would express the majority's views, and under the amended charter, six judges constituted a quorum. The Soviet and Filipino justices went along with the plan. But the agreement collapsed with the arrival of the Indian justice. In an analysis of the incident, Judge Röling wrote me on September 20, 1982, "After this decision, Pal entered. He declared: 1) not to be bound by the decision taken by the nine judges, and 2) the intention to write a dissenting opinion." With that declaration, the former decision collapsed. As it developed, the Indian judge had arrived in Tokyo with his mind made up to dissent before he had even heard the evidence.

Pal appears to have thrown more than one monkey wrench into the organization and work of the bench. On April 25 the judges then in Tokyo signed an affirmation in which they pledged that "we will duly administer justice, according to law, without fear, favor or affect, and according to our conscience, and to the best of our understanding, that we will not disclose or discover the vote or opinion of any particular member of the Tribunal upon the finding or sentence but will preserve inviolate the secrecy or the counsel of every member." The original of this document, in the U.S. National Archives, bears the signatures of all the judges except Pal. Nor was this an oversight. Pal arrived in Tokyo in May and Jaranilla in June. Yet the document bears Jaranilla's name and the initialed date "June 1946." Pal declined to bind himself to the affirmation.

Whatever the case, the IMTFE, like a ship ghosting along in a lifting fog, gradually began to acquire a recognizable form. The charter, judges, and prosecution were in place, and the defense was beginning to take shape.

5

The Defense,
the Prisoners,
and the Charges

To some observers the defense of the war criminal suspects seemed to come to the Allies almost as an afterthought in their plans for the trial. In fact, it was not until April 5, 1946, that a Defense Division (DD) was formally established. As announced by the tribunal's general secretary, Colonel Vern Walbridge, an American, the division was to provide "counsel for the major war criminals at the forthcoming trials." The initials DD never caught on. In the transcript the defense was referred to as the Defense Section (DS), and the reporters and others at the trial referred to it as simply "the defense."

The question of a defense had arisen earlier, on January 7, when a pair of well-dressed Japanese paid a call on SCAP's legal section and asked whether two of their friends detained at Sugamo as Class A suspects, one a former foreign minister and the other a member of the *zaibatsu,* would be permitted to select their own defense counsel. "I was not absolutely sure about that," the SCAP officer in charge later said, "but I felt that within reasonable limits that might be the case." The Japanese proposed as defense counsel Dr. Theodore Sternberg, a German Jew who had lived in Japan since 1913 and was a professor of law at Tokyo Imperial University. Sternberg, they contended, was "the best available counsel in Japan for matters of this kind." But the officer said that he did not know whether a German alien could serve as counsel to the Japanese defendants. As it turned out, Sternberg, seventy-two years old and ailing, did not join the defense, although he maintained contact from the sidelines with Kenzo Takayanagi, a colleague on the faculty of Tokyo Imperial who played a prominent role in the defense.

In Sternberg's only known published comment on the trial, made in late 1948, he was quoted in the periodical *Yukan Miyaka* as saying he had maintained no "personal" connection with the defendants during the trial but that "I think they were led to commit these crimes because they subscribed to an erroneous ideology." However, he continued, "from the point of jurisprudence, I am absolutely opposed to the imposition of the death penalty on them."

Most of the Class A war-criminal suspects confined to Sugamo were quick to acquire defense counsel, but for reasons of security, no Japanese attorney was permitted to interview a client who was not indicted. However, from outside Sugamo, three Japanese attorneys took command of the impending defense by remote control. One was Ichiro Kiyose, who had served in the prewar Diet for eight terms. Though he had been purged by SCAP as an ultra-rightist with military connections, he impressed both the IPS and the American defense counsel during the trial. Joseph Keenan characterized him as "very astute and able." George Furness, one of the American defense attorneys, described him as "one of the top lawyers in the world." After the 1952 Japanese peace treaty, Kiyose returned to politics and was reelected to the Diet, where he became speaker of the house. I especially remember him for his white beard and ill-fitting, poor-quality suits.

Kenzo Takayanagi was another heavyweight on the Japanese defense. A legal scholar who had studied under Roscoe Pound at Harvard, he wrote many theoretical briefs for the defense. Takayanagi, I recall, was of slim build with a bald head and a short, black brush mustache.

The third member of the trio was the scholarly Somei Uzawa, president of Meiji University and a renowned legal authority. Shortly after the war, Uzawa told a press conference that personally he held Tojo responsible for the war but that Tojo should be given a fair trial, "although I am not sure he deserves it." Uzawa initially served as the defense's "utility infielder," assisting the counsel of several accused. When the trial opened, he was nominated unanimously by the defendants as chief of the defense. Kiyose, who was elected his deputy, set the tone of the defense on March 16, 1946, when he told a press conference that the Tojo case was "defensible." No single individual or group of individuals, Kiyose contended, could be responsible for a conflict of the magnitude of the Pacific War.

This was followed up within a fortnight by Takayanagi's lengthy analysis of the forthcoming trial, which ran on the editorial page of the *Nippon Times*. It served notice on Joseph Keenan and his staff that there would be a strong defense at the IMTFE.

Takayanagi held that the trial was an "act of necessity," that the Japanese were honor-bound to submit to a trial after accepting the Potsdam terms, and that MacArthur, "whatever [his] personal opinion regarding this historic trial"—a confirmation that some Japanese were privy to MacArthur's opposition to the trial—must carry out the trial since SCAP was charged with implementing Potsdam. Takayanagi also held that the Allies were themselves forced to stage a trial "not only by their previous declarations but the state of current public opinion in their respective lands."

Given the Anglo-Saxon composition of the tribunal, the Japanese defense felt ill prepared. "It is apparent that the procedure by which the tribunal is to conduct the trial has been drafted with Anglo-American law in mind," Takayanagi said.

Accordingly, with the consent of the as yet unindicted Class A war-criminal suspects, the Japanese government appealed to MacArthur on February 14 for British and American trial lawyers to assist the defense. However, British barristers as a matter of law were barred from practicing in a foreign jurisdiction. Sir William Webb, of course, was aware of this problem, and as president of the tribunal he told Joseph Keenan that the court would approve a role for advisory (read U.S.) counsel only if the accused "always have the fullest right to select their own counsel and advisers."

The man who was universally considered number one on the Allied war-criminals list, Hideki Tojo, assented to Allied legal assistance—on one condition. "That condition was that we did not shove off responsibility for the war on the emperor," one of the American defense attorneys revealed to me recently. When the American defense lawyers arrived on the scene, they warned Tojo that without implicating the emperor, his defense would be difficult. But Tojo was adamant: "I want nothing said or presented that will bring the emperor into this; I know they are going to hang me." Even under such restrictions, the American defense at the IMTFE put up a vigorous fight, a fact that was widely acknowledged by the Japanese defense attorneys, the accused, and their families.

On February 21 and 28 Keenan appealed to Washington to send "fifteen to twenty attorneys" to Tokyo to assist their defense. "SCAP asks for military personnel for defense counsel," Keenan said, "but if not available, civilian counsel would be desired." On March 11 Washington notified him that it had "arranged for fifteen defense attorneys, principally civilians," to fly to Tokyo. Despite SCAP's pleas for haste, most of these attorneys did not arrive in Tokyo until May 17. This was two weeks after the indictment and the formal opening of the trial, but two and a half weeks before the prosecution's opening statement on June 4. Thus, in the pretrial maneuvering the case for the defense had been carried by a number of Japanese attorneys engaged by the individual suspects and by six American lawyers who were already in Japan. Captain Beverly Coleman, a U.S. Navy officer and a lawyer in civilian life, had been appointed chief of the defense team. Coleman and his colleagues had done what preparatory work they could as they awaited the indictments.

Meanwhile, Joseph Keenan and his prosecutors had been working long hours, trying to decide who among the more than eighty Class A suspects in Sugamo Prison should be indicted. In the beginning, the case had appeared to be relatively simple, at least to the Americans: Try Tojo for Pearl Harbor. MacArthur admitted as much in his memoirs, and the Dutch judge, Röling, later disclosed that SCAP repeatedly expressed a preference for "only a short court-martial about Pearl Harbor." But as even the most naïve and shortsighted prosecutor quickly saw, to concentrate on Pearl Harbor was akin to cleaning up polluted water without investigating the source of the poison. It became the job of the IPS to trace down the source.

The Kido diaries had provided good early leads to the investigators, but it was the ongoing interrogation of the suspects held in Sugamo that now provided some of the most fruitful information. Many of the Japanese prisoners were voluble and frank, but others, such as former premier Koki Hirota, were tight-lipped, volunteering no information and giving only terse answers to all questions. Several of the generals, notably Akira Muto, feigned ignorance and played out the role of childish innocence. Muto denied knowledge of the mass-scale Japanese atrocities at Nanking in 1938 and Manila in 1945, even though he had been a senior staff officer at both places in both those time frames. Other suspects were evasive, but their evasions often provided the prosecution with damaging testimony against other defendants.

Several of the statements obtained by the prosecutors were so startling—for example, that Japan had maintained no prisoner-of-war camps in China because there had been no war in China, only an "incident"—that some critics suspected that the Americans were either using force or bribing the suspects. One of the British assistant prosecutors, a man named Christmas Humphreys, was a bit anti-American, and suspicious of the U.S. investigators. In a posttrial memoir he wrote, "So full were the confessions obtained by American lawyers . . . that I made it my business to attend one or two [interrogations] to see if, in fact, an inducement or threat was used. Nothing of the sort occurred, and indeed most of these Japanese one-time national leaders were grateful for the chance to express, at inordinate length, their own part in national affairs for the last fifteen years and many of them, indeed, boastingly took upon themselves a responsibility greater than warranted by the facts."

Despite the confessions, the deeper the Allied prosecutors probed, the more uncertain they became in trying to fix responsibility for the war. One of the problems was simple ignorance. "Rarely," Solis Horwitz confessed, "has any group of men undertaking a project of similar size or scope been less prepared for their task." Few prosecutors had a specialist's knowledge of Japanese affairs, much less any appreciation of the magnitude of the venture they were undertaking.

The delicate task of selecting whom to indict was placed in the hands of the prosecutors' executive committee, chaired by Arthur Comyns-Carr, although Joseph Keenan, as chief Allied counsel, later said, "I had the ultimate and final responsibility for the selection of the accused." But in holding together the Allied prosecutorial team, Keenan had the good sense to go along with the majority recommendations of the committee. Keenan's only insistence was that the executive committee's choices "stand up in history."

That was easier said than done, and Comyns-Carr recognized the pitfalls. On one occasion Admiral Okada, a former premier and a leader of the prewar peace faction, told prosecutors that he had devoted years of his life unsuccessfully to attempting to find where the real responsibility rested. The Japanese government traditionally operated behind a *shoji* screen in a dangerous game of shifting combinations and alliances between families and political factions, including secret societies and military cliques. In that situation, it was anyone's guess who held the true reins of power. The only constant in Japan was the emperor. But was he puppet or puppeteer?

The status of Emperor Hirohito was a major recurring problem for Joseph Keenan and his staff. One question was asked over and over again: Would the emperor be indicted? The question of Hirohito's responsibility and culpability had always been included in the Allies' consideration of what to do about Japanese war crimes. While the Australians and Soviets had been eager to see the emperor in the dock, the Americans were inclined against making any moves against the head of state most Japanese considered to be divine. At his first news conference after being appointed chief prosecutor, Keenan brushed aside questions about Hirohito. But the issue would not go away. In my research at the U.S. National Archives I made a startling discovery. At a London meeting of the UN War Crimes Commission on January 9, 1946, the Australians revived a proposal they had made the previous August and moved again to indict Hirohito as a war criminal. They offered "Australian List No. 1 of Major Japanese War Criminals and Memorandum in Support Thereof," which contained sixty-two names and was accompanied by a seventeen-page analysis. The names appeared in alphabetical order; Hirohito was number four.

On January 16 this material was transmitted to the office of the U.S. judge advocate general, and nine days later Washington radioed the list to the IPS in Tokyo, citing "particularly the charge against Hirohito." These communications were classified top secret. Until my own discovery of this material, I had shared the conventional belief that Australia's demand for the emperor's trial, proposed the day Japan surrendered, had been quietly shelved and forgotten. But this later statement from Canberra made a strong case for Hirohito's indictment, citing Justice Jackson's words at Nuremberg: "Any head of state who launches aggressive war is personally guilty as a war criminal." The Australians did concede, however, that "there appears to be little doubt that Hirohito has personally had peaceful aspirations and ideas."

MacArthur brushed aside the legal aspects of the case in a stern cable to Washington: "His [Hirohito's] indictment will unquestionably cause a tremendous convulsion among the Japanese people, the repercussions of which cannot be overestimated." MacArthur added that all the intelligence he had gathered indicated that Hirohito's connection with affairs of state had been "largely ministerial and automatically responsible to the advice of his counsellors." Then the Allied Supreme Commander warned that if Hirohito was put on trial, it would be "absolutely essential" to increase the Allied forces in Japan by a minimum of 1 million troops, to provide the occupation with a completely new civil service of "several hundred thousand," and to establish an overseas supply base to maintain the occupation.

MacArthur's assessment shattered Canberra, Washington, and London, and abruptly ended any official consideration of whether or not to indict Hirohito. Indeed, according to associates on Keenan's staff, MacArthur told the chief Allied prosecutor that the emperor was not only off limits as a defendant, but also as a witness at the trial. For that matter, Hirohito was not even to be interrogated. Seiichi Yamazaki, Keenan's Japanese secretary, in the September 5, 1959, issue of *The Japan Weekly,* revealed that at first, Keenan had thought the emperor should be indicted, but MacArthur had changed the Allied chief prosecution's mind. When Keenan reported back to the Allied associate prosecutors the U.S. decision to protect the emperor, there was a flap. In his curt fashion Keenan told his colleagues on the IPS, "If you can't agree with the SCAP's decision, by all means go home immediately," Yamazaki wrote. "We are no longer asking your agreement on this matter." The Americans, as the principal occupying power, had vetoed all Allied opposition.

Despite this contretemps, the IPS executive committee continued its work of identifying those Class A detainees who would be indicted. The committee agreed that no one at Sugamo should be indicted unless he could be charged with "crimes against peace"—actively plotting and launching an acquisitive war. The committee also agreed that those indicted must be leaders who bore responsibility as policy-makers. As one committee member put it, "General Tojo's orderly or chauffeur may have had the general's ear and advocated things that influenced the general, but it is very doubtful that either should be brought to trial as war criminals because General Tojo was responsible as premier." Keenan's only order to Comyns-Carr, other than hands off the emperor, was that the cases against those indicted must be air-tight. Walter Lee Riley, in a paper on the law of the IMTFE, observed that these tests as the basis for an indictment "can be classified as unprecedented and novel."

The committee also sought to limit the number of defendants to fifteen, but this proved hopeless. Then it was informally agreed that each prosecuting nation should exercise the right to indict two Class A suspects, raising the number to twenty-two. In the background of this numbers game was the growing realization that most of the war criminal suspects would never be brought to trial. There were simply too many of them. For example, of the sixty-two war criminal suspects listed in the controversial Australian memorandum, only thirteen were later indicted and tried by the IMTFE.

The mechanics of indicting a Class A suspect are illustrated in the executive committee's decision to put Dr. Shumei Okawa on trial. Okawa was interrogated at Sugamo by Hugh B. Helm, who had served as a legal liaison officer in Okinawa. Helm delivered his bill of particulars against Okawa to Comyns-Carr on March 15.

Virtually unknown outside of Japan, Okawa was a revolutionary intellectual, a one-man think-tank for the military clique. Like any good fanatic, Okawa was also a combination ideologue, paranoiac, propagandist, racist, and terrorist. He was the author of more than a dozen scholarly works, including translations of Shakespeare's sonnets into Japanese. Okawa believed in a one-party system and advocated the regimentation of the Japanese people for a war of world conquest. He operated a school for radicals in which each year twenty bright young boys of peasant background were trained in his fascist doctrines and sent into the hinterland to develop activist cells. As a cover for his activities, Okawa directed the East Asia Research Institute, which was partly financed by the financial interests behind the South Manchurian Railway. Okawa also participated in three abortive coups d'état in the early thirties against cabinets that opposed the politics of the militarists and right-wing fanatics. One of the coups resulted in the murder of the premier.

In his interrogations of Okawa and his burrowing into the Japanese court and police records, Hugh Helm discovered that Okawa had furnished weapons and money to those involved in the assassination of Premier Inukai in 1932. "It is interesting to note,"

Helm said in his report, "that Dr. Okawa still believes in all this and his only regret today is that Tojo refused to listen to his advice in 1940 and started the war for Greater East Asia too soon." Helm was captivated by his subject. "This man's scholarship is great; his power was real; and his principles are constant," he said.

The last paragraph of Helm's three-page brief read as follows: "Recommendation: That Dr. Shumei Okawa be indicted under Section II, Article 5, paragraph (a) of the Charter of the International Military Tribunal for the Far East, in that he did commit crimes against peace by planning and initiating a war of aggression and a war in violation of international law, treaties, agreements and assurances, and in that he did participate with Col. Kingoro Hashimoto, General Hideki Tojo, General Koiso et al. in a common plan for conspiracy for the accomplishment of the foregoing."

Sometimes the evidence on a Class A prisoner was inconclusive or borderline. "We were being rushed," Robert Donihi, an American assistant prosecutor, confessed recently in an interview. "The question in the executive committee was: Is he indictable? In evaluating the evidence we had so many scorecards that even we were confused in telling who the players were."

Donihi was in charge of the cases being developed against General Sadao Araki, a former war minister who talked freely at Sugamo, and former premier Koki Hirota, who was persistently close-mouthed. Both suspects were inexorably bound up with Japan's China policy in the thirties. "I recommended that both should be put on trial," Donihi said. "I was reluctant to do so in Araki's case because of his age [he was then nearing 70], but he was involved in palace and army affairs from the beginning of Hirohito's reign as crown prince."

Donihi also had doubts about Hirota. "I liked Hirota immensely and I had doubt that he was a prime suspect," he said. "But we included him as a borderline case toward the end." Former foreign minister Shigenori Togo was still another suspect against whom the executive committee found the evidence conclusive. "He was hard to judge," Donihi observed wryly. "He was a professional diplomat." Even the Japanese themselves considered Togo "inscrutable"—the Occidental stereotype of the Oriental. In the end, Togo was indicted for his role as the foreign minister in Tojo's cabinet in the delivery of Japan's declaration of war to the U.S. Embassy *after* the attack on Pearl Harbor and to the British Embassy *after* the attacks on Hong Kong, Singapore, and Malaya.

By mid-April of 1946, after much pushing and shoving, the executive committee pared down the eighty-odd Class A inmates at Sugamo to twenty-six men against whom there seemed to be strong cases. This was one more than had been indicted at Nuremberg and four more than the IPS's self-imposed limit of two indictments for each nation represented on the bench.

No sooner was the list completed than the Russians arrived in Tokyo. Major General Zarayanov, the Soviet judge, and Minister Golunsky, the Soviet associate prosecutor led a small army of functionaries. "The Russians inundated us," Frederick Mignone recalled during a recent interview. The Soviet staff numbered more than fifty lawyers, clerks, and interpreters, with hundreds of chauffeurs, gardeners, cooks, and others, many of whom appeared to fall into no particular category. The United States had barred a direct Soviet role in the occupation, and Moscow fell back on the IMTFE as a wedge for making its presence felt in Japan.

When Joseph Keenan presented Golunsky with the list of the accused, the Soviet prosecutor nodded approvingly but then observed that several names were absent. Keenan himself recognized that names were missing but, as he later told the Far East Commission, some candidates "were omitted for convenience and clarity in presenting the case." Golunsky pointed out that the Soviet Union had not been represented on Keenan's staff when the list was drawn up and that he wished to exercise the prerogative of naming two defendants. Keenan sighed, and agreed. Golunsky surprised the Allied prosecution and confounded SCAP by naming the two representatives of Japan who had signed the instrument of surrender, Foreign Minister Shigemitsu, a former ambassador to Moscow, and General Umezu, who had commanded the Kwantung Army in Manchuria along the Soviet frontier from 1939 to 1944. Neither was then in custody. The prosecutors had toyed with the idea of indicting Umezu, the Imperial Japanese Army's last chief of staff, but Shigemitsu was an acknowledged leader of the peace faction and had been selected as a witness for the prosecution.

On April 28 an astonished Shigemitsu and a sullen Umezu, who had long been contemplating *hara kiri,* were arrested and brought to Sugamo Prison.

The very next day the judges met in chambers for the first

time. With the Filipino and Indian judges still absent, nine of the judges conferred with the prosecutors to fix a date of arraignment. At the same time, Sir William Webb, the tribunal president, disclosed that chief defense counsel Beverly Coleman had requested that the arraignment be delayed two weeks. In his application, which Webb read, Coleman argued that the defense had been unable to organize properly "for the reason that the identity of the accused has not been known until now," and that of the thirty American defense lawyers assigned to the defense only six had arrived in Tokyo. The judges agreed to hear Coleman in person.

"Will you tell us in detail how you became chief defense counsel?" Webb opened. Coleman said he had been appointed "under instructions of GHQ." Webb arched an eyebrow. "But you have no authority from any Japanese, have you?" Coleman replied, "No, sir." Webb refused to hear him further on the ground that the tribunal would listen only to a defense attorney who spoke with a defendant's approval. Coleman protested that until that very day there had been no Japanese defendants and that therefore there was no one whom he could represent. Catch-22. Webb was adamant, and Coleman was dismissed.

Webb then instructed Keenan "to serve copies of the Indictment and Charter on each of the accused forthwith, the service to be undertaken by an officer of the Court, namely, the Marshal; and we fix Friday, the 3rd day of May, at ten-thirty, at the Tribunal's court in Tokyo as the time and place when the accused will plead to the charges in the Indictment."

6

The Indictment: Tojo, Not Hirohito

As completed, the indictment represented a signal achievement for Keenan and his prosecutorial team. They had put together a carefully reasoned and well-documented case against twenty-eight Japanese leaders. The indictment ran forty-three single-spaced typewritten pages and was spread over no less than fifty-five counts. Among the accused were nine civilians and nineteen professional military men. This was almost the direct opposite of Nuremberg, where seventeen of the twenty-two defendants were civilians. In Japan the military leaders—in particular, the expansionists who dominated the army—had gained control over the government beginning in the late twenties. In Germany, just a few years later, Hitler and his gang coopted the armed forces.

The indictment named the following men:

- Four former premiers: Hiranuma, Hirota, Koiso, Tojo
- Three former foreign ministers: Matsuoka, Shigemitsu, Togo
- Four former war ministers: Araki, Hata, Itagaki, Minami
- Two former navy ministers: Nagano, Shimada
- Six former generals: Doihara, Kimura, Matsui, Muto, Sato, Umezu
- Two former ambassadors: Oshima, Shiratori
- Three former economic and financial leaders: Hoshino, Kaya, Suzuki

• One nobleman and imperial adviser, Kido; one radical theorist, Okawa; one admiral, Oka; and one colonel, Hashimoto

The central theme of the indictment was that since 1928 Japan's foreign and domestic policies had been dominated by a "criminal militaristic clique." The defendants were accused of thirty-six counts of crimes against peace, sixteen counts of murder, and three counts of crimes against humanity, or conventional war crimes. Twenty-one of the defendants were charged specifically with planning and initiating aggressive war against China, beginning with the invasion of Manchuria in 1931. All the defendants except Okawa and Shiratori were charged with conventional war crimes and/or crimes against humanity in violation of the Hague and Geneva accords. The majority of the accused were charged with plotting aggressive war against the United States, United Kingdom, or USSR, singly or collectively. Significantly, Marquis Kido, the emperor's adviser, was charged on all three counts in addition to initiating a war of aggression in violation of international treaties against China in 1937.

The language of the indictment was brutal. It accused the defendants of promoting a scheme of conquest that "contemplated and carried out . . . murdering, maiming and ill-treating prisoners of war [and] civilian internees . . . forcing them to labor under inhumane conditions . . . plundering public and private property, wantonly destroying cities, towns and villages beyond any justification of military necessity; [perpetrating] mass murder, rape, pillage, brigandage, torture and other barbaric cruelties upon the helpless civilian population of the over-run countries." After Count 17 the indictment named names; for example, a dozen defendants were named in Count 45 as involved in the Rape of Nanking. Seventeen of the accused were named in Count 39—the "Pearl Harbor Count"—for ordering the attack on the United States, in which they "unlawfully killed and murdered Admiral Kidd and about 4,000 other members of the naval and military forces of the United States of America and certain civilians whose names and number are at present unknown."

"It may seem strange to include charges of murder in an indictment before an international tribunal," Joseph Keenan conceded in a press statement issued with the lodging of the indictment. "But it is high time, and indeed was so before this war began, that the promoters of aggressive, ruthless war and treaty-breakers should be stripped of the glamour of national heroes and exposed as what they really are—plain, ordinary murderers."

The core of the Allied case was that the accused had engaged in a conspiracy to wage aggressive war in violation of international agreements. Although there was a debate over whether or not there was a statute in international law to support this charge, an appendix was attached to the indictment citing forty-seven treaties, conventions, protocols, and other international agreements the Japanese had violated.

Brendan F. Brown, dean of law at Catholic University, prepared an exhaustive brief for Keenan and the executive committee on this key conspiracy charge. In his brief, reprinted in part by the *American Bar Association Journal,* Brown sought to demonstrate that the conspiracy or common-plan concept at the trial was common to all the major legal systems of the world. He contended that the conspiracy doctrine that the IPS asked the Tokyo tribunal to adopt was modest compared to the conspiracy concepts that permeate Anglo-Saxon and Soviet law. The IPS concept, he felt, was more consistent with the concept of conspiracy as it appears in French, Chinese, German, and Japanese law. Under this more flexible interpretation of conspiracy, any Japanese leader who entered into an agreement, combination, or association with anyone else to wage war was guilty of criminal conspiracy "even though he did not authorize or actually participate in the preparation of the ultimate unlawful act or acts or in the preceding illegal means, as long as he failed expressly to withdraw from the evil combination." This interpretation of the conspiracy or common-plan charge was to generate unremitting controversy among international lawyers and was to play a role in the judgment ultimately handed down by the tribunal.

Another source of controversy was the allegation that there were four glaring omissions in the indictment. No leaders of any ultrapatriotic secret society, no chiefs of the Kempeitai, and no members of the *zaibatsu* were indicted, and there was no mention of the emperor. In the Allied countries there were howls of indignation. The *New York Sun,* a conservative daily, observed dryly, "There are notable omissions."

The USSR was particularly incensed over the absence of any members of the *zaibatsu* in the dock. Minister Golunsky, the Soviet associate prosecutor, fumed in Moscow's *New Times:* "The big capitalist concerns exercised a very great influence on the entire political life of Japan. It was they that were the mainsprings of piratical aggression. Wherever the Japanese armies appeared, the giant monopoly octopuses stretched their tentacles." Even so, when the Soviets had been given the opportunity to select two defendants, they had named no one from the *zaibatsu*.

But the absence of big business hardly caused a stir compared to the outrage in Allied countries over the failure to indict Hirohito. Following the line laid down by MacArthur and the Truman administration, Keenan and his staff argued that in both theory and practice the evidence showed that "the Emperor's role [was] that of a figurehead." But to his credit, Keenan admitted after the trial that "we gave a good deal of thought" to indicting him and that "strictly legally Emperor Hirohito could have been tried and convicted because under the Constitution of Japan he did have the power to make war and stop it." That, of course, was the Australian argument when it demanded that the IPS indict Hirohito.

Yet, in a true sense, the emperor was in the dock. Hideki Tojo was universally regarded as the biggest name among the accused—a "celebrity," like Hermann Göring at Nuremberg—but clearly Tojo was not the most important defendant at Tokyo. Marquis Kido, Hirohito's alter ego, was the *only* figure among the accused to be indicted solely because of his relationship to the emperor. Kido brought the presence of the emperor into the trial in a way the Japanese public understood, subtly and indirectly. Thus, in many ways, Kido was the centerpiece of the prosecution's case against the Japanese leaders.

The indictment was splashed across the front pages of Tokyo's press, and newsboys hawked four-page extras that carried the full text. Like a pregnancy, it had taken nine turbulent months to organize the trial of the Japanese war criminals.

At Sugamo Prison, now designated U.S. Army XI Corps Stockade No. 1, a grim and gray set of square, squat, ugly three-tier buildings containing some 700 cells, the accused read the indictment. Stripped of power and pomp, robbed of their dignity, for the most part they appeared to be a group of tired old men who would have moved unnoticed on any Tokyo street. To paraphrase Mark Antony's verdict on Lepidus, they appeared to be small, unmeritable men, meant to be sent on errands. Yet, they had once ruled an empire stretching from Korea to the borders of

India, their every whim an imperial edict. Here were the emperor's advisors, field marshals, admirals, cabinet ministers, financial wizards, and political mythmakers confined to cheerless cells while awaiting trial as gangsters and murderers. And all this time the gods of Japan mocked them while they themselves contemplated their fate.

The trial was finally about to begin.

7

The Trial Opens: Challenges and Decisions

For a fleeting moment, May 3, 1946, the attention of a distraught world was focused on Tokyo as the first public session of the International Military Tribunal for the Far East was called to order. The anticipated peacetime calm of the postwar era was breaking apart, and the world seemed to be descending into a maelstrom of conflict and uncertainty. The newspapers of that day told a sad story. The Arabs threatened a holy war if there was a mass immigration of European Jewry to Palestine. The Socialist Polish labor minister expressed fear of Moscow's intentions toward his newly liberated nation. Chiang Kai-shek returned in triumph to Nanking, only to face a bloody civil war. Hjalmar Schacht, Hitler's financier, completed three days of testimony at the Nuremberg trial, now entering its eighth month. Uneasy armed truces between nationalists and colonialists prevailed in Indonesia and Vietnam. The divisions of Germany and Korea were solidifying as Soviet and Allied troops took up their positions on the newly drawn borders. And all over the world streams of refugees continued their unhappy journeys away from terror and oppression, privation and despair.

In Tokyo that morning the sun rose behind a bank of clouds, and the day began overcast but springlike. Spectators began trudging up Ichigaya before 7 A.M., hoping to get a seat at history in the making. The hill rose over the city of Tokyo like an acropolis, dedicated, like Troy, to the god of war. The Supreme Commander for the Allied Powers, General MacArthur, had chosen the former War Ministry buildings as a fitting site for the trial of the Japanese leaders who had been indicted as Class A war criminals. The main headquarters atop the hill, an immense three-story building that resembled a pillbox, was still in good shape, having been spared by Allied bombers. There was only one major entrance to the site, simplifying security measures. Ichigaya's auditorium, measuring about 90 by 115 feet, had been transformed into an impressive courtroom by thousands of Allied and Japanese workers who had been on the job almost around the clock for over four months. There were now about 1,000 seats in the courtroom, including 660 in the balcony for spectators. Each seat was wired to the translators' booth, a glass-enclosed workroom that was on a small balcony overlooking the "stage." There were two principal channels on the translation system, one for Japanese and one for English, and a third channel that was generally used for Russian (the Soviet judge and others in the Soviet delegation spoke neither Japanese nor English).

In sum, General MacArthur's interior designers and construction crews had turned Ichigaya into a fitting stage for the international drama that was to be played out there. A press section and a camera booth held places of prominence in the room, assuring that this would be no Star Chamber, conducted in secrecy. Klieg lights hung from the ceilings, there to illuminate the proceedings for the cameras and to bring sweat to the brows of the participants on the muggy summer days common to Tokyo.

Twenty-six of the twenty-eight indicted Class A war criminals had been held at Sugamo Prison ever since their arrest. Isolated from the rest of the prison community in their individual cells, these men were finally to have their day in court. On opening day they breakfasted earlier than usual and were then whisked to Ichigaya in a bus with papered-over windows. Accompanied by a convoy of American military police, the bus drew up at the west entrance of the courtroom at 8:30 A.M., Army Time. The tribunal was scheduled to begin proceedings at 10:30. As they had been doing for the past many months, the defendants waited.

At Sugamo, Yoshio Kodama, who was awaiting indictment or release, wrote in his diary that he gazed out his cell's solitary window and saw Tojo entering the bus that day. During the war he had often seen Tojo driving across the plaza of the Imperial

Palace in an army sedan with a military escort, as premier and war minister of the empire. "Now, when I see him being carried off in a bus guarded at the front and rear by American MP's, I feel that nothing makes sense," Kodama wrote. "But I suppose that, seen in the light of history, it makes quite a good sense."

Perhaps the most conspicuous arrivals that morning were the judges. They arrived in long, shiny-black limousines. The scene resembled a funeral procession. All wore suitably sober expressions: Webb of Australia, the president of the tribunal, and North-croft of New Zealand, Bernard of France, Zarayanov of the Soviet Union, Mei of China, Higgins of the United States, Patrick of Great Britain, McDougall of Canada, and Röling of the Netherlands. (Jaranilla of the Philippines and Pal of India had not yet reached Tokyo.)

A few minutes before 10:30, when the tribunal was scheduled to convene, the huge courtroom buzzed with the talk of participants and spectators. The press gallery, on the north side or main entrance to the courtroom, was crammed with Allied and Japanese correspondents. A team of military police, wearing white gloves to match their white helmets, swarmed through the dock, running their open palms over and under each chair in search of secret messages, weapons, and other contraband. This routine would be carried out daily thereafter. The prisoners filed in accompanied by four military policemen and the officer in charge, Colonel Aubrey Kenworthy. Each of the accused knew in advance where his permanent seat would be, and as they entered, everyone in the courtroom glanced at his scorecard, which bore the printed legend "Court Room Seating Diagram."

General Kenryo Sato, in a khaki uniform bereft of medals and insignia, led the small band of men who had held the fate of the Japanese Empire in their hands for almost a generation. The once plump Okinori Kaya, the financial brains of the war machine, had lost considerable weight in prison, and his double-breasted business suit looked two sizes too large for him. Former foreign minister Mamoru Shigemitsu appeared in a long black coat with tails and striped trousers; only his top hat was missing. He looked haggard, as if he had not slept the night before, and he supported himself on his one leg with a walking stick. The Tiger of Korea, Kuniaki Koiso, also entered supporting himself on a cane, as did the intellectual and war-lover Shumei Okawa, who had removed his jacket and revealed his wrinkled white shirt. He was the only prisoner to arrive at Ichigaya that morning wearing the traditional Japanese *geta* or wooden clogs, and he was made to remove them before entering the courtroom.

Former foreign minister Yosuke Matsuoka entered the dock at a painfully slow gait, his face pallid, his cheeks sunken. Ex-premier Kiichiro Kiranuma's equine face looked longer and more melancholy than ever. Admiral Osami Nagano, another aged militarist, wore his naval dress blues stripped of all emblems and badges. The figure most familiar to both Japanese and everyone else in the courtroom, Hideki Tojo, strode in wearing a dapper khaki bush jacket. Tojo appeared alternately bemused and dispirited but looked remarkably healthy for a man who had shot himself in a failed suicide attempt just months before. Marquis Koichi Kido looked ill at ease, almost embarrassed. As the emperor's close adviser he had generally been hidden from the public behind the palace gates, and here he was in full view. Shigenori Togo, the career diplomat who had been foreign minister at the time of the Pearl Harbor attack, wore his customary enigmatic expression. He would have been a great poker player! Hiroshi Oshima, general turned diplomat, Japan's ambassador to the Third Reich, was still dapper, sporting a bow tie and a large white handkerchief tucked into his pocket. General Suzuki maintained his scowl. Thought by many to be the number one power broker in Tokyo, he was accustomed to arriving at Ichigaya in circumstances very different from those of the trial.

Other generals were there at their old headquarters, too: the aging Sadao Araki, a relic of the 1930s; Iwane Matsui and Shunroku Hata, at different times commander of all the Japanese forces in China; Jiro Minami and the man who succeeded him in 1938 as commander of the militant Kwantung Army, Kenji Doihara, together with their partner in murder and intrigue, Colonel Kingoro Hashimoto; Yoshijiro Umezu, chief of staff at the end of the war and signer of the surrender aboard the U.S.S. *Missouri*. Alone among the nine generals in uniform, Akira Muto wore his tropical outfit, a jungle-green jacket with the white collar of an open-throated shirt protruding over his lapels. In addition to the uniformed Nagano, the other admirals in the dock were Shigetaro Shimada, wartime head of the Navy Ministry, and his close associate, Takasumi Oka. Rounding out the civilians then in the dock were the wartime cabinet secretary Naoki Hoshino, ex-premier Baron Koki Hirota, and Toshio Shiratori, who had been ambassador to Italy when the Axis Pact was signed. Not yet in the dock were two generals who had been scheduled to arrive from their prison in Bangkok: Seishiro Itagaki, the terror of Southeast Asia, and Heitaro Kimura, under whose command thousands of prisoners of war and civilian slave laborers lost their lives in the construction of the ill-fated Burma-Siam Railway.

The appointed hour of 10:30 came and went. Sir William Webb and his colleagues lounged in chambers, hopeful that the wayward generals would soon arrive. They didn't—until 2:20 P.M. that afternoon. Finally, after waiting forty minutes, the judges decided to move ahead. At 11:13 a bell tinkled gently, like the bell under the eaves of a Buddhist temple, and a hush fell over the courtroom. The massive wooden doors at the entrance slowly closed, like the gates of an Assyrian walled city, and military police carrying sidearms took up their positions around the room. Seven minutes later everyone rose as Webb, bulky and formidable in his black robes, led the single file of judges to their places on the elevated bench. When the judges were seated, Captain van Meter, the red-haired marshal of the court, intoned, "The International Military Tribunal for the Far East is in session and is ready to hear any matter brought before it."

Flashbulbs exploded and motion picture cameras whirred. The historic moment compelled Webb to deliver a few introductory remarks. He first disclosed that each present member of the court had that morning signed a joint affirmation to administer justice fairly (Judge Pal of India would refuse to sign). The president of the tribunal then warmed to his theme. "We fully appreciate the great responsibility resting upon us," Webb said. ". . . To our great task we bring open minds both on the facts and on the law. The onus will be on the prosecution to establish guilt beyond reasonable doubt." He described the judges as "a court of plain men" and, ignoring the Nuremberg trial, said of the Tokyo tribunal, "There has been no more important criminal trial in all history."

A Japanese newspaper reported that when the reading of the Japanese translation of Sir William Webb's statement ended, "some of the defendants began looking around the courtroom like actors of a play waiting for applause from the audience. Seldom was there a more attentive and quiet audience."

The reading of the indictment was undertaken in relays. When the clerk of the court reached Count 22—charging that several defendants "on or about the 7th December, 1941, initiated a war of aggression and a war in violation of international law, treaties and agreements against the British Commonwealth"—the court was thrown into an uproar. Shumei Okawa, who sat in the dock directly behind Tojo and had been alternately clasping his hands in prayer and buttoning and unbuttoning his shirtfront, half-rose from his seat and struck Tojo on top of the head. Tojo was startled, and a flash of anger crossed his face. The military police pounced on Okawa just as he slapped Tojo a second time. This time Tojo smiled. Okawa was hustled from the courtroom, and in the corridor, in English, he croaked, "I must kill Tojo." Asked why, he replied, "It will be good for my country, if I do."

When court reconvened the next day, Saturday, the first order of business was an application from Okawa's defense attorney for his client's removal from the dock and transfer to a hospital for examination by psychiatrists. Under the tribunal's charter the court was empowered to determine the mental and physical capacity of the accused to stand trial. Accordingly, the tribunal approved the defense's request providing the IPS appoint one psychiatrist and the defense another to "ascertain whether he is mentally capable of pleading."

The court settled down again to the business at hand, and the marshal returned to reading the indictment. ". . . The defendants Hata, Kido, Koiso, Sato, Shigemitsu, Tojo and Umezu, prior to the 18th June, 1944, and on succeeding days, by unlawfully ordering, causing and permitting the armed forces of Japan to attack the city of Changsha in breach of the Treaty Articles mentioned in Count 2 hereof and to slaughter the inhabitants contrary to international law, unlawfully killed and murdered thousands of civilians and disarmed soldiers of the Republic of China, whose names and number are at present unknown. . . ." The marshal droned on, and yesterday's excitement receded before today's morning calm.

On May 6, when the court convened to hear the defendants plead, the tribunal was again thrown into disarray. As the judges took their seats, they found the bench littered with copies of an anti-Japanese tract, *Japan's Record and World Security*. "It was most improper for that document to be placed on the tables of the members of this court," Sir William Webb said angrily. Though he did not order the marshal of the court to undertake an investigation, he stated firmly that the court "will not be, in the slightest, influenced by anything in that pamphlet."

Webb then called upon the accused to plead. But Ichiro Kiyose, deputy chief of the Japanese defense counsel, interrupted: "We would like to challenge the judge." A murmur swept the courtroom. Speaking in English, he explained, "It is not proper from the standpoint of justice and fairness that Sir William Webb should conduct this trial. . . . Sir William Webb has investigated the case of Japanese atrocities in New Guinea." Pandemonium ensued, and the marshal of the court rapped for order. "May I ask the spectators to remain quiet!" Captain van Meter shouted as the court declared a recess.

After about fifteen minutes, the court reconvened with New Zealand's Justice Northcroft as acting president. "The members have asked me, who presided at their conference, to make announcement of their decision," he said. The tribunal, he continued, rejected the defense's challenge on the ground that the charter instructed MacArthur to appoint the judges, and thus "it does not rest with the tribunal to unseat any one appointed by the Supreme Commander." Nonetheless, Webb felt constrained to clarify his position when he returned to the microphone. Before he accepted his appointment to the tribunal, Webb said, he had considered the effect of his work in New Guinea. "I came to the conclusion without difficulty that I was eligible," he said, adding that the best legal opinion in Australia concurred. Unknown to most of those in the courtroom, so had MacArthur when the prosecution raised the issue three months earlier.

"I now call on the accused to plead," Webb said, moving the trial forward. "Araki, Sadao, how do you plead, guilty or not guilty?"

The aging general stood up in the dock, a picturesque figure out of the past with a bristling handlebar mustache. Araki said his counsel would plead for him, but Webb insisted that he plead for himself. Raising his voice, the former war minister launched into what promised to be a long explanation. "We want a plea," a vexed Webb interrupted, "not a speech."

"I plead not guilty," Araki shouted and promptly sat down.

All the accused pleaded not guilty, with some variations in wording. The American-educated former foreign minister Yosuke Matsuoka, supporting himself on a cane, declared in English, "I plead not guilty to all and every charge." And Hideki Tojo said firmly, "On all counts, I plead not guilty."

After taking all the pleas, the tribunal recessed, reconvening a week later to meet the first of a series of protracted legal challenges to the proceedings. The first debate was fought largely over the court's jurisdiction. The defense's attack was launched by Ichiro Kiyose and strongly supported by three American defense attorneys, Ben Bruce Blakeney, George Yamaoka, and George Furness. The gist of their argument was that Germany had surrendered unconditionally, but Japan had not. The Potsdam terms were conditional. Some of the defendants appeared shocked when Kiyose observed parenthetically, "As regards German war criminals, the Allies, if I may be permitted to say so, could just as well have punished war criminals without trial." Shades of Stalin, Churchill, and Hull.

Echoing the deliberations of the Supreme Council for the Direction of the War in the days before Japan's surrender, Kiyose averred that Japan had accepted the Potsdam terms "on the understanding that the punishment of war criminals will take place in accordance with the commonly accepted understanding of that term"—that is, conventional war crimes. To accuse the defendants of crimes against the peace and against humanity "overstepped the bounds of international law." No such crimes existed in international law. For the tribunal to try the accused on such charges was to impose *ex post facto* law on the defendants. Moreover, the period covered by the indictment was faulty. Japan had accepted the Potsdam Proclamation to end the 1941–45 war. It was "absolutely unthinkable" that incidents unrelated to that war, such as Japan's conquest of Manchuria in 1931, should be cited in the indictment. Even one of the nations represented on the bench and in the prosecution, the Soviet Union, had diplomatically recognized the emergence of Manchukuo as a nation-state in Manchuria following that "incident." Kiyose also cited other "highly inconsistent" elements in the indictment and demanded that the indictment be thrown out.

The next attorney to speak for the defense, Ben Bruce Blakeney, wore the uniform of a U.S. Army major. In the course of his impassioned attack on the IMTFE's jurisdiction and the law of the case, he felt it necessary to make sure that the motives of American defense counsel were clearly understood. "We speak for American, for Anglo-Saxon, for Anglo-American, for democratic views of justice and of fair play. We speak for the proposition that observing legal forms, while ignoring the essence of legal principles, is the supreme atrocity against the law. . . . The responsibility before history of this tribunal, and of us who play our several parts here, is tremendous; it is awe-inspiring. That responsibility goes far beyond the fate of these twenty-eight men here on trial.''

Blakeney charged that the judges were Allied nationals and that therefore "a legal, fair, and impartial trial is denied to these accused before this tribunal." As representatives of the Allied powers, the justices, no matter how great their personal and professional integrity, could not be impartial. Why weren't the accused being tried by judges from neutral nations? "War is not a crime," Blakeney continued, warming to the defense. "The very concept of war implies the right legally to use force. . . . Never in the history of civilization have the planning and waging of wars been tried as crimes by a court." The Allies, as victors, could have imposed on the defendants any terms they wished—exile, imprisonment without trial, "or shoot them out of hand." Since the Allies had decided to handle the disposition of the vanquished through judicial proceedings, the Allies were committed to established principles of law. Since waging war was not a crime, the accused could not be charged with crimes against the peace. Moreover, charging the accused with "murder" was ludicrous. Killing in war was not murder because war was legal. Legalized killing, however repugnant and abhorrent, had never been thought of as imposing criminal responsibility on an individual. If the attack on Pearl Harbor had resulted in the "murder" of 4,000 persons, how about Hiroshima? "We know the name of the chief of staff who planned that act, we know the chief of the responsible state," Blakeney said. "Is murder on their consciences? We may well doubt it . . . because the act is not murder."

Furness and Yamaoka followed and buttoned up the defense's arguments.

At the IPS table the British associate prosecutor, Arthur Comyns-Carr, sat unflappable, as did Australia's associate prosecutor, Judge Mansfield, and many other Allied prosecutors. Joseph Keenan, however, the chief of counsel, was unable to restrain himself. When he approached the podium to deliver a rebuttal, he abandoned fine points of law and plunged into violet-hued oratory.

"Mr. President, members of this international military tribunal, can it be that eleven nations represented on this tribunal and in this prosecution, and in themselves representative of orderly governments, of countries containing one-half to two-thirds of the inhabitants of this earth, having suffered through this aggression the loss of a vast amount of their resources and deplorable and incalculable quantities of blood due to the crimes of murder, brigandage, and plunder, are now totally impotent to bring to trial and punish those responsible for this worldwide calamity; that these Allied nations, having brought about, as they were compelled to do so by sheer force, the end of these wars of aggression, must now stand idly by and permit the perpetrators of these offenses to remain without the reach of any lawful punishment whatsoever?''

The veins on Keenan's neck protruded, and the color of his face almost matched his prose. Webb looked unhappy. "Mr. Chief Prosecutor," the president asked dryly, "do you think those rhetorical phrases are fitting at this juncture?''

The consensus among the prosecutors was that if Keenan did not die of a stroke on the spot, he would survive to the end of the trial.

Stung by the chief judge's admonition, Keenan quietly rebutted the defense's arguments. Both Potsdam and the instrument of surrender authorized the Allied Supreme Commander to take steps "as he deems proper to effectuate the terms of surrender," including a trial. As for the suggestion that the accused be tried before a panel of neutral judges, Keenan brought laughter to the courtroom by suggesting that it would be necessary to wait until man landed on Mars in order to find "some neutral nations or people to come and sit upon judgment of those responsible for aggressive war.''

As for the subject of war itself, Keenan accused the defense of making light of the subject. "They treat it as something abstract, something that has a legitimate purpose in the world, a rather sacred purpose enshrined in a certain manner by tradition, and by legal precepts and, as far as I can determine, by justice.'' But Japan was a signatory to international treaties after World War I that outlawed aggressive war, he pointed out, quickly adding, "Of course, there is a dearth of precedent—that we all recognize.'' But the failure to punish the perpetrator of a crime had never been the basis of sound legal or moral reasoning for denying the existence of the crime itself. He conceded there would always be a question of justice where power and force were brought to bear. "We admit today and with no apology that the Allies are in control of Japan," he said. "We admit that great force and violence, including the Hiroshima bomb, have been employed by the Allies, and we make no more apology for that than does a decent, innocent citizen walking home from his office, his factory or shop to his home and his family who employs the use of force to prevent his life being taken by an outlaw."

The defense's attack on the tribunal's fairness, he said, was the result of a misconception. It made no difference who the judges, prosecutors, defense counsel, or, for that matter, the accused were. Eleven neutral nations could preside over the trial, and that would still not be a test of fairness. "The test of the fairness and of the impartiality will be made manifest in an open court where every proceeding is subject to the scrutiny of the press and observers and the Japanese people. . . . Will this court require ample evidence of the guilt of these accused? Will the court permit an adequate opportunity for defense of the accused? These are the tests of fairness . . ." Keenan declared. "History will answer."

Australia's associate prosecutor, Alan Mansfield, followed Keenan to the lectern and tackled the defense's *ex post facto* argument. The Kellogg-Briand Pact, or Pact of Paris, in 1928 outlawed war, he stressed. Therefore, war was no longer a discretionary prerogative right of the sixty-two nations that had signed the treaty, including Japan. As for the argument that the indictment was faulty because it went back to the Mukden Incident, Mansfield held that it was a legal absurdity for the leaders of a nation to order their armed forces to carry out warlike acts and then seek to absolve themselves by arguing that because they had omitted a declaration of war there had been no war. If there had been no war, as the defense claimed, then there had been no possible justification for killing millions of people in China. This therefore constituted murder, and murder was a crime triable by the law in every land. In an allusion to Pearl Harbor, Mansfield added that to attack without warning was also to murder, and to attack without warning was in violation of the Hague Conventions to which Japan was a signatory.

The first round of debate created a sensation among the Japanese. They had not expected so much push and shove. The legalistic minds among the defendants, notably the two ex-foreign ministers, Togo and Shigemitsu, as well as Marquis Kido and ex-premier Hiranuma, were noticeably pleased and attentive; Hideki Tojo took copious notes. Most of the Allied prosecutors took the first round in stride, but the Soviet representatives at the IMTFE were upset. This would be reflected later in Judge Zarayanov's memoranda to his colleagues and the frequent denunciation of the trial in Moscow's controlled press. The commentary of V. Berezhkov in *New Times* was a fair sample. In an attack on Sir William Webb, Berezhkov wrote, "Instead of ruling out statements of the defense counsel which are extraneous to the trial, he willingly allows them the floor." As for the role of the American defense counsel, the Russians were mystified. "Another peculiar feature of the trial is that the defense includes a score or more American lawyers," he wrote. "They are no less zealous than their Japanese colleagues in whitewashing the criminals whose hands are stained with the blood of thousands of American citizens."

The American Bar Association took immediate notice of the debate and rushed Blakeney's argument into print. The August issue of the ABA's *Journal* cited his remarks as "an outstanding demonstration of the lawyer's performance of the traditions of his profession to say all that can be said in behalf of his client's cause, to the end that justice may be done according to law." The *Journal* added that "the argument shows the far-reaching character of the questions presented in such a trial." The periodical did not mention Keenan's rebuttal. Score one for the defense.

The legal wrangles continued over the next several days. On May 17 the Indian judge, Pal, took his seat for the first time, sitting next to the Dutch judge, Röling. That same day the tribunal dismissed, "for reasons to be given later," the defense's motions challenging the court's jurisdiction. The stage was now set for the prosecution to deliver its opening statement.

8

The Missing Defendants

Before the prosecution could make the opening statement set for June 4, another defendant was hospitalized.

On May 8, two days after he pleaded innocent to the charges against him, Yosuke Matsuoka, the former foreign minister and confidant of Hitler and Stalin, was examined at Sugamo by Dr. Denji Teraro, a member of the Tokyo Research Institute of Tuberculosis, and declared unfit to stand trial. "Matsuoka does not have the physical capacity to proceed to trial without causing permanent injury to his health and endangering his life as well as the lives of those people around him from contracting such a contagious disease," Teraro's report to the IMTFE said. Matsuoka, who had been in and out of the hospital since 1941, was racked by tuberculosis. On the basis of this report Matsuoka was transferred from Sugamo to the U.S. Army's 361st Station Hospital, which had become the dispensary for the accused (before the trial ended, almost every defendant would be treated there).

On June 3 Matsuoka's attorneys arranged for his transfer to the isolation ward of the Tokyo Imperial University Hospital and called on the court to strike his name from the indictment. The IPS vigorously objected on the ground that physical disability provided no cause for dismissal of the charges against him. The tribunal reserved its decision, but Matsuoka's condition deteriorated rapidly thereafter. Within a month he was dead.

With Matsuoka's demise ended the career of one of the most flamboyant diplomats of the thirties and forties. His power had lain in his intimacy with the militarists, particularly the Kwantung Army clique. He had been their mouthpiece and openly championed aggressive war. It was Matsuoka who led Japan out of the League of Nations in 1933 after the league condemned Japan as an aggressor in Manchuria. He lacked the polish of a Prince Konoye but served in the latter's second cabinet as foreign minister during the critical years 1940–41. Matsuoka's great feat in that period was engineering both an alliance with Hitler's Germany and a neutrality pact with Stalin's Russia.

Matsuoka had firsthand knowledge of American life. At the age of fourteen he had been sent to the United States, where he acquired idiomatic mastery of American English and joined the Catholic Church. He graduated from the University of Oregon in 1900 and entered the Japanese diplomatic service. Given Matsuoka's role in later events, it is extraordinary to record that in 1910 he told A. E. Wearne, a Reuters correspondent in East Asia, "I foresee that in thirty, forty, perhaps it will be fifty years, Japan will make war against the West, and after a desperate struggle will be completely destroyed by a combination of the powers."

On the morning of June 27, 1946, Matsuoka died. In a poem left to posterity, he penned, "With no regret nor grudge shall I proceed to the other world." A funeral service was held for him at the Kanda Catholic Church. Later that same day the indictment against Matsuoka was dismissed. Sir William Webb announced in court that the action was a "decision of a majority" of the justices. At Ichigaya there was speculation that General Zarayanov, the Soviet judge, opposed discharging the indictment.

The other defendant whose indictment was under question, Shumei Okawa, had been transported from Ichigaya to the 361st Station Hospital for psychiatric examination after his strange outburst in the courtroom on May 3.

In the days that followed his removal to the hospital, Okawa's hallucinations ran riot. According to the official U.S. Army psychiatric report, Okawa felt he was the embodiment of Jesus Christ, Mohammed, Lord Buddha, and Jehovah. To achieve paradise on earth, Okawa declared that he must ascend the throne as emperor. To achieve this, he said he was willing to accept U.S. citizenship. Asked why he had struck Tojo, Okawa said he wanted to kill him because he loved him and wished to protect Tojo and his family from "the humiliation of the trial." One wondered, reading these reports almost forty years later, whether Okawa was twitting the psychiatrists. The army psychiatrists should have pondered Guildenstern's observation that Hamlet's behavior smacked of "a crafty madness." As it turned out, only one psychiatrist, in his report to the tribunal, raised doubts about Okawa's insanity—and that psychiatrist was a Japanese.

On May 11 Dr. Y. Uchimura, a professor of psychiatry at Tokyo Imperial, examined Okawa and was puzzled by his ranting. Uchimura's skepticism emerged in his official report to the court. The report quoted liberally from Okawa's "raving." At one point he said, "The international tribunal is not an object of jurisprudence, but of the science of war. Overlooking such an obvious fact, and taking this for a real trial, [the Japanese] say flatteries in order to curry favor with MacArthur and give interpretations that are to the disadvantage of our miserable war criminals. At Sugamo they were all discussing how to escape the sentence, but I told them they've all got to die since it's a natural force. . . . General MacArthur comes to take his meals here. He's a very nice person. He's like General Yamashita in wisdom and like General Itagaki in his pluck." And so on.

Were these the observations of a madman? "I wondered whether [his remarks] were not said by way of a joke or on purpose," Uchimura confessed in English in his report. He added that Okawa reacted with "ill humour" when his insanity was challenged. Among the American psychiatrists, however, there was no doubt about Okawa's mental condition. He suffered grandiose delusions, visual hallucinations, and defective judgment; his right knee jerk was absent and the left sluggish, clearly symptoms of syphilitic meningoencephalitis. But the Americans did not consider Okawa permanently insane. Both Uchimura and the U.S. Army doctors agreed that with the latest therapy there was a possibility that Okawa would recover from his pathological mental condition.

In a sworn deposition dated May 23, 1946, the chief of the hospital's neuropsychiatric staff concluded: "This patient is considered unable to distinguish right from wrong, and incapable of testifying in his own defense." In court on June 3 the defense requested that Okawa's name be struck from the indictment and that he be transferred to a Japanese asylum for treatment. The prosecution argued that the defendant's mental disability constituted no ground for dismissal of the charge against him, and the tribunal reserved judgment. On June 28 the court ordered Okawa to undergo further examinations to determine if his insanity was "temporary or permanent."

Okawa was a fascinating character. Born in a small village in the hinterlands, he converted to Catholicism at the age of seventeen. In his twenties he came under the influence of a Buddhist monk and turned to mysticism. At Tokyo Imperial University, where he majored in Hindu philosophy, he mastered Chinese, English, Sanskrit, German, and French. His studies led him into a deepening interest in Japanese history and he became increasingly nationalistic. He soon plunged into the twilight world of secret societies and political intrigues, and by the early thirties he was one of the most influential figures in Japan. Okawa was involved in several assassination plots and the wildest scheme of all—the seizure of Manchuria, China's granary, in preparation for war against the United States.

When Okawa was tried for complicity in a political murder in 1934, he turned the witness box into a pulpit for his theories, preached the glory of war, and was acquitted as a great patriot. "If a Japanese-American war is unavoidable," he admonished the court, "this war will probably be a protracted one. Since Japan will be confronted with food and other economic difficulties, the Manchurian problem should be settled first. . . . Japan and Manchuria as a unit are capable of withstanding a protracted war."

Okawa's medical history was a psychiatrist's delight. He engaged in his first sexual intercourse at the age of thirty-three, and contracted gonorrhea. Thereafter he frequented houses of prostitution and wound up with syphilis. Because he suffered from venereal disease, he put off marriage until the age of forty-one. During this period he "experimented" with hard drugs, chiefly heroin. It is a sad commentary on the modern state that the fate of a great nation and a great people—Japan and the Japanese—was so strongly influenced by a self-confessed drug abuser and half-mad syphilitic.

While Okawa sat out the trial in the relative comfort of a psychiatric ward, there continued to be speculation and debate about the state of his mind. Was he insane, or simply a very clever fake—or both? At least one judge believed him sane. B.V.A. Röling wrote me in 1982 his opinion that "Okawa deceived . . . the Court and first of all the psychiatrists." In 1947 the newspaper

Dai Ichi Shimbun carried a report that Okawa appeared to have "recovered" and was "normal." He had regained his appetite and was heartily eating meals sent from home. The Japanese newsman who interviewed him said that "it is difficult to imagine that this quiet, normal individual was the one time 'unbalanced' Okawa who created a furor at the international tribunal." As a result of this dispatch, the court ordered another examination of the accused. A copy of that examination has never turned up in any archive, but Okawa was not released from the hospital.

In 1948, a few days after the trial ended and the sentences were carried out, Okawa's attorneys asked SCAP if any further action would be taken against him. MacArthur was relieved that the IMTFE was behind him and his legal section chief, Colonel Carpenter, announced that all charges had been dropped against Okawa and that no further charges would be instituted. Under Japanese law, persons held to be insane may be released any time the physician in charge decides that the person has "regained his faculties." On December 31, 1948, a week after Hideki Tojo was hanged for crimes against peace and crimes against humanity, Okawa was discharged from the hospital as mentally fit. He died in bed of a heart attack on Christmas Day, nine years later, the only major Japanese war-criminal suspect who did not plead before the IMTFE.

While all these developments unfolded, the defense counsel continued to work diligently to upstage the prosecution before the opening statements. At one point the defense submitted two petitions to Sir William Webb requesting that the tribunal poll world figures for an advisory opinion as to the legality of the IMTFE. The petitions urged that one questionnaire be directed to the "chief exponents of human wisdom" and the other to the "most eminent American authorities on international law." In all, the defense suggested twenty-seven questions. Webb and his colleagues were startled by the maneuver. The names submitted by the defense as the "chief exponents of human wisdom" included Pope Pius XII, Mahatma Gandhi, Karl Barth, Rabbi Stephen Wise, Hu Shih, H. G. Wells, Aldous Huxley, and Roscoe Pound. Among the questions to be put to them were: Does humanity favor the imposition of penal sentences by the victors on their defeated enemies? Does an international war-crimes trial inhibit the future conduct of foreign affairs since the policies of statesmen may be given a criminal interpretation? Is not the ruin of a defendant's country and personal fortunes sufficient retribution for his acts?

The second questionnaire, which was addressed to a dozen law professors of the caliber of Quincy Wright of the University of Chicago, asked: Does the law of nations bind individual members of each state? Does the Kellogg-Briand Pact's renunciation of war "render illegal forcible acts of self-defense"? Is not the imposition of *ex post facto* law condemned by all writers on morals and legislation?

Only five of the defendants put their names to the petition, although the original documents reveal that two others had signed them and later obliterated their names. The five were Shigemitsu, Umezu, Hiranuma, Kaya, and Suzuki, a disparate group even if they were lumped together in the same dock. The idea for the petitions originated with Kenzo Takayanagi, who had been educated in the United States and was Shigemitsu's chief defense counsel.

The tribunal took no judicial note of the petitions, and they were soon forgotten in the rush of events.

9

The Prosecution Begins

In most criminal trials the prosecution's opening statement briefly and succinctly states the parameters of the case and the nature of the evidence the prosecution intends to produce to prove its case. But everything at the IMTFE was on a gargantuan scale, and Joseph Keenan's statement was no exception. It ran about 20,000 words.

"Mr. President," Keenan said crisply, "this is no ordinary trial, for here we are waging a part of the determined battle of civilization to preserve the entire world from destruction." The threat came from the deliberate, planned efforts of individuals, singly and in groups, to plunge the world into war in their ambition to dominate the globe, Keenan asserted. He then pointed to the accused and paused for dramatic effect: "They declared war upon civilization."

All the defendants, including those who were fluent in English, listened to the Japanese translation over their headphones. Hideki Tojo sat with his hands behind his back; Togo and Shigemitsu, the twin foreign ministers, stared blankly ahead. Most of the accused sat stonily, seemingly immovable. Occasionally there was a movement in the dock as a defendant shifted in his seat or took notes.

In answer to the accusations of "victor's justice," Keenan insisted that the tribunals were unrelated to vengeance. The purpose of the trials, he said, was to confirm the already recognized rule that individuals who planned aggressive war were "common felons and deserve . . . the punishment for ages meted out in every land to murderers, brigands, pirates, and plunderers." He dismissed outright the charge that the defendants were being tried *ex post facto.* "To this we believe there is a short answer," he said. In the Allied view, this principle of law meant that a person should not be punished for an act that was not a crime at the time it was committed. "Every offense charged against these accused was well recognized as a crime in international law long before the dates stated in the indictment," he claimed.

Keenan cited chapter and verse in support of the Allied view that crimes against peace existed in international law. The Hague Conventions of 1907 directed states to settle their disputes by pacific means whenever possible and that in the event of war, one side "must not commence without previous and explicit warning." Japan was a signatory to those conventions. At the end of World War I the Allies, of whom Japan was one, declared at Versailles in 1919 that "a war of aggression constitutes an international crime." The Kellogg-Briand Pact of 1928, which Japan signed, renounced war "as an instrument of national policy." Accordingly, Keenan concluded, "To initiate a war of aggression is thus not only a crime, but the chief of war crimes."

Keenan then singled out as the most important feature of the case the liability of the individual for the commission of crimes in the name of the state. "All governments are operated by human agents, and all crimes are committed by human beings," Keenan said passionately. "A man's official position cannot rob him of his identity as an individual nor relieve him from responsibility for his individual offenses. The personal liability of these high-ranking civil officials is one of the most important, and perhaps the only new question under international law, to be presented to this tribunal. That question is being squarely presented."

Thus, he skirted perilously close to *ex post facto* law, admitting that the question of whether individuals could be prosecuted for violations of international law broke new ground. No international body had ever codified such a law, he conceded, but over the years a sufficiently developed body of such laws had gradually crystallized to make this proposition "cognizable by courts of justice."

"When we add to this general rule the additional rule that every person is liable for the natural and probable consequences of his criminal acts, we find that these men, who held positions of power and influence in the Japanese government . . . planned, prepared, initiated and waged illegal wars, [and] are responsible for every single criminal act resulting therefrom," he declared. Again stressing what the Allies considered the core issue at Tokyo, Keenan held that "individuals are being brought to the bar of justice for the first time in history to answer personally for offenses that they have committed while acting in official capacities as chiefs of state. We freely conceded that these trials are in that sense without precedent."

The reference to chiefs of state was either sloppy language or a Freudian slip. No chief of state was on trial at Tokyo, although there were several chiefs of *government* (premiers) in the dock. There had been only one chief of state in Japan between 1928 and 1945, Emperor Hirohito, and he was not present in court. His absence continued to weigh heavily on the IPS, and Keenan was defensive about the failure of the prosecution to indict him. "This is not, and will not be, the only trial of Japanese war criminals," Keenan claimed. "It is obvious that a substantial share of the responsibility rested upon persons now dead or in such a state of health that they cannot be brought to trial." The next line, which clearly referred to Hirohito, should have been set out in italics: *"It may well be that if all the facts were now known to us, there are persons not now on trial whom we might have charged in preference to some of the accused."* Many eyes in the courtroom turned to Marquis Kido, the emperor's stand-in.

The record would demonstrate, Keenan went on, that Japan had attacked China in 1931 at Mukden in Manchuria without notice or warning and struck at Pearl Harbor similarly a decade later. The record would also show that in waging aggressive war, Japan had ignored "the laws and customs of war." In support of this statement, Keenan recited a litany of well-known atrocities such as the Rape of Nanking, the Bataan Death March, and the Burma-Siam Death Railway before turning to "lesser-known but equally infamous crimes," including the massacre of Australian nurses at Bangka, Indonesia; the bayoneting to death of 450 Vietnamese and French prisoners of war at Langson, Vietnam; the slaughter of 18,000 Filipino men, women, and children at Lipa, the Philippines; the murder of 3,000 Chinese at Liaoning, Manchuria; the Double Ten Massacre at Singapore; the murder of all Europeans at Balikpapan, Borneo. ". . . These atrocities were not merely accidental or isolated individual misbehaviors but were the planned results of [a] national policy," Keenan charged. "These killings were contrary to international law even if the warfare in which they occurred had been lawful in itself."

Although the prosecution accused the defendants of acting in concert, Keenan acknowledged that the evidence would not show that they were a united band who were in agreement with one another, as was the case among the Nazi war criminals on trial at Nuremberg. On the contrary, the evidence would show sharp differences of opinion among the defendants and in some cases "fierce rivalries." Some of the accused had directed their venom primarily against China, others toward the Soviet Union, and others against the United States and Britain. Even so, he added, they were all dedicated to a policy of aggrandizement through aggressive war or threat of war.

Many courtroom observers found Keenan's opening statement to be flawed. In addition to being filled with gratuitous remarks— Keenan's calling card—it was also marred by outrageous misinterpretations of history. As Judge Webb commented wryly, "Opening statement contains high language." A glaring example of Keenan's thoughtlessness was his charge that the Japanese sought to destroy "democracy and its essential basis—freedom, and respect of human personality; they were determined that the system of government of and by and for the people should be eradicated and what they called a New Order established instead." From an Asian viewpoint, of course, this was absurd. On the bench and at the prosecutors' table were representatives of imperialist powers, notably Britain, France, and Holland, that still held hundreds of millions of Asians in colonies that enjoyed neither representative government nor civil liberties. And, of course, there was always the shadow across the IMTFE of Stalin's Soviet Union, which had emerged from World War II as the world's principal totalitarian power.

Despite these problems, the prosecutor's statement, lengthy excerpts of which appeared in the Japanese press, encouraged soul-searching among many people, and herein lay a true value of the trial. The IMTFE provided the Japanese with a daily dose of information about prewar and wartime Japan that was foreign to them. Even General Seishiro Itagaki, a hardline leader of the Kwantung Army clique who now sat in the dock, wrote in his diary on January 20, 1947, "[At the trial] I am learning of matters I had not known and recalling things I had forgotten." Many others among the accused made similar comments. If the defendants were in the dark on many matters, what could be said of the Japanese public? "Chief Prosecutor Keenan was fully justified in stressing the individual responsibility of each defendant in his opening address," the *Oriental Economist,* Tokyo's financial and economic weekly, observed on June 22, 1946. "We, the Japanese, however, should go a step farther and think deeply, once again, why the individuals of this kind were ever developed in Japan. Then, we shall come to find that . . . Japan was so organized as to give birth to men of this kind. . . . The IMTFE in Tokyo is extremely significant in that it has given a chance to the Japanese people to reflect deeply upon this fundamental problem."

The *Yomiuri Shimbun,* the smallest of the Big Three dailies, followed up Keenan's opening statement by sampling non-Japanese Asian opinion in Tokyo. Ri Ken Sho, the editor of *Chuka Nipponsha,* a Chinese-language journal, doubted that "the Japanese people, still under the influence of old ideas, can properly digest the meaning of Keenan's words." However, he supported the Japanese defense's view that judges from neutral nations should sit in judgment of the accused. He went a step further. "I think it would be an excellent idea if some of the cultured Japanese who were staunch opponents of the war were added to the bench," the editor said.

George Theodoro, a Filipino correspondent in Tokyo who recalled the visits of an arrogant and strutting Tojo to Manila during the war, studied the ex-premier's face while Keenan read the opening statement. "Although I perceived a sort of resolution in his expression," Theodoro said, "I could not detect any sign of submissive repentance." A young Indonesian nationalist, Abdullah Kamil, who had arrived in Japan shortly *before* the war ended as a member of a group representing an "independent" Indonesia, said he was embittered to learn in Tokyo that Indonesia would be no more free under the Japanese than it had been under the Dutch. "In the arraignment the defendants pleaded not guilty," Kamil said. "What audacity!" As for Keenan's high resolve that Nuremberg and Tokyo would put an end to aggressive war, the Indonesian dryly remarked, "That depends on God's will, and the will of mankind." (Kamil later became a diplomat and was Indonesia's ambassador to the United Nations from 1978 to 1982.)

The reaction of the defendants to Keenan's opening statement varied. General Sato, former head of the powerful Military Affairs Bureau, told his attorney, "I will yield to the judgment of the court in good grace." On the other hand, General Doihara, who had masterminded opium trafficking and acts of terrorism against the Chinese, was unmoved. "Even if the whole nation speaks ill of me," he said defiantly, "I will stand as firm as a rock, and the value of my life shall not at all be impaired." Like many of the defendants, Doihara realized that some of the accused had been talking to the prosecution and that the Allies were getting evidence from "confidential informants." Doihara was bitter. "It is against the duty of a warrior to become a traitor," he said.

Hideki Tojo, recovering from his attempted suicide, told Japanese reporters that he had taken notes on Keenan's opening statement and had already planned a defense to "confute" it. Others among the accused, such as Colonel Hashimoto, withdrew into themselves. Itsuro Hayashi, his attorney, sighed, "It appears to me that Hashimoto has lost his vigor."

The opening statement, with its indirect reference to the emperor, stirred interest in whether or not Hirohito would be called as a prosecution witness. When Japanese reporters asked whether the emperor would be subpoenaed, an IMTFE spokesman replied, "That will be decided at the proper time." This prompted a Japanese newspaper to comment, "The still unsettled question will probably be raised again." Indeed it was, despite the secret decision by Truman and MacArthur six months earlier to keep the emperor clear of any personal involvement in the trial.

10

Trouble in the Tribunal

Outwardly the trial appeared to be off and running, but beneath the surface there was great turmoil involving defense, prosecution, and bench. At times it bordered on scandal.

The defense had been in trouble almost from the beginning. Because of some hesitation about who was responsible for the defense, SCAP had not provided much support. There were not even enough desks to go around at Ichigaya, much less offices. The prosecution had 102 translators, the defense 3. The secretaries and stenographers finally assigned to the defense by SCAP did not take up their positions until the first week of June. "The defendants came in with stacks of books and documents for translation," one defense lawyer protested to Webb in chambers. "It was ridiculous—a mess." Among the most unhappy defense attorneys was Floyd Mattice, a former special assistant to the U.S. attorney general and an authority on criminal law who taught at the University of Indiana Law School. He was appalled by the time consumed in organizing the case for his client, General Itagaki. "We find that when we talk to Japanese counsel, or through an interpreter to defendants, that far more time than the usual time is required," Mattice said. "We find that when we go to the various offices to be, what it seems to be known in military circles as 'processed,' it takes about four times as much time as it takes back in our country to do a similar thing."

On June 3, the day before Joseph Keenan delivered the prosecution's opening statement, Mattice spoke for the U.S. defense attorneys who had arrived in Tokyo on May 17, appealing to Webb for additional time to prepare the defense: "If we are to be of any real assistance to this tribunal, to the defendants, to the Japanese counsel, we reasonably should have some time. We have not had it." And this angrily: "I wonder why we are here."

How much time would the defense need? Webb asked. "We have not agreed upon a time," Mattice acknowledged. The defense lawyers had rowed inconclusively over the length of the recess. Some favored two weeks, others as many as twelve.

Although the accused shared the same indictment, they did not share the same legal interests. The counsel for former premier and foreign minister Koki Hirota, whose wife had died in May, recognized this predicament and filed a motion with the court for a separate trial. The motion pointed out that Hirota had never occupied any military office. "The joining of this defendant with a large number of military and naval officers of the Japanese government renders it impossible, from both a legal and practical standpoint, for this defendant to obtain a fair and impartial trial," the motion, drafted by Tadashi Hanai and David F. Smith, said. To be tried with Japan's military leaders, they averred, "hopelessly prejudices [Hirota's] defense."

George Furness, counsel for former foreign minister Shigemitsu, also found himself isolated. "Shigemitsu was against the war from the beginning," Furness told me in 1981 in Tokyo, "and I did not want his defense governed by any others." Another defense attorney, Aristides Lazarus, was not as diplomatic in the presentation of his strategy. At a meeting of defense counsel at the end of May, Lazarus declared, "I intend to hang twenty-seven of the accused to save Field Marshal Hata, my client; my first and only loyalty is to my client."

Lazarus recalled his strategy at an interview in Yonkers, New York. "I told the meeting that I would keep the trial going two years," he said. "If we stalled long enough for a Communist takeover in China—the civil war was heating up—there would be a different atmosphere in the courtroom. I warned my colleagues that if this trial ended in three months, every one of the accused would hang." Clearly, given this divergence of views on the defense it was inconceivable that the chief of the defense, Beverly Coleman, could direct a unified courtroom strategy.

There were other problems on the defense, including interservice rivalry. When Coleman took control of the defense as chief counsel, the quip at Ichigaya was that "the navy has taken over." Coleman, of course, was a navy captain, but his crew also had naval backgrounds—his deputy, Valentine Deale; John Guider, a graduate of Annapolis; Charles T. Young, a Virginian from the naval judge advocate general's office; Norris N. Allen, who had served with Coleman at Guadalcanal; and Joseph F. Hynes, a wartime officer and former assistant to Wendell L. Willkie, the Republican presidential candidate in 1940. "We were not only rivals in defense of our clients, but we were also service rivals," a member of the defense with an army background said. "The navy had assumed direction of the defense, and this gave rise to resentment among defense counsel from other branches of service."

Finally at an emergency meeting of defense counsel, the crisis broke. "We were earnestly concerned not only as lawyers for justice but also for the good name of the U.S.," Coleman, his bright blue eyes belying his eightieth year, said over lunch in January 1981 at the National Press Club in Washington. "I thought that our role was the most delicate in the whole setup. If the U.S. was going to provide defense counsel, the U.S. must see to it that it was the best defense available. If we sent people to defend our enemies and they did a bum job, the good name of the U.S. in history would be marred."

Coleman and many others in his group were on active duty and could not resign. They could, however, seek reassignment, and that is what they resolved to do. Coleman visited SCAP and told MacArthur's chief of staff, Major General P. J. Mueller, that "we want out." Mueller's eyebrows rose appreciably, and late that night, he received an order to see MacArthur the following morning. Coleman took along Guider, whose father-in-law was Frank Hogan, MacArthur's personal attorney and later New York's district attorney. "MacArthur filled his pipe and began walking up and down," Coleman recalled. "He looked at us and said, 'Ridiculous! We asked for volunteers. You knew what you were getting into. Now you are dissatisfied because of administrative problems, and you're ready to quit.' "

At that point, Coleman said, he wanted to blurt out, "General, you don't understand," but he held back. "I felt it was better to let MacArthur get the steam off his chest," Coleman reminisced.

When MacArthur finished dressing them down, Coleman said,

"General, we are more interested in the trial now than when we started. We've met the defendants and we don't want to desert them, but we need more time to go back to the leading legal firms in the States and get people to put up a first-rate defense."

MacArthur shook his head vigorously. "It is too late for that." The court was now an independent body, beyond SCAP's control, and he did not have the authority to interfere in the proceedings. "He made clear that his hands were tied," Coleman said. But the defense chief felt the situation on the defense was intolerable. He told MacArthur that their only hope was to take a dramatic step to alert Washington to the situation. Thus, when he and Guider withdrew, they left behind their requests for reassignment.

On June 5 Coleman and his naval team resigned en masse, and the next day they notified the IMTFE. These developments did not reach the public until June 15, when the *Nippon Times* reported the American attorneys' withdrawal from the case. "No official explanation was given for the sudden resignation," the newspaper said. In the aftermath, the defense was restructured. The designation of chief of American defense counsel was abolished, although George Yamaoka, a prominent Japanese American attorney who was bilingual, gradually filled the role. A man of great personal integrity, Yamaoka was respected by all sides and valued as a bridge between the Japanese and American lawyers on the defense team.

While the defense went through this turmoil, the Allied prosecution was swept up in a crisis of its own. After delivering the prosecution's opening statement, Joseph Keenan left Tokyo immediately for Washington and was gone for several weeks. According to some, he flew home for "consultations"—that is, to keep abreast of political developments. Others claimed he returned to "dry out." Whatever the truth, in his absence a group of American prosecutors arranged for a meeting with MacArthur and appealed directly to the Allied commander to remove Keenan from the case. They complained about Keenan's drinking, his bullying, his egocentrism—and about what appeared to be the makings of a severe personality conflict between an aggressive Keenan and a churlish president of the court, Webb. MacArthur shook his head. "Mac told them that he was not in a position to act on their request," Robert Donihi, one of the assistant prosecutors, recalled in an interview at Andrews Air Force Base, Maryland.

MacArthur then added that there were a dozen nations represented in the prosecution and that even the prosecutor's critics had to admit that Keenan had a talent for organization and diplomacy. "Mac had a high regard for Keenan," Donihi said.

The issue of Keenan's removal never again rose formally during the trial. But shortly after his return to Japan, Keenan learned of the palace revolt, and thereafter his relations with the ringleaders became more acrimonious than ever.

The turmoil buffeting the IMTFE also affected the bench.

On Friday, June 8, the Filipino judge, Delfin Jaranilla, arrived in Tokyo and that weekend attended a party at which he met, among others, David F. Smith, the American defense counsel for ex-premier Koki Hirota. Smith thus learned that Jaranilla had been in the Bataan Death March and spent the war as a Japanese POW. The next day Smith and Hirota's Japanese counsel, Tadashi Hanai, drafted a "motion suggesting the disqualification and personal bias of the Philippine justice of the tribunal." On June 12 Smith argued the motion in Webb's chambers. "It is personally very embarrassing to me to present this matter," Smith said. "The Philippine justice is a graduate of Georgetown University Law School, of which I have the honor to be a graduate." Hirota's defense attorneys, in their motion, held that since the Bataan Death March was part of the prosecution's evidence, Jaranilla "has and maintains in the legal sense a personal bias and prejudice against this defendant [Hirota]" and that Hirota would therefore be unable to obtain "a fair and impartial trial."

Sir William Webb countered with the observation that the bench had "no power to set aside an appointment by General MacArthur." The president pointed out that this was the position taken by his colleagues when the defense had challenged his own presence on the bench. Smith, however, took the view that "every court and tribunal, anywhere in the world, is always called upon to determine the qualifications and competency of its own members." The defense argued hotly that Jaranilla "has facts, of his own personal knowledge, which may creep into the case." Smith suggested that Jaranilla disqualify himself. Webb now raised a curious point: "If a judge retired voluntarily at this point, it would be difficult to replace him. It is going to create a long delay and it is wholly unfair to the other judges that he should get out unless there is every reason for thinking his qualifications are not beyond challenge." Webb held that Smith's motion did not present clear grounds for challenge. The motion was denied. The next day, June 13, Jaranilla took his seat on the bench and sat alongside New Zealand's Justice Northcroft. "This tribunal is now fully constituted for the first time," Webb said with a sigh. But the bench was no sooner fully constituted than the IMTFE was thrown into panic.

The U.S. judge, John P. Higgins, had gained access to Keenan's scorching cables to Washington about Higgins's appointment, including the cable describing the judge as a "distinct embarrassment." In retrospect, it seems likely that whoever leaked the cables to Higgins may have sought to embarrass Joseph Keenan following the failure of the palace revolt to oust him as chief prosecutor. If the hope was that Keenan would now resign, it was dashed. John Higgins did.

Higgins felt humiliated, and he promptly notified Washington that he intended to resign. A shaken Washington in turn signaled Keenan by teletype at 11 P.M. on July 3 of Higgins's plans. Keenan was asked to notify MacArthur and was informed that Major General Myron C. Cramer, the army's judge advocate general, "is available to replace him immediately."

The next day was July 4, and the occupation and the IMTFE closed down—in court Webb referred to American Independence Day as "Remembrance Day," confusing it with the slogan "Remember Pearl Harbor." On July 5 Keenan summoned an emergency meeting of the IPS. All were present except the associate Filipino prosecutor, Pedro Lopez, who was not in Tokyo, and Britain's associate prosecutor, Arthur Comyns-Carr, who, according to an internal IPS memo from Keenan, had "expressed his views to me privately." Comyns-Carr was represented at the meeting by an aide, Rex Davies. A dreadful row ensued. The Australians, Canadians, New Zealanders, and Dutch took the view that MacArthur had no power to replace a member of the bench. If Higgins resigned, so be it. The charter merely stated that the tribunal would consist of not less than six members nor more than eleven. Why couldn't the trial proceed with ten judges? The French, British, Chinese, and Soviet prosecutors, on the other hand, held that the IMTFE was a Big Five responsibility and that the Americans must be represented. The Chinese prosecutor, Judge Hsiang, was adamant. "[China] especially does not like to see the nonrepresentation of the United States of America on the bench," he said emotionally.

The Americans felt that if Higgins was not replaced, a ludicrous situation would develop at the IMTFE. After all, the United States had carried the burden of the war in the Pacific just as China had carried it on the mainland, the chief Allied prosecutor was an American, there were Americans on the Japanese defense team, and the United States was financing the trial. The Big Five felt that MacArthur had a right to replace Higgins and noted that earlier MacArthur had appointed Henri Bernard to replace Henri Reimburger as the French judge. All the prosecutors agreed, however, that "as a matter of policy it would be most unfortunate for Justice Higgins to be permitted to resign." This implied that Higgins's resignation should not be accepted. The prosecutors also agreed unanimously that it was bad form for a new judge to be appointed to the court after it had been in session one month.

The following day, July 6, Higgins met with MacArthur, who attempted to dissuade him from resigning. Failing this, he extracted a promise from Higgins to "stay on the bench for approximately one week." MacArthur then appointed Washington's choice, Major General Cramer, to the tribunal.

All this maneuvering was kept from the public until July 15, when Sir William Webb made the announcement in open court that "Chief Justice Higgins of the Massachusetts Superior Court, with the consent of the Supreme Commander, has withdrawn as a member of the tribunal." Webb's official reason differed from the view of those behind the scenes. The president of the court claimed that since Higgins's arrival in Japan, his successor in office had died and the present acting chief justice was in advanced years and frail health. Higgins felt he could not put the burden of responsibility for running the Massachusetts court on his successor, as Webb expressed it, "for the period of time it will take to try this case."

According to one attorney at the IMTFE, Higgins believed the trial would run at least two years and that "he could not afford to take two years out of his career." It was said that Higgins met with several defense attorneys in chambers "to tell us that he had resigned and was going home." Aristides Lazarus, who was present at this meeting, recalled that Higgins told them that he considered the trial a fiasco or farce or "something like that" and that "he congratulated us on the fight we were putting up and urged us to stay on course." Lazarus said that Higgins warned the defense that "if we ever quoted him, he would deny all."

Another defense attorney, Owen Cunningham, who was in Washington at the time, observed that "the resignation of Justice Higgins caused considerable comment and indignation in our nation's capital when it was made public." He reported that at Nuremberg there was shock. Judge John J. Parker, the American alternate judge there, was said to have expressed "great concern" over the legal aspects of the move.

As for the prosecution, Joseph Keenan's reaction is not known, but Robert Donihi, one of his assistants, admitted to me that many IPS members felt that "bringing Cramer in midstream was not fair."

Many years later, in his preface to the first publication of the complete judgment of the IMTFE in 1977, the Dutch judge described Higgins's decision as "a matter for regret." Röling added dryly, "Judges should be present during the entire proceedings." For that matter, he continued, it was likewise "improper" that, after the proceedings had already commenced, India and the Philippines each took the opportunity to contribute a judge." And in a letter to the author dated November 12, 1981, thirty-five years after the incident, Röling added with vigor, "I have always thought the USA was a bit ashamed about what happened there, [especially] since Cramer . . . had opposed the opinion that aggressive war was a crime."

This comment had its basis in a book published in 1981. In *Road to Nuremberg,* European historian Bradley F. Smith published documents from the U.S. archives revealing that Cramer had initially had misgivings about a trial of Axis war criminals on the charge of crimes against peace. Cramer felt strongly that war criminals must be dealt with through trials, not summary executions, but by this he meant conventional war crimes—the shooting of civilian hostages, the murder of prisoners of war, and so on. At that time Cramer did not believe there was any basis in international law for the charge of war criminality in connection with preparing and launching aggressive war. However, by the time he was appointed to the Tokyo tribunal, he had come around to the viewpoint that aggressive war was a crime if one state attacked another without a declaration of war in violation of the Hague Convention. By illustration, the Japanese attacks on China, the United States, and Britain were of this character. According to Smith, Cramer engaged in "foot dragging" before accepting the Allied thesis that aggressive war was a criminal act.

Cramer arrived at Ichigaya on July 22 and took Higgins's seat between Webb and Britain's Lord Patrick. His appearance in the courtroom ignited legal fireworks and publicized the divergent interests of the defense.

The attorneys for three of the civilians among the twenty-six defendants immediately challenged Cramer's presence. Owen Cunningham, on behalf of former ambassador Oshima, accused MacArthur of violating his own charter, which empowered him to appoint up to eleven judges; Cramer was the twelfth (thirteenth if Henri Bernard was included). Cunningham argued that the appointment of Cramer would open a floodgate of resignations and appointments to the bench in the course of the trial. "This would result in a ridiculous situation as far as a just trial for the accused is concerned," Cunningham said. He also attacked the appointment itself. "Having served as a high-ranking general in the armed forces of one of the leading victorious accuser nations," the defense lawyer said, "impartiality is incompatible with this relationship and his past official duties." Cunningham called on Cramer to disqualify himself, and he moved that the court declare a mistrial.

David Smith and George Furness, on behalf of Hirota and Shigemitsu, also called for a mistrial. The proceedings had been in progress for a month, Smith said, and "the new judge has lost the benefit, and the defendants have been deprived of the right, of the American judge to see and hear the witnesses and to appraise their credibility."

The conflicting interests of the defendants were now silhouetted. Major Franklin E. N. Warren, the defense counsel for General Doihara and Admiral Oka, warmly welcomed Cramer to the bench. Until now there had been only one military member on the tribunal, Russia's General Zarayanov, Warren pointed out, and the defense should like "another one who understands" the military mind and military law. "We do not join in the motion," Warren declared. U.S. Army Captain Samuel J. Kleiman also announced that he and his client, former premier Hiranuma, welcomed Cramer to the bench. "I know the background of General Cramer, his reputation for fairness, and I welcome him," Kleiman said. It is also worth asking: Did Kleiman know that Cramer had once staunchly opposed charging the war criminals with crimes against the peace, the bottom line of the Tokyo indictment?

At 2:45 P.M. court recessed, and a half hour later Webb announced: "The tribunal, by a majority, holds that General Cramer, the American representative, is eligible to sit as a member of this tribunal and dismisses the motion.'' Cramer took no part in the decision, and the reference to ''a majority'' indicated that the bench, like the prosecution and defense, was split on the issue. Whatever the case, the IMTFE now settled down to what would prove to be a long run.

11

The Army in the Dock

The initial phase of the prosecution's strategy was threefold. First, the IPS wanted to illuminate the police-state mentality in Japan in the thirties, the milieu within which the men in the dock had operated. Then, through the testimony of two former premiers and the son of an assassinated premier, the prosecution would seek to demonstrate how the militarists had stage-managed "incidents" to consolidate their power. Finally, the Allied prosecutors had to pick their way through the intrigues among the army fanatics and the civilian rabble-rousers who had been the key figures in promoting aggressive, expansionist wars.

Superficially, prewar Japan had boasted the trappings of the modern state—political parties, a parliament (the Diet), the secret ballot, trial by jury. The prewar Constitution was Prussian in origin and embodied British legal trappings and a French system of local government. But behind the *shoji* screen of representative government, Japan was a police state. The country was terrorized by the Kempeitai, a military police apparatus unlike any other in the world. In war and peace, the Kempeitai was responsible primarily to the War Ministry. Its principal jobs were "thought control" and counterespionage, and it was given a free hand in dealing with both civilians and the armed forces. Like civil policemen, Kempeitai officers considered themselves agents of the emperor. Prestige or official rank in office was meaningless to them in the

122

performance of what they saw as their duty. There was a deadly parallel here between the Kempeitai and the Gestapo in Hitler's Germany and the KGB today in the Soviet Union.

Canada's associate prosecutor, Brigadier Nolan, handled this phase of the case with the assistance of a team of Allied prosecutors. He introduced into the record the instructions given to the police before and during the war. The Kempeitai (and the civil police, for that matter) were directed to "decide whether or not a person is suspicious from his external appearance, such as his features." This, of course, was the Chinese pseudo-science of physiognomy, or face-reading. The police were empowered to question a "suspicious" person about the origin of his journey and his destination. If the policeman's suspicions were strengthened, he was trained to "ask questions on other points which do not touch upon the main point of the case"—thus, the "suspicions" have, without evidence, turned into a case. Any man or woman, irrespective of rank or position, could be detained at a police station on "suspicion." In addition, the police operated a "peace preservation section" whose duty, in effect, was thought control. No public meeting could be held without police approval. The police were also empowered to shut down a speaker and/or close a meeting if they thought the subject matter subversive. Public morals were also under police control; the police licensed prostitutes. A books and publications section in the police department censored "all books, magazines and newspapers." In practice, few books were banned because they were censored in manuscript form. In effect, the police exercised prior restraint.

As a policy, official warnings were sent to newspaper offices to tell them what could not be printed. When the Gestapo chief in the Far East, who later became Hitler's envoy to Japan, visited Tokyo in 1940, the Japanese press was warned that "nothing is to be mentioned of the coming to Japan, presence here or movements of Heinrich Stahmer, a German minister, who will be at the German Embassy on a certain mission." In a country with a free press, such a notice from the government would serve only to evoke curiosity, but in Japan a failure to obey the order could result in a fine, imprisonment of the editor, or the closing down of the paper. The result was that the Japanese press in the thirties published little besides propaganda tending to justify and glorify Japan's militaristic and aggressive policies.

A prize witness in this phase of the prosecution's case was

Goro Koizumi, a stocky, high-ranking prewar police official. "In connection with law enforcement," Koizumi told the court, "the police enforced the censorship laws over newspapers, publications, writings, books, moving pictures, plays and other forms of entertainment, public speeches, public gatherings . . . and when persons infringed upon any law such persons, they were then put in prison." Between 1931 and 1941 Koizumi ran several prefectures as chief of police. He testified that the policeman's job was to "watch over the activities of anyone who was opposed to the policy of the Japanese government. . . . No one in Japan was permitted to express opposition to the war with China." Those who did were arrested under the Peace Preservation Law. Koizumi hastened to add, however, that this did not apply "if a mother whose son was a soldier in the Japanese army in China, should say, 'I wish the war was over and my boy was home.' "

The prosecution put a dozen witnesses on the stand to spell out the authoritarian nature of prewar Japan in which the twenty-six defendants had operated.

Hyoe Ouchi, a professor at Tokyo Imperial University, had been purged with eight others on the faculty for criticizing Japan's invasion of China proper in 1937. Ouchi had spent eighteen months at Sugamo, the very same prison that now housed the war criminals. In his testimony Ouchi fingered two men in the dock, General Araki, the former war and education minister, and Marquis Kido, the emperor's adviser and briefly an education minister. Araki, he said, had forced military training into the curriculum, and Kido had been instrumental in purging the university of opponents to the China war. As a sign of things to come, during his cross-examination the defense engaged in blatant delaying tactics, raising the specter of an endless trial. For instance, when Ouchi referred to a law passed in 1939 to make military training in schools compulsory, defense attorney Kleiman asked, "You have just used the word 'passed' . . . by that you may mean passed by the Diet?" Kleiman kept asking questions in a similar vein until an exasperated Sir William Webb raised his voice. "I cannot allow this to go on . . ." Webb boomed. "If you are going to have every 'i' dotted and every 't' crossed in this case, we will never finish." He added gruffly, "We have heard enough of you!"

Tamon Maeda, a former editorial writer of the *Asahi Shimbun,* one of Japan's most popular newspapers, described the atmosphere in Japan after 1928 as "tense" as the militarists, in league with ultrapatriotic groups, jockeyed for power. Maeda singled out Shumei Okawa, now consigned to an asylum, as the theoretician for rabid nationalism and aggressive war. After 1931, Maeda testified, Japan's newspapers were censored heavily. A typical example of this pressure occurred in 1936, when he had warned in an editorial that by deepening her Nazi ties Japan was "isolating herself from the rest of the world." Two colonels, one from the War Ministry and the other from the general staff, visited his office the next day and expressed disapproval of his views. "[They] instructed me that in the future when writing or speaking about such subjects to do so in a more favorable aspect," Maeda said. "While no actual threats were made to me, there was much rattling of their sabers."

Another witness, Nobufumi Ito, a former president of the government's Board of Information, acknowledged from the stand that the board had been essentially a propaganda ministry that imposed censorship and disseminated views "of an inflammatory nature for the purpose of preparing the Japanese people for war." A high official of the Japan Broadcasting Corporation testified that the network had been controlled by the government and that "broadcasting scripts were first censored in the Ministry of Communications before being released to the public." The witness who provoked the most curiosity among the Allied spectators was Akio Saki, the president of a firm that manufactured "paper theatre productions." He explained that these were "large picture cards with a story on the back of each." Bubble-gum cards! In prewar Japan censorship and propaganda had been tuned so finely that bubble-gum card manufacturers were told what to print. The cards introduced at the IMTFE as evidence were cartoons that showed Japan and Germany as staunch, peace-loving friends and Britain and the United States as the villains responsible for the Sino-Japanese War.

One of the witnesses balked, either out of fear or for reasons of misguided patriotism, and altered his testimony on the stand. Tokiomi Kaigo, an assistant professor at Tokyo Imperial for a decade, took one look at the accused in the dock—some of whom, notably the bushy-browed General Itagaki, glowered at him—and then began to squirm uncomfortably in the witness box. Valentine Hammack, a former assistant U.S. attorney for southern California and later a special assistant who handled war fraud prosecutions, endeavored to get Kaigo to recite chapter and verse on the militarization of Japan's educational system. Hammack failed. Over and over again he said, "Will you please answer that question?" Each request set off Kaigo on a reply more circuitous than the one before. At one point the defense accused Hammack of trying to lead the witness. "If it please the Court," Hammack protested, "I respectfully submit that up to date the witness has not answered any questions, and I am endeavoring to expedite by leading him slightly."

Webb shook his mane. "You are not entitled to lead him, even slightly," the tribunal's president said. "Do you want to have him declared a hostile witness?"

Webb made this remark in jest but Hammack mistook the suggestion. "I ask to have the witness declared hostile, and I would like the privilege of impeaching my own witness on the ground that we were taken by surprise."

Now Webb was surprised. "That is a very serious step," he said. "I was trying to be facetious." But Hammack charged that Kaigo's answers "so far have been . . . wholly in conflict with the answers given to me heretofore."

Once again Hammack tried to elicit answers to his questions and once again Kaigo proved evasive. "Your . . . witness is rather devastating, Mr. Hammack," Webb remarked dryly.

This scene was repeated often during the trial. But for the first time since 1928, the year the military consolidated their power, new voices were being heard in Japan. A fresh breeze was blowing across the charred wasteland that had once been a great nation.

As George Orwell might have expressed it, in Japan all cabinet ministers were equal except that the war minister was more equal than others. Theoretically, all cabinet ministers had the right of access to the emperor. But the war minister—and to a lesser extent the navy minister—exercised a right greater than all the other ministers and co-equal with that of the premier: *iaku joso,* direct access to the throne. The subjects the war minister discussed with the emperor were generally kept secret from other cabinet ministers except the premier, and even the premier was often left in the dark.

The war ministers of Japan were generals; the portfolio was never held by a civilian. In the twenties these officers were drawn from the reserve list. In 1936, however, Premier Koki Hirota, one of the men in the dock, accommodated the militarists and dramatically altered the selection process. Thereafter the ministers were drawn from the active list. Thus, the army chief of staff directly controlled the government since an officer on the active list was under his orders. In the case of the war minister, he was selected by a triumvirate consisting of the army's chief of staff, the outgoing war minister, and the inspector general of military education, this last an innocuous-sounding title but one usually held by a firebrand who was responsible for whipping up the army's fighting spirit.

For all practical purposes, then, the army ran the empire.

By failing to appoint a war minister, the army could prevent the formation of a government. By ordering a war minister to resign, the army could bring down a government. By exploiting the right of *iaku joso,* or access to the emperor, the army could force the adoption of policies that an entire cabinet, including the premier, might oppose.

"It will be shown time and time again throughout the course of these proceedings that, entrusted with the defense of the nation, the supreme command has challenged the power of the cabinet over many matters on the ground that they were matters of national defense," Brigadier Nolan, the Canadian associate prosecutor, told the court. "They have thus claimed and exercised the right to advise the emperor and to formulate policy on matters relating to the declaration of war, foreign relations, treaty negotiations, the ratification of international conventions, and many internal matters because of their relationship, however remote, to national defense."

The Allied prosecution introduced voluminous evidence to prove the point. The Tanaka cabinet of 1929 had been forced to resign because the others were powerless to control the war minister in connection with the punishment of Japanese Army officers responsible for the murder of Marshal Chang Tso-lin, the principal Chinese warlord in Manchuria. Two years later the Wakatsuki cabinet was compelled to resign when it refused to go along with the army's defense of fanatics who had created another incident in Manchuria, this time at Mukden, and used it as a pretext for the invasion of China's northernmost provinces. In 1937, when the army conspired to provoke another incident, this time at Marco Polo Bridge, the Japanese peace faction thought they had found a way to get around the army's control of the war minister. They induced Emperor Hirohito to invite General Kazushige Ugaki, who had served as war minister from 1929 to 1931, to form a new cabinet. But the generals recalled that in 1924, when the peace faction was riding high, Ugaki had reduced the size of the army. The army hotheads considered this a traitorous act. Ugaki had little difficulty putting together a cabinet list until he came to the appointment of a war minister. No general on the active list accepted the portfolio, and Ugaki's effort collapsed. In the same year, too, the cabinet of Admiral Mitsumasa Yonai fell when the war minister, the same Field Marshal Hata who was now in the dock, resigned his portfolio after the cabinet blocked Japan's entry into a tripartite alliance with Germany and Italy.

The IPS introduced evidence that during this political turmoil the army had reinforced its power plays by the strategy of terror and the tactic of assassination. In 1930 Premier Osachi Hamaguchi had been assassinated because he cut the army's budget and pushed for the ratification of the London Naval Treaty restricting the size of the Japanese Navy. Two years later Premier Tsuyoshi Inukai was murdered, along with his finance minister, for trying to trim the army's budget and pursuing a "good neighbor" policy toward China. Four years after that, in 1936, an attempt was made to murder Premier Keisuke Okada.

The IPS called as witnesses for the prosecution several of the principal surviving figures of these troubled times. The first witness to take the stand was Baron Kijuro Shidehara, who had served as foreign minister between July 2, 1929, and December 12, 1931, and had been for a brief time acting premier. During this time, at the height of his career, Shidehara had fought the army's expansionists, but they bested him and eventually forced him out of the government. Then, in October 1945, MacArthur had called Shidehara out of oblivion to take over the reins of government as premier. Thus, Shidehara had been present at the rise of the empire in 1931 and at its collapse in 1945, a period strewn with the bodies of millions of his dead and wounded countrymen.

Shidehara, who was now seventy-four years old, shuffled to the stand. His face was tired but his words were crisp. "Shortly before the Manchurian Incident [in 1931], as foreign minister, I received confidential reports and information that the Kwantung Army was engaged in massing troops and bringing up ammunition and material for some military purpose," Shidehara told the tribunal, "and knew from such reports that action of some kind was contemplated by the military clique." The Kwantung Army by treaty patrolled the Japanese-leased South Manchurian Railway, Manchuria's lifeline.

Shidehara paused and gazed stonily at the men in the dock. Among the defendants was General Jiro Minami, who had held the portfolio of war minister in the same cabinet. Shidehara recalled that he and Premier Wakatsuki had "made every effort to control the army and prevent further territorial expansion but [we] were unable to do so." The militarists had laughed at their efforts and denounced Shidehara's "weak-kneed policy" toward China. He lost face. "This was a great embarrassment," the aged Japanese leader said gravely. He testified that the cabinet's policy had been to contain the incident and that the defendant Minami had agreed to this policy. The following exchange ensued between Hugh Helm, an American assistant prosecutor, and Shidehara:

HELM: These instructions were issued to General Minami?

SHIDEHARA: The cabinet had no authority to give orders to the war minister.

HELM: Well, following the war minister's agreement with the cabinet on this policy, did the Manchurian affair cease?

SHIDEHARA: As everyone knows, the Manchurian incident did not cease. And in spite of all the efforts of General Minami, the incident continued to develop and expand. . . .

HELM: Were any of the officers . . . disciplined in any way for the spread of the Manchurian incident?

SHIDEHARA: The cabinet was not in a position to discipline either the army in Manchuria or any army anywhere.

Under cross-examination, Shidehara admitted that the accused Minami had described the Japanese Army's action at Mukden as "self-defense," but "even so, the cabinet considered that it was wrong that this affair should be extended to other districts and bent every effort to prevent this further expansion."

During redirect questioning Shidehara dropped a bombshell. As an example of the autonomous nature of the army he described how, as the Kwantung Army swept across Manchuria, the Japanese forces in Korea, which was then a Japanese colony, had crossed the border and linked up with the Kwantung Army. "I know," the former foreign minister said, "that the army in Korea [acted] without the knowledge of the cabinet." Had this army acted with the emperor's approval? "I understand," he continued haltingly, "—it is my understanding—that they entered Manchuria without the imperial sanction." In the gallery the Japanese spectators, especially the young people, sat with their mouths agape.

Three witnesses followed Shidehara to the stand, and their testimony gave the trial, for the first time, the character of a criminal proceeding. They accused Generals Koiso and Itagaki, Colonel Hashimoto, and the absent Shumei Okawa of conspiring to seize the government to further their plans for aggressive war.

The first witness was Konosuke Shimizu, at one time a disciple of Okawa, who recounted that in March 1931, at the Kinryutai Inn, one of Okawa's favorite geisha houses, over cups of warm saké, Colonel Hashimoto and Okawa had unfolded a plot to topple the government. "My part in the plot was to throw some bombs outside the Diet building during a demonstration by Dr. Okawa's followers," Shimizu told an amazed tribunal. "It was further planned that Dr. Okawa was to lead this mob into the Diet and proceed to take over the government." For this purpose the plotters obtained 300 bombs from the army. But for a reason that never emerged at the trial—though there were hints that the navy had embarked on a similar conspiracy itself and that the army preferred staging an incident in Manchuria—the army had a change of heart, and General Koiso, the defendant who was then chief of the Military Affairs Bureau in the War Ministry, ordered "that this plot be abandoned."

Shimizu added that he had continued to meet with Okawa at the Kinryutai Inn, and in August of that year, when Okawa was drunk, Okawa had confided that a group of colonels, including Itagaki, who was then vice chief of staff of the Kwantung Army, "would bring about an incident in Mukden sometime later on."

The defense jumped on the witness. "You realize that the statements that you have made about this plot are self-incriminatory, do you not?" a Japanese defense counsel asked sharply. "What induced you to give these answers? Were you promised a gift, or were you threatened by anyone in any way if you refused to answer?''

Shimizu retained his aplomb. He did not testify for a ''cowardly motive,'' he said, and added that he felt these ''little incidents'' had nothing to do with the trial now in progress.

Another of Okawa's intimate political associates, Yoshichika Tokugawa, confirmed from the witness stand that despite the failure of the plot to seize the Diet, Okawa had continued to make plans ''to place the militarists in control of the government.'' The witness testified that General Koiso had told him he was in trouble with the army after the plan was abandoned because Shimizu refused to return the bombs. Koiso had implored Tokugawa to get the bombs back and ''to pay money, if necessary.'' A triumphant witness said he had persuaded Shimizu to return the bombs ''without payment.'' During this testimony General Koiso sat slumped in his seat in the dock, Colonel Hashimoto took notes, and General Itagaki radiated menace.

The provocative action that went down in history as the Manchurian or Mukden Incident was the first important move the army made on its own, without government sanction. The incident was a manufactured crisis that led to the Japanese invasion and occupation of Manchuria and was the first major step toward all-out war with China.

The tribunal heard the story of the Mukden Incident from the man ostensibly most qualified to relate what was happening inside the government at the time. Reijiro Wakatsuki, the prime minister when the army staged the Mukden Incident, took the stand. Now eighty-one years old, his hair as white as the snow on Mount Fuji's crest, Wakatsuki talked about the crisis as if it had happened yesterday. There was added drama to his words because the premier who preceded him, Hamaguchi, and the premier who succeeded him, Inukai, had both been murdered in office. Wakatsuki was in fact the only premier to survive in office in the critical years 1929–32, though he, too, had been a target of assassins.

The testimony of Wakatsuki echoed and amplified what had been said by Shidehara. On September 18, 1931, Kwantung Army agents had planted bombs that blew up parts of the Japanese-controlled South Manchurian Railway. Charging sabotage, the army promptly went on a war footing—though no war was declared—and within a short time occupied all of Manchuria. The day after the incident, Wakatsuki testified, the cabinet told the war minister, the defendant General Minami, that the affair was to be "terminated at once." Minami agreed, but the next day newspaper correspondents at the front reported that the Kwantung Army was continuing to expand the area under its control. Minami explained hastily to the cabinet that "this was only a protective measure and would in no sense be expanded." On the following day, however, the army continued to race across Manchuria even as Minami reiterated that the area of Japanese control "would not be enlarged upon." The ex-premier added with a touch of frustration in his voice, "This same performance was repeated on the 22nd."

On September 23 the Japanese troops in Korea crossed into Manchuria, without the emperor's sanction, to join the Kwantung Army. Wakatsuki testified that he had demanded "these operations in Manchuria must cease immediately, and War Minister General Minami agreed to put this cabinet policy into effect with the army at once." But in the days that followed the area of military operations continued to spread.

"I was shown maps daily on which the aforesaid General Minami would show by a line a boundary which the army in Manchuria would not go beyond, and almost daily this boundary line was ignored and further expansion was reported, but always," Wakatsuki sighed, "with assurance that this was the final move."

In perhaps one of the saddest commentaries of the trial, Wakatsuki told the IMTFE: "I tried everything I could think of in an effort to control this situation, but without success." The warlords in the dock had thirsted for combat and nobody was going to stop them, least of all a Japanese premier.

The defense was devastated.

During the cross-examination, in the hope of introducing an element of mitigation in Minami's case, the defense startled the court by drawing from the witness the admission that young army hotheads had plotted to kill him a month after the Mukden Incident but that Minami had intervened to save his life. "The younger officers contemplated an attempt on my life, and the gendarmes stopped his attempt," Wakatsuki acknowledged. As war minister, of course, Minami exercised control over the secret police.

Who, the defense counsel asked, was primarily responsible for the advances in Manchuria? "I suppose there is some military man responsible for them," Wakatsuki said slowly, ". . . [but] the government does not know who is responsible for matters of the Supreme Command. Therefore, I cannot definitely state that it was the chief of the army general staff or not." Once again the true source of power in Japan was hidden behind a *shoji* screen. If the leaders of the Japanese peace faction did not know—and the integrity of their statements has never been effectively challenged—how could the Allied prosecution ever learn the true state of affairs? This key question persisted throughout the trial.

Excitement rippled through the courtroom when the prosecution summoned its next witness, General Kazushige Ugaki, who was unable to find a war minister for his own cabinet after the emperor had given him a mandate to form a government to stifle the army's adventurism abroad.

In early 1931, Ugaki testified, he received reports that Shumei Okawa was involved in some kind of plot against the Diet, but he "did not take this too seriously at the time." To his horror, however, Ugaki then learned that the plotters had set him up as the front man for the military regime they hoped to put in power. The defendant General Koiso, who was then army chief of staff, told him that there was a plot and that he was scheduled "to become head of this revolutionary government." Ugaki immediately ordered Koiso to stop the plans for a coup, he said, and then he resigned from the cabinet and went into seclusion.

As evidence of these bizarre events Ugaki surprised the defense by fishing out of his jacket a handwritten letter he had received from Shumei Okawa on March 6, 1932, and which was marked as Prosecution Exhibit No. 163, Part 2. Okawa proclaimed wildly in the letter, "Signs of disorder are already pressing around us. . . . The ready-made parties have entirely lost confidence under heaven. . . . Every mouth among the people has cursed parliamentary politics. Vital now is the need for a great man of ability to overcome disorder, and vindicate righteousness. Who else but you! . . . The life of the Empire hinges on your decision."

Another witness who gave an insider's account of the Manchurian affair was Ken Inukai, a member of the Diet who in 1930 and 1931 had been private secretary to his father, Premier Inukai. In the dock sat his father's war minister, General Sadao Araki. Inukai approached the witness box with the air of a man who had a lot to get off his chest.

As a child, he testified, he had sat on the lap of Sun Yat-sen, the founder of the Chinese Republic who was an intimate friend of the Inukai family. His father had also been a close personal friend of the young Chiang Kai-shek. "During my father's tenure of office as premier, he was opposed to the extension of the Manchurian Incident and was in favor of having the Japanese Army withdraw from Manchuria," he testified. He said his father sought to defuse the situation by going directly to Hirohito and asking the emperor to issue an imperial rescript withdrawing the army from Manchuria. His father also sent a secret envoy to Nanking to negotiate a peaceful resolution of the Mukden Incident with Chiang Kai-shek.

Both moves misfired. "Prime Minister Inukai had an audience with the Emperor," the son testified, "but was not successful in having the army withdraw from Manchuria." As for the mission to China, "this secret delegate communicated with the premier by code, which code, however, was intercepted by the military."

On May 8, 1932, Premier Inukai delivered an anti-army speech at Yokohama, and a week later a group of terrorists shot him. As he lay mortally wounded, the son testified, "he told me that several young naval officers had forced their way into the official residence and that one of them had shot him." These terrorists also attacked the homes of the two top advisers to the emperor, the minister of the imperial household, and the lord keeper of the privy seal.

The reference to Hirohito in Ken Inukai's testimony apparently touched an open wound, and Marquis Kido, the emperor's alter ego among the accused, hastened to cauterize it. On cross-examination, Kido's defense attorney, Shigetaka Hozumi, asked the witness why his father's appeal to the emperor had failed. "There were various reasons," the witness said; ". . . one is the opposition of the army." But, the defense counsel persisted, if the emperor did not grant the premier an imperial rescript ordering the army out of Manchuria, "this statement can mean to me that the emperor was also responsible for this matter." Accordingly, Hozumi asked the witness to clarify his remark with "a very clear statement." Inukai retreated. The emperor, he said, was "a strong advocate of peace and had a very strong desire for an amicable settlement of the Manchurian Incident." This, anyway, was what he meant to convey in his testimony. The defense was satisfied, but to make certain, Hozumi asked Webb if the tribunal was satisfied. The political implications sailed over the head of the Australian, who was confused. "I cannot understand," he said. The interpreter rephrased Hozumi's request. The defense counsel said he was satisfied with the witness's clarification, but was the court? "I have heard enough," an irritated Webb said.

Webb's colleagues on the bench did not agree with him. That evening, at the Imperial Hotel, several judges complained to Webb that they wanted to hear more on why Hirohito had not issued a rescript ordering the Japanese Army to withdraw from Manchuria. The following day, June 28, Webb announced in court that "some of the members of the court would like to hear the witness make a fuller statement on the emperor's position to clear up a contradiction, if there be one, in his own evidence."

Ken Inukai returned to the witness stand. In the British tradition Webb took personal charge of the witness. "Yesterday, witness, you were guilty of an apparent contradiction in your evidence," Webb said, leaning over his microphone. "We would like to hear you fully now."

The wound bled anew. Inukai's reply was enlightening, not so much for its insight but because of the muddle it created and because it revealed the state of mind of the Japanese toward their emperor irrespective of whether they were associated with the war or peace faction. "As the learned President will probably understand," Inukai said, "it is the feeling of the Japanese to avoid bringing the name of our emperor into this argument—and, in line with this feeling, I hesitated somewhat yesterday and gave only a rough explanation of the details of the incident."

Inukai now subtly shifted ground. He was "not sure" whether his father had asked the emperor directly for a rescript ordering troop withdrawals or whether his father went through an intermediary such as the lord keeper of the privy seal. Whatever the case, Inukai continued, he was convinced that the emperor had told his father that he did not want the army to control Japanese politics. "I have no proof . . . but I believe that . . . my father would not lie to me, as a son, in an important matter as this. . . . Also I am convinced that my father would have staked his life in following the imperial wishes."

Inukai's statement on the role of the emperor filled nine pages of testimony in the transcript and left the contradiction where it was originally. "Mr. Witness," Webb said wearily, "we have heard enough. Only a fraction of what you have said bears on the Emperor's position or attitude."

Joseph Keenan and his Allied prosecution, coming into the trial cold and sorely lacking a background in Asian much less Japanese affairs, had done well. They had successfully penetrated the shifting Japanese political scene in the 1930s, and they had established the police-state mentality that gripped Japan in the thirties and the unique control the army exercised over the Japanese government. As for the emperor in this situation, the trial left his role in suspension. The record showed that at a minimum he had acquiesced in the army's occupation of Manchuria. But the nagging question, the riddle that the IMTFE would never solve, was whether Hirohito was puppet or puppeteer. It is a peculiar commentary on the shadowy political situation in Japan in this period that a strong case could be made for either view. Perhaps the answer is that the emperor was like a pendulum. When he was pushed strongly in one direction, the laws of motion took over and pushed him just as strongly in the opposite direction. When the pendulum was not pushed, it was stationary, at peace with itself—the role of the emperor in Japan today.

12

The Invasion of Manchuria

If it is true that there exists a moment in time when history can still choose between war and peace, the Allied prosecution's next witness pinpointed that moment for Japan. Admiral Keisuke Okada, premier between 1934 and 1936 and twice navy minister, was another figure the IMTFE brought from the past to give damaging testimony against the accused. He held moderate and peaceful political values and, like Wakatsuki, he had narrowly avoided the fate that befell other peaceful premiers like Hamaguchi and Inukai. His brother-in-law had been mistaken for him and killed by the "ultras."

Okada, nearing eighty, had a long score to settle with the warlords who had led Japan to ruin, and he threw Japanese politeness to the winds. He started his tale in 1928, the year Marshal Chang Tso-lin was murdered in Manchuria—a murder he attributed to "a clique" in the Japanese Kwantung Army. "They arranged on June 4, 1928, that the train on which Chang Tso-lin was traveling from Peiping to Mukden should be wrecked by explosives placed on the track," he testified, adding, "Chang Tso-lin was killed in this wreck as planned."

The admiral categorically declared that "this incident, plotted and instituted by the clique in the Kwantung Army, represented the *first* overt army move . . . to project itself into the formulation of the policies of the government" (italics added). Here was the start of the events that led to Pearl Harbor, and beyond. And here, too, was that delicate moment when the fortunes of history could have been reversed. The then premier Giichi Tanaka, gravely shaken by these events, reported fully to the emperor on the role of the army in the murder of the *de facto* ruler of Manchuria. "The emperor told him that he considered that this was the time to take strong disciplinary action with respect to the army," Okada testified. This was the Voice of the Crane, and this was his first opportunity to assert authority.

Hirohito's father had died on Christmas Day, 1925, two and a half years earlier, and the twenty-year old crown prince had succeeded him that same day. However, Hirohito's coronation was still being planned—the ceremony would not be held until November 10, 1928—and he had not moved into the Imperial Palace when Chang Tso-lin was murdered. There was a fatal gap in the throne's full authority. Is this why the army struck when it did?

According to Okada, the premier relayed the youthful emperor's desires to the war minister, but "when the war minister took the matter up in the war ministry, he encountered such strong opposition on the part of the general staff and other army officers, that he was unable to make any headway or progress whatsoever.

"After the murder, the influence of the army insofar as participation in the formulation of policy on the part of the government with respect to Manchuria was concerned grew progressively stronger," said Okada, who had had a ringside view of the struggle between the army and the civilians in the government. The behavior of the arrogant generals, who were prepared to throw Japan's 60 million people into a war against 400 million Chinese, "created a great deal of anxiety on my part," Okada said sorrowfully.

After the Mukden Incident, Okada testified, "the army was completely out of control by the government, and no restraint could be placed upon it." In 1934, when he was asked to form a cabinet, it was considered a "navy cabinet" because the navy was known to oppose the army's aggressive, expansionist plans on the Asian mainland.

The militarists and the ultrapatriotic societies plotted "many occurrences" aimed at toppling him, the admiral testified, "culminating in the attempt at my assassination in February of 1936, which resulted in the assassination of my brother-in-law, Mr. Matsuo, who was mistaken for me." The incident, Okada continued, "constituted an embarrassing situation to the emperor as it was a somewhat public manifestation of the inability of my cabinet to control the military." Okada resigned as premier the following month.

"The army was completely without the control of the Japanese government and remained so up until the Great War in 1941," he continued. And, turning philosophical, he explained what motivated him to take the stand against those in the dock. Above all, he was a Japanese patriot. The army's behavior had always caused him untold anxiety and anguish. "Japan has been done a most grave injustice," he said.

The Japanese defense counsel tried to impeach the witness by charging that he had been blackmailed by the Allies into testifying against his former comrades-in-arms. "When you appeared before the International Prosecution Section, did not some friend solicitous for your safety tell you that unless you offered an affidavit favorable to the prosecution that you, yourself, would be in danger of standing trial?"

Okada glared at the accused. "I have never received such advice or cautionary advice from any person." Well, asked the defense lawyers, had he ever heard rumors to that effect? "I have never heard such a rumor," the witness said.

On this note the aged sea lord left the stand, and the Allied prosecution followed up by bringing the sensational Kido diaries into play. The IPS tendered in evidence several excerpts, starting with the entry dated August 7, 1931, when the Japanese Army plotted the Mukden Incident and the conquest of Manchuria. It was "regrettable," Hirohito's adviser complained in his secret memoirs, that Japan was sliding under the army's control. "Recently," Kido wrote, "the army group has been getting very strong. There is a danger of strong antagonism between the civilians and the army."

A September 22 entry, written four days after the Mukden Incident, confirmed the struggle between Premier Wakatsuki and War Minister Minami recounted earlier in court. "The army is so strongly determined in its positive policy toward Manchuria that orders given by the central authorities may not be carried out," Kido wrote. He added that the emperor sought to put a rein on the army and that the army was "indignant" over the emperor's interference. By October 1 Kido was frightened. "The army is trying to destroy political parties and parliament and establish a military dictatorship," he wrote, "[and] it is very difficult to devise a countermeasure." The only way of restraining the militarists, the lord keeper of the privy seal concluded, was to "guide" them. And this was precisely the policy Kido pursued up to and including his recommendation that General Hideki Tojo be named premier in 1941, a policy of appeasement that led to Pearl Harbor and Hiroshima. Even in rolling with the army's punches, Kido feared that the policies of the militarists would damage the nation and result in unnecessary sacrifice. "It is a national calamity," he wrote sorrowfully. As these entries were read in open court, Marquis Kido sat motionless and downcast in the dock. He did not even look up at Ben Sackett, the American assistant prosecutor who was reading them aloud. Kido was inscrutable, as the bright shafts of light from the klieg lights above shone down on his pink, balding head, and as the gallery and press strained forward in their seats.

The next witness proved to be one of the most controversial to take the stand. Before the trial ran its course, Major General Ryukichi Tanaka would testify for the defense as well as the prosecution, and part of his testimony would ultimately be discredited. Tanaka had been in Manchuria during the Mukden Incident, and his military career ended in 1942 when Premier Tojo dismissed him from the Military Affairs Bureau because he had suffered a nervous breakdown. Like most former Japanese generals who took the witness stand, he did not speak normally but shouted his answers, a product of his training.

In January 1942, he testified loudly, when the War Ministry was being moved to Ichigaya, where the IMTFE was now in session, in the course of packing he had discovered a top-secret dossier marked "Urgent File of the Chief of the Military Affairs Bureau."

Among the papers was a report on how elements in the Kwantung Army had carried out the murder of Marshal Chang Tso-lin in 1928 "to create a new state under Japanese control." Under questioning, Tanaka was asked if the Mukden Incident was also a Japanese Army plot. "Yes," he replied. Did he know the conspirators? Yes, he knew three of them, all defendants at the trial— Shumei Okawa, General Itagaki, and Colonel Hashimoto. Well, did he personally know, for example, Colonel Hashimoto? "Yes," Tanaka said. "He is my friend." Is he in the courtroom? "Yes," Tanaka said, turning his head to the left and gazing into the dock.

"To the extreme left, second row." Hashimoto grimaced.

Hashimoto, Tanaka said, had told him that the ultimate objective of the Mukden Incident was "to make Manchuria a base from which to bring about the revival of Asia." The independence of Manchuria had been his ideal since his youth; however, Hashimoto confided, since there would be a strong international reaction to Japan's move into Manchuria, he felt it expedient to turn the region into a Japanese puppet state to protect it. Hashimoto was convinced, the witness said, that the conquest of Manchuria would be "the first step in the emancipation of Asia." In a manner of speaking, of course, it was; in the aftermath of the 1931–45 East Asian War, the backbone of European colonialism and imperialism in the Far East was broken.

Ben Sackett now asked Tanaka if he knew the accused General Itagaki. "Yes," the witness replied, "I am very much indebted to him." Was Itagaki in the courtroom? "Extreme right, second row," Tanaka said.

The Tanaka testimony strengthened the case against Itagaki, who had been deputy chief of the Kwantung Army at the time of the Mukden Incident. Tanaka testified that Itagaki had arranged clandestinely to move big guns, with a range of fifteen miles, into Mukden, one aimed at the Chinese Nationalist Army barracks and the other at the Mukden airfield. The installation was completed September 10, eight days before the incident. "[Itagaki] said that the installation of the guns should be kept top secret," Tanaka testified, "and that to the outside world it should be said that a well was being dug." The dismantled cannons were assembled and hidden within the Japanese compound in the city; the weapons shipment had been authorized by the War Ministry. On the night of the Mukden Incident, Itagaki brought the big guns into play. When the Chinese heard the roar of heavy artillery, they panicked and fled Mukden. "The element of surprise [attack] is very essential in war," Itagaki had told Tanaka.

On the eve of the incident, Tanaka testified, Major General Tatekawa, who is believed to have committed *hara kiri* after Japan's surrender, was sent to Mukden by War Minister Minami with a letter ordering the Kwantung Army to abandon its plot, as demanded by Premier Wakatsuki and Foreign Minister Shidehara. Later in the trial evidence would indicate that Tatekawa also carried with him a letter from the emperor. But Tatekawa was privy to the plot, favored it, and lusted for war, so he and the defendant

General Doihara cooked up a ruse. Doihara arranged for Tatekawa to arrive in Manchuria on the night of September 18, 1931, putting him up at a geisha house for a "rest" before delivering his message the following morning. "At midnight the roar of heavy artillery so frightened the geisha girls," Tatekawa later laughingly told him, "that they began to tremble." The general "slept soundly," however, until the following morning when he delivered his message—too late. "But at that time the Incident had already occurred and he was unable to carry out his mission," Tanaka explained. And so the army betrayed the emperor, premier, foreign minister, and ultimately the Japanese people. While Tatekawa caroused that night, the imperial orders to stop the war before it broke out nestled in his coat pocket.

When the Japanese defense lawyers cross-examined Tanaka, they concentrated on challenging his motives and impugning his testimony. "Your intention was to escape punishment, yourself, wasn't it?" a defense lawyer asked.

"I am a soldier," Tanaka replied, "and I have said very definitely that if there are any charges against me I shall gladly go to Sugamo Prison, but to this day the prosecution has not found any charges against me. . . . I am not the kind of person who would act because of threats or because of certain reciprocal suggestions, or a person who would try to misconstrue the truth."

"Do you receive renumeration from the Allied forces?"

"I am very poor," the witness replied, "and I would like to, but to this date I have received nothing."

Following Tanaka's testimony, the prosecution surprised many in the court by introducing voluminous Gaimusho—Foreign Ministry—files on the Mukden Incident. These had been deliberately saved by ministry officials. On September 19, the day after the incident, the Japanese consul general in Mukden reported to Tokyo that "according to confidential information" from a director of the South Manchurian Railway, when a crew was sent to repair a section of track damaged during the night by bombs, Japanese Army officers had prevented a Japanese consular official from approaching the spot to make a firsthand investigation into the incident. And the Japanese consul general also reported that "putting this and that together, it is considered that the recent incident was wholly an action planned by the army." Another Gaimusho report said the consul general pleaded with "staff officer Sagaki"—apparently a typographical error for the accused Itagaki—to avoid aggravating the incident and to stop the fighting between the Japanese and Chinese armies, but the staff officer claimed that the prestige of Japan and the army was at stake and that the army was determined "to see it through."

This segment of the trial ended when the IPS tendered in evidence newspaper reports in the *Japan Times* of August 6, 1931, quoting a bellicose War Minister Jiro Minami on the Manchurian situation. General Minami's American defense counsel, William J. McCormack, demanded that the original text be submitted as evidence, not a newspaper account. Webb agreed. "You ought to get it, Mr. Hyder," Webb said, and Elton Hyder, an assistant prosecutor, replied, "I would be delighted." He thereupon introduced a letter from the Central Liaison Office, which served as a link between the Japanese government and SCAP, to the effect that the text could not be found, "probably because it was among the documents destroyed at the time of surrender." McCormack insisted that the prosecutor possessed a copy of the text. "I know they have got it," McCormack declared.

An extended row erupted, and when McCormack was unable to support his claim, the following dialogue ensued:

WEBB: We think the proper course for you is to withdraw and apologize. We are not going to allow this tribunal to be used for the making of false accusations by one side or the other.

McCORMACK: I am sorry.

WEBB: Well, you withdraw, do you?

McCORMACK: Pardon?

WEBB: You withdraw the accusation and you apologize?

McCORMACK: Yes.

WEBB: You didn't do it very gracefully.

During this period the tribunal acquired a new look. The appearance of so many Japanese ministers, generals, and admirals as witnesses for the prosecution to the secret struggle within Japan between the forces of good and evil had a salutary on Allied public opinion. The wartime myth that *all* Japanese were monsters began to fade. The testimony at the IMTFE put the Japanese in a new light: Like all other people, the Japanese were a mix of good, bad, and indifferent. The trial of the major war criminals thus acquired a new dimension—humanizing the enemy.

As the testimony and documentary evidence during the Manchurian phase accumulated, the IMTFE often produced dramatic, revealing, and at times scandalous information. No only were the Japanese and Allied publics fascinated, but also the accused. Former foreign minister Shigemitsu, in his posttrial memoirs, recalled that "day after day, I had the opportunity of listening to a great deal of evidence by the prosecution, and rebuttals thereto by the defense counsel," adding significantly, "Included in these exchanges were incidents of which up till then I had not known; also developments of many others which I had not previously understood and which became clear for the first time." This admission was by the man who had been ambassador to China at the time of the Mukden Incident, later ambassador to the Soviet Union and Britain, and, finally, foreign minister during the terrible years 1943–45. If much of what he listened to was news to him, how much of it must have been news to the average Japanese citizen, whose newspapers, magazines, books, and other sources of information had been heavily censored or controlled during the period of the indictment?

At Sugamo Prison each day's account of the trial was read avidly. "Since the Ichigaya trial is now in full swing," an inmate wrote, "we Class A prisoners eagerly wait for the newspapers each day and devour them hungrily when we get them."

When the sordid details emerged about the plotting of coups and wars by Okawa and men of his ilk, accompanied by ribald scenes of heavy drinking, prostitution, and debauchery, some of the Sugamo prisoners became depressed. They felt that the court and history were being deceived as to the brave new world their Japan hoped to bring into being. "This is not pleasant reading for someone like myself, who was one of the young nationalists in those days, revering the nationalist leaders almost like gods and not minding being thrown into jail for one's convictions," Yoshio Kodama, who was still waiting to be indicted, wrote in *Sugamo Diary*. "It is a sad thing that by exposing and emphasizing only the follies of those times while ignoring the facts as a whole, the convictions of the young men of those days, who were inspired by hopes and ideals for a New Japan, should be cast in the light of sin or crime."

13

Lawyers at War

The running account of the tribunal presented here is somewhat misleading. The trial did not flow smoothly in narrative form. Each line of testimony was accompanied by a cacophony of legal skirmishing of a dubious, technical nature. This was hardly surprising, given the presence of more than 100 lawyers in the courtroom, but these problems should have been kept to a minimum by the Tokyo charter, which, like its sister at Nuremberg, expressly held that the court should not be bound by technical rules of evidence. The fact of the matter is that these endless interruptions in the narrative occurred with increasing frequency and often turned into tests of will among bench, prosecutors, and defense counsel. Who would score the most points? Very often, the same ground was gone over again and again; for example, the defense's challenging of the tribunal's charter. "If every point raised here is going to be submerged in a discussion of the Charter generally," Webb said wearily on one occasion, "we will never finish."

The situation demanded a tribunal president who was even-tempered and diplomatic; Webb was neither. He was aware of his shortcomings and attributed his asperity to terseness—a characteristic of Australians, he claimed. "It is said I speak with some asperity and the qualification is made that I do so naturally," he observed after he was criticized in the Japanese press. "Whether that is a compliment or not, I cannot say, but I can assure you that sometimes terseness is mistaken for asperity."

Part of the problem, perhaps, lay in the nature of the case. The Allied prosecutors were a model of unity. They shared a common determination to prove to history that Japan had engaged in aggressive wars on a massive scale in disregard of treaties and conventions, and that Japanese leaders had swept aside the customs of war in waging them. But the defense had twenty-six separate interests to protect. Thus, when an important witness such as Baron Shidehara was on the stand, so many different defense counsel—Japanese and American—wanted to cross-examine him on behalf of their clients that Webb expressed alarm that the trial would descend into "very disorderly proceedings" if there was a continual procession to the lectern every time a witness testified. In chambers, and over dinner at the Imperial Hotel, the justices evolved a scheme by which one counsel alone for each side was permitted to conduct the examination-in-chief. Cross-examination by several attorneys was permitted only if the questions stuck firmly to direct examination.

The trial continued by trial and error. The bench kept modifying the rules to speed up the proceedings. One of the major changes in procedure involved Rule 6b of the tribunal's rules of procedure, which held that "a copy of every document intended to be adduced in evidence by the prosecution or the defense will be delivered to the accused concerned or his counsel or to the prosecution. . . ."

Early in the trial the IPS threw up its hands in despair. The prosecution pointed out that a 300-page book in Japanese took 30 translators 10 days to render into English and that out of the entire book the prosecution might only have to introduce a paragraph or a page. Preparing for the defense 30 copies of 5,400 excerpts from the Kido diaries consumed all the photographic material immediately available in occupied Tokyo. Worse, the prosecution planned to introduce about 100 pages of testimony from a trial of Japanese terrorists in the thirties whose trial transcript filled sixty-five 750-page volumes. To reproduce a complete set for each defense counsel, as prescribed under Rule 6b, would involve making half a million copies. Other evidence would require 15 million copies. These revelations were made in 1946, it must be remembered, long before the photocopy machine.

Although the IPS said it was "loath" to ask for relief, it had no choice. The prosecution successfully proposed that only relevant excerpts from a document or book be copied for the defense and that the original be placed with the IMTFE's secretariat for study by the defense, judges, or "anyone." But the defense demurred. "It just isn't fair at this stage of the proceedings, in the middle of the trial so to speak, to put any part of the burden which the prosecution had under Rule 6b upon the defense," an American defense counsel charged. He argued that the prosecution should be compelled to translate completely documents of 100 pages and less or "the first thing we know, they will get down to documents of five or six pages." The court, however, agreed with the prosecution.

In addition to modifying Rule 6b, the tribunal accepted an IPS proposal that witnesses testify in affidavit form to save "the vast amount of time" involved in the tortuous translation of a prosecutor's question in English into Japanese and a Japanese witness's reply into English. Again, the defense objected strenuously. "Sir, I know of no foundation in law, I know of no precedent ever having been set which would require an accused to cross-examine a living person upon an affidavit which he previously made under the supervision, under the entire control, of the prosecution but without a single member of the defense being present," said defense counsel Warren.

But there was a precedent—Nuremberg, whose charter also said that the tribunal was not bound by technical rules of evidence. The use of affidavits by witnesses was found to save one third of the time it would take to examine a witness on direct questioning. Yet something intangible would be lost. Captain Alfred W. Brooks, the American attorney for former premier Koiso, observed that there is a certain moral effect produced in court upon a witness brought face to face with the accused and that the use of affidavits would rob the defense of the "elusive and incommunicable evidence of a witness's deportment while testifying."

Ichiro Kiyose, the associate chief of the Japanese defense, described the court's ruling as having "a grave effect on the interest of the defendants."

When the bench ruled in favor of affidavits, Warren asked if the defense would be permitted to secure affidavits for their crossexamination. Webb's face clouded. "That is just a taunt," he said angrily, "and we ignore it."

Warren replied, "I am sorry that your Honor feels that way because, sincerely, sir, I didn't mean it in that manner."

Webb was still upset. "I was speaking for myself," Webb groused. "I took it in that manner, but I accept your apology." Such outbursts between Webb and defense—and the prosecution, for that matter—dot the trial's 50,000-page transcript.

Another change in legal procedure involved the prosecution's presentation of excerpts from the lengthy interrogations of the accused at Sugamo. William Logan, Marquis Kido's defense counsel, objected strongly. "It is sound law, and I believe universally recognized, that where part of a confession or declaration by the accused is offered by the prosecution, that the balance of the document may be introduced and excerpts read by the accused on the prosecution's case." As an example, he cited the practice at Nuremberg. The bench ruled that the court would accommodate the defense on this point. But Webb exploded like a Roman candle when Nuremberg was mentioned.

"Talking about the Nuremberg decision," Webb said, "I want to remind you for what it is worth, that there are four nations represented at Nuremberg; those four are represented here and seven other nations besides, and you are wrong if you think we are going to slavishly follow Nuremberg." Webb seemed fascinated with the phrase "slavishly follow Nuremberg," for he used it three times within a couple of minutes. Nuremberg, of course, was a sore point with him and with many others at the Tokyo trial, who felt largely obscured by Nuremberg's shadow. The IMTFE never got out from under that shadow, which is one of the reasons why the Tokyo tribunal has been given less than its due in the history books.

Webb's remark about "slavishly following Nuremberg" later misled academicians writing articles or papers on the IMTFE into claiming that Webb was hostile to Nuremberg. These scholars did not do their homework. In point of historical fact, the IMTFE judges relied heavily on Nuremberg and were relieved to have Nuremberg as a beacon. The Nuremberg transcript was flown by pouch to Tokyo daily. It was closely digested on points of law by bench, prosecution, and defense. Both prosecution and defense dispatched special missions to Germany not only to secure documents for the Tokyo trial but also to keep abreast of legal developments there. Since Nuremberg and Tokyo were accused of breaking new ground in international law and of practicing *ex post facto* law, the judges at Tokyo were anxious to fall back wherever possible on Nuremberg as a precedent.

Another precedent-shattering procedure initiated at Nuremberg and followed at Tokyo involved the bench granting the prosecution, and later the defense, permission to make a preliminary opening statement before the introduction of each piece of documentary evidence. This helped place the complex sequence of events in a framework. In many respects, the prosecutors' case resembled a jigsaw puzzle—precisely how they described it on one occasion. The trial was difficult to follow even if one attended daily or had access to the complete daily transcript, since a missing piece of evidence in one phase of the case often turned up in another phase. Thus, the IPS held that a preliminary explanation of the evidence was designed "only to show what we believe to be the ultimate facts supported by the evidence." Nevertheless, the defense objected to this procedure on the ground that the prosecutor was testifying and that the evidence introduced should "speak for itself."

Each legal row took time away from the trial itself and plunged the court into debate over what seemed to most spectators to be arcane technicalities. Sometimes the discussion drifted far afield. In the course of the argument over the court's ruling that the IPS would be permitted to introduce excerpts of translated documents as evidence from lengthy documents, defense counsel McCormack charged that the U.S. Army was holding 95 percent of the defendants' evidence in the form of confiscated material. Raising his voice, Webb said, "I do not care to listen to an allegation of this kind unless there is a motion before us. Confiscation of documents by the army is a very serious charge. I do not believe it. They may be holding documents for legitimate reasons."

The IPS immediately rebutted McCormack's accusation. The only documents the army had seized were official Japanese records, "that is, the ones that were not burned at the time of the surrender," an Allied prosecutor declared, and about 95 percent of them were available to the court. "There are still five percent which we have not got," Australian associate prosecutor Mansfield added. The IPS never did get them, and it is anybody's guess what they were all about. Today the supposition is that they dealt with such sensitive matters as the Japanese drive to acquire nuclear weapons, the Soviet Union's spy ring in Japan, Japan's use of Allied prisoners of war for experiments in germ warfare, and possibly incriminating evidence involving Emperor Hirohito.

The flow of the trial was interrupted by other problems. The

Japanese counsel, for example, had a penchant for turning a question into a speech. On one occasion, when the chief of the Japanese defense, Somei Uzawa, addressed the court, Webb displayed bad manners. "He could go on forever," the president said in a loud aside. But there were times when Japanese defense counsel would try anyone's patience, including that of a Japanese. Here is a sample of a Japanese attorney questioning a Japanese witness:

> Q: In your affidavit you say that "I was arrested on September 1, after the outbreak of the Manchurian Incident." Is that correct?
>
> A: Yes, it is correct.
>
> Q: What do you mean by "On September 1, after the outbreak of the Manchurian Incident"?

Webb cut the defense attorney short. "That is a futile question as far as I am concerned."

Most Japanese counsel, out of politeness, also prefaced a question with the phrase "With the permission of the president of the tribunal, I should like to . . ." Webb summarily put an end to this custom one afternoon in what was, for him, the epitome of courtesy. "When a Japanese counsel comes to the lectern, all he needs to say is, 'My name is . . . I appear for . . .' and then proceed to put questions," Webb said. "That will help shorten the proceedings very much. We appreciate your courtesy; nevertheless, we would like to shorten proceedings by eliminating every unnecessary word."

As president of the tribunal and spokesman for his fellow judges Webb came to dominate the court proceedings. When those who were at Ichigaya think back to the trial today, Webb's name is almost invariably the first to be recalled. Even Hideki Tojo has faded by comparison. (In Nuremberg the chief prosecutor, Supreme Court Justice Robert Jackson, emerged as the dominant figure, rivaled only by the boastful Hermann Göring.)

For all his bluffness and asperity in public, Webb was a soft-spoken, pleasant, and witty character in private. He was embarrassed by his dominant role on the court and emphasized to visitors that he held the only microphone on the bench by the agreement of his colleagues. One day, in open court, Webb reflected on this awkward situation. "I should like to say—and I say this with some hesitation and some reluctance—that I have as my colleagues ten able and charming men who have given me every support. There is not a question of any importance that comes before us on which I do not get the maximum assistance from each of them. My table is cluttered with notes from all ten members of this court."

The flow of the trial was often interrupted not only by a running Blackstonian guerrilla war but also by the language barrier. Japanese does not lend itself to being translated readily into English, and the defense raised an ongoing series of objections from the first day about the quality of the translation of documents, including the indictment. Kido's diaries in particular were the subject of innumerable linguistic rows. William Logan, Marquis Kido's defense counsel, objected strenuously that the prosecution often delivered to the defense two different sets of translations of the same document. The tribunal acknowledged these difficulties and retreated. "Well, it is utterly impossible for this court to itself adjust differences between translations," Webb said. "All it can do, it has done; that is, set up a Language Section to discharge that function. We regret to hear these things, but we can do no more than we have done." Curiously, the simultaneous translations of the courtroom dialogue over the IBM system, then in its infancy, generated fewer objections than the translations of documentary evidence.

Sometimes the translation issue bordered on farce, especially when a witness spoke a language other than English or Japanese. The first time this occurred was during the Manchurian phase, when a Chinese general took the stand. Rightly, the defense objected that his Chinese was being translated into Japanese and then from Japanese into English—and that something was being lost on the way.

Major L. M. Moore, the chief of the Language Section, which arbitrated language disputes, explained that "we don't have anyone who speaks Chinese and English; we only have a Japanese-English and a Chinese-Japanese interpreter." In an amazed tone, Webb said, "There must be translators in Tokyo who can do this!"

The Chinese associate prosecutor, Hsiang Che-chun, interjected that all the Chinese on the prosecution were fluent in English but that it would be unethical for Allied prosecutors to serve as interpreters. The progress of the trial appeared temporarily stymied, but then Judge Mei, the Chinese member of the tribunal, sitting on Webb's right, passed the president a note. Mei's secretary, W.F.S. Fang, was pressed into temporary service as a Chinese-English translator, and he was sworn in on the spot.

The trial never fully overcame the language problem. On one occasion, a prosecutor acknowledged that the prosecution could not, "as a physical possibility, translate half the documents we need." By the end of the first year the IPS had about 150 translators working in shifts almost around the clock; the defense had about one-third that number, though it did have the advantage of fluency in Japanese. Even so, the defense experienced "grave difficulty," as one defense counsel put it.

Webb brushed aside these complaints, observing that "translation difficulties can be overcome by the expenditure of money on both sides [and] we expect it to be spent." He continued, "If money is a consideration in this case, this trial may never conclude." The defense protested, however, that the defendants' assets were frozen. On the prosecution side it was not so much a financial as a physical problem. The setting for the trial was a land in ruins: Transportation was scarce and dilapidated; virtually everything was in short supply; one of MacArthur's biggest problems was simply feeding the Japanese. The IMTFE, however, did hold one "A" priority. MacArthur authorized SCAP's duplication service to give first priority to the tribunal. While there is no official estimate of the cost of the trial, the consensus in Tokyo was that it cost the U.S. taxpayers about $7 million.

As if these problems, legal and linguistic, were not enough, the summer of 1946 was one of the hottest and most humid in Tokyo's history. Thermometers climbed into the nineties, and in the courtroom, it was hotter. Only one side of the courtroom had windows and they were sealed, as were the doors. When the battery of overhead klieg lights went on for the benefit of camera crews, almost everyone broiled. "The conditions of heat in this courtroom are causing great discomfort to one of my colleagues, who will decline to sit if this lighting is continued at its present intensity," Webb complained in late June. "I want those lights to be reduced to a minimum." Britain's Lord Patrick was feeling the heat. Most of the judges and accused, it should be borne in mind, were men over fifty. By mid-July, in chambers, the judges agreed that "the heat is most oppressive" and that something had to be done about it. "This is one of the gravest cases ever tried and for its proper trial, of course, we should have reasonable comfort," Webb declared.

Much thought had been given to moving the proceedings to one of the mountain resorts outside Tokyo, but this was seen to be impractical. The logistics of transporting lawyers, judges, translators, and support personnel—to say nothing of the defendants and their guards—proved to be beyond the capabilities of the occupation forces. But Colonel Walbridge, the tribunal's general secretary (housekeeper), reported that the U.S. Army Corps of Engineers planned to air-condition the courtroom by June 20.

The great day came and went without air conditioning. The army's problem was that the water supply on the hill was uncertain, as it was in much of battered Tokyo. Another problem was that there was only one factory functioning in Japan that made the necessary fluid for a large air-conditioning unit and three fourths of it was bombed out. "However," a SCAP spokesman announced, "we have borrowed fluid from all over Japan and we now have that problem solved."

By early July Webb announced that the heat and humidity were so bad that "we are seriously thinking of adjourning until air conditioning is installed." An army medical officer reported to Webb that the situation in the courtroom, especially for judges and accused, was serious enough to warrant an adjournment. Former premier Hiranuma and ex-generals Araki and Minami, all in their seventies, looked especially peaked. July 10 was unusually oppressive, and Webb peremptorily adjourned the court "on the grounds that the conditions of heat are such that we cannot discharge our duties in the way we think we should." Several days later the army succeeded in getting the air-conditioning equipment to work, and the temperature in the courtroom dipped to the high seventies. The trial resumed.

During this period, MacArthur maintained his ten-hour-a-day, seven-day-a-week work schedule at SCAP headquarters. The building was not air conditioned.

At Sugamo, the prisoners also complained about the heat and about an infestation of mosquitoes. Although they did not get air conditioning, the army installed mosquito screens in each cell, ending the mosquito problem but reducing ventilation. But then, these were the first screens ever installed in the cells in the sordid history of the grim and gray prison, and few complained about the loss of fresh air.

14

The Emperor of China Speaks

In the middle of 1946 the IMTFE was back on the front pages. For eleven days in August the tribunal was dominated by the presence of one of the most extraordinary figures in modern history, a man who entered the world as a character out of a fairy tale and who left it in a nightmare.

Accompanied by a detail of Stalin's secret police, the witness for the prosecution landed at Tokyo on August 9, wearing a cheap, poorly cut blue-serge suit, a black Russian workingman's cap—the style popularized by Lenin in the twenties—and white socks. He was the last emperor of China—living history, a page out of the past yet very much a part of the present. Twice he had sat on the Dragon Throne in Peking and ruled over a fourth of mankind. His titles included Lord of Ten Thousand Years, He Who Is Above, the Enthroned One, the Lord of Myriad Years, the One Who Faces South, the Celestial Emperor, the Emperor of Cathay, the Emperor of the Middle Flowery Kingdom, and, above all, the Son of Heaven, a title he shared with Hirohito.

To the world he was better known as Henry P'u Yi, onetime emperor of the puppet state of Manchukuo, which the Japanese set up after their conquest of China's Manchurian provinces.*

---

*In 1975 I wrote the first complete biography of P'u Yi, *The Last Emperor* (New York: Scribner's). In 1980 the book was reissued as *The Prisoner of Peking* (New York: Van Nostrand Reinhold). The biography carries P'u Yi's story to his death during the Great Proletarian Cultural Revolution unleashed by Mao Tse-tung and his myrmidons in 1965.

P'u Yi mounted the throne for the first time at the age of three in 1908 and later recalled that "whenever I think of my childhood, my head is filled with yellow mist." In imperial China the color yellow was reserved exclusively for the emperor. The tiles on the floor of the palace and the tiles on the roof were glazed yellow. The emperor sat on a yellow cushion; the lining of his clothing was yellow; the porcelain dishes from which he ate were yellow; his bedcover was yellow brocade; his writing brushes were wrapped in yellow silk. The imperial standard was a five-clawed dragon, emblazoned on a yellow field.

P'u Yi was swept up by the Chinese Revolution in 1911 and forced to abdicate by Dr. Sun Yat-sen, the first president of the Chinese Republic, the following year. During World War I, while Europe's attention was distracted by the ghastly trench warfare in France and Belgium, a royalist coup put P'u Yi, at the age of twelve, back on the Dragon Throne. The restoration was short-lived, and he was soon forced to flee Peking. P'u Yi took up residence in the foreign concession at Tientsin, where he remained in relative obscurity until he was contacted by Doihara, then a colonel, who offered to put him back on a throne as emperor of Manchukuo. To underline the importance of P'u Yi's acceptance of the offered throne, Doihara sent him a basket of fruit that also contained a disarmed bomb. He got the message, and the arrangements were completed by Itagaki, then also a colonel, who gave a banquet for P'u Yi. The warm saké flowed freely, and the geishas of the evening, *korobi,* gave their bodies freely. "Itagaki fondled and embraced the girls," P'u Yi recalled later, "without bothering about the conventions of polite behavior." Thus, his bargain with Japan was sealed among prostitutes and drunken Kwantung Army officers, two of whom were now on trial as major war criminals.

The Allied prosecution had brought P'u Yi to Tokyo to testify on the brutalization of Manchuria by the Japanese. He was a key witness and, indeed, was on the stand longer than any other witness for the prosecution. Stalin, who retained P'u Yi as a trump in the event that he could pry Manchuria from China during the Chinese Civil War and establish a puppet regime of his own, as he had done in Mongolia, approved sending the former Manchu emperor to Japan. Moscow's only condition was that the U.S. Army return him to Soviet custody after he testified. This was readily agreed to by MacArthur, who was embarrassed by P'u

Yi's presence. SCAP wanted the ex-emperor out of Japan as quickly as possible for fear that his appearance in the witness box would raise new demands that Hirohito also be called to the stand. What was good enough for the emperor of China surely was good enough for the emperor of Japan.

By the time P'u Yi arrived in Tokyo that August, the Allied prosecution at the IMTFE had tendered overwhelming evidence that Manchukuo was a Japanese satellite state. Among the chief documents was a Foreign Ministry file that had not been burned after the surrender, entitled "Confidential Records Concerning Manchurian Affairs." One peek at that file would be enough to satisfy any independent observer that Japan ran Manchukuo, and P'u Yi.

As early as November 3, 1932, the Kwantung Army prepared a secret policy directive that outlined the rules for "guiding Manchukuo." The language was direct and mirrored the Japanese adage that only a fool, if he has power, displays it. "Officials of Manchukuoan lineage shall outwardly assume charge of the administration as much as possible, while officials of Japanese lineage must satisfy themselves by controlling its substance," the directive stated.

Japanese civilians working as officials in the Manchukuo government retained their Japanese citizenship. A Japanese vice minister served alongside each minister in the Manchukuo cabinet. Each department in the Manchukuo government was directed by a Japanese. But the fanatical Kwantung Army did not even trust its own countrymen, and consequently *all* Japanese officials in the Manchukuo government were placed directly under the army's authority.

As for Manchuria's 25 million people, the Japanese Army followed the principle "Let the people follow blindly." A secret army directive held that they should have no voice in government. "Political parties and political bodies shall not be permitted to exist, and we do not welcome the rise of political ideas among the people," the directive, introduced as evidence at the trial, said. To ensure the population's docility, "thought control" edicts similar to laws in Japan were introduced and implemented. In foreign affairs, all of Manchukuo's diplomatic actions had to be first submitted to the Japanese ambassador "for thorough and unreserved deliberation." The commander in chief of the Kwantung Army served as Japan's ambassador. The economy was also placed under state control, to avoid "the evils of uncontrolled capitalist economy." (In Japan the ultrarightists and the military clique opposed the capitalist system because it placed the economy beyond their complete political control and inculcated an independent-minded spirit among entrepreneurs.)

When P'u Yi entered the courtroom on August 16 for the first time, the press and spectator galleries were jammed. Joseph Keenan, who had been conspicuously absent from the lectern since delivering the prosecution's opening statement, reappeared suddenly and took command of the witness. His critics complained that he did so because he realized that P'u Yi was a headline maker.

P'u Yi was accustomed to exploding flashbulbs and gawking crowds. He stage-managed his entrance, holding an exquisite ivory fan in his right hand (the air conditioning was off again), and walked to the witness box in a deliberate, authoritative manner. He wore black-rimmed spectacles and was immediately recognizable from his frequent appearance in the Sunday supplements of the twenties, thirties, and forties. In many ways, unless Emperor Hirohito himself were put in the box, no witness at the IMTFE possessed so close a relationship to the accused as the last Manchu emperor. Twenty-four of the twenty-eight defendants had been directly or indirectly linked to him.

Hideki Tojo, a former head of the Kempeitai in Manchukuo, was later chief of staff of the Kwantung Army, as were two of the other accused, Generals Koiso and Itagaki. General Doihara was in charge of the Kwantung Army's spy organization; General Umezu was commander of the Kwantung Army from 1939 to 1944; General Minami was war minister at the time of the Mukden Incident; Field Marshal Hata was war minister in 1940 when P'u Yi visited Hirohito to "strengthen the bonds of friendship" between the two emperors; Koki Hirota was awarded Manchukuo's First Order of the Chrysanthemum; and General Kimura was once director of the Manchurian Land Development Corporation. P'u Yi also had links to Okinori Kaya and Naoki Hoshino, the financial men who ran the Manchurian Affairs Bureau; General Araki, who was war minister when P'u Yi was installed as emperor of Manchukuo; Shigenori Togo, the career diplomat whose first posting abroad was at Mukden; General Sato, who was secretary of the Manchurian Affairs Bureau at the time of Pearl Harbor; and General Muto, who started his military career in Manchuria as a

Kwantung Army staff officer. P'u Yi's links even stretched to Admiral Oka, who once served as secretary to the Manchurian Affairs Bureau, and Mamoru Shigemitsu, the former foreign minister who, as a diplomatic troubleshooter, was dispatched to Manchukuo as early as 1936.

For the first time, the prosecution's strategy of tying the defendants together in a historical setting moved into the open.

Each of the accused watched as P'u Yi walked across the hushed courtroom that hot, humid August day. The defendants' faces were wreathed mournfully in anticipation of what was to come, except for General Itagaki, who was unaccountably cherubic. He smiled broadly as though welcoming an old business associate to the party.

For a few seconds—it seemed much longer—the tribunal was caught up by history. Even Sir William Webb hesitated to speak. Here was the last of the Chinese emperors, whose line receded to the dawn of history, before the Pharoah Tutankhamen reigned, before the Trojan War was fought.

Webb snapped the court out of its reverie. "Mr. Chief Prosecutor," the president intoned.* Joseph Keenan approached the lectern. "We call the next witness," the Allied chief of counsel said, "Henry P'u Yi." The voice of the marshal of the court boomed across the tribunal: "Mr. President, the witness is in court and will now be sworn."

P'u Yi's performance in the box was bravura. Until this first public appearance, he had been derided by observers as slow-witted, if not mentally retarded, a cardboard figure. On the stand, however, P'u Yi proved himself wily, the master of cunning, guile, and downright deceit. He outdueled Sir William Webb, Joseph Keenan, and both the Japanese and the American defense. He alternately infuriated them and teased them, and in the end he got them fighting one another. If P'u Yi had been a free man, his performance would have been impressive. But given the peculiar circumstances in which he found himself, his performance was truly remarkable. On the bench sat General Zarayanov, whose Soviet Union held P'u Yi a political prisoner. To Zarayanov's right sat Judge Mei, whose China had branded P'u Yi a traitor. Simultaneously, P'u Yi was under the military jurisdiction of a third

---

*Webb had fallen into the American custom of addressing persons with or without rank as "Mr." His use of the term could be dubbed the Americanization of Sir William Webb.

member of the bench, Judge Cramer of the United States. Perhaps P'u Yi's only solace was that his Japanese enemies were in the dock.

In this situation, it is hardly surprising that P'u Yi considered himself a defendant, and the defense lawyers treated him as if they were prosecutors. "We are not trying the witness," Webb repeatedly admonished counsel.

From the outset of his testimony P'u Yi adopted the Chinese strategy of retreat by advancing. He told how General Itagaki had offered him the Manchurian throne. "If I refused," he testified, "my life was threatened." And then, in a deft maneuver, he admonished the Allies. "At that time the democratic nations were not trying to resist the Japanese militarists," he said slyly. "I alone as an individual was hardly able to resist them."

Over and over again he claimed that all the acts he had committed since 1931 were under duress and that since he had not been a free man he disclaimed responsibility for them. Thus, unlike Hirohito, who had told MacArthur that he was ready to assume responsibility for every political and military decision made by Japan during the war, the last Manchu emperor not only shook off responsibility for his acts but blamed his advisers for his behavior. Repeatedly, he claimed that he had sought to oppose Japan. But "under the threat of military force and the advice of my advisers, I had to [retreat] to save my own life."

After several days of this posture, the flinty Webb was moved to exasperation and gratuitous comment. "I hate to make this observation," Webb said, going on to make it. "We are not trying the witness, of course, but we are concerned about his credibility. Now, danger to life, fear of death, does not excuse cowardice or desertion on the battlefield; neither does it excuse treason anywhere. All morning we have been listening to excuses by this man as to why he collaborated with the Japanese. I think we have heard enough."

During this exhibition as one week's testimony blended into another, the familiar names of the accused repeatedly turned up while they looked on either defiantly or resignedly. Doihara stared at the witness, his flabby face twisted in anger; Umezu looked askance; Muto, still wearing the tropical uniform of a Japanese general, was unsettled; Minami appeared annoyed; and Hoshino was upset when his name cropped up for the first time. Itagaki alone continued to enjoy the spectacle. Occasionally he appeared to restrain himself from bursting into laughter. Itagaki either was hysterical or, more likely, considered P'u Yi's performance comic.

The defense had a field day discrediting the witness. "We have here a witness who willingly testified that in the past on numerous occasions, under the threat of force, he has distorted the truth," Major Ben Bruce Blakeney, Umezu's American defense counsel, said disparagingly. "I intend to impeach him." Blakeney said his purpose was to show that P'u Yi was not a prisoner or puppet of the Japanese but that he "desired, planned for, and eagerly seized the opportunity to obtain restoration to a throne."

Blakeney successfully implanted the notion that if P'u Yi had not been free to speak his mind during the Japanese occupation of Manchuria, he certainly was in no position to do so while the Allies occupied Japan. "When you walked into this tribunal for the first time," Blakeney asked innocently, "were two Soviet guards with you?" Keenan flushed, and objected. Webb sustained the objection. Blakeney tacked. "Do the Chinese plan to try you as a war criminal?" he asked. Again Keenan objected, and again Webb sustained him.

Yet, masterfully, P'u Yi continued to exercise his hypnotic effect on the courtroom. The representatives of the barbarian nations beyond the borders of China listened attentively to the voice of the Celestial Emperor. Frequently, he took charge of the questioning. "You don't have to ask me all those questions," the witness snapped once. At another point, he said, "I don't think it advisable to waste any more time on this." And on one occasion, when he was asked to check his notes during the noontime lunch break, he returned to the courtroom at 1:40 P.M. and said brazenly, "During the lunch hour I was rather busy; I didn't have enough time to locate them."

Judging by P'u Yi's behavior on the stand, it appeared that he often understood a question in English before it was translated into Chinese, the language in which he was addressed. A Japanese defense counsel asked innocently at one point, "By the way, do you speak English . . . Mr. P'u Yi?"

The former emperor replied evenly, "Some [of the questions] I understand, and some not." Trying to pin him down was like trying to catch a leaf in a gust of autumn wind. The daily cross-examination, intended to wear down the witness, instead wore down the bench, translators, prosecution, and defense.

The subtlety of P'u Yi's court Chinese presented the translators with a formidable problem. The witness rarely answered a

question with a simple "yes" or "no" but with so many grada-
tions of tone that it was difficult to translate the shade of meaning.
Of course, an emperor is trained to be evasive, so this should
hardly have been surprising. P'u Yi's Chinese was so sophisticated and slippery that Webb personally appealed to MacArthur
for more Chinese-English interpreters, and on August 26 Mac-
Arthur sent his personal Chinese interpreter to assist the IMTFE.

Periodically P'u Yi deftly and cleverly threw the courtroom
into an uproar and, in the process, deflected attention from himself. Thus, on one occasion the defense presented him with a letter bearing his "chop," or seal, which he had allegedly sent General
Itagaki in 1931, expressing a desire to accept a Manchurian throne
under Japanese patronage. P'u Yi glanced at the letter and, in a
dramatic gambit, leapt to his feet. The American MPs jumped to
attention. So did the Soviet detail of plainclothes secret police.
Above the ensuing din in the gallery, Sir William Webb shouted
from the bench, "Keep your seat!"

Coolly, P'u Yi shouted back, "Your honor, this is a fake!"
The former emperor slipped back into his chair.

"Just answer the question," Webb said. "Did you send that
letter?"

He had not, P'u Yi replied, charging that the defense "should
be [found] guilty of counterfeiting this document."

Near the end of his lengthy cross-examination, an exasperated
Blakeney told the tribunal, "I should like to direct the attention
of the tribunal that, from the beginning of this witness's testimony
until the conclusion at the present time . . . he has palpably and
willfully lied to the tribunal."

P'u Yi shrugged. "I don't blame you, being counsel for the
defense," he said, properly imperious. "Of course, you would
like me to distort the truth."

"The witness has taken up a certain stand that he was wholly
under the direction of the Japanese," Webb said, cutting off the
debate. "It is a simple stand. No amount of cross-examination is
going to dislodge him from it. That is obvious."

On another occasion, the qualifications of the IMTFE's language arbitration board were called into question. "Mr. President," Major Moore, the chief of the board, told the court, "since
my qualifications have been called into question, I hope the tribunal will indulge me in saying that I have had thirty years of
experience in Oriental question and answer, and it is an estab-

lished fact that an Oriental, when pressed, will dodge the issue."

The courtroom shuddered, and Webb was aghast at the racial implications of the remark. "Well, now, Major Moore, you have said a thing which you should not have said," Webb admonished him. "It is quite beyond your province to comment on the nature of evidence given by Orientals, and I ask you to withdraw that comment."

Under visible strain, Moore apologized. "With all due respect to this tribunal, sir, I apologize for my remarks," Moore said sheepishly. "I was pressed."

The Chinese prosecutors were outraged. "I think it is quite a gratuitous charge against Oriental people," Chinese associate prosecutor Hsiang shouted. And Joseph Keenan stepped forward in support of Hsiang and decried the suggestion that "Orientals have the invariable habit of dodging the issue."

"I think I can safely say on behalf of every member of the court," Webb said, closing the issue, "that we do not share Major Moore's view."

In the end, so deftly did P'u Yi handle himself at the IMTFE that when Sadako Oagata undertook almost twenty years later to write, from a Japanese perspective, her definitive work on the Mukden Incident, she ruefully concluded that "the degree of his willingness to assume the leading role [in Manchukuo] remains unclarified."

In retrospect, as I look back on the testimony of P'u Yi in the witness box, one statement stood above the others amid the flotsam and jetsam littering the sea across which he was swept by the currents of history. It was this: "I can do nothing but weep."

This simple truth summed up the life and times of the Chinese emperor. Could the same be said for Hirohito?

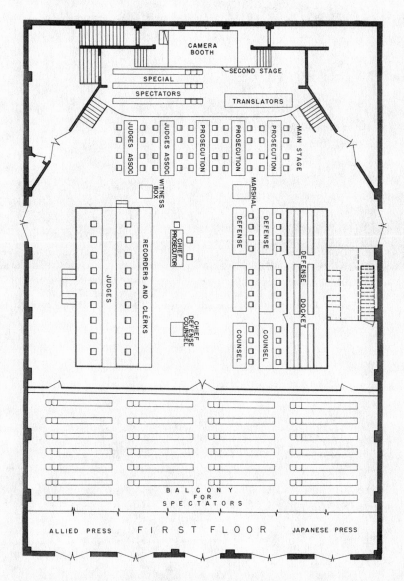

Diagram of the courtroom at Ichigaya. It was about 100 feet in length, with separate sections for the defendants, their attorneys, the prosecutors, translators, press, spectators, and of course the eleven judges.

The bench. From left to right: Pal (India); Röling (Netherlands); McDougall (Canada); Patrick (Great Britain); Cramer (U.S.); Webb (Australia), president; Mei (China); Zarayanov (USSR); Bernard (France); Northcroft (New Zealand); and Jaranilla (Philippines).

The prosecution—Joseph Keenan (U.S.), chief, with the associate prosecutors. Seated, from left to right: Vasiliev (USSR), Comyns-Carr (Great Britain), Keenan, Borgerhoff-Mulder (Netherlands), Mansfield (Australia). Standing: Nolan (Canada), Hsiang (China), Oneto (France), Lopez (Philippines), Quilliam (New Zealand). Missing: Menon (India).

The defense. Among the principal defense attorneys were, from left to right, the chief of the Japanese defense counsel, Somei Uzawa, and the Americans Joseph Howard, Alfred Brooks, William Logan, Jr., John Brannon, Lawrence McManus, Michael Levin, George Yamaoka, and George Francis Blewett.

The defendants. From left to right, back row: Hashimoto, Koiso, Nagano, Oshima, Matsui, Hiranuma, Togo, Shigemitsu, Sato, Shimada, Shiratori, Suzuki, Itagaki. Front row: Doihara, Hata, Hirota, Minami, Tojo, Oka, Umezu, Araki, Muto, and Hoshino. Missing from the photo are Kaya, Kido, and Kimura, along with Okawa and Matsuoka, who were severed from the trial for medical reasons.

Shumei Okawa being removed from the dock after his assault on Tojo as the indictments were being read. Psychiatrists declared him unfit for trial, and he never returned to the courtroom.

Four of the defendants listening pensively to the proceedings through their earphones. From left to right: General Teiichi Suzuki, Marquis Koichi Kido, General Heitaro Kimura, General Seichiro Itagaki.

The defendants often closed their eyes as they listened to damaging testimony. From left to right, front row: Naoki Hoshino and Okinori Kaya, both civilian members of the wartime cabinet. Back row: Admiral Shigetaro Shimada.

An overall view of the defendants in the dock, at one side of the vast courtroom.

During one of the many recesses in the trial proceedings, General Kenryo Sato (*left*) and Ambassador Toshio Shiratori play the game of *go*, as Baron Koki Hirota watches with interest.

Three of the defendants eating lunch served on standard GI mess trays at Ichigaya. From left to right: Admiral Takasumi Oka, Okinori Kaya, Ambassador Hiroshi Oshima.

Hideki Tojo in the witness box. As premier from 1941 until 1944, he assumed responsibility for conventional war crimes and crimes against humanity committed by Japanese forces during the war.

Hideki Tojo with his pipe looked more like a scholar than the fierce military leader that he was. The former premier never lost his composure during the trial.

The author, then a young reporter, in the witness box, being questioned by Sir William Webb about a news story previewing the defense attorneys' opening arguments. Webb called the premature article "gross contempt of this court."

NOTE :

1. No smoking in court at any time.

2. Use of cameras in courtroom is prohibited except by accredited photographers.

3. Spectators leaving at any recess forfeit right to return to courtroom for that session.

4 A. M. spectators must be seated not later than 0915. P. M. spectators must be seated not later than 1315.

5. Pass will be surrendered to Military Police on request.

6. Use only the headphone provided at your seat. Operate the selector switch located there until you hear the desired language. Russian is heard on position #3, English and Japanese on position #1. and #2.

7. When Judges enter courtroom stand and remain silent.

8. After the departure of the Judges all persons are required to be seated until defendents leave the courtroom.

One of the cards distributed to the spectators laying down the rules of the court. On the reverse side were printed the seating arrangements.

15

Holocaust in China

Following the conquest of Manchuria and the establishment of the papier-mâché Manchukuo regime with P'u Yi as emperor in 1934, the Japanese militarists resumed their methodical march across China, setting up regional puppet regimes as they went. Incidents were routine. The watershed event, however, did not occur until the night of July 7, 1937, at Lukouchiao, about ten miles southwest of Peking, the old capital of China.

Most of the world does not remember and cannot even pronounce the name Lukouch'iao, but a railroad bridge in the vicinity, bearing the venerable name Marco Polo, is unforgettable and is remembered to this day in the Far East as Sarajevo is in Europe. Literally millions of people perished in the aftermath of the Marco Polo Bridge Incident, which loosed the bloody Sino-Japanese War.

A parade of Chinese, Japanese, and American witnesses provided a refresher course on that grim incident. A high-ranking Chinese official, Wang Len-ch'ai who had been on the scene on July 7, summarized the episode: "The war of Lukouch'iao was started as a consequence of the Japanese military maneuvers which they performed upon Chinese soil freely without any treaty rights and without notifying the local Chinese authorities beforehand." At 11 P.M. that night, he recalled, "a few shots were heard." The next thing he knew, the Japanese Army commander General Matsui—the man now glowering in the dock—telephoned him to say that Chinese soldiers had fired upon a Japanese unit engaged in night maneuvers and that a Japanese soldier was missing. Matsui instructed Wang to investigate the matter, but "no missing soldier was ever found." The Japanese had invented another incident.

At the time, General Joseph Stilwell, the American military attaché in China, ordered his assistant, Colonel David Barrett, to investigate the matter. Early in 1946, almost a decade later, Stilwell, who by then had achieved renown as the commander of Chinese and American armies in the China-Burma-India theater of the war, was unable to come to Tokyo, but he encouraged Barrett to testify at the IMTFE. In the witness box, the leathery-looking Barrett recalled that "as far as I could determine, the clash had been on a very small scale . . . [and] I believed the incident could easily be settled if the Japanese really so desired." But the Japanese militarists were spoiling for an all-out war, and nothing was going to stop it. Events moved rapidly thereafter, and by July 31, when Stilwell and Barrett toured the outskirts of Peking, they saw the scenes of desolation that would become commonplace in China until the end of World War II. "We found hundreds of dead bodies of men and quantities of material lying on the road, indicating that Chinese units had been attacked while in close column." Apparently, the Chinese had been the victims of a Japanese sneak attack. "Hundreds of corpses, rotting in the summer heat, were still jammed in the trucks in which Chinese troops had been riding when the Japanese attacked," Barrett testified. "It was evident that the Chinese unit had been taken by surprise and had had no time to deploy."

In the first year of the carnage, 124,130 Chinese soldiers were killed in action and 242,232 wounded, according to evidence introduced by the IPS. The number of civilians killed and maimed is not known, nor will it ever be. The killing went on year after year until the Japanese surrender in 1945. By then, Chinese Army casualties had surpassed 3.2 million killed and wounded; Japanese losses were about one third of that.

Among the witnesses who testified during the China phase of the prosecution's case was John Goette, the chief China correspondent of the International News Service from 1924 to 1942 and the correspondent of London's *Daily Telegraph* from 1927 to 1940. On the night of the Marco Polo Bridge Incident, Goette had been at dinner with Stilwell, Barrett, and the U.S. ambassador to China,

Nelson T. Johnson. All four were puzzled by the Japanese announcement that their forces would conduct night maneuvers southwest of Peking.

Between 1937 and 1941, Goette testified, he had traveled "some 20,000 miles" as a news correspondent with the Japanese invaders. One of Keenan's assistants, Kenneth N. Parkinson, a Cambridge-educated Washington lawyer, handled Goette on the stand. "Will you describe briefly what you saw, if anything?" Parkinson asked.

Goette's reply was graphic. "I, of course, visited towns and cities and villages; some of them completely destroyed and flattened by shellfire, and by aerial bombardment; others with great property damage; villages without a living thing, not only not a living person, not an animal or beast, nothing left, just the hand of death on the villages. I saw numerous civilians shot dead, with their hands tied behind their backs. I mean I saw the bodies—not actually shot."

The remainder of his testimony was equally unsettling. "The formal demand by the Japanese army on local Chinese officials to provide women for the use of the Japanese army was a commonplace thing," he said. At Taiyüan, a provincial capital, the Japanese Army, he recalled, erected a war memorial to its dead above the main city gate. Every Chinese passing through the gate was forced to leave motorcar, cart, or rickshaw and walk, rather than ride, under the gate "in tribute to that Japanese war monument."

The cross-examination by the defense attorneys lacked the intensity of their attack on P'u Yi's credibility. Rather than challenge what John Goette said he had seen firsthand, the defense came up with such churlish questions as "Mr. Goette, you state that you were the dean of newspaper correspondents in northern China. Will you tell us whether that is an honorary title conferred on you by the members of your profession?"

An annoyed Webb interrupted. "We all know what it means," the tribunal's president said, "and we know it isn't conferred."

But if Goette troubled the defense, worse was ahead. The IPS introduced more excerpts from the exhaustive interrogations that the accused had undergone at Sugamo during the months preceding the trial. The first interrogation read was that of the defendant General Muto, who had been a senior officer on the Japanese general staff in China in 1937—a post he also held under Yamashita eight years later during the Battle of Manila. The excerpt tendered was lifted from his interrogation at Sugamo the preceding April 16.

> Q: . . . Of course, you took prisoners from the Chinese armies?
>
> MUTO: No. The question of whether Chinese captives would be declared prisoners of war or not was quite a problem, and it was finally decided in 1938 that because the Chinese conflict was officially known as an "incident" that Chinese captives would not be regarded as prisoners of war. . . .
>
> Q: As a matter of fact, the Chinese "incident" was a war, was it not?
>
> MUTO: Actually, yes, but the Japanese government looked upon it as being an incident.
>
> Q: So that you . . . carried on a policy of not treating the Chinese captives as prisoners of war?
>
> MUTO: Yes.
>
> Q: What regulations governed the treatment of Chinese that were not treated as prisoners of war?
>
> MUTO: We had no connection whatsoever with this matter. . . .
>
> Q: In 1939, 1940, 1941, the Japanese army was fighting in China, is that correct?
>
> MUTO: Yes.
>
> Q: They took large numbers of prisoners, did they not?
>
> MUTO: . . . We received no reports of how many prisoners were taken and only read in the papers that such and such elements of the Chinese Chungking army surrendered. . . .
>
> Q: Very frequently your army took prisoners, did it not?
>
> MUTO: There were very few prisoners taken at this time. . . .

Q: What were the orders given by your command with respect to the treatment of the Chinese captured by you in the course of the fighting?

MUTO: . . . I have no recollection. . . .

The interrogation of the defendant Field Marshal Hata at Sugamo on January 14 gave an even more sinister cast to the issue of prisoners. Hata had been appointed commander in chief of the Japanese expeditionary force in China in 1938 and, among other campaigns, captured Hankow, hurling upward of 400,000 Japanese troops into the battle.

Q: How many Chinese troops did the army capture in this operation? How many prisoners were taken?

HATA: I don't think there were so many. I didn't worry about figures of prisoners. . . .

Q: Did the General [sic] study international law in his staff college?

HATA: Yes. In the War College.

Q: Did the General know that Japan had treaties in which they promised not to invade China and not to wage war against China? . . .

HATA: What is this treaty called?

Q: The Nine-Power Treaty.

HATA: Yes, I know it.

Q: Well, did he think that they were breaking that treaty or not?

HATA: I know of the existence of this treaty, but I do not know the terms.

Q: But suppose the treaty says they are not to resort to armed force until they have made a treaty for peace?

HATA: I am not well acquainted with the Nine-Power Treaty. I merely know its existence.

When the prosecution began the Nanking phase of its case, the trial came to life once again. The dimensions of the Rape of Nanking were so vast that two witnesses, independently of each other, said from the stand in an awed tone of bewilderment: "I don't know where to begin."

In 1928 the Chinese Nationalists had moved their capital from Peking to Nanking, a bustling metropolis on the southern bank of the Yangtze River that had been founded during the Ming dynasty 500 years earlier. The city normally held about 250,000 people, but by the mid-1930s it had swollen to more than 1 million. Many of them were refugees, fleeing from the Japanese armies. Nanking had long been a cultural and intellectual hub, the location of the University of Nanking, Ginling College for Women, and other institutions of higher learning. When the Japanese Army approached Nanking in November 1937, Generalissimo Chiang Kai-shek decided not to defend the capital, to the dismay of many Chinese, but to withdraw deeper into the interior of China to consolidate his forces. About half the population of the city also fled. So did all the foreigners except twenty-two, largely Americans and Germans with a sprinkling of Danes and Englishmen. Hastily the foreigners organized an international rescue committee and cordoned off a section of Nanking as an international safety zone for refugees.

The first prosecution witness to take the stand was Dr. Robert O. Wilson, a surgeon who had been born and raised in Nanking and educated at Princeton and the Harvard Medical School. Wilson testified that he had told his hospital staff of Chinese physicians and nurses that "under martial law they would have nothing to fear in Nanking after the city fell." On the night of December 12 all Chinese Army resistance ended, and the following day the first Japanese military columns freely entered the Chinese capital. Immediately, Wilson testified, "the hospital filled up [and was] kept full to overflowing" during the next six weeks. The patients usually bore bayonet or bullet wounds; many of the women patients had been sexually molested.

A sixty-two-year-old official from the Chinese Ministry of Railways followed Wilson to the stand and described the Japanese soldiers as "rough" and "barbarous." "They shot at everyone in sight," Hsu Chuan-ying said in broken English. "Anybody who run away, or on the streets, or hanging around somewhere, or peeking through the door, they shoot them—instant death." Three days after the Japanese entered the city, the streets were littered with corpses. "I saw the dead bodies lying everywhere, and some of the bodies are very badly mutilated," Hsu continued. "Some of the dead bodies are lying there as they were shot or killed, some kneeling, some bending, some on their sides, and some just with their legs and arms wide open." On one boulevard he started to count the number of corpses and got as far as 500 when he felt that there were so many that "it was no use counting them." The Japanese also entered the refugee zone and took into custody any male with calluses on his hands, ostensibly from carrying a rifle. The prisoners were tied in batches of 10 and 15 and marched away. On a single day as many as 1,500 men and boys were carted off in this fashion. At night, from the safety zone, the refugees could hear the incessant chattering of machine guns.

But it was the women who suffered the most. "The Japanese soldiers—they are so fond of raping—so fond of women," the witness said haltingly in English, "that one cannot believe." Young girls and women of between thirteen and forty were rounded up and gang raped. Hsu said he had visited one home where three of the women had been raped, including two girls. "One young girl was raped on a table," he testified, "and while I was there blood spilled on the table was not all dry yet."

Hsu was a member of the Red Swastika, the Chinese equivalent of the Red Cross, and after several days of indiscriminate killing, the Japanese, fearful that the decomposing bodies would create an epidemic, organized a burial detail. Hsu estimated that the Red Swastika had buried 43,000 bodies in the following weeks but that the true number was probably higher and could not be verified because the Japanese had not permitted the organization to keep records. Most of the corpses had their hands tied, sometimes with rope, sometimes with wire. "It is our sacred practice to have a dead body all unloosed if it is tied," Hsu explained. "We wanted to unloose everything and bury them one by one. But with these wires, now it is almost impossible to do that. In many cases, these bodies were already decayed so we would not be able to bury them one by one. All we can do is simply to bury them in groups."

Sir William Webb raised his right hand. "You need not go into all these details," he said quietly, breaking the silence in the courtroom. "The method of disposal of the bodies is hardly helpful."

Another Chinese witness, Shang Teh-yi, testified that the Japanese had arrested him and his elder brother, a cousin, and five neighbors. Their wrists were roped together and they were marched to the bank of the Yangtze, where they joined more than 1,000 men sitting along the bank. Machine guns faced them at a distance of about forty yards. In late afternoon a Japanese staff car arrived and ordered the hostages to stand. "I slumped to the ground just before the firing started, and immediately was covered with corpses and fainted," Shang said.

The defense lawyers declined to cross-examine him. They also waived their right to cross-examine the next witness, a thirty-eight-year-old rice merchant who testified that he had been rounded up with 300 others and marched to the west gate of the city, where a steep slope ran to a canal. At bayonet point the prisoners were driven through the gate and shot as they emerged, their bodies spinning down into the canal. The bullets missed him and he rolled down the slope and feigned death. A Japanese soldier walked over the killing ground, bayoneting those who had not fallen into the canal. The merchant was bayoneted in the back but "lay still as if dead."

David Sutton, an American assistant prosecutor, asked the witness to remove his shirt and show the court the bayonet scar. Marquis Kido's counsel, William Logan, objected. "If the tribunal please, the defense objects to any such exhibition."

Webb was not interested, either. "We do not wish to see the wounds," the president of the tribunal said, "unless the defense questions their existence."

Among the most damaging witnesses for the prosecution was Miner Searle Bates, a slim, bespectacled American and professor of history at the University of Nanking who held degrees from Oxford, Yale, and Harvard. "I, myself, observed a whole series of shootings of individual civilians without any provocation or apparent reason whatsoever." One Chinese had been taken from his own house and killed. "From my next-door neighbor's house two men, who rose up in anxiety when soldiers seized and raped their wives, were taken, shot at the edge of the pond of my house, and thrown into it," Bates related. "The bodies of civilians lay on the streets and alleys in the vicinity of my own house for many days after the Japanese entry. The total spread of this killing was so extensive that no one can give a complete picture of it."

Bates and a colleague estimated that 12,000 civilians had been slain inside Nanking's walls "within our sure knowledge." Thousands of civilians were also killed outside the city's walls, but he said nobody would ever know the number. "This is quite apart from the killing of tens of thousands of men who were Chinese soldiers or had been Chinese soldiers."

Bates also accused the Japanese of "treachery," for example by posting proclamations and persuading Chinese to come forward as voluntary workers for the Japanese Army's labor corps. "If you have previously been a Chinese soldier or if you have ever worked as a carrier or laborer in the Chinese army," the local Chinese were told, "that will all now be forgotten and forgiven if you will join this labor corps." One afternoon, Bates said, 200 men accepted the Japanese offer on the campus of Nanking University "and were marched away and executed that evening."

But, he continued, lowering his voice, "the roughest and saddest part of the whole picture" was Japanese conduct toward the women. Women in three neighboring homes were raped and, he said, "on five different occasions, which I can detail for you if desired, I, myself, came upon soldiers in the act of rape." Japanese soldiers, he said, in gangs of fifteen or twenty roamed through the city in search of women. A friend of his witnessed the rape of a Chinese woman by seventeen soldiers in rapid succession. "I do not care to repeat the occasional cases of sadistic and abnormal behavior in connection with the rapes, but I do want to mention that on the ground of the university alone, a little girl of nine and a grandmother of seventy-six were raped." The international committee estimated that within six weeks of the Japanese occupation, 20,000 women were raped, and many of them subsequently murdered or mutilated.

In addition to murder and rape there was wholesale looting, and "on one occasion I observed a supply column, two-thirds of a mile long, loaded with high-grade redwood and blackwood furniture," he testified. After the first week the Japanese soldiers, some of them drunk, put torches to buildings and at night fires in the city were commonplace. "We could not see any reason or pattern in it," Bates said. Shops and department stores, foreign churches, embassies, houses large and small, buildings of all descriptions were set afire. German firms flying the Nazi swastika were also burned.

On December 15, Bates testified, thirty college girls were raped on his campus in one building alone. Three days later eighteen girls were raped in six different locations on campus. The remaining women at the university were in a state of hysteria. Until this point, the courtroom had been eerily still, but a suppressed gasp went up among spectators and others when Bates off-handedly remarked that his university, the University of Nanking, was located next to the Japanese Embassy. The implications were plain. Not only had the Japanese high command in Nanking been aware of the deplorable situation, but so had Japanese officials in the embassy. And the terror covered a six-week period.

For the first time since the Nanking phase of the prosecution opened, the prosecution asked the question that logically cried out to be answered. Who had been in command of the Japanese troops at Nanking?

The defendant General Iwane Matsui, Bates said, and all eyes in the courtroom involuntarily turned to the dock where the aged and gaunt Matsui looked as if he wanted to flee. His ferretlike face was tense, and he perspired liberally. To the front and right of Matsui sat Koki Hirota, who had been foreign minister during the Rape of Nanking. Hirota sat frozen, as did Marquis Kido, who had held two portfolios in that particular cabinet, education and welfare. Okinori Kaya, who had been finance minister at the end of 1937 and into 1938, rounded out the trio in the dock who had been cabinet ministers during the atrocities at Nanking. The premier, Prince Konoye, had committed suicide the previous December rather than face the IMTFE; his war minister, General Sugiyama, had done likewise after the Japanese surrender.

The defense blundered during Bates's cross-examination. The witness testified that he had sent reports of these incidents to the Japanese Embassy. Had the embassy forwarded these reports to Tokyo? "Yes," the witness replied. Had he personally seen the messages? "No," the witness admitted. The usually astute William Logan now violated a cardinal rule in a criminal trial—never ask a question unless you know the answer. "So, Mr. Bates, not having seen the messages," Logan said triumphantly, "I assume you do not know of your own knowledge to whom they were sent in Tokyo, is that right?"

But Bates's reply stunned Logan, and the tribunal. The U.S. Embassy in Nanking, he said, had shown him messages from the American ambassador in Tokyo, Joseph Grew, in which Grew referred "to these reports in great detail and referred to conversations in which they had been discussed between Grew and officials of the *Gaimusho,* including Mr. Hirota."

In the dock Koki Hirota looked as if a live wire had fallen on him. Jerkily, he sat upright in his seat. A rapid, three-way exchange followed among defense counsel, witness, and bench:

LOGAN: I ask that the answer be stricken. . . .

BATES: I should be glad to give you some more evidence from Japanese sources on that.

LOGAN: If your honor please, I ask this witness be directed not to give, no—to volunteer statements.

WEBB: His answer will stand. He must, of course, confine his answer to the question. But he may add any explanation.

An American Episcopal minister, John G. Magee, testified that a Japanese vice consul had asked him to accompany him on a tour of the northern quarter of Nanking to point out foreign-owned property, as he wanted to post a notice in Japanese to protect them from the Japanese Army. "We turned into an alley to take a shortcut," Magee said, "but soon ran into so many bodies that the car had to back out of the alley, as we couldn't possibly get through without driving over so many bodies." At one point they saw, at the bottom of a grade, three piles of dead, roughly 300 to 500 bodies in all. "The clothing was burned off these bodies, and many of them were charred," Magee continued. "Evidently, they had been set on fire." During the trip they turned down a main boulevard leading to the railway station. The road was littered with bodies. On December 22, he testified, he took motion picture films of a group of sixty Chinese men on a road and women kneeling in the streets before the Japanese begging for their menfolk.

In addition to eyewitnesses, the Allied prosecution tendered in the stilled courtroom diaries written by the handful of foreigners residing in the city. The story they told was spontaneous and terrifying. George A. Fitch, a China-born American, wrote, "Many hundreds of innocent civilians are taken out before your eyes to be shot or used for bayonet practice, and you have to listen to the sound of the guns that are killing them. It seems to be the rule here that anyone who runs must be shot or bayonetted." James M. McCallum wrote in his diary on December 19, 1937, "It is a horrible story to try to relate; I know not where to begin nor to end. Never have I heard or read of such brutality. Rape Rape

Rape—we estimated at least 1,000 cases a night, and many by day. . . . People are hysterical. . . . Women are being carried off every morning, afternoon and evening while the Japanese army seems to be free to go and come anywhere it pleases.'' An entry ten days later read, ''Girls of 11 and 12, and women of 50, have not escaped. Resistance is fatal. The worst cases come to the hospital. A woman six months pregnant, who resisted, came to us with 16 knife wounds in her face and body, one piercing the abdomen. She lost her baby, but her life will be spared.''

After the introduction of the diaries, the prosecution focused attention on random bayoneting and arson in the city during the six weeks of hell. Three Chinese eyewitnesses, a rice dealer, a day laborer, and a widow, who had been flown to Tokyo to testify for the Allies, recounted more tales of terror. Civilians had often been bayoneted for sport, for practice, or for no reason whatsoever. A sixteen-year-old blind girl was raped. A house was put to the torch one night so that a Japanese patrol could ''keep warm.'' Japanese soldiers practiced their martial arts on young Chinese. If the Chinese won, he was bayoneted. The Kempeitai, always looking for new kinds of amusement, poured kerosene down a victim's throat, whipped prisoners with long clubs, left prisoners out overnight on exposed ground to freeze to death, or forced Chinese laborers to carry heavy loads and beat them senseless if they faltered. The report of the Chinese War Crimes Commission, tendered as evidence, pointed out that many men had been forcibly removed from Nanking in trucks to unknown places and that nothing had been heard from them for eight years. ''The manner in which they were probably killed is still unknown.''

The Rape of Nanking was not the kind of isolated incident common to *all* wars. It was deliberate. It was policy. It was known in Tokyo. For that matter, it was front-page news in the world's press. This was what the IMTFE was all about.

During this phase of the case one prisoner in the dock, Mamoru Shigemitsu, who had been a leader of the peace faction, sat with his head buried in his hands. He had had nothing to do with Nanking, but like so many Japanese, he felt the shame so deeply that he hid within himself.

On March 8, almost two months before he was indicted, General Matsui, the field commander at Nanking, had given his version of events to Allied interrogators at Sugamo. This interrogation, put in evidence by the prosecution, read in part:

Q: When did you first hear, if you did hear, that Europe and America got the idea that your troops committed many outrages in Nanking?

MATSUI: Almost as soon as I entered Nanking.

Q: You heard about it?

MATSUI: Yes.

Q: From what source did you hear about it?

MATSUI: From Japanese diplomats.

Q: . . . You were relieved from command because of this Nanking situation and replaced in February by General Hata. Is that correct?

MATSUI: No, that is not the reason. I considered my work ended in Nanking and wished to doff my uniform and engage in peaceful pursuits.

Q: . . . The charges also are made that the discipline of troops that captured Nanking was very bad.

MATSUI: I considered the discipline excellent but the conduct and behavior not.

Q: Of the soldiers?

MATSUI: Yes.

Q: This was at Nanking?

MATSUI: Yes. I think there were some lawless elements in the army.

Q: . . . Why do you say that it is your opinion that the behavior of the soldiers was bad? On what do you base this statement?

MATSUI: On account of their behavior toward the Chinese population and their acts generally.

Q: Were there any general orders that preceded the capture of Nanking from your headquarters?

MATSUI: I always advocated the maintenance of strict discipline and the punishment of all evildoers. . . .

The interrogation brought out that Matsui himself had first entered Nanking December 17 and remained there a week. He gave the opinion that his army had consisted of "experienced troops officered by experienced men." The first column of Japanese troops to enter Nanking was led by Lieutenant General Prince Asaka, Hirohito's uncle, and in Japan there had long been whispers that the prince was the real villain at Nanking and that Matsui felt it necessary to cover up for him. The spectators at the IMTFE stirred restlessly when the interrogation turned to the emperor's peripheral involvement. Matsui was asked about the rumors that Prince Asaka had been responsible for the Rape of Nanking but that "little or nothing was said about it." Matsui vigorously denied the prince's responsibility and put the blame on the prince's subordinates. Matsui was asked what he thought about the Chinese War Crimes Commission's report that hundreds of thousands of persons had been massacred at Nanking. "That is absolutely untrue," Matsui protested. ". . . This I can state upon my honor." The following exchange developed:

Q: After you got back to Japan in February, were you ever asked to make a report about the behavior of your troops at Nanking, either by the chief of staff or the war minister or anyone else?

MATSUI: . . . No, I was not asked to make a report. If there had been any such incidents, I would naturally have made a report on my own responsibility.

Further along in his Sugamo interrogation, Matsui confessed that he had maintained a diary during the campaign and that the only entries concerning the behavior of his troops were the court-martials of an officer and three soldiers for rape. Asked to produce the diary, the general said that his log and *all* his other records had been destroyed during an air raid late in the war.

Another senior officer in the dock, General Muto, who sat in front of Matsui and to the left, was also linked directly to Nanking. Akira Muto had served as head of the notorious Military Affairs Bureau in the early days of the Pacific War; as the Japanese Army commander in Sumatra, where many prisoner-of-war and civilian internee camps were located; and as the chief of staff to General Yamashita at the Rape of Manila in 1945.

During his interrogation at Sugamo on April 20, Muto confirmed that he had been at Nanking for about ten days, December 14–25, 1937, as adjutant to the chief of staff, and that "I had not heard of the Japanese soldiers acting up." He acknowledged, however, that he had seen a report that Japanese troops looted and raped. But, according to Muto, only "ten to twenty incidents were reported." Weren't there thousands? "I can't imagine that there were so many incidents," he said. Well, did he read the newspapers of the period? "I did not read the papers." As adjutant, what were his duties? "To assist the chief of staff."

Matsui's and Muto's feigning of ignorance was shown for what it was as the prosecution introduced into evidence seventy reports filed with the Japanese Embassy in Nanking over a six-week period by the international rescue committee. The reports cited the names, dates, and places of literally thousands of cases of Japanese depravity. In report after report the committee asked: What happened to the honorable tradition of the samurai warrior? A December 27 note to the Japanese Embassy concluded: "Shameful disorder continues and we see no serious efforts to stop it. The soldiers every day injure hundreds of persons most seriously. Does not the Japanese army care for its reputation?" In retrospect, another note was historically interesting because it employed a phrase that was already haunting the men in the dock. The note appealed to the Japanese to stop the slaughter in Nanking "in the name of humanity." The Allied indictment, of course, charged the defendants with "crimes against humanity."

In addition to the flow of notes, the committee sent delegations of foreigners almost daily to the Japanese Embassy to protest the carnage. The evidence showed that among the Japanese officials with whom they talked was Toyoasu Fukuda, who was now the chief secretary to Premier Shigeru Yoshida. But the foreigners absolved Fukuda and other Japanese diplomatic personnel of complicity in the terror. When Miner Searle Bates was on the stand, for example, he too was asked about the behavior of Japanese civilian authorities. "These men were honestly trying to do what little they could in a very bad situation," Bates testified, "but they themselves were terrified by the military, and they could do nothing except forward these communications through Shanghai to Tokyo."

Also placed into evidence was a stream of telegrams and dispatches from the files of the U.S. Embassy in Nanking, some marked "confidential" and others "secret," in which American diplomatic officers described the situation at Nanking as "a ruthless reign of terror." One dispatch observed that from the windows "we have seen them [Japanese soldiers] stop unarmed civilians on the road, search them, and finding nothing, calmly shoot them through the head." Among the documents was "confidential information," provided by a British diplomat, that the Japanese Army was rampaging in a similar fashion in other Chinese cities, towns, and villages. The British believed that "the army was deliberately turned loose . . . as a punitive measure," and British diplomats suggested that the only solution was publicity "so that the Japanese government would be forced by public opinion to curb the army." But in Japan the Rape of Nanking went unreported. Japanese editors were afraid to print foreign news-agency eyewitness dispatches for fear of inflaming the army or the Kempeitai.

Among the foreign embassies, perhaps the best informed was the German, since the chairman of the international safety committee was a German, John H. D. Rabe. The old saw about the kettle calling the pot black is a perfect characterization of the report sent by the German ambassador in China to Foreign Minister Joachim von Ribbentrop in Berlin on February 16, 1938, and marked "strictly confidential." The embassy report was initially prepared by the Nazi military attaché in China, General von Faulkenhausen, who was sickened by the Japanese Army's behavior as a "brutal military mob." The message reported disgustedly that "the Japanese soldiers raged like savages." The reaction in Berlin is not known, and the prosecution pursued the matter no further.

The evidence of Japanese depravity at Nanking, with the approval, tacit or otherwise, of the high command and with the knowledge of Prince Konoye's cabinet, was conclusive. This was partly reflected in the feeble cross-examination of the witnesses for the prosecution. The defense strongly objected that the prosecution had excluded from the evidence favorable comments about the Japanese at Nanking. Alfred Brooks, the American defense counsel for General Koiso, drew attention to one prosecution document that read, "Although the Japanese Embassy staff has been cordial and tried to help us out, they have been helpless." Another Allied document referred to "some very pleasant Japanese." Sir William Webb, however, dismissed these objections. "Well," the president of the tribunal said, "we take it for granted that wherever there are Japanese in large numbers, there are sure to be some fair Japanese among them. The defense can read that as part of their case later."

The strangest objection came from Lawrence McManus, the counsel for General Araki, who argued as a point of law that the accused were being smeared with charges of onerous crimes and that if a defendant was acquitted he would be "besmudged forever." The bench was bemused. "That applies to every accused who has ever been acquitted of a crime," Webb said in a tone of wonder. "I have allowed you to speak at length so that the absurdity of your remarks would be borne on the face of the record."

During this time the Japanese gallery was packed, and many of the spectators were young women. Yoshiko Yokoyama, a pert eighteen-year-old, admitted she was not "too shocked" by the tales of horror because since the surrender she had read about atrocities in the Japanese press. The IMTFE testimony, she said, convinced her of the "utter nonsense of the Japanese army's boast that Japanese soldiers were the model of honor and discipline the world over." Another spectator at the trial, a forty-one-year-old dentist, Takeshi Uetani, told the press that the testimony on Nanking confirmed rumors he had heard when he visited the city six months after its capture, but at the time he had had no way of corroborating the stories of rape and murder.

If the Japanese-contrived Marco Polo Bridge Incident of four and a half months earlier had been the prologue to the Sino-Japanese War, the Rape of Nanking was Act I, Scene 1. Thereafter, between 1938 and 1945 the Japanese launched four major invasions of central and south China, imposed a naval blockade along the China coast, and bombed the Chinese hinterland. Gradually, Japan occupied an ever-expanding slice of China, while the armies under Chiang Kai-shek fell back deeper into the mountainous interior, finally establishing a provisional capital at Chungking. One by one the great cities of China fell to the Japanese—Peking, Shanghai, Hankow, Canton. Rape, pillage, and murder were the order of the day. A stream of prosecution witnesses testified as to time, date, and place of incident after incident. Albert Dorrance, the chairman of the American Chamber of Commerce at Hankow, was in that industrial metropolis the day the Japanese entered, October 25, 1938. At the customs wharf abutting on the Yangtze

River, he testified, the Japanese collected "several hundreds of Chinese war prisoners." The rest of Dorrance's testimony, given in starts and stops, sounded like something out of Kafka:

> The soldiers, the Japanese soldiers, who were at the head of this gangplank would occasionally walk up to this crowd of Chinese soldiers—well, Chinese people, most of who were soldiers according to their dress—would select at random three or four of them and apparently with no personal selection, just more or less point for three or four to walk on down. These several would walk on down this long gangplank, and as they passed the Japanese soldiers, the sentries, why they would casually walk out, walk behind them on down to the water's edge. When they arrived at the water's edge, the Japanese sentries who had been following them down—apparently extremely impersonal the action, the disinterest impressed you, the impartiality of it all the way through—arriving at the water's edge where the water was deep, the soldiers would kick these Chinese into the water and shoot them when their heads appeared above water.

The mounting evidence was taking its toll on the men in the dock. General Umezu, who had been vice minister of war during the Rape of Nanking, sat glumly, almost in a daze. Toshio Shiratori, the dapper former ambassador to Italy, stared, head down, at his shoes. Fleet Admiral Nagano appeared to have lost a great deal of weight, and several of the other defendants looked as though they had passed sleepless nights in their cells. In the Allied press room, where an informal scorecard was kept, the consensus was that the evidence in the Manchurian and Chinese phases had seriously damaged ten of the accused: Generals Doihara, Itagaki, Koiso, Matsui, Muto, Araki, and Minami, Colonel Hashimoto, and two civilians, Shumei Okawa and Koki Hirota. Matsui and Muto, it was felt, were certain to get the death penalty.

The defendants suffered even greater discomfort when the absurdities of their prewar postures and statements were held up to the light. The IPS introduced examples of Japanese double-think and double-speak on Mukden, Marco Polo, and the entire China "incident," among them the commentaries of such accused as former premier Hiranuma, Ambassador Shiratori, Foreign Minister Matsuoka, and Colonel Hashimoto. Matsuoka had described

Mukden as "an exaltation of the national spirit" and Japan's war in China as "liberation." As for Japan's withdrawal from the League of Nations, Matsuoka termed it "the day on which Japan set the world on the road to the establishment of a true and real peace." In Matsuoka's florid language Japan was a "divine country." Given the ultimate outcome of the China incident—a prostrate Japan—even Matsuoka had read the future: "The fact that our country is a divine country means, in a way, that there will be the grace of Heaven when our country will go forward in accordance with divine will and, if we act against it, we will be punished by Heaven."

In their lust for war Japan's militarists and political fanatics had misread the will of heaven.

16

Unconventional Warfare: Drugs and Disease

The Japanese Army not only set up jackboot governments in China, it also trafficked in narcotics to finance the occupation. As the Allied indictment put it, successive Japanese cabinets, through their military and naval commanders and civilian agents in China, pursued a deliberate policy of weakening the Chinese people's will to resist not only by systematic atrocities but also "by directly or indirectly encouraging increased production and the importation of opium and other narcotics and by promoting the sale and consumption of such drugs among such people."

Part of the prosecution's case on the drug trade had emerged earlier. Japan's narcotics policy in China, like a periscope, revealed itself intermittently and briefly amid the evidence on the Rape of Nanking. The first time the subject of drugs arose during the trial was in the testimony of the American surgeon Robert O. Wilson, who casually observed that it had been a capital offense to sell drugs in Nanking—and elsewhere in Nationalist China— until the arrival of the Japanese. But within a year of the Japanese occupation public opium dens had sprouted like reeds along the banks of the Yangtze. Another witness recalled that with the coming of the Japanese "heroin was very easy to get" in Nanking and that Chinese laborers, so-called coolies, whose ages ranged from ten to thirty years, were often paid off in heroin cigarettes.

The most telling evidence on the drug situation, however, was offered by Miner Searle Bates, who independently had made several studies of the opium trade in occupied China. Within a year of Nanking's capture, he testified, the sale of opium in the former capital had become rampant and the Japanese Army's special services branch did a brisk $3 million monthly business in opium, heroin, and morphine. Bates conservatively estimated that 50,000 people, or one eighth of the city's population, had been heavy users of drugs early in the Japanese occupation. As a corollary, he observed that there was a strong relationship between narcotics and crime. He noted that robberies by addicts in Nanking had reached epidemic proportions, "a serious matter for everyone." But the highlight of his testimony was in connection with his visit to Tokyo in 1939. At the Foreign Ministry he had conferred with a Japanese expert in opium trafficking who had recently returned from a two-month inspection tour of central China. "He told me that he was greatly distressed at the terrible addiction that he saw in Hankow and other cities of the Yangtze Valley," Bates testified. "When I asked him if there was any hope for improvement, he shook his head sadly and said, 'No, the general told me that so long as the war continues, there is no hope of anything better because no other good source of revenue has been found for the puppet government.' "

According to one of Bates's studies, by 1940 there were 600 licensed opium emporiums in Peking, 460 in Hankow, and 852 in Canton. "The situation through the occupied areas was one of the open sale of opium in government shops or licensed shops, and the aggressive peddling of heroin," he said. "In some cases, there was attractive advertising of opium; in some cases, Japanese soldiers used opium as payment for prostitutes and for labor engaged on military supply dumps."

China's associate prosecutor, Hsiang Che-chun, handled the main phase of the IPS case on narcotics. Wherever the Japanese trod in China, he charged, they had created opium monopolies under the guise of suppressing the use of opium. The monopolies served as a conduit for the distribution and sale of opium and its derivatives, heroin and morphine, to Chinese men, women, and children. The Japanese, however, dealt harshly with Japanese soldiers or Japanese nationals in China using drugs. Japan's opium operations, Hsiang said, had a double objective: to weaken the Chinese people's will to resist and to provide substantial revenues "to finance Japanese military and economic aggression." Japan's trafficking in narcotics, moreover, was in contravention of international treaties to halt the spread of drugs that the Japanese themselves had solemnly signed. Among these were the Hague Convention for the Suppression of the Abuse of Opium and Other Drugs; the Covenant of the League of Nations with Respect to the Traffic in Opium and Other Drugs; and the Geneva Convention Relating to Narcotic Drugs.

The Allies' evidence was overwhelming.

As early as June 4, 1932, the chief of staff of the Kwantung Army in occupied Manchuria, with Tokyo's approval, set up an opium monopoly to finance the creation of the state of Manchukuo. Joseph Keenan's investigators had discovered a contract in the files of the Industrial Bank of Japan to finance Manchukuo's establishment by the floating of 30 million yen worth of bonds. Several *zaibatsu* banks, including Mitsubishi, Yasuda, Kawasaki, Sumitomo, and Mitsui, formed a consortium to underwrite the sale of the bonds. Article 4 of the financial arrangement read, "These bonds shall be secured by the profits of the opium monopoly. . . . The principal and interest shall be paid preferentially from the monopoly profits."

In addition, a financial incentive was provided to the growers of the poppy in Japanese-occupied areas. Farmers engaged in the production of foodstuffs could borrow $1.80 an acre at 7 percent interest per year for every acre they planted. For those who cultivated the poppy, the source of opium, a loan of $12 per acre at 2.3 percent interest could be obtained. Even so, according to a report from a U.S. Treasury Department agent stationed in Shanghai, tendered as evidence, the loans were rigged to deceive the Chinese peasants. "Many farmers who anticipated considerable profit from the cultivation of poppy found that, owing to the compulsory order requiring them to sell their opium exclusively to the Japanese . . . at a fixed price which was much below market value, they were unable to make any profit at all," the report explained. "After the harvest, many of the farmers could not repay their loans and their lands were confiscated."

Although hundreds of thousands of acres of land were turned over to poppy cultivation in occupied China—more than 150,000 acres in Manchuria—the Japanese authorities were unable to meet the insatiable demand of addicts whose ranks were swelling into the millions. The Japanese resolved the problem by importing opium from abroad, principally Iran. Once again the *zaibatsu* surfaced at the trial. Mitsubishi, according to the evidence at the IMTFE, controlled narcotics shipments and distribution in Manchukuo while Mitsui handled central and south China. North China, however, was a source of contention. "The distribution for North China shall be shared equally by the two companies," a contract drawn up in 1939 read.

The war in Europe put a crimp in these plans. Because of the uncertainty of international shipping, the Imperial Japanese Navy was ordered into narcotic-trafficking convoy duty. In one instance two destroyers were dispatched under secret orders to Ceylonese waters to convoy an Iranian drug cargo to the China coast, following a telegraphic message from Japanese agents that one of the tramp steamers carrying opium "will not proceed further for fear of German submarines." The freighter carried 1,000 cases of opium with a value of $30,000 per case. Thus, one shipment alone was valued at $30 million in 1940 dollars, or better than a quarter of a billion dollars in today's marketplace.

Manchukuo was the first Japanese-occupied territory to feel the impact of these policies. A third of the country's 30 million people were turned into addicts within a relatively short period. In the witness box Tsunekazu Namba, the former vice director of the Manchukuo Opium Monopoly Bureau—the director was a Manchurian—claimed that his goal had been to establish a strict prohibition on the use of narcotics and thus to reduce the number of addicts. Pressed by New Zealand's associate prosecutor, Ronald Quilliam, Namba admitted, however, that during Manchukuo's ten-year opium-suppression program the monopoly bureau's profits had risen. But Namba did not attribute this to the increase in the number of addicts as much as to the amount sold and higher prices. The witness considered this a "favorable sign."

During his testimony it emerged that the defendant Naoki Hoshino, who had controlled Manchukuo's financial affairs, had played the principal role in Namba's appointment. Did Hoshino expect him to increase the profits from opium sales as vice director of the monopoly bureau? "I do not recall accurately," Namba replied. Did Hoshino tell him the Japanese Army in Manchukuo expected bigger revenue from opium sales? "I have no recollection whatsoever," the witness said. Quilliam then sprang a document dated June 4, 1932, from the chief of staff of the Kwantung Army to the vice minister of war in Tokyo, warning that Manchukuo would run up a deficit in maintaining "law and order" and recommending that the deficit be covered by raising revenue from customs "and opium sales."

During the testimony of several Japanese witnesses no comment was made about whether or not Japanese nationals in Manchukuo had also used opium. Quilliam asked Namba to clarify the situation. For example, had Japanese nationals in Manchukuo required permission to purchase opium from the monopoly bureau? "I thought that that was unnecessary to point out," the witness said, "because Japanese nationals were strictly prohibited from anything to do with opium by Japanese laws."

By the time the Japanese witnesses left the stand, the financial manipulators among the accused emerged as little more than glorified drug peddlers. In the dock Hoshino, Kaya, and Suzuki sat like lizards on a rock, motionless except for the involuntary blink of their eyelids.

The IPS flooded the court with evidence, most of it statistical, compelling Webb at one point to dam the flow. "You must be approaching the saturation point," the tribunal's president suggested. "The evidence must be reaching the stage at which it will become cumulative." But the tragedy of addiction was also brought home forcefully in a more personal manner. In a confidential report from Mukden on October 13, 1936, American Consul William R. Langdon wrote about his visit to a rag-pickers' market, situated near a reeking open sewer and in an area dotted with the hovels of prostitutes who dispensed narcotics. "Demonstrating with peculiar force the relation of cause to effect, there lay on an ash heap just behind the narcotic brothels seven naked corpses which had evidently been stripped of their rags by fellow addicts. It is generally stated that this is a daily sight, despite the regular removal of the bodies by the Red Swastika Society. There was offered no other explanation than that these dead met their end through narcotic poisoning."

Within a short time the garbage dumps of Manchuria had become so notorious that a Japanese-controlled Chinese-language newspaper, *Sheng Ching Shih Pao,* complained in a February 18, 1937, editorial about the presence of bodies strewn on Mukden's ash heaps, their hair disheveled, their faces dirty, their upper garments and trousers stripped from their bodies. "They could be recognized at a glance as morphia-addicts," one newspaper story tendered by the prosecution said. It added, with a touch of concern for civic pride, "It is deeply hoped that the municipal government and philanthropic organizations will, at an early date, dress these corpses for burial, so as to show regard for humanity and to improve the appearance of the city.''

What had all this to do with Tokyo? A Japanese prosecution witness established the link in a deadly manner. He was Genshichi Oikawa, a former director of the Ko-A-In, or China Affairs Board, which the late premier Prince Konoye had established in 1938 to oversee political, economic, and cultural affairs in occupied China. The opium trade came under the directives of this official Japanese umbrella organization. Konoye himself, and successive premiers, served as presidents of the Ko-A-In. The agency's four vice-presidents were the ministers of war, the navy, finance, and foreign affairs. Accordingly, every figure in the dock who held one of these posts between 1938 and 1945 had exercised a direct hand in the trafficking of drugs as state policy. It was as if the Mafia had taken control of the Japanese government. "The Ko-A-In studied the opium needs in different parts of China and arranged for the distribution of the opium . . . to North China, Central China, and South China," Oikawa related matter-of-factly. "This distribution was done through Chinese organizations."

Scant wonder that Prince Konoye had committed suicide on the eve of his arrest the previous December. In the press room at Ichigaya the consensus among foreign correspondents covering the trial was that if Konoye had stood trial, on the basis of the evidence produced during the opium phase alone, he would have been convicted of crimes against humanity, and executed.

During the first four months of the trial, as the prosecutors dealt largely with Japanese internal affairs, the conquest of Manchuria, and the invasion of China, it was clear that for reasons of security, relating to either the occupation or the emergent cold war, the Americans barred certain areas of inquiry to Allied prosecutors. Hirohito's role was the most obvious example of this. By the autumn of 1946 it was plain that the emperor would not be subpoenaed as a witness for the prosecution or defense, although his name turned up repeatedly in the transcript. The zaibatsu also seemed to be out of bounds, although it was clearly impossible to omit all references to the financial and industrial monopolies that dominated business activities in Japan.

But there were two other areas of far greater sensitivity: Japan's programs in nuclear weapons and in bacteriological warfare.

The former does not appear once in the trial's 10-million-word transcript, although the IMTFE record is dotted with references to Hiroshima. The latter surfaced inadvertently and then submerged swiftly and mysteriously.

On November 17, 1945, the IPS cabled the Chinese War Crimes Commission at Nanking and asked for a summary report of its investigations into Japanese war crimes in occupied China. The report was prepared by the procurator of the District Court, Nanking, and assistant U.S. prosecutor David Sutton read parts of the document into the record of the IMTFE. Under the subheading, "Particulars Regarding Other Atrocities," Sutton read three sentences: "The enemy's TAMA Detachment carried off their civilian captives to the medical laboratory, where the reactions to poisonous serums were tested. This detachment was one of the most secret organizations. The number of persons slaughtered by this detachment cannot be ascertained." This was the first hint at the IMTFE that the Japanese had engaged in experiments on humans in connection with bacteriological warfare.

Sutton droned on about unrelated matters when Sir William Webb interrupted him. Webb was puzzled and annoyed. "Are you going to give us any further evidence of these alleged laboratory tests for reactions to poisonous serums?" he asked. "That is something entirely new, we haven't heard before. Are you going to leave it at that?"

Sutton's reply was surprising. "We do not at this time anticipate introducing evidence on that subject," the Allied prosecutor said. He then returned to the Chinese document and proceeded to list nine Japanese Army units known to have carried out "wholesale murders" of Chinese in occupied territories, a forerunner of the Nazi *Einsatzgruppen,* or death squads, that would later operate in occupied Russia. But the defense, also caught unaware, thought it was dangerous to permit the reference to bacteriological warfare to slip by unchallenged. Alfred Brooks, the defense counsel for General Koiso and Shumei Okawa, objected. He suggested that the allegations that the Japanese had experimented with poisonous serums may have been confused with a public health program in occupied China. "We would like to inquire of the prosecution if this does not consist of a series of vaccinations of these people [prisoners]," he said. Brooks's colleague, the burly Michael Levin, counsel for the financiers Okinori Kaya and Teiichi Suzuki, joined in the objection. "Mr. President," Levin said, "I believe the defense ought to have some protection against the use of a document of this character."

Webb agreed. "The evidence I take you to be objecting to is that referring to tests on Chinese apparently with poisonous materials. Subject to what my colleagues think, that appears to me to be a mere assertion unsupported by any evidence." Levin nodded approvingly and observed that the Allied prosecutors owed a duty to the tribunal, the defense, and public to exercise discretion in the presentation of "matters of this kind." Webb reiterated his concurrence and declared that the bench rejected unsupported statements as evidence.

That was the end of the legal pavane, and the question of bacteriological warfare was never again mentioned during the trial.

Like several other observers at the trial I was puzzled and intrigued. As a layman, I thought this was the sort of thing the IMTFE should concern itself with instead of the seemingly endless debates on technical aspects of the law. But I did not follow up on the incident nor did I mention it in my United Press dispatch that day. The reason was uncomplicated: I, like the other correspondents at the trial, was overwhelmed by testimony. Within the transcript were more than 1,001 tales, and it would require a Scheherazade to tell them all.

After the Tokyo tribunal had concluded its work, the February 23, 1950, issue of *Izvestia,* the Soviet government daily, assailed Joseph Keenan for "his weakness toward eminent war criminals" and charged that Soviet prosecutors had turned over to Keenan, as chief of Allied counsel, hard evidence of Japan's experiments in bacteriological weapons: ". . . Keenan closed his eyes when, in September 1946, the Soviet prosecution at the Tokyo trial delivered to him, as the main American prosecutor, the evidence of the leading officials of this [TAMA] detachment. . . . This evidence exposed the Japanese militarists in preparation of bacteriological warfare and in bestial experiments performed on living people." That same year Moscow published the transcript of the December 25–30, 1949, trial of twelve former members of the TAMA detachment, whom the Soviets had captured in Manchuria along with several hundred thousand other Japanese troops. The twelve were convicted of conducting experiments in bacteriological warfare on Allied war prisoners and Chinese civilians and were sentenced to prison terms, along with the chief of staff of the Kwantung Army, Lieutenant General Otozo Yamada, the implication being that he had been privy to experiments on living people, who were infected with plague, cholera, typhus, anthrax, and gangrene microbes. (Three of the accused in the dock at the IMTFE were former Kwantung Army chiefs of staff and therefore linked to these experiments—Generals Hideki Tojo, Seishiro Itagaki, and Yoshijiro Umezu. Among these, it will be recalled, the Soviet Union had insisted on Umezu's indictment.) The Soviet trial was largely ignored by the world. Stalin's rigged purge trials in the thirties, which sent millions to their death, had completely discredited the Marxist-Leninist concept of justice.

Years later, however, in 1976, the Tokyo Broadcasting System confirmed the existence of the TAMA detachment. A Japanese journalist after three years of research had tracked down five living members of the top-secret operation who told him that they had escaped indictment as war criminals in return for divulging their research to U.S. authorities. In Japan the story caused a sensation, and since then a book on the detachment, *The Devil's Insatiability*, has sold more than 1.5 million copies in Japan—one of the few books on Japanese atrocities to appear in Japan's postwar literature.

In the Western world the first detailed report on the TAMA detachment appeared in 1981 in the *Bulletin of Concerned Asian Scholars*, an obscure left-of-center periodical published in the United States. The author of the article later wrote a similar piece for the October 1981 issue of the *Bulletin of Atomic Scientists*, which was picked up by American news agencies and widely reported in the United States. There is an element of irony in this. The author of both articles was John W. Powell, who had remained in China and operated there freely after the Communists ascended to power in 1949 and who had been charged with treason by the United States for his activities during the Korean War. The charge was later dismissed after a grand jury failed to vote an indictment. His father, John B. Powell, a well-known journalist in prewar China, was a key witness for the prosecution at Tokyo during its China phase of the case. The father had lost the use of his legs in a Japanese civilian internee camp during the war.

The Japanese experiments in bacteriological warfare, it was alleged, included infecting prisoners with diseases, freezing portions of their bodies, and exposing prisoners to fragmentation bombs. Chinese women were infected with syphilis to develop vaccines. Prisoners were infected with plague, typhus, typhoid, hemorrhagic fever, cholera, anthrax, tularemia, smallpox, and dysentery. Prisoners were given doses of horse blood and had their livers destroyed by prolonged exposure to X rays. Allied prisoners were dissected alive. POWs were tied to stakes and canisters of bubonic plague and other horrible viruses exploded nearby while Japanese army technicians in protective clothing, holding stopwatches, measured how long it took the prisoners to die. The experiments were carried out in Manchuria and on the outskirts of Nanking, and included the bombing of Chinese cities with plague. Periodically, medical teams in the Chinese Nationalist Army reported on the mysterious outbreak of plague in several areas in wartime China. The experiments ended abruptly with Hiroshima.

In 1983 I pursued the question of the suppression of information on bacteriological warfare with the robust, seventy-nine-year-old former surgeon general of the Chinese Nationalist Army, General Yang Wen-tah, a pioneer in public health in China. He felt that the whole story should be told in the name of "righteousness and truth" and provided me with many facts and with a two-page affidavit from his predecessor, Surgeon General Chen Li-kai, now an octogenarian, who confirmed that in February 1940 he had personally witnessed a naval amphibian plane flying at about 300 feet over Changteh, Hunan Province, dropping packages of "cotton substances." A fortnight later plague broke out at Changteh. The suspicious General Chen promptly slapped a sixty-day quarantine around the city (forty days was the normal period) and had the population inoculated against plague. In the joint opinion of Generals Yang and Chen, "The outburst of bubonic plague in February 1940 in Changteh, Hunan, China, [was] definitely implanted by a certain foreign invasion military force during World War II." To this day, for fear of offending Japanese sensibilities— the isolated Republic of China is in dire need of Japanese political support—neither physician was willing to identify the "foreign invasion force" as Japanese. "But there was no other foreign military force invading China in 1940," General Yang observed. "No other conclusion could be drawn." He felt the Chinese had not pressed the matter at the IMTFE or elsewhere because other terrible crimes, on a broader canvas, had to be dealt with at that time.

In retrospect, given the testimony at the IMTFE on Japan's narcotics policy in occupied China, it appears that the plague experiments coupled with the opium program and the use of death squads were designed to reduce China's "surplus" population. In Taipei, Shih Mei-yu, former head of the Chinese War Crimes Court, told me that the Chinese government possessed evidence that the Kempeitai had recommended to Tokyo that "Japan wipe out all Chinese from the map," a Japanese version of Hitler's "final solution" in handling gypsies and Jews.

In 1982, in the face of various reports, the Japanese government formally acknowledged that *more than* 3,000 Allied prisoners of war and Chinese civilians had been used as guinea pigs in biological and medical experiments. "It is most regrettable from the point of view of humanity," State Minister Kunio Tanabe told the Diet in April. Four months later the Kyodo News Agency, Japan's premier news service, reported that behind the bacteriological warfare experiments had been the hope of developing a plague weapon for use in the war against the United States. Japan was lagging in nuclear technology and hoped that germ warfare would prove to be its ultimate weapon.

Washington's decision to grant these Japanese war criminals immunity and to suppress evidence of bacteriological warfare at the IMTFE was motivated by a desire to prevent Stalin from acquiring the top-secret information about Japan's atomic bomb project. At the time of the IMTFE, it should be remembered, the United States had a monopoly on nuclear weapons.

Nonetheless, the U.S. decision to suppress evidence at the IMTFE was questionable. The last surviving judge at Tokyo, B.V.A. Röling of the Netherlands, recently expressed the view that the United States should be "ashamed because of the fact they withheld information from the Court with respect to the biological experiments of the Japanese in Manchuria on Chinese and American prisoners of war." In a comment in the *Bulletin of Atomic Scientists* Röling was sharper. "As one of the judges in the International Military Tribunal for the Far East," he wrote, "it is a bitter experience for me to be informed now that centrally ordered Japanese war criminality of the most disgusting kind was kept secret from the Court by the U.S. government."

Thus, the horror stories emanating from the IMTFE in the fall of 1946 were not, even at their worst, the whole book on Japan's war crimes.

17

The Axis on Trial

After skirting the issues of Japanese bacteriological experimentation and nuclear research, the IMTFE next addressed the formation of the Berlin-Tokyo Axis. The alliance was as logical as it was sordid. The leaders of both countries were expansionist and racist. Each possessed a police-state mentality. Among the documents introduced by the Allied prosecution as evidence were the secret minutes of a 1940 conference of Japan's leadership at which the emperor presided. The voluble Yosuke Matsuoka, who as foreign minister orchestrated the alliance with Germany and Italy, revealed at the meeting intimate details of his conversations with Joachim von Ribbentrop, his Nazi counterpart. Matsuoka said he had defined for the Nazis what Japan meant by a "New Order" in Asia and the Pacific. "For the present," he said, the New Order would embrace French Indo-China, Thailand, Burma, Malaya, the Netherlands East Indies, and the Southwest Pacific." Japan's colonial empire would displace the European. When Japan consolidated control over these areas, Matsuoka added, "the meaning [of New Order] would be gradually changed" to include Australia and New Zealand. Matsuoka, however, prided himself on his restraint. "I did not refer to India," he told the imperial conference.

For their part, the Germans laid claim to the whole of Europe and exhibited their own restraint by making no mention of Africa.

But once German and Japanese hegemony had been established in their respective regions, Matsuoka said, Ribbentrop "pointed out the possible necessity . . . for common action" against the United States.

The Allied case at Tokyo was based largely on documents captured when the Allies had overrun Germany and on the interrogation of the accused at Sugamo, notably Hiroshi Oshima, the primly dressed general and diplomat who had served in Berlin first as Japan's military attaché and later as ambassador, the man the Japanese termed "more Nazi than the Nazis."

Amid the welter of material introduced—Sir William Webb again complained that the prosecution swamped the proceedings—two dates acquired significance. The first was February 4, 1938, when Hitler, a civilian, assumed supreme command of the German armed forces, and the other, July 18, 1940, when, to all intents and purposes, the Japanese high command completed its takeover of the civilian Japanese government. Between those two dates, for a fleeting six months, the Japanese peace faction made a desperate attempt to end the war in China and to halt Japan's slide into a world war. Admiral Mitsumasa Yonai, who bitterly opposed an alliance with the Nazis, emerged as premier.

Once again—to the shock of the Japanese spectators in the gallery—the IPS demonstrated that the militarists had reverted to government by assassination to get their way. Excerpts from the Kido diaries were read into the record. Seven government leaders, including Premier Yonai, had been marked down, as Kido delicately put it, as "proposed objectives." Hit squads were set to go into action at 7 A.M., July 5, 1940, but ninety minutes beforehand, acting on "secret information," the civil police thwarted the plot by raids that netted them the would-be assassins and an arsenal of pistols, hand grenades, Molotov cocktails, and other weapons. The emperor's primary adviser added matter-of-factly, "The conclusion is that a cabinet change is inevitable in order to face this grave situation."

Foiled in their assassination attempt, the militarists now resorted to a familiar political strategy to bring down Admiral Yonai. Field Marshal Hata, the war minister, submitted his resignation, toppling the cabinet. On July 18, while the civilians labored to put together a new cabinet, the army silently seized power. Invoking *iaku joso,* the right of direct access to the emperor, Hata visited Hirohito and, Kido's diaries revealed, "secretly recommended Tojo

as war minister." The emperor was stunned by the army's dicta-
tion and accused Hata of acting "out of order." But at this point
Hirohito was powerless to oppose the demand of the militarists.
Later that day Prince Konoye, in the role of the army's front man,
formed his third and last cabinet. His war minister? Hideki Tojo,
an enthusiastic champion of the alliance with Hitler who dreamed
of bigger and better wars, the man who more than any other would
lead Japan into a war with the United States a year and a half
later.

One of the new cabinet's first actions was to rubber-stamp the
alliance with Nazi Germany. Less than ten weeks later the Tripartite Axis Pact, with Mussolini's Italy as a junior partner, came
into existence.

The evidence at the IMTFE made it patently clear that many
influential Japanese knew they had mounted a tiger and that there
would be a problem in dismounting. The IPS tendered into evidence the minutes of a Privy Council meeting chaired by a former
premier, Baron Hiranuma, who now sat in the dock looking more
glum and haggard than ever. Emperor Hirohito had attended the
council meeting and sat as silent as a stage prop as the council
unanimously approved the Axis arrangement. But the meeting did
not run as smoothly as indicated by the surface manifestation of
unity. "Because I deeply fear that the enforcement of this alliance
is apt to invite grave disasters, I wish to give a few outspoken
opinions concerning this draft," a member of the Privy Council
said bluntly. "There is not a single country that has gained any
benefit from allying itself with Germany. . . . I believe that Chan-
cellor Hitler of Nazi Germany is a character of no little danger.
. . . From whatever angle we view it, we cannot believe that Nazi
Germany under the leadership of Hitler can be a loyal friend of
Japan." Then, not daring to go any further, the councillor sat down
and joined in the vote for the pact. Many others were uneasy
about the alliance but were in no position to thwart the dogmatic,
chilling ambitions of War Minister Tojo, who had emerged as the
most powerful man in Japan.

Despite their mutual mistrust, the German and Japanese high
commands plunged into an active collaboration. Evidence at the
IMTFE revealed that they had swapped intelligence reports and
technical assistance. German dive-bomber specialists visited Japan to train Japanese naval pilots in 1940. The Germans provided
Tokyo with the details of their assault on the Maginot Line to

assist the Japanese in their attacks on Britain's fixed fortresses at Singapore and Hong Kong. Hermann Göring personally pledged that "all experiences which Germany had during the course of the war will be made available to the allied Japanese armed forces." Best of all, as a token of their close collaboration, Nazi Foreign Minister von Ribbentrop offered the Japanese a secret weapon, "the greatest military mind at the present time." The Führer himself. Alas, the Japanese reaction to this vainglorious gesture perished in the bonfires of the immediate postsurrender period.

For their part the Japanese provided the Germans with seventy advanced aerial torpedoes that were far superior to anything in Western arsenals. Hitler was elated and personally acknowledged Germany's "backwardness" in this area of weapons development; he thanked Japan for her "great assistance." A wing of the German Air Force, he notified the Japanese, was being organized immediately for their operational use.

The most terrifying aspect of the evidence presented at the IMTFE was the imperturbable manner in which the Japanese and German leaders discussed military operations. The evidence at the IMTFE in this phase clearly demonstrated that Berlin and Tokyo were jointly bent on war, and no appeasement was going to stop them. Although it seems inconceivable that they were plotting a wider war at a time when the Battle of Britain was still being fought indecisively and the Japanese armies were bogged down in China, nevertheless, it is a fact that Berlin and Tokyo devoted most of their secret deliberations to the question of when and where to strike next. Neither side, however, took the other into its confidence.

With the demise of Admiral Yonai's cabinet, the Germans were jubilant. They expected Japan to pursue "a more active anti-British policy," and they were not mistaken. With Yonai out of the way, the Japanese Army's high command told Hitler in strictest secrecy that they had completed their plans for an attack on Hong Kong. But the Germans were far more anxious to get Japan to attack Singapore, Britain's greatest naval bastion east of Suez. The Nazis feared that Roosevelt would concoct another lend-lease agreement under which the British would turn Singapore over to the U.S. Pacific Fleet in return for the stepped-up delivery of American military aid. On February 28, 1941, Ribbentrop advised Ambassador Oshima that "Japan should attack as soon as possible. . . . The occupation of Singapore must take place with lightning speed"—a blitzkrieg. The Germans were convinced the United States would not intervene because "she was not yet armed and would not risk her fleet west of Hawaii." Hitler explained to his inner circle that Japan's entry into the war against Britain was imperative and that Singapore was the key. This would divert America and tie up her fleet, he said. But something else was in the back of Hitler's mind: "No hint must be given to the Japanese concerning Operation Barbarossa"—the invasion of Russia.

For that matter, while Oshima, Matsuoka, and other senior Japanese officials discussed plans with the Germans to attack Singapore and Hong Kong, the Japanese said nothing about their major objective, Hawaii. Yet the Japanese hinted about the possibility of a war between Japan and the United States. In March 1941, for example, Matsuoka visited Hitler and asked what, in that era, was the sixty-four-dollar question: What would Germany do if war between Japan and the United States developed? The Führer replied unhesitatingly. "Germany," he said, "would strike without delay in case of a conflict between Japan and America." Tokyo was elated; if the attack on Pearl Harbor required final approval, this was it.

Oshima, in his conversations with Joachim von Ribbentrop, hinted even more broadly that something was in the Pacific wind. By May, he said, Japan would complete preparations for the invasion of Singapore, but he added cautiously, "For safety's sake, preparations must be made not only for war against England but also against America."

Adding to the wealth of documentary information in Tokyo, the prosecution introduced the diaries of Count Galeazzo Ciano, the suave, indecisive Italian foreign minister who had been the Prince Konoye of Mussolini's circle. On December 3, 1941, as the Japanese fleet steamed secretly for Pearl Harbor, Ciano's entry for that day revealed that the Japanese had informed him that the U.S.–Japanese talks on China had arrived at a "dead end" and that Japan formally requested Italy's declaration of war against the United States when hostilities erupted. "The interpreter translating this request was trembling like a leaf," Count Ciano wrote.

Interestingly, Ciano's diary reported that Hitler's reaction to the Japanese request was less enthusiastic than Mussolini's. Even so, neither Germany nor Italy knew when or where or how the Japanese would start their war with the Americans, only that Tokyo had opted for war. As late as December 5, with the Japanese fleet now taking up its final position north of Hawaii, Heinrich Stahmer, the Gestapo agent and German ambassador to Tokyo, sent Berlin a *"most urgent!"* message to report that a break in U.S.–Japanese negotiations was imminent and that Japan was poised to attack. The Germans, like most Americans and others, thought Japan would strike at French Indochina. Reports of Japanese troopships moving off the coast of Vietnam and in the Gulf of Siam were so commonplace that even news agencies reported their movements. Amusingly, Toshio Shiratori, the former ambassador to Italy and sharp-tongued spokesman for the Foreign Ministry—who now sat in the dock at the IMTFE—told Stahmer that leading Japanese believed the United States wanted to enter the European war through an Asian back door. This was the Ciano line, in fact; Shiratori had probably picked it up in Rome and was now feeding it back to Axis-occupied Europe. If this had been the case, of course, Berlin and Tokyo could have short-circuited Roosevelt's foreign policy simply by avoiding a Pacific war. But Tokyo wanted war. Thus, in the next breath, Shiratori—listening in the dock—was quoted by Stahmer as confessing that for reasons of internal Japanese affairs, "it is unavoidable to declare the existence of a state of war or to declare war on America simultaneously or after the beginning of hostilities."

Berlin and Rome rejoiced on December 7, 1941, the evidence at the IMTFE showed. Mussolini was "happy," Ribbentrop "overjoyed," and Hitler in ecstasy. As an outward sign of Hitler's enthusiasm, he awarded Ambassador Oshima the Grand Cross of the Order of the Merit of the German Eagle in gold for his valiant effort in getting Japan to strike against the United States. The sneak attack on Hawaii appealed to Hitler's sense of honor. "You gave the right declaration of war!" Hitler told an elated Oshima at the investiture ceremony. "This method is the only proper one . . . strike as hard as possible, indeed, and not waste time declaring war." The Führer, according to the prosecution's captured documents, then compared Japan's desire for peace to Germany's and praised Japan for its "angelic patience" in dealing with Roosevelt. According to Hitler, everyone knew that Germany and Japan sought to avoid war but had been forced into it. Hitler also took America's fighting spirit lightly. "How could troops whose god is the dollar hold firm to the last?" the Führer asked. Oshima and Hitler, in their delirium, must have laughed heartily at this assessment.

Among the accused in the dock, the most badly mauled by the evidence of plotting aggressive war were Oshima and Shiratori, and twin Axis ambassadors, particularly the former. The evidence also proved that Oshima had not been simply an ambassador of the Japanese Foreign Ministry in the classic sense but also the ambassador of the War Ministry. General Oshima had also directed Japanese intelligence and counterespionage activities. Through his American defense attorney, Owen Cunningham, Oshima waged a futile courtroom fight to block the prosecution's introduction of his diplomatic correspondence and conversations into evidence.

Cunningham argued vigorously that Oshima's acts had been those of an ambassador or military attaché in Berlin. "His acts were privileged under the diplomatic-immunity rule of international law," Cunningham declared, "and it is an inviolable rule of the law of nations." He contended that Oshima was exempt from punishment or criminal responsibility for his acts and that his arrest and detention by the Allies in themselves were violations of international law. Webb overruled Cunningham's objection and said the tribunal was determined to hear the evidence, adding, however, "Now, although it may seem to be an extraordinary thing that an ambassador, guilty of crimes against international law, should be beyond the reach of the long arm of international law, nevertheless, you will be able to argue that at the conclusion of the case."

The evidence against Oshima was devastating. Among other things, he had handled Japan's agitprop and terrorist operations in Europe. The evidence of this was found in the private papers of Heinrich Himmler, the arch-murderer of the Nazi regime who had operated the concentration camps, and in Oshima's voluble admissions during his pretrial interrogations at Sugamo. According to the Himmler evidence, Oshima had purchased a "safe house" at Falkensee, Germany, and trained White Russian assassins there for missions within the Soviet Union in collaboration with the Abwehr, the German counterintelligence organization. Oshima boasted to Himmler that he had sent "ten Russians with bombs across the Caucasian frontier . . . with orders to kill Stalin." Other agents had also been dispatched, but they "had been shot at the frontier." Oshima also sent balloons from German-occupied Poland into Russia, carrying pamphlets, "when the wind was favorable." In addition, he clandestinely operated a motorboat out of a Romanian Black Sea port, using it to ship propaganda leaflets into the Soviet Crimea. Oshima also planted an agent in Afghanistan, but the agent was expelled because "he was suspected of wanting to overthrow the Afghan government." This prompted Himmler to tell him, "I have a police officer there, and the two could work together very well once [you] again had a man there."

These disclosures tantalized the tribunal, but the prosecution never followed up. Perhaps there was no need; there certainly was no time. The IMTFE was trying to write a living and documentary history of 1928–45 in 50,000 pages, and the evidence barely skimmed the political and military complexities of that tumultous period.

18

Trouble Among the Allies

As the trial rattled along, it was becoming increasingly apparent that the prosecution's case was often unevenly presented. The Allied case was being compressed, sometimes unintelligibly, to save time, and it was cluttered with obscure names, dates, and places. The testimony of a Chinese witness, Colonel Kiang Chen-ying, is a fair example of this compression. He testified that Japanese atrocities in China had been so numerous that he could recite only "a few remarkable instances." In its entirety, here is one instance:

"Commander Mizuno, chief intelligence officer Kagawa, assistant intelligence officer Ebi of the 38th Battalion of the 4204 Japanese Army Unit, massacred 128 innocent women and children by swords or by burying them alive, on the 24th day of the third month, Chinese lunar calendar, at 1945, at Chuan Tweng-tseng village, 4th District, Chiao Ho Hsien, Hopei province. This was covered by a report of the local government of Chiao Ho Hsien which includes a list of the victims."

This single paragraph cried out for amplification. Yet it was only one slaughter among literally *thousands* committed by the Japanese, and nobody had the time to go into it. The banality of evil is such that atrocities, after a while, all sound alike. This difficulty was compounded at Tokyo by the prosecution's penchant for calling witnesses out of turn, thereby losing whatever track the IPS was exploring. Too often the explanation was given that "the evidence will be connected up later"—that could mean in hours, days, weeks, or months, if at all.

In fairness to the prosecution, it should be observed that the decision was not of its making. The logistics of the trial were incredibly complex. Witnesses were flown to Tokyo from Singapore, Australia, China, the United States, and elsewhere, housed in a Tokyo billet, and told to stand by for their court appearances. But as the legal wrangles at the IMTFE intensified, the witnesses waited almost interminably. The first time an Allied prosecutor introduced witnesses out of order, he told the court that they had been sitting in Tokyo for more than a month and "their own circumstances are such that they cannot remain longer without great embarrassment." For its part, the defense often complained that it was caught unaware and unprepared by these prosecutional maneuvers. Ichiro Kiyose, on behalf of Japanese defense counsel, charged that "one of the causes for the confusion here is that witnesses are introduced out of order." Sir William Webb was enraged. "There has been no confusion," he said angrily. But there was confusion, and almost everyone in the courtroom agreed with Kiyose.

On another occasion the IPS informed the court that it "must deviate from the order of procedure . . . due to the processing of faulty translations," and then summoned several witnesses out of order. Webb asked whether the deviation would affect the logical sequence of the evidence. "It does affect it," the prosecutor acknowledged. As the first witness, a Japanese, entered the courtroom, Webb asked, "Could you present more documents instead of calling this witness? The Indian representative, of course, is not here."

This exchange pinpointed three problems: calling witnesses out of turn, translation problems, and the repeated absence of judges. Judge Pal was indisposed that day.

Both the prosecution and defense, meanwhile, alternately exhibited a strange sense of values. Time was wasted when one prosecutor asked a witness the size of the piece of rail that the Japanese Army claimed had been damaged at Mukden. "How far are you going to carry this?" an irritated Webb asked. "We have no interest in the size of the rail. . . . Give us something more useful!"

The defense provided its own share of misplaced concern. A

classic insight into the value system of the generals in the dock occurred during the Chinese phase. S. Okamoto, the defense counsel for General Muto, expressed dismay that the Japanese press had misquoted the interrogation of Muto relating to the Rape of Nanking. The *Asahi* had reported that Muto said that General Matsui, his co-defendant who was field commander at Nanking, had been reprimanded by his staff. This was inaccurate, Okamoto pointed out. Matsui had reprimanded his officers. "We are not here to correct what appears in the Japanese press," Webb growled. But Okamoto persisted in his desire to clarify the record. Incredible as it seems, Generals Matsui and Muto were more troubled about army protocol than the terrible deeds of their army at Nanking.

Often the court added to the confusion by changing rules in midstream. After lengthy argument and a court ruling that witnesses might testify by affidavit—a decision Webb said the bench rendered with "grave misgivings"—the court later amended the rule and compelled witnesses who spoke English to testify without affidavit. This change led to more argument among the lawyers, wasting time and distracting further from the narrative of events. Frequently, too, Webb and the lawyers on both sides clashed on matters of technical procedure and tied up the court, for example, on whether an attorney should object *before* or *after* a document was admitted into evidence. Webb held out for the latter, prompting the perplexed American defense counsel for Baron Hiranuma, Samuel J. Kleiman, to comment, "This practice is so different from the practice that we have in the United States, I've had difficulty in understanding the ruling."

If lawyers encountered difficulty in following trial procedures, where did that leave press and public? These squabbles over law served to cloud the Tokyo trial and provide the IMTFE's shriller critics with the grounds for a continuous assault on the proceedings. These critics devoted more attention to legal procedure than to evidence.

Purple prose was another problem that disrupted the narrative of the trial. The attorneys frequently forgot that the IMTFE was a trial by judges, not jury, and consequently continued to indulge in overblown language. In opening the China phase, the prosecution referred to the Japanese occupation of that country as a "tale of horror without parallel since the days of Attila the Hun." The bench retreated in horror. "These inflamatory statements . . . only tend to antagonize the tribunal," Webb warned. "We are being treated as a jury, not as eleven sober judges." What witness could be called to testify that the Japanese behaved worse than Attila? he asked sarcastically.

The president of the tribunal, however, did not help matters with his own extravagant style. Early in the trial he claimed that there had been "no more important trial in all history" than the IMTFE. This statement hung around his neck like a dead albatross. His critics guffawed with delight. How about Nuremberg, for openers? Webb obviously regretted his enthusiasm and, as the trial progressed, retreated by referring to the proceedings as "one of the most important trials in history."

The Western press, particularly the American, soon lost interest in the trial. As Russell Brines, the chief of the Tokyo bureau of the Associated Press, later wrote, "Something went wrong." He believed that the theme of the trial had been lost in the prolonged legal battles and that the quarrels among the lawyers were often more vigorous than the testimony. In the *Texas Law Review* Frederick Mignone, the young assistant prosecutor from Connecticut, complained that American press coverage was "skimpy and begrudging," and added, "Perhaps, the distance barrier is responsible for the lack of interest in this important unveiling of criminality in the Far East."

But these explanations did not completely explain the collapse of interest in the IMTFE as the trial wore on, although it should be noted that even in the United States the tribunal passed through bullish and bearish periods of news coverage, not unlike the UN today. Yet to gauge global, especially Asian, interest in the IMTFE by what the U.S. press printed was foolishness, for the U.S. press was and is generally provincial. The Tokyo trial received good play in China, the Philippines and, of course, Japan, among other places. Even the trial's critics conceded the point. "Japanese newspapers covered the trial well, considering newsprint shortages," The AP's Brines acknowledged, "and periodically summed up the evidence with editorial pleas that this 'national shame' should not be repeated. But the press could report only what went on in the courtroom. So its story followed the long, disjointed, unclear outlines of the conspiracy, wading through masses of testimony that perhaps carried great legal weight but had little emotional appeal." And A. Frederick Mignone observed that "in Japan and in the Orient in general, the trial is one of the most important phases of the occupation. It has received wide coverage in the Japanese press and revealed for the first time to millions of Japanese the scheming, duplicity, and insatiable desire for power of her entrenched militaristic leaders, writing a much-needed history of events which otherwise would not have been written.''

Another problem that permeated the IMTFE from the start was the questionable credibility of several of the powers represented on the bench and in the prosecution. In the aftermath of the Axis phase of the trial, this situation became more evident, notably with the introduction of the Dutch, French, and Soviet cases against the Japanese.

Nobody could fault the Dutch and French for bringing against the defendants charges of crimes against humanity and conventional war crimes. But these charges were held back for later. The initial Dutch and French (and Soviet) cases dealt with crimes of aggression—and the charges had a hollow ring. The Dutch and French accused Japan of invading and occupying the East Indies and Indochina, respectively, and of exploiting them economically—precisely what the Indonesians and Vietnamese accused their former colonial overlords of having done. With Japan's surrender, Indonesia on August 17 and Vietnam on September 2, 1945, had proclaimed independence. As the Dutch and French phases of the Allied case at the IMTFE opened, both countries were engaged in colonial wars aimed at restoring their prewar Southeast Asian empires. The Dutch colonial war in Indonesia lasted until 1949, the year after the IMTFE adjourned; the French war in Vietnam went on until 1954, when Vietnam was divided into two independent states, one Communist and the other non-Communist. No matter how strong the Dutch and French cases against Japan—and their cases were strong—it was difficult for the two European nations to shed their colonial and imperialist image.

The multilingual Dutch presented their case in English. But the French embroiled the IMTFE in three days of wrangling over a language crisis that was really a diplomatic crisis reflecting France's loss of prestige and power in postwar East Asia.

The IBM simultaneous-translation equipment at Ichigaya operated on three channels—English, Japanese, and Russian. Under the charter, however, English and Japanese were the tribunal's only working languages. Since the Russian judge, General Zarayanov, spoke neither English nor Japanese, as a courtesy, he and his private interpreter were given the third, otherwise idle channel. There was no secret to this arrangement; every correspondent who snapped on headphones could pick up the dialogue in English, Japanese, or Russian. But for some inexplicable reason this arrangement was not generally known. On July 16, 1946, after attending the China phase, Lieutenant General Chu Shih-ming, the chief of the Chinese mission to Japan, "discovered" the third or Russian channel and fired off a letter to the Chinese judge, Mei Ju-ao, in which he complained that if there was going to be a third language, "it seems to me that Chinese certainly should be included."

Mei relayed the protest to Webb, who explained, in a memorandum dated July 23, that "Russian is really not a third language at the trial." He also explained the Soviet judge's need for a private channel. The Chinese were placated.

In September, as the French prosecutors prepared their case, the French judge learned of the Russian arrangement, probably through the Chinese protest, and on September 6 wrote Webb a sharp note. Judge Bernard stated that the French government considered the Russian arrangement "prejudicial to the French Delegation." Webb repeated to Bernard the same explanation he had given the Chinese. But, unlike Judge Mei, the French judge pressed the issue and got a majority of the judges to agree to permit the French phase to be conducted in French; as a practical matter, the documentation, however, would continue to be read in English. On September 28, two days before the French opened their case, Canada's Justice McDougall warned Webb that while Canada did not object to the French speaking French as "an act of courtesy," he thought it might violate the charter, and "if the defense object, this question will have to be further considered." Earlier, in a note to Webb, Bernard had observed that the "text of the Charter no way forbids the use of the French language."

Robert Oneto opened the French case, and the defense immediately objected to the use of French. Ichiro Kiyose contended that as long as English and Japanese were used, it was relatively easy for the bilingual members of the defense to monitor the translations for accuracy and completeness. But the addition of a third language constituted a "very great danger" that they would no longer be able to do so; in addition it would "unduly prolong the proceedings." The bench overruled the objection, and Oneto took over the lectern. Oneto could read and write English well, but his accent left much to be desired. It was not long before the interpreters' booth and court reporter asked Oneto to speak only French when handling documents because his "English is not understandable." A long, pointless argument ensued; the problem was that a Japanese document translated into English would now have to be translated into French and then back to English. Webb grew testy and cut off the debate with the announcement "The court insists on the use of English throughout."

Joseph Keenan, the binder who had held the IPS together, was aghast and pleaded with the bench to reconsider its decision and "in a matter of this importance" announce the decision of each member of the tribunal individually. Webb conferred with his colleagues and agreed to hear further arguments by Keenan. But before Keenan could speak, Oneto grabbed the lectern and began to shout volubly and excitedly in French. Webb was dumbstruck. "He is still speaking French," the president croaked. "That is almost contempt." Oneto grew more excited in his native tongue, and Webb abruptly rose from his seat, announced, "The court will adjourn," and led the judges in a walkout. The court was in an uproar as Oneto, gesticulating wildly, continued shouting in French. The official trial transcript does not contain Oneto's remarks since, at that point, the bench had ruled against the continued use of French.

During the trial I normally sat next to Maurice Chanteloupe, the Agence France-Presse correspondent, who was later taken prisoner by the Communists during the Korean War. From Chanteloupe I got a copy of Oneto's remarks, as follows: "I represent the great country of France. I demand the right to be heard. If I am not heard, I shall withdraw from the case."

When the court reconvened ten minutes later, Webb announced that Oneto's behavior "appears to constitute contempt of court," and concluded, "He may have a satisfactory explanation or he may be prepared to apologize. Failing in one or the other," Webb went on, "he will be liable to proceedings for contempt of court." Since it was late afternoon, the court adjourned and gave Oneto a night to sleep on the incident.

The following morning, October 2, before the court reconvened, Webb found a letter on his desk from his French colleague, Judge Bernard, who wrote, "I believe that it is my duty to retire from the bench until the final solution of the incident." Webb may have sensed that he was losing control of the court.

He and his colleagues rushed to Bernard's chambers and pleaded with him to remain on the bench in the interests of Allied harmony and juridical authority. Bernard agreed.

Before Oneto presented his defense in the tense courtroom that sunlit morning—with the accused in the dock looking on as fascinated spectators—Webb made it clear that the court was dealing not with France but with an individual who represented that nation. "If a British or American or Australian or Netherlands prosecutor behaved before this court as did Mr. Oneto, he would be dealt with in exactly the same way," Webb observed. "No member of this tribunal entertains any national prejudice. . . . Now," Webb said, "we would like to hear Mr. Oneto in English or French in explanation of his position."

Oneto stuck to French. He attributed the flare-up to "confusion"—the same word Ichiro Kiyose had used earlier to describe the proceedings—and he expressed "regret that a misunderstanding arose." Oneto attributed the incident to the court's hybrid nature, observing that Anglo-Saxon and French courtroom procedure are "very different." Graciously, he concluded, "I can assure the court of my complete cooperation at all times."

Oneto's apology was accepted, and he proceeded with the case in French. This time, though, Frank Tavenner and Solis Horwitz, two assistant American prosecutors, took turns reading in English the documents on which France based her accusations against the defendants.

To the amazement of some observers, Oneto introduced the 1941 pact between Vichy and Tokyo as an example of Japanese pressure on the French in Indochina. Under its terms, both parties "promised to cooperate militarily for the joint defense of French Indo-China." The Japanese signatories were the premier and the war, navy, and foreign ministers, in that order. Japanese troops subsequently poured into Indochina, and a secret German diplomatic message to Berlin made it clear that even the Nazis considered it an "invasion of Indo-China that has all the signs of an occupation calculated to last for a long period of time." The Japanese Army's attitude, while arrogant, was correct, except for the mistreatment of Vietnamese laborers who were employed to build Japanese military bases and were regularly and brutally beaten in the process.

The evidence showed that the French had sat out the war in Indochina in an uneasy collaboration with the Japanese. Why the

French themselves would want to put this sordid business in the record was unfathomable. Worse, the defense had a field day with French witnesses during cross-examinations in trying to pin down whether the witness was a Vichyite or member of the Free French movement. For example, the Japanese defense tied into knots Captain Ferdinand Gabrillagues, an officer who had been sent to Indochina after the Japanese occupation of Indochina. He had been put in the witness box to testify about atrocities committed by the Japanese troops in Indochina. The defense counsel asked Gabrillagues in whose army he had served during the war.

Q: Was that under the Vichy government or was that in the Resistance Army?

A: In the French Army in Africa.

Q: Was that as a member of the Resistance Group or as a member of the forces of the Vichy government?

A: It was as a French citizen who was still under military obligations.

WEBB: It is suggested to me that if you use "Free French" instead of "Resistance," you might get more satisfactory answers.

Q: Were you a member of the Free French?

A: Since February 1, 1943, I belonged to the French army of Africa, the only army which was in Africa.

Q: Were you under General Le Clerc?

A: I did not say that I was in Africa. I was in West Africa—in French West Africa.

Q: I didn't ask you that. Were you under General Le Clerc?

A: General Le Clerc was not in the West of Africa.

Q: Were you under him?

A: Absolutely not.

Q: Then were you under some general of the Vichy government?

A: I do not think so.

Q: Do you seriously want this tribunal to understand
        from your testimony that you were fighting for France
        but you didn't know which army you were in?

A: I was only thinking of fighting for France.

In exasperation, Webb cut off the cross-examination with the observation that whether Gabrillagues was Vichyite or Free French was "trifling."*

By the beginning of 1945, both the Japanese and the French expected an American invasion of Indochina. Vichy tottered as the Allied armies raced into Germany. The Japanese suspected—correctly—that the French in Indochina would greet the Americans with open arms, and on March 9, 1945, Tokyo served an ultimatum on the French to surrender their weapons. The French resisted valiantly and were cut down. Meanwhile, according to Robert Oneto's evidence, "the activities of the Vietnamese in North Indo-China became more and more vigorous . . . as the Vietnamese sought to dispel Japanese forces in order to accomplish full independence for their people." Oneto even quoted from a French document that described the Vietnamese desire for sovereignty as "a mistaken idea of independence and race-consciousness." This from the prosecutor of a nation that had just been liberated from a foreign invader.

In the light of postwar Vietnamese history these IMTFE documents strike a poignant note. Here were the French and Vietnamese dying side by side in a vest-pocket war against the Japanese while awaiting an American army of liberation. A prompt acknowledgment by the French of Vietnam's right to independence at this crossroad in history might have obviated all the agonies in Vietnam to this day.

The Soviet phase of the prosecution's case, which followed the French, was just as bad. Actually, it damaged the Russians more than it hurt the defendants.

As noted earlier, the Soviet role at the tribunal had been controversial from the first. Not only was the Soviet Union a police state but also, like Japan, it had been expelled from the League

---

*Junji Kinoshita, a well-known Japanese playwright, used this sequence in his *Kami to hito to no aida (Between God and Man)*, a satirical play about the trial, first produced in 1970.

of Nations for waging aggressive war (in Russia's case against Finland). Like Japan, the Soviet Union had entered into a pact with Hitler (for the division of Poland). Worse, the periodic border wars in the thirties between Russia and Japan formed the basis of the Soviet case. But these wars had been waged on Chinese territory. Moscow and Tokyo had fought acquisitively over Manchuria and Mongolia, neither of which was Russian nor Japanese.

The Soviet team at Tokyo was capable. S. A. Golunsky, a minister of state with an excellent command of English, was the Soviet associate prosecutor. His supporting cast included Major General A. N. Vasiliev, the Moscow district attorney; Major General V. S. Tadevosyan, the assistant Soviet attorney general; Colonel S. J. Rosenbilt, the chief assistant to the Red Army's judge advocate general; and Colonel A. I. Ivanov, the chief of the Red Army's department of investigation. As in the French affair, a language dispute erupted immediately when the Russians requested the court's permission to conduct their phase in Russian. Again the defense objected strongly. Owen Cunningham, the American defense counsel for Ambassador Oshima, charged that the French incident had disrupted, delayed, and prolonged the trial and that the use of yet another language "involved political considerations."

Webb bristled. "That language is offensive, Mr. Cunningham," the president said aggressively. "You cannot address the court in those terms and expect to be immune from action by the court."

Cunningham flushed. "If this statement is offensive to the tribunal, and I had no intention of it being so," he replied, "I withdraw the statement."

The testy courtroom atmosphere could not be attributed to a heat wave; this was autumn. It could be traced, however, to a malaise that had overcome the proceedings, a feeling that there was no light at the end of the tunnel, and that the trial was drifting further and further afield. Days were being consumed in wrangles that had nothing to do with war criminality.

Ichiro Kiyose also objected. "We object to the use of the Russian language for the same reason for which we objected to the use of the French language before," he said. He also skillfully raised the issue of "political considerations" after Joseph Keenan, in the course of his argument in favor of Russian, disclosed that before the trial started SCAP had reached an agreement with the Soviets to use Russian in their phase of the case. Webb, taken aback, insisted that the dispute be settled only on the basis of the charter. Kiyose slipped into the opening and subtly raised the question of a fair trial. "I earnestly hope that in a court no considerations will be given to promises between governments of a political nature, and that the only consideration given will be to the interests of justice and a fair trial," he said triumphantly. Nonetheless, the bench ruled that the Soviet Union would be permitted to conduct its case in Russian. The tribunal's deference to French and Russian ruffled the Chinese; they had not conducted their phase of the case in Chinese.

Golunsky launched the Russian phase with an opening statement that ran sixty-five pages, longer than Keenan's opening statement for all the Allies. A good part of it dealt with the Russo-Japanese War of 1905, which predated the Hague Conventions of 1907, certain Geneva accords, and the Kellogg-Briand Pact—the tripartite legal plinth on which the Allied case was built. The defense complained bitterly that the purpose of an opening statement is to provide a brief, concise summary of what will be proven. The Soviet opening statement by contrast, was argumentative and inflammatory. Webb, however, fobbed off these objections by restating the theme that the bench was not a jury and that "we can be trusted to hear things that might prejudice a jury but which would not influence us."

As it turned out, there was a good deal in the Soviet case that was unlikely to influence anyone. If the French phase caused Allied discomfort, the Soviet phase was an embarrassment. The Russians based their case in large part on affidavits of witnesses who were either dead, were in custody in Moscow, or were "too ill" to travel to Tokyo to submit to cross-examination. These "affidavits" were used as evidence to support Soviet charges that Japan initiated border wars against Russia in Mongolia and Manchuria.

The first affidavit, that of Grigori Mikhailovich Semyonov, a Russian who had collaborated with the Japanese, jarred the courtroom. Semyonov had been interrogated in the Soviet Union on April 16, 1946, thirteen days before the IMTFE opened. His affidavit was filled with conclusions and opinions, and he was not in court when the affidavit was read. Ben Bruce Blakeney, the American defense counsel for General Umezu, shocked the bench with the disclosure that Semyonov had been executed by the Russians "within the last three weeks," a revelation that Golunsky waved aside with the observation "In what way the fact that the man had been hanged can attack his credibility is for the tribunal to object, but I don't think that it can be an obstacle to the admission of this affidavit."

The affidavit was admitted but, with the exception of Judge Zarayanov, the bench appeared visibly unnerved. "Throughout this trial we have made quite a feature of the right to interrogate a deponent who is not called here, but that right has been destroyed by the country offering the evidence," Webb said solemnly. "Upon the merits of that country's action I express no opinion." And he added, "As an Australian judge, I may not think the [affidavit] has any value, but my views do not prevail here. There are eleven nations, and they may have different views, or some of them may have different views."

When the Soviets introduced the affidavit of Lieutenant General Kyoji Tominaga, who had been captured in Manchuria at the war's end, Tominaga was not in the courtroom either. "We wished to bring witness Tominaga to be examined before the tribunal in Tokyo because his testimony is very important," Colonel Ivanov explained. "But due to the illness of the witness we are bereft of this opportunity."

It quickly developed that the tribunal was also bereft of the opportunity of examining Lieutenant General Keisaku Murakami in the witness box. "I present a certificate of the illness of Murakami, in connection with which he could not be brought here before this tribunal," Ivanov said.

Among the questions in the affidavit put to Murakami was "Whom do you consider to be the most important war criminal?" The defense attorneys leaped to their feet. "In the first place," William Logan, Marquis Kido's attorney, said angrily, "this witness is not qualified as either a lawyer or a judge or a student of international law; and, in the second place, there is no evidence, at least there has been no conclusion up to the present time, that there were or are any war criminals. That is a fact to be determined by the tribunal."

The defense won this one. "The objections," Webb announced, "in the opinion of a majority of the tribunal, are well taken and are sustained."

The Soviet prosecutor then introduced the affidavit of Konstantin Vladimirovich Rodzaevsky, the leader of the Russian Fascist Union, "to prove that Japan was preparing for war against the U.S.S.R." As a point of information, the defense inquired "whether he is presently alive or dead and whether he will be produced for cross-examination." When S. A. Golunsky told the court that "Rodzaevsky was sentenced to death," Blakeney exploded. "We wish to enter our strong protest to the second example of a deliberate removal of a witness whose testimony was known to be material here," the American defense counsel said. "As these instances multiply, we submit that the tribunal must find that the reception of this testimony is inconsistent with the barest minimum of a fair trial."

Now it was the Russians' turn to become inflamed. Golunsky objected heatedly to Blakeney's description of the act of Soviet justice as a "deliberate removal of a witness." Webb lowered the thermostat by suggesting that Blakeney's remarks had been misunderstood and that he merely meant Rodzaevsky's removal as a witness by a judicial process.

And so it went. On one occasion, when the affidavit of a Japanese diplomat detained in the Soviet Union was presented to the court and the defense asked sarcastically whether the imprisoned witness was "going to be tried as a war criminal, or, was being tried as a war criminal, or, that he had been tried already as a war criminal," Golunsky told the court, "I cannot tell at this moment." As it turned out later in the trial, the Russian prosecution section was as much in the dark about the status and whereabouts of its witnesses as anyone else in the courtroom.

There was an almost audible sigh of relief on October 21, 1946, when Golunsky announced, "This concludes, Your Honor, the presentation of this phase of the trial." There was also an air of disbelief in the courtroom. The Russians had confounded almost everyone. Here was their big opportunity to indict the emperor or the *zaibatsu* in open court as they did almost daily in their propaganda broadsides. But they passed.

19

Judgment at Nuremberg

The French and Soviet antics at the IMTFE in September and October 1946 were mercifully obscured by news from Nuremberg. On October 1, just about eleven months after the trial of Nazi war criminals had begun there, the tribunal returned a verdict of guilty in the trial of major Nazis, condemning twelve to the gallows, sentencing seven to imprisonment for terms ranging from ten years to life, and acquitting three. The prosecution had sought the death penalty for all defendants.

In Tokyo the accused appeared to receive the news impassively. They did not ask for whom the bell tolled. Despite the efforts of Japanese and Allied correspondents to elicit their views through defense attorneys, every one of the defendants declined public comment. It is likely they did so on advice of counsel; however, according to several defense attorneys, the defendants were stirred by the verdict. The three acquittals at Nuremberg gave them grounds for hope.

Japan's press played the judgment at Nuremberg on the front page, and the editorial tone was set by the *Mainichi* on October 4. "As in the case of the Tokyo trial, the penalties decided upon are a judgment brought by civilization. . . . The world must profit in every way from the lessons of the Nuremberg trial. Especially we, the Japanese, have the obligation to go out of our way to learn much from these lessons."

The Nuremberg judgment was, as one British correspondent observed, "a remarkable piece of literature." It was, of course, revolutionary. For the first time in history a nation's political and military leaders were held criminally responsible for waging aggressive war. The theme of the judgment's 50,000 tightly drawn words was that aggressive war is "the supreme international crime."

The chief criticism of Nuremberg (and later of Tokyo) was that even if the tribunals were correct that aggressive war was unlawful, it was not a crime in the accepted sense of the word, since there were no laws defining the crime, providing penalties, or establishing courts to try such crimes. In legal parlance the accused were tried *ex post facto*—after the fact. But the Nuremberg judgment held that it was just to punish a person for doing what he must know was wrong. When the defendants invaded peaceful countries, broke international treaties, and violated the Hague and Geneva Conventions on the customs of war, they had known they were doing wrong. The judgment observed that a man who burns a baby alive when it is not a crime has not been unjustly treated if afterward such action is made criminal and he is punished. He must have know that he was doing wrong and should not feel aggrieved if his wrongdoing is later made punishable. By contrast, a man who does something he cannot know is likely to be a breach of the law—for example, drinking beer after 10 P.M.—has been unjustly treated if he finds that his act has later been made a crime. At the time he drank the beer the act appeared innocent.

In essence, Nuremberg confirmed the existence in human affairs of natural law, mankind's innate sense of right and wrong. In the last analysis the Nuremberg and Tokyo trials derived their legal basis from the existence, before recorded history, of natural law.

Beyond that, as the British periodical *Round Table* pointed out in a review of the Nuremberg trial, "The most remarkable feature of the case was the fact that the defendants cooperated a hundred percent in making the trial a success." The same could be said of Tokyo. If any of the Japanese entertained other thoughts, they were dashed by the behavior of their counterparts at Nuremberg, at least up until the night of the executions there. For the Japanese accused who had turned their backs on *hara kiri,* there was a deep psychological necessity to match the behavior of their Nazi counterparts and thus assure an orderly completion of the Tokyo trial.

One participant at the IMTFE attended both the beginning and the end at Nuremberg—Owen Cunningham, Ambassador Oshima's American defense counsel. On September 7, 1946, he conducted a three-hour interview with Hitler's foreign minister, Joachim von Ribbentrop, in English, "in which he gave me answers to questions which were prepared in advance in cooperation with my Japanese co-counsel," Cunningham said later. The Allies put one condition on the interview: Cunningham was not to make it public until after Ribbentrop was sentenced. When Oshima later took the stand at Tokyo in his own defense, Cunningham produced the Ribbentrop interview.

Nuremberg had impressed Cunningham. "They have done things in a much bigger way in some respects than here," he told his colleagues in a fourteen-page typescript report. He observed that each of the four judges there had a microphone in front of him and participated directly in the trial. "It is difficult to try a case before judges who you have never even heard utter a word," Cunningham said of Tokyo. "It's like carrying on a one-sided conversation." Of course, there were eleven judges at Ichigaya.

Cunningham had returned to Tokyo in a spirit of optimism. "It is my thought that the defendants in the Tokyo trial have a much better chance of acquittal than the Germans for four reasons." He enumerated them as follows: "(1) We have nothing comparable to the Jewish question here; (2) we had no continuing government or set of officials making the permanent policy; (3) . . . the inability of Chiang Kai-shek to make peace now that the Japanese influence is out of the picture indicates that the blame for the former situation must at least be shared; (4) the events since the surrender have shown that at least some of the fears of the Japanese were well-founded." The latter remark was a veiled reference to the postwar Communist seizure of Manchuria.

The Cunningham mission to Germany had been monitored by U.S. intelligence. By error, the defense at Ichigaya received copies of a message from the War Department in Washington to the prosecution section. The defense boiled. The message read: "Owen Cunningham, defense counsel, en route to Nuremberg informed Col. Hornaday the defense staff is expected to establish the defense Japan was forced into the attack on Pearl Harbor by America's diplomatic moves and economic sanctions. This is the same type of political defense the Germans tried at Nuremberg and the tribunal consistently refused to admit on the objections of the prosecution. Thought you might like to be forewarned," the message concluded, "if you have not previously learned of defense intentions."

The American defense attorneys rightly complained to American correspondents that such action by the War Department was in "bad taste" and did not inspire confidence in the men the department hired to do a fair and earnest job of defending the accused. The defense was right.

The Nuremberg judgment was read ravenously at Tokyo. An indication of how deeply the IMTFE was influenced by the trial in Germany appeared in open court on November 1, when the prosecution turned to Japan's preparations for the Pacific War and the events leading up to Pearl Harbor. Captain Robinson of the U.S. Navy handled the opening statement and was citing a 1934 document when Webb interrupted him. "Captain Robinson," Webb said thoughtfully, "we have received copies of the Nuremberg judgment. We have just received them, and the court there stresses the point that evidence of a conspiracy should not go too far back; it should be comparatively recent. . . . When you consider the Nuremberg judgment you may decide to cut down some of the material you intend to put before the court." Clearly, if Nuremberg started a revolution in international law, Tokyo would consolidate it.

Two hours before the condemned Nazi war criminals were to be hanged on October 16, an American military guard outside Göring's cell saw the *Reichsmarschall,* who scheduled to lead the procession to the gallows, writhe on his cot, his face contorted. Göring was dead by the time the prison physician reached him; he had taken potassium cyanide. After a brief delay the hangings were carried out with Ribbentrop, Oshima's intimate associate in plotting global war, replacing Göring at the head of the procession. Later the bodies of Göring and his collaborators in murder and mayhem were cremated and the ashes thrown to the wind to preclude the possibility of future Nazi piligrimages to their burial place.

Görings's suicide sent shock waves through the whole world. R. W. Cooper, the Canadian-born correspondent at Nuremberg of the London *Times,* captured the feeling of the day in the observation that Hitler's deputy "for a day made sport of Nuremberg, above all of American security and its year of pin-pricks." This message was not lost on the authorities in Tokyo. Orders soon came down from SCAP. None of the accused at the IMTFE would be afforded the opportunity to make sport of the Tokyo tribunal or American security. For the first time in months my jeep was stopped at Ichigaya's gates, and I had to produce my SCAP press-accreditation card to gain entry. I also had to show credentials each time I entered the courtroom, even though I was known personally to the MPs. But these were minor inconveniences compared to what the accused went through.

At Sugamo the dental fillings of all the defendants were X-rayed for secretly implanted vials of poison. Almost daily, at different hours, the cells were searched while each defendant stood naked with his face to the wall. The crowning humiliation was the order that the accused had to strip and step into different clothes before they left for court and on their return to the prison. Inmates at Sugamo who were subpoenaed to testify at the trial were subjected to the same personal indignity. General Itagaki told a fellow inmate, "They made me feel so embarrassed by even peeping into my anus." Itagaki and the other defendants realized that this new regimen stemmed from the Göring incident. The accused in Tokyo, having failed to commit *hara kiri* at the time of Japan's surrender, now despised Göring not only for the security mess but for his "cowardly" act in taking his own life. "We are determined not to do such a cowardly thing as to sneak into the cells bits of glass with which to commit suicide behind the guards' back," the unindicted inmate Yoshio Kodama wrote in *Sugamo Diary*. "But this feeling is not understood by the other party [the Americans]."

A roguish fellow who never lost his sense of humor while imprisoned, Kodama wrote amusingly of the rectal search after each day at court. "It was a grand sight," he said lightly, "if you want to call it that. Prisoners returning from the trials would form in a line with a row of MPs standing behind them. The prisoners are ordered to stoop down on all fours—stark naked, of course. The MPs would then put their hands on the buttocks of the prisoners and peer into each anus. If anyone should have released any gas by accident, it would have been a real comedy."

The defense protested the new security precautions. "While we have no desire whatsoever to interfere or make any recommendations respecting security measures," William Logan said in a November 12 press statement, "we do wish to call the tribunal's attention to the fact that part of the measures appear to us to be unreasonable and closely connected with a fair trial to the accused."

On Valentine's Day, 1947, the seven news agency correspondents covering the trial daily—British, Chinese, French, Russian, and three Americans, including me—were invited to visit Sugamo, the first tour of the prison by outsiders since the start of the occupation. The tightened security measures in the aftermath of Göring's suicide proved to be warranted, Kodama's views notwithstanding. That morning at 12:45 A.M., one of the Class C prisoners, on trial at Yokohama for torturing Allied POWs, cut an artery in his left arm with a rusty nail and two copper-clad pen points. He was discovered by a guard wriggling under his blanket; the guard pulled back the blanket and found blood on the sheet. The prisoner was rushed to the hospital, where he later recovered. We were shown the cell, the prisoner's mattress, and the dried blood stains. "We are continually fighting the laws of probability," the prison commander, Colonel Francis W. Carey, said as we walked down a corridor, which was painted in blue, green, and cream. "The challenge is to beat probability, and it is all against us." The sprawling prison, covering four acres, held 1,073 indicted and unindicted inmates and 365 guards. In the "museum" Carey showed us the objects the MPs had recovered from guilt-ridden inmates (guilty over either their failure to commit *hara kiri* at the time of surrender or their criminal behavior during the war)—bits of glass, wires, scissors, ropes, nails, needles, pieces of broken pottery. Of greater interest were a piece of paper impregnated with potassium cyanide sewn into the lining of a prisoner's kimono and cyanide crystals wrapped in paper in the lining of a shoe. Our biggest surprise was the contraband taken from the now-familiar faces in the dock. A *haramaki,* a six-foot sash used by many Japanese soldiers as an athletic supporter, had been found on Hideki Tojo, and confiscated. "He could have hanged himself with that," a guard said. A piece of steel wire, whetted on a wall, had been taken from General Itagaki's cell. A pair of false-bottom shoes of Italian design had been found on Toshio Shiratori, the former ambassador to Italy. Several months earlier a pair of chopsticks shaved into stilettos had been removed from the cell of Admiral Nagano, one of the most nondescript individuals in the dock, the man who had approved the day, hour, and minute for the attack on Pearl Harbor.

The highlight of our visit was viewing the environment in which the accused led their lives outside of the courtroom. The MPs in the cell block were unarmed and were locked into the tier with the defendants. Each defendant was confined to a single cell, the door of which had been removed—"They get more heat that way," a guard explained, "and we can get at them quicker if they try something." A guard sat posted in front of each cell twenty-four hours a day; a naked electric bulb burned in each cell day and night.

I was in my early twenties when I walked softly and slowly by the doorless cells of the major Japanese war criminals. My memory of that walk is imperishable. Here, before my own eyes and within little more than an arm's reach, were characters out of history books. As chess pieces they had once been the queen, knights, rooks, and bishops of Kipling's great game. In exercising their power they had left no evil undone. Now they were reduced to pitiful pawns. The bushy-browed Itagaki was writing and did not look up. The sallow, unshaven Sato was reading. Oka, the admiral, played solitaire. Hoshino was lying down, a U.S. Army blanket thrown across him; Suzuki and Kimura were asleep on their *tatami* mats. The crutch of the one-legged Shigemitsu leaned against the wall of his cell. Shiratori smoked one of his daily allotment of five cigarettes. The sly, diminutive Kido and the burly Oshima were lost in reveries. Kaya stared blankly back at me. Araki was writing, a brush in his hand and a pink bottle of ink nearby. Tojo, to me, presented the most startling portrait of all. The Tojo I saw that day wore a kimono, and viewing Tojo in a kimono was seeing him for the first time.

When we were about to leave, the commander at Sugamo pointed in the direction of a small, squat building bearing the designation Block 5C. The death house. In the building's inner courtyard, he said matter-of-factly, several new scaffolds had been erected. Yoshio Kodama, the diarist of Sugamo, was wrong. Even if someone had broken wind, there would have been no real comedy.

20

Remember Pearl Harbor

For more than a month, between October 23 and November 27, 1946, the tribunal turned its attention to what Webb called "the most important documents of the trial," regarding the attack on Pearl Harbor. The prosecution's evidence was based on the interrogations of the accused at Sugamo, the Kido diaries, captured enemy documents, the discovery at the Foreign Ministry of top-secret reports of imperial conferences attended by Emperor Hirohito in 1941, and the congressional Pearl Harbor hearings at Washington.

The evidence was bountiful. It knocked into a cocked hat the claims of the hardcore American isolationists that Roosevelt had induced Tokyo to attack so that America could get into the war against Germany.

In fact, there was incontrovertible proof of long-range Japanese preparation, planning, and duplicity. Most of this was news to the Japanese public. For the rest of the world, it was lost in the labyrinth of the trial. The defense bitterly contested the presentation of evidence by former U.S. cabinet secretaries Cordell Hull and Henry Stimson and former ambassador Joseph Grew by affidavit and not in person. The affidavit of the former secretary of war was a case in point. "If further examination of Mr. Stimson is desired by the defense, it could be done on commission in America, or by way of interrogatories," Sir William Webb ruled and, citing Nuremberg, added, "We can see no need for his attendance here; he is a statesman in the highest category, and no such statesmen were called in Germany."

Japan's decision to carry out within a few hours synchronized attacks against the international settlement at Japanese-occupied Shanghai, Kota Bharu in Malaya, Singora in Thailand, Pearl Harbor, Singapore, Guam, and Hong Kong—in that order—on December 7 (Washington time), 1941, was not concocted overnight. If it were not for domestic American political considerations, it is hard to understand why such a torrent of evidence had to be produced to make such an obvious point.

The prosecution went for the jugular at the outset by introducing a series of ten directives dating from January 16, 1941, each marked top secret and bearing the seals of the Japanese war and finance ministers. These directives, apparently based on decisions taken late in 1940, ordered the preparation of plates for the printing of occupation currency for the Philippines, Malaya, Singapore, Hong Kong, and the Netherlands East Indies in lots of 37 million pesos, 45 million guilders, and $45 million. One directive bore the signatures of four defendants, Generals Tojo and Kimura, Admirals Shimada and Oka. The currency was to be used "to defray war expenditures . . . [in the] southern regions." The first delivery of currency went into the vaults of the Bank of Japan, wrapped in burlap and secrecy, in May 1941.

During 1940 and 1941 the Japanese high command also rushed to completion military geographies, health bulletins, and propaganda booklets in preparation for the massive offensive. As early as April 30, 1940—before Hitler overran Europe—the Japanese Army secretly prepared a military geography of Malaya. A year later a pamphlet about New Guinea was printed bearing the descriptive notation in Japanese "Future Treasure of Japan." Japanese-Indonesian language phrase books were printed, and booklets on tropical hygiene were stockpiled. On November 10, 1941, Japanese troops massing for assaults were handed a booklet whose frontispiece displayed a map of south China, French Indochina, Thailand, Burma, Malaya, the Netherlands East Indies, and northwest Australia. "It's length and the nature of the contents are such as to indicate original preparations as a date considerably prior to this," the prosecution observed icily.

Why did Japan attack? "By the Imperial will for the peace of the Orient," the pamphlet explained; ". . . to bring about the happiness of the natives of the South Seas and India." The pamphlet railed against the white race and amusingly explained in twisted logic: "Understanding this war as one between races, we must enforce our just demands on the Europeans—excluding Germans and Italians." Less amusing was the failure to explain why the Chinese resisted "liberation" by Japan. The booklet conceded that "over one million [of our] comrades exposed their bones on the continent," and claimed that the Chinese arms that had "killed these comrades were sold mostly by England and America." But obviously, the Sino-Japanese War was not the yellow race against the white race. In another pamphlet, "Message to Warriors in the South Seas," also issued that November, Japanese troops were urged to "swiftly bring the Holy War to a successful termination, and thereby carry out the sacred Imperial desire."

Perhaps the most explosive evidence of Japan's extensive preparations for war was the diaries of Japanese officers and men killed in the field and randomly retrieved by the Allies. A lieutenant colonel wrote in his diary that he had been mobilized at Hiroshima on September 12, 1941, and within a month "we made preparations for the landing operations which were to accompany the war for Greater East Asia." A Japanese private confided in his diary that between October 12 and November 14 he had "prepared for Malayan operations in the vicinity of Shanghai." Another wrote on November 15, "We have now set out for the field." In a November 26 entry, after leaving Japan aboard a transport, still another Japanese soldier wrote, "Our battle zone will be Guam."

To the astonishment of the Japanese spectators in the gallery, the evidence showed that Japanese commanders often misled their troops into thinking war had been declared *before* December 7. The diary of a soldier at sea contained this notation: "December 4 . . . At 0930 we proceeded southeast to 'X.' We received an order announcing the declaration of war." Another wrote, "December 4 . . . Japan and America at war! Men have no greater love than this. Convoy to sail 0901! Now, prosper, fatherland!"

The evidence showed that in preparation for these troop movements, the Japanese over a span of years had prepared forward supply bases among the mandated islands in the southwest Pacific that she had acquired from Germany after World War I on condition that they would not be fortified. Depositions by dozens of Micronesians were introduced to prove that Japan had violated this condition for administration of the islands even after pledging again as late as 1936, under the terms of the London Naval Treaty that year, not to fortify the mandated isles. In 1939, a Micronesian chief testified, the Japanese placed ten-inch guns on Saipan and rounded up men and young boys for "forced labor." Gasoline tanks were buried on Yap. Caves for storing supplies and as fortified strong points were dug at Truk. In 1940 camouflaged hangars, warehouses, ammunition dumps, and barracks were built throughout the islands, which soon became naval bases. This was a time when the American peace movement, led by isolationists, pacifists, Axis sympathizers, and plain Roosevelt-haters, was reaching a crescendo. The United States was sleepwalking into the future.

Politically, the most fascinating disclosure was the depth of opposition to widening the war among Japan's civilian and naval leaders, providing new insight into the Tokyo government's subservience to the generals in the dock. During this phase of the case the man who personified the army mentality, Hideki Tojo, busily took notes. Even then he did not realize how poor a strategist he had been and how badly he had misled Japan. To this day, his strategy of attacking America and Britain while bogged down in a massive war in China defies rational analysis.

An entry from the Kido diaries on July 31, 1941, disclosed that Fleet Admiral Nagano had told the emperor that he and his predecessor as chief of the navy general staff, Prince Fushimi, believed that "we should try to avert [an American] war as much as possible." Nagano assailed the Axis alliance with Germany because it made for bad relations with the United States and he warned Hirohito that if Tokyo went to war against America, Japan would barely have a one-and-a-half-year supply of oil to wage the war. When Hirohito asked if Japan could beat the Anglo-Americans as they had beaten Russia in 1905, Nagano replied courageously, "It is doubtful whether or not we would ever win, to say nothing of as great a victory as in the Russo-Japanese war." A diary entry in August revealed that Premier Konoye also visited the emperor with similar views, describing a war with the United States as "hopeless." For his part, Hirohito was also alarmed, and as late as November 26, with the die cast, he convened an extraordinary conference of senior statesmen for "broader and more complete discussions on the matter." By now it was useless; the army had pulled down Konoye's third cabinet, and Hideki Tojo had emerged as premier and war minister. An October 12 entry in the Kido diaries put the responsibility for the war in Japan's—not Roosevelt's—hands. "Now this country is standing at the crossroads, having two ways to choose," the emperor's closest adviser quoted the navy as telling him in secret. "One is restoration of friendly relations by diplomatic negotiations; the other, a declaration of war on the U.S." The choice was Japan's.

At this juncture the IPS tendered evidence from the grave. The prosecution introduced the last testament Prince Konoye had written before swallowing cyanide. The Hamlet of Japanese politics dropped his indecision and subtlety, flatly characterizing the army in this period as "boisterous"—in effect, as other premiers before him in the thirties had discovered, beyond control. The testament also disclosed that Admiral Oka, the former chief of the naval affairs bureau now sitting immobile in the dock, had confided to him, "The brains of the navy don't want a Japanese-American war."

In a final desperate attempt to check the army, Konoye brought his war and navy ministers together in the same room alone with him in the hope that, by going two on one, he and the navy could bring the army to its senses. But the war minister at this stage was Hideki Tojo, and at the conference the tide went out and the rock was revealed. "There is absolutely no hope for a successful conclusion of the diplomatic negotiations," Tojo said firmly. The United States was insisting on Japan's withdrawal from China and a Japanese assurance of "nondisturbance of the status quo in the Pacific except as the status quo may be altered by peaceful means," a formula that provided for the dissolution of Europe's colonial empires.

The navy minister pointed out that until now Japan had been "making preparations for war on the one hand, while carrying on diplomatic negotiations on the other," but that Japan had reached "the crisis stage of peace or war." The navy proposed that the premier decide the issue. But Tojo balked. "This great problem cannot be left solely in the hands of the premier," he said with finality.

"On looking back," Prince Konoye, thrice premier of the empire, wrote as he prepared to take poison, "I cannot help but feel my flesh creep." And the flesh of literally millions of future war dead, he should have added.

In July 1941 Japan's ambassador to Washington, Kichisaburo Nomura, dispatched an "urgent–top secret" cable to Tokyo warning that the flow of Japanese troops and supplies into Indo-China was being viewed by American officials and public opinion as "the first step which will eventually lead to Singapore and the Dutch East Indies." There was also suspicion, the Japanese ambassador reported, that Tokyo was preparing to move southward while talking peace and that "the Secretary of State is being deceived."

In the prosecution's documentation a theme of Japanese deception runs like the phosphorescent wake of a ship at night. The fear of duplicity was especially widespread within the Japanese camp. According to the Kido diaries, Hirohito expressed misgivings about a war with the United States and, suspecting what was afoot, the emperor insisted "wholehearted efforts should be made in the conduct of negotiations with the U.S." On October 21, 1941, the credibility gap within the Japanese inner circle widened. Ambassador Nomura, a man of unquestioned integrity, cabled Foreign Minister Togo, "I don't want to continue this hypocritical existence, deceiving other people," then warming up, continued, "Please do not think I am trying to flee from the field of battle, but as a man of honor this is the only way that is open for me to retreat. Please send me your permission [to return to Japan]. Most humbly do I beseech your forgiveness if I have injured your dignity, and I prostrate myself before you in the depth of my rudeness." The transfer request was denied. Tojo had set up Nomura, and a special envoy sent to bolster him, Ambassador Saburo Kurusu, as the December 7 fall guys.

The diplomatic traffic between Tokyo and Washington was intercepted and decoded by the U.S. Navy, a fact widely publicized at the congressional Pearl Harbor hearings. Thus, it was manifest to the intimate group around Roosevelt—and to Asia-watchers—that Japan was preparing to strike. But where? Nobody knew. When? Nobody knew. U.S. and British intelligence thought Singapore or Thailand or some point in Southeast Asia to be most likely. For that matter, as revealed in the documentation at the IMTFE, the Japanese themselves were not unanimous about the direction they should take. The evidence at the trial revealed that those in the know in Tokyo debated whether to strike first to the west or south; those not in the know thought north or south.

On November 16 Nomura, in the dark in Washington, warned Tokyo that the United States feared the approach of war and was making preparations "to prevent us from a thrust northward or a thrust southward." He suspected, however, like everyone else in

Washington, that the Japanese high command would strike south. But Admiral Nagano, in his cold Sugamo cell, acknowledged during his 1946 interrogation that the Japanese navy had been divided into two factions, one favoring an attack against Pearl Harbor and the other anxious to waylay the American fleet in the southwest Pacific, using the illegally fortified mandated islands as bases. Nagano said he had favored the latter plan but decided in favor of Pearl Harbor because the commander of the combined fleet, Admiral Isoroku Yamamoto, whom the Americans shot down and killed later in the New Guinea theater, threatened to resign and plunge the navy into a crisis if he did not get his way. Yamamoto and his staff were elated by Nagano's decision; Admiral Ito, Yamamoto's chief of staff, boasted that the U.S. Pacific Fleet at Pearl Harbor "will be utterly crushed with one blow . . . while America is still unprepared."

As the IPS introduced as evidence transcripts of other Sugamo interrogations, the defendants in the dock grew increasingly uncomfortable. At one point Admiral Nagano was asked when the plan to attack Pearl Harbor was first brought to his notice. "I found out about this plan *officially* in October 1941," he replied (italics added). Not in April, when he was appointed chief of the naval general staff? "No," he lied. When was the plan called to his attention *unofficially*? "About July," he said. But excerpts from the Sugamo interrogations of the weak-willed Admiral Shimada, Tojo's navy minister who was despised in the navy as the army's sycophant, torpedoed Nagano's claim. When was the Pearl Harbor plan proposed to the high command? "January of 1941," Shimada replied evenly.

In most war plans, chance plays a decisive role. The Japanese surprise attack on Pearl Harbor was no exception. On December 5, 1941, for example, Japanese spies in Honolulu reported to Tokyo—accurately—that three battleships had returned to Pearl Harbor after eight days at sea and that an aircraft carrier and five heavy cruisers had slipped their moorings the same day. That same aircraft carrier turned up at Midway in 1942 and helped turn the tide against Japan in one of the great air-sea battles of the Pacific War.

Did Roosevelt plan that, too?

I thought at the time—in retrospect I think the more so—that the Allied prosecutors wasted time during the Pearl Harbor phase of the IMTFE. They could have made their case against the accused—that they had launched aggressive war without warning in contravention of established international law—more expeditiously simply by concentrating on the Japanese surprise attack at Kota Bharu, a small port perched on the northeast coast of the Malay Peninsula, then a British protectorate. The Japanese attack there was cut and dried, as lawyers are fond of saying; it lacked the red herrings that surrounded Pearl Harbor. The Japanese and British were engaged in no negotiations about Kota Bharu when the Japanese shelled the port and landed an amphibious force. There were no intercepted and decoded diplomatic cables, no delayed messages, and above all, no domestic American politics to divert attention from the core issue—launching premeditated, aggressive war without advance notice. Better still, the Japanese attacked Kota Bharu *before* they struck Pearl Harbor.

While Pearl Harbor was understandably the centerpiece of the events on December 7, 1941, it was only one element in Japan's strategy. The Japanese offensive that day unfolded in clusters of four major attacks on the Allies *before* Ambassador Nomura belatedly delivered Japan's "final note" to Secretary of State Hull, and four major attacks *after* its delivery. The first twelve hours that fateful day, as viewed from Tokyo, looked like this:

0045	Japanese troops seize Shanghai Bund (international settlement).
0140	Kota Bharu attacked from the sea.
0305	Singora and Patani, southern Thailand, invaded.
0320	Pearl Harbor attacked.
0420	Nomura hands "final note" to Hull.
0520	British gunboat sunk in Chinese waters.
0610	Singapore attacked from the air.
0805	Guam attacked.
0900	Hong Kong attacked.
1140	Emperor Hirohito issues imperial rescript declaring war on Britain and the United States.

The seizure of the Shanghai Bund would have made a good case, too, but as in the case of Pearl Harbor, there were too many red herrings. The Japanese seized it without a shot, and the Japanese Army had long since occupied the rest of Shanghai, China's premier port. But the attack on Kota Bharu was an unquestionable act of open aggression. The forces defending the area—chiefly British and Indian troops—fought courageously but were overwhelmed. Major General Arthur Percival, the British commander for Malaya and Singapore, who was destined to surrender his forces to Japan's General Yamashita, testified at the IMTFE that his troops at Kota Bharu "were eventually wiped out almost to a man."

Sir Orme Gaston Sargent, Britain's permanent undersecretary of state for foreign affairs, in a legal document tendered at the trial, also testified that "the Japanese did not, before opening hostilities, deliver to Britain or any of its representatives, or to any member of the British Commonwealth, any previous explicit warning in the form either of a declaration of war—giving reasons—or of an ultimatum with a conditional declaration of war, in accordance with the provisions of the Hague Convention of 1907." In another affidavit, Robert Craigie, the former British ambassador to Japan, testified that when Foreign Minister Togo summoned him to his residence at 7:45 that morning, "I had received no intimation whatever of any state of war." Togo simply told him that Japan had decided to break off negotiations with the United States. Craigie was handed a copy of Japan's "final note," which he hastily perused and "discovered there was not a word in it about war." Craigie, however, took the occasion to express Britain's concern about press reports that Japanese warships and transports were proceeding across the Gulf of Siam. Togo, impassive as ever, coolly explained that Japan had ordered troop movements because "of large concentrations of British and Indian troops on the frontier of Siam, disposed for purposes of attack."

To think that Britain, battling for survival against Hitler, planned to start a new war in Asia is so absurd that to this day even the revisionists have failed to pick it up for a thesis.

But the IMTFE swiftly passed over the Kota Bharu attack. Percival, Sargent, and Craigie never appeared in court; they testified by affidavit. Their statements were unchallengeable, and their presence in Tokyo, the prosecution felt, could add nothing further to the trial. The bench apparently thought likewise because it overruled repeated defense demands that they be subpoenaed to appear in Tokyo for cross-examination. "We know they have testified to serious matters, but is their testimony seriously questioned?" Sir William Webb asked the defense. "Have you any information upon which you could hope to cross-examine with any success?" The defense provided none.

Another reason a large part of the Pearl Harbor testimony could have been skipped was that much of it was drawn from the voluminous U.S. congressional hearings into Pearl Harbor. Even so, the IMTFE shed new light on the attack. For example, the term "sneak attack" offends Japanese sensibilities to this day. But, based on the evidence produced at the IMTFE, it was hard to describe the assault in any other way. Hideki Tojo, at his Sugamo interrogation, excerpts of which were tendered in evidence, claimed that Hirohito "warned me many times" to be certain that the "final note" to the United States was delivered *before* the attack. Prior notice should have been a routine matter, as a matter of national honor, and the acknowledgment that the emperor raised this point with his premier and war minister "many times" indicates that Hirohito was worried that something else was afoot. Whether or not Tojo testified honestly about Hirohito's concern is questionable, however. During his interrogation he claimed that he himself did not know about the impending attack on Pearl Harbor until the week before it took place(!).

When asked if such an attack in the absence of a declaration of war was "nothing but murder," Tojo replied, "I think it was perfectly legal." However, Tojo eventually conceded that the "final note" was not a declaration of war. "I think it was a final note," he said.

John W. Fihelly, the American assistant prosecutor who handled the Tojo interrogations, pressed the former war minister. "You have not answered the question," Fihelly said. "Do you agree with him [Ambassador Nomura] that it was not a declaration of war?"

Tojo hesitated. "It was a note breaking off diplomatic relations," he said, "but it was different from a declaration of war." Thus, even if the "final note" had been delivered *before* the attack, the bombing of Pearl Harbor would have come as a surprise. As in their intercepts of Japanese diplomatic traffic, the Americans would have remained in the dark, knowing a Japanese attack was in the wind but not knowing either when nor where. Fihelly asked Tojo why a declaration of war had not been made *before* the assault on Pearl Harbor. Tojo never answered the question.

From the Japanese public's standpoint, perhaps the most appalling aspect of the Pearl Harbor testimony was the disclosure that when the two Japanese envoys at Washington, Nomura and Kurusu, in a desperate attempt to avert war, proposed to Tokyo that Roosevelt and Hirohito exchange messages of goodwill, "thereby not only clearing the atmosphere, but also gaining a little time," Hirohito was not informed of the recommendation. The Sugamo interrogations of Foreign Minister Togo were now brought into play. Had the foreign minister told Hirohito about the proposal? "I did not mention that telegram to the emperor," Togo said. Why? "Such a step would not contribute toward the satisfactory settlement of negotiations," he said.

Nonetheless, on December 6, Roosevelt seized the diplomatic initiative and dispatched a message of goodwill directly to Hirohito, over the heads of Tojo and his co-conspirators in the dock. But, as it turned out, the Japanese Army had ordered all incoming foreign cables to be held up for as long as ten hours before delivery. Hirohito did not receive the Roosevelt message until *after* Japan had attacked Hawaii.

If Roosevelt knew about the impending Japanese attack and closed his eyes to it to get the United States involved in a war against the Nazis, he failed. The U.S. Congress, at the President's request, the next day declared war on Japan only. Germany was home free. Britain's political ally was diverted from Europe by a separate war. But Hitler must have been privy to Roosevelt's plot, to carry the absurdity of the historical revisionists to a logical conclusion, for it was Hitler, not Roosevelt, who now declared war and embroiled the United States in the European conflict. The evidence at the Tokyo trial was conclusive. A secret diplomatic cable from Japanese Ambassador Oshima in Berlin to Tokyo revealed that he had gone to Foreign Minister von Ribbentrop immediately after the Pearl Harbor attack and asked for a German declaration of war. The Japanese ambassador was told that Hitler was drafting it, and then Ribbentrop dropped a blockbuster. "Ribbentrop told me that on the morning of the eighth," Oshima informed Tokyo, "Hitler issued orders to the entire German navy to attack American ships wherever and whenever they may meet them." The directive was issued *before* a Nazi declaration of war, in character with Hitler's earlier admonition to the Japanese on the efficacy of sneak attack. "It goes without stating," Oshima went on, "that this is only for your secret information." The Americans were already at war on two fronts and did not know it.

The Japanese Foreign Ministry, alarmed at the world's reaction to the sneak attack, commissioned a study by the Japan International Law Society. The report, introduced by the IPS as evidence, was startling. It held that Japan's final note "can scarcely be regarded as a declaration of war because it included no preliminary notice that independent action is being taken or that hostilities are being opened, though it states, 'Japan recognizes that the continuance of negotiations henceforth in the hope of a solution is useless.' "

The study then dealt with the Hague agreement of 1907, which held that hostilities could not be started without preliminary notice in the form of an ultimatum that included a declaration of war. The Japanese legal experts felt that the treaty did not prevent a country from delivering a declaration of war in the attacker's capital and then attacking the victim before the victim's embassy could transmit it. Accordingly, the Japanese experts considered the 1907 treaty a bluff or simulacrum and concluded that there "is no need to respect such a childish treaty at the outbreak of a war."

Hideki Tojo and his generals loved war, and their brilliant initial victories in the Pacific and Asia only served to heighten their lust for greater conquest. The Nazi ambassador in Tokyo cabled Hitler on January 29, 1942, that the Japanese high command now planned to conquer the Dutch East Indies, which it did by March 8, and Australia, and to complete the conquest of China. Ambassador Eugen Ott reported, "According to confidential military information, in Australia, Port Darwin is to be conquered first." He added, however, that Japan was exercising "great restraint" on India and had no intention of invading because India was more a liability to the Allies than an asset to the Axis. Ott ended his transmission with optimism. Influential Tokyo circles, he said, expressed the view that "after Darwin, Japan must turn on Russia . . . and must seize Vladivostok, the coastal province and North Sakhalin, in order to finally secure herself in the north also."

21

Atrocities in
the Philippines

After Pearl Harbor the tribunal's focus shifted to the Philippines and, inescapably, to mass-scale atrocities. The atmosphere in the courtroom was cold and heavy, like the air under a shroud.

The Philippine phase was handled by Pedro Lopez, the black-haired, immaculately attired associate counsel of the Philippines. The Filipino judge, who had been taken prisoner on Bataan, voluntarily excused himself from the courtroom. Each day the marshal of the court intoned, "For the tribunal, the same as before with the exception of Honorable Justice D. Jaranilla, member of the Republic of Philippines, not sitting."

Owen Cunningham led the defense's fight to block the presentation of the Philippine case. Cunningham objected that the Philippines had not been a sovereign power in 1941 and was not a signatory to the Geneva Red Cross Convention or the Geneva Prisoners of War Convention of 1929, the two international agreements upon which the prosecution planned to build its Philippine case. Sir William Webb dismissed the objection by pointing out that there was only one Allied chief prosecutor and he could get around Cunningham's objection by simply assigning the Philippine atrocities to the American phase. Next, Cunningham objected that "full criminal responsibility" for the Philippine atrocities had already been adjudicated in the trials of Generals Homma and Yamashita, both of whom had been tried, convicted, and executed at Manila as war criminals. Webb was disgusted. "We are trying the accused whom the prosecution assert are responsible for what was done by Yamashita and Homma," Webb said sourly. "The position is so elementary as to be incapable of argument, and I resent the waste of time involved in listening to you."

Another defense counsel, William Logan, was more adroit. He asked the court to force the IPS, before proceeding, to prove there was a prima facie case against the accused they intended to hold responsible for atrocities. This, he reminded Webb, was "the ordinary procedure which is adopted in a law suit."

Webb agreed and, on one of the rare occasions that he revealed the workings of the bench, disclosed that he had called on Alan Mansfield, the Australian associate prosecutor, "the other day" to explain to the bench how the prosecution proposed to prove a connection between the accused and the violations of the Geneva Conventions. "And after hearing him," Webb disclosed, "we were satisfied to let evidence of this type go."

Unknown to prosecution and defense, the judges had already raised the prima facie question among themselves. The white-haired Judge Northcroft of New Zealand circulated a memorandum among his colleagues December 3, 1946, in which he expressed the view that "we should be *first* satisfied that the prosecution can make at least a prima facie case" linking the accused to atrocities, before permitting the IPS to move into the atrocity phase. "A mere assertion that it can be proved is not enough." He added, "It may be that the misbehavior of the Japanese in this matter should go on record, but this is not the concern of this court." And he concluded, "I am not conscious as yet of any basis for holding any of the defendants responsible for the wrongdoings of individual Japanese officers and other ranks in charge of prisoners of war. . . . I would like this matter to be debated among the judges."

Northcroft's memorandum astounded Webb, Lord Patrick of Britain, General Cramer of the United States, and several other members of the bench. Within twenty-four hours the New Zealand justice retreated. Northcroft was embarrassed when several of his brethren overnight called to his notice Article 26 of the Geneva Convention dealing with prisoners of war. It held that "commanders-in-chief of belligerent armies . . . in accordance with the instructions of their respective governments" bear responsibility for the treatment of POWs. The following morning, December 4, Northcroft hurriedly dispatched a second memorandum to his colleagues in which he acknowledged that "my attention was drawn by Lord Patrick to the Indictment, which charges breaches of the Geneva Convention of 1929, and in particular to Article 26 of that Convention." Northcroft admitted that he was routed. "In these circumstances," he continued, "it may be the purpose of the prosecution to prove widespread breaches in many camps in different theatres of war. If that be proved, the court might then be asked to infer (in the absence of rebutting evidence) that the evidence necessarily points to a breach by the Commanders-in-Chief and by the Government of Japan to carry out the duties imposed upon them by Article 26."

Atrocities and the Philippine phase were inseparable. The essence of the Allied case was that in the Philippines between 1942 and 1945 the Japanese had carried out a broad, calculated plan of atrocities on orders from Tokyo. The purpose of the mass-scale terror was to cow the newly occupied islands into submission. "A part of the pattern of these crimes has already been delineated with the presentation of the Chinese case," Pedro Lopez said in his opening statement. "We shall now proceed to unfold more of that pattern." The exact number of prisoners of war, civilian internees, and civilians who "met a horrible death by murder, cruelty, starvation, assaults, and mistreatment" was not known, but Lopez provided evidence to account for 131,028 murders; this was a bare minimum because many Filipinos and Americans murdered by the Japanese were later mistakenly listed as either killed in action or missing in action.

"Hundreds suffered slow and painful death in dark, foul, and lice-infested cells," the Filipino prosecutor continued, "for whom the quick, scientific mass extermination in the lethal gas chambers at Camp Dachau would have been a welcome alternative."

In sickening detail Pedro Lopez ran through a roster of names and incidents: the case of Lucas Doctolero, crucified, nails driven through hands, feet, and skull on September 18, 1943; the case of a blind woman who was dragged from her home November 17, 1943, stripped naked, and hanged; and on and on. The particulars on group killings were terrifying: In Manila, at St. Paul's College, 800 men, women, and children were machine-gunned. At Calamba, the birthplace of José Rizal, the founder of the Philippine national liberation movement, 2,500 were bayoneted or shot to death. At Ponson, in the south Philippines, 100 people were bayoneted and machine-gunned to death inside a church while 200 on

the outside were hunted down like game and slaughtered. At Ma-
tina Pangi 169 villagers were lined up and bayoneted or shot in
cold blood. One prosecution submission alone was literally a book
of horrors in itself, IPS Document 2726. It consisted of 14,618
pages of sworn affidavits, each describing attrocities carried out
by the Japanese authorities over the two-and-a-half-year period of
their occupation. After a while, as in the China phase, the statistics dulled the senses.

Even more damaging evidence came from the Japanese themselves in some official orders that miraculously survived the destruction of documents at the close of the war. In addition there
were the diaries of Japanese officers and men.

"When killing Filipinos," one Japanese directive read, "as-
semble them together in one place as far as possible, thereby saving ammunition and labor." As in the case of the Nazis, disposal
of bodies was "troublesome." The final solution? Throw them
into a river or stack them in a house wired for demolition.

The diary of a Japanese warrant officer, dated October 24, 1944,
read, "We are ordered to kill all the males we find. . . . All in
all, our aim is extinction of personnel." A soldier's diary explained how "we dug holes here and there in the coconut grove,"
lined up thirty Filipinos in front of the holes, their hands tied behind their backs, and bayoneted them. "My turn was the second
one," the diarist confided. "The moment I bayonetted the victim,
he cried, 'Ah,' and fell into the hole behind him. He was suffering
but I had no emotion at all. That may be because I was so excited. After bayonetting them, we covered them with soil and laid
coconut leaves on top. We returned to the company singing a military song at 2200 hours."

An entry dated February 17, 1945, in a diary picked off the
body of a dead Japanese soldier: "In various sectors we have
killed several thousands (including young and old, men and women,
and Chinese)." Another diary contained this entry: "Every day
is spent hunting guerrillas and natives. I have already killed well
over 100." A captured notebook read like a laundry list: "7 Feb.
'45—150 guerrillas were disposed of tonight. I stabbed [bayo-
neted] 10. 9 Feb. Burned 1,000 guerrillas tonight. . . . 13 Feb. At
1600 all guerrillas were burned to death." Another official report,
compiled by a Kempeitai unit and classified "most secret . . . to
be kept five years," consisted of 978 pages filled with gruesome
accounts of torture. "Indeed," the Japanese author of the report

wrote, "the Japanese army does extreme things."

Lately, particularly in the West, there has been a plethora of romantic novels glamorizing Bushido, the code of the samurai, part of which directs the conqueror to extend benevolence to the conquered. With the militarists in control of Japan, the Japanese Army did not even respect the honor of a brave enemy. The general commanding the 16th Imperial Japanese Army Division, according to one prosecution document, told his troops that prisoners of war and surrendering troops were to be killed indiscriminately on the battlefield, if possible. "By prisoners of war we mean soldiers and bandits captured on the battlefield; by surrenderors we mean those who surrender or submit prior to the battle." Troops were advised to kill "cautiously and circumspectly, with no policemen or civilians to witness the scene, and care must be taken to do it in a remote place and leave no evidence." Obviously, the general knew it was wrong—criminal.

Another set of directives, prepared by a Kempeitai detachment, dated April 3–21, 1944, ordered, "When prisoners are taken, those who are not worth utilizing shall be disposed of immediately. . . . Surrenderors found to be malicious after the interrogations performed on them . . . will be immediately killed in secret and will be disposed of so as not to excite public feeling."

The most memorable atrocity of the Japanese occupation of the Philippines was the Bataan Death March. In April and May 1942, 76,000 American and Filipino troops surrendered on Bataan and Corregidor and were marched to a POW camp. Over 10,000 men died on the 7-day, 120-kilometer march. Some of the survivors were placed on the stand in Tokyo.

Staff Sergeant Samuel B. Moody, his forehead furrowed, testified that the only food they received on the march either was thrown to them by Filipinos or consisted of stalks of sugarcane grabbed from alongside the road. Water came from caribou wallows and ditches, and those who drank from the former usually contracted dysentery. "We were beaten," Moody recalled in an almost inaudible voice. "The men were bayonetted, stabbed; they were kicked with hobnail boots. . . . If any man lagged to the rear of the road, fell off to the side, he was immediately bayonetted and beaten." The road was dotted with bodies. "I saw many dead men, many of whom were my friends," he testified. "I also saw two dead women, one of whom was pregnant. . . . Many times I could look ahead and see my friends stabbed and beaten.

Quite often I could hear groans of men behind me that had received beatings from someone in the rear."

Another witness, Donald F. Ingle, recalled that during the march Filipinos who gave the men food had done so "at the risk of their lives, and a lot of civilians did lose their lives trying." Men, he said, were sometimes taken out of the column and bayoneted or shot for no reason.

During cross-examination, defense attorney Logan asked Ingle, "You don't know what the rank the officer had who was in charge of the march itself, do you?"

Ingle replied, "How could I?" prompting Logan to counter, "I do not know, Mr. Witness, I was not there; I thought you might know."

At the end of the cross-examination, Logan suggested, "You sound rather bitter about this, Mr. Ingle. Are you?"

Ingle appeared to count to ten. "Well, there are several thousand buddies that aren't here today that would be here if it weren't for that. Use your own judgment." The courtroom was deathly still.

"No further questions, Your Honor," Logan said.

Other than Bataan, the world does not remember nor does it care about the other great massacres that took place in the Philippine Islands during the Japanese occupation. On Palawan, for example, 150 American POWs, almost double the number massacred at Malmédy, Belgium, during the Battle of the Bulge, were slaughtered—and forgotten. But the deed is indelibly printed in the transcript of the IMTFE. On December 14, 1944, the Japanese claimed the Americans were planning to bomb the Puerto Princesa camp on Palawan and ordered all prisoners into the tunnels that served as makeshift air raid shelters. Then Japanese soldiers flipped a lighted torch inside and followed it with a couple of buckets of gasoline. The gasoline exploded and set the occupants aflame. "As screaming men ran from the shelter," said a report based on the eyewitness account of three survivors, "they were mowed down by machine guns and rifles." Realizing that they were trapped, several prisoners ran to the Japanese and asked to be shot in the head, but the Japanese laughingly shot or bayoneted them in the stomach.

In another now-forgotten incident, Lieutenant Colonel Austin J. Montgomery testified to conditions at the Davao penal colony in the southern Philippines, were 2,000 prisoners of war were incarcerated. When 10 prisoners escaped, 600 men, including Montgomery, were punished by being placed in cages about three feet high, three feet wide, and six feet long for two months. Periodically, they were beaten or whipped. Who gave the order of punishment? Pedro Lopez asked. "The commanding officer of the camp, Major Maeda, announced to us that he had received the notification of the punishment to be imposed from the high command."

At another camp, among the horrors witnessed by Colonel Guy H. Stubbs were five Filipinos thrown into a latrine and buried alive; a Filipino spread-eagled on the ground and both his legs dislocated; a Filipino suffering from dysentery made, on one occasion, to "eat everything he eliminated."

Colonel Franklin M. Filinau, who was taken prisoner at Iloilo City in the central Philippines, described the terrible beatings he had received in a Japanese torture chamber, "a bare room, no chairs and no tables." He testified that he had witnessed 100 other beatings (usually the victim was beaten unconscious, awakened by buckets of water, and then kicked back into unconsciousness). "I was told by the captain in charge when I protested the beatings of different individuals that he had orders from his superior to punish us," Filinau said. Who were the superiors? "On every occasion, the only words used were 'the high command.' "

The court, which was sickened by these stories, was jarred when Filinau observed that the Filipinos had taken more of a beating than the Americans.

Of all the colonial territories overrun by the Japanese in the aftermath of Pearl Harbor, the only territory where the population waged a massive guerrilla war in collaboration with the former colonial power was in the Philippines. During the cross-examination of Filinau the defense suggested the guerrilla war had incited Japanese misbehavior. "Colonel," Owen Cunningham asked, "did you have any part in the training of the Filipinos for guerrilla warfare before the surrender?"

Webb halted him. "The question is irrelevant."

Cunningham persisted. "Of course, I disagree with Your Honor, and it is too bad," he said, "as I have a line of questions along that line which would show that the U.S. Army, I believe, contributed to the situation which existed in the Philippines with this guerrilla warfare and mistreatment; and I am sorry that I cannot go into that line of questioning."

Clearly, during this phase of the proceedings, the defense was desperately trying to find something to offer to counter the evidence that had sickened the court. It failed.

The atrocities in the Philippines were inextricably interwoven with the broader charges against the Japanese of conventional war crimes and crimes against humanity across the Pacific and Asia. Alan Mansfield, the bright, articulate Australian associate prosecutor, followed an exhausted Pedro Lopez to the lectern and introduced a filing cabinet of diplomatic notes to and from Tokyo that dealt with Japanese bestiality in the Philippines and elsewhere. This correspondence linked several of the accused with the policy of mayhem and murder in the Japanese-occupied territories. Before Mansfield could proceed, however, Owen Cunningham, who was rapidly becoming the tribunal's gadfly, moved to block its admission as evidence. He described the correspondence as "incompetent, irrelevant and immaterial [because] the documents are not in compliance with the provisions and rules of land warfare."

Sir William Webb was aghast. "To employ the expression of another member of the bench," the president of the tribunal said, "the objection is overruled as puerile."

The correspondence established that the ruling powers in Tokyo had been aware of the atrocities in the field, not only in China and the Philippines, but wherever the Japanese Army trod. Six men in the dock were singled out as privy to these frightful events. The diplomatic notes of protest had been sent to the Japanese foreign minister, who had in turn passed them on to the war minister. They were also seen by the vice war minister and the chiefs of the Military Affairs Bureau and the Prisoners of War Information Bureau. Among the accused, Shigenori Togo and Mamoru Shigemitsu had served as foreign minister; Hideki Tojo, as war minister; General Kimura, as vice war minister; and Generals Muto and Sato, as chiefs of the Military Affairs Bureau. Muto in particular always seemed to have been at the wrong place at the wrong time; he was at the scene during the Rape of Nanking in 1937 and the Rape of Manila in 1945. Throughout the testimony he sat unmoved, his hair closely cropped, his lips tightly drawn, his black eyes dull and glazed like two pieces of unlit charcoal. His track record was written in blood.

Although Japan had signed the 1929 Geneva Conventions, Tokyo did not ratify the Prisoners of War Convention. On December 18, 1941, however, Washington contacted Tokyo through their mutually appointed intermediary, Switzerland, and expressed the hope that "nevertheless," Japan would subscribe to that convention. On February 4, 1942, Foreign Minister Togo notified the Allies in writing that "first: Japan is strictly observing the Geneva Red Cross Convention as a signatory state; second: although not bound by the Convention relative [to the] treatment of prisoners of war, Japan will apply *mutatis mutandis* provisions of that Convention to American prisoners of war in its power." This correspondence was tendered in evidence.

By late 1942 there was a steady stream of reports about Japan's inhuman treatment of prisoners of war, civilian internees, and civilian populations in the occupied territories. The Allies responded by showering written, detailed protests on Tokyo through various intermediaries. On April 5, 1943, Washington warned Tokyo that "the American government will visit upon the officers of the Japanese government responsible for such uncivilized and inhumane acts the punishment they deserve." The warnings increased in intensity as the war progressed. Specific atrocities, such as the Palawan massacre, were the subject of dire protests. Washington flatly informed Tokyo, "The Japanese government cannot escape responsibility for this crime."

Tokyo's replies to the unremitting flow of protests were either insipid or dissembling. As early as February 14, 1942, Washington notified Tokyo that it had received "disquieting reports" about the Japanese treatment of American civilians in the Philippines. Ten days later, in its reply, Japan claimed, "Conditions applied to them are more favorable than contemplated by Convention." Another Japanese note decried American protests over the treatment of Filipino and American POWs, saying that the "apprehensions [of the] American government based on information from unknown sources and citing no exact facts are therefore without foundation." Later, when Tokyo was confronted with "exact facts," the Japanese dismissed them as Allied fabrications.

During this phase of the case, as the horrors of one day transcended the horrors of the day before, the Americans at the trial found it hard to reconcile the evidence inside the courtroom with the evidence outside. After all, we now lived among the Japanese and found most of them to be decent and likable. How could they and their government have behaved like the monsters depicted in the testimony? We found part of the answer in the prosecution's evidence, the diaries of the Japanese who had committed the atrocities.

Thus, a Japanese private wrote in his diary on December 19, 1944, "Taking advantage of darkness, we went out to kill the natives [Filipinos]. It was hard for me to kill them because they seemed to be good people. The frightful cries of the women and children were horrible. I myself . . . killed several persons." Another soldier told how he watched his comrades torture Filipino prisoners. "It is pitiful, and I couldn't watch. They also shot them and speared them to death with bamboo lances." The most poignant word here is "they," a Japanese soldier describing his comrades-in-arms as strangers.

In another diary a soldier wrote that he had killed many defenseless civilians and that "the naïveté I possessed at the time of leaving the homeland has long since disappeared; now I am a hardened killer and my sword is always stained with blood." As a postscript he added, ". . . It is sheer brutality. May God forgive me! May my mother forgive me!" A Japanese officer inspected a prison camp in the southern Philippines and wrote, "Even though they are foreigners, my heart goes out to them. The prisoners are Filipinos and Chinese. There are also a few Westerners." He concluded, "We, who are at war, must not lose to the Allies or our fate will be worse. Certain victory!"

In this period the American chaplain at Sugamo, Captain Francis P. Scott, left for home. In a farewell interview with *Stars & Stripes,* a U.S. Army–sponsored daily newspaper, he revealed that he had questioned many of the convicted POW camp commandants as to their reasons for the barbaric treatment of prisoners. In the end, Scott said, he put together a composite explanation. "They had a belief that any enemy of the emperor could not be right, so the more brutally they treated their prisoners, the more loyal to the emperor they were being." The chaplain ascribed this to Japanese education, training, and conditioning. In literature as well as history this has a familiar ring. Thus, in *War and Peace* Tolstoy described one of Napoleon's aides as "unable to express devotion to his monarch except by cruelty."

Against this backdrop of testimony of the IMTFE, the arrest of war criminal suspects continued. In late 1946 seventeen more Japanese Army and Navy personnel, including a lieutenant general, were imprisoned at Sugamo. The trials of Class B and C suspects, meanwhile, continued apace at Yokohama and else-where in the Far East. In the New Guinea area—Sir William Webb's old stamping ground—twenty-seven Japanese war crimi-nals, including two colonels convicted of committing atrocities against POWs and the Papuan and Polynesian population, were executed. One officer escaped a firing squad by committing sui-cide.

At Sugamo there was a noticeable change in the atmosphere as the IMTFE delved into Japan's crimes against humanity. Sev-eral of the Class A defendants, in search of inner peace, turned to Lord Buddha. General Matsui, the commander during the butchery at Nanking, requested a volume of Buddhist scripture; so did ex-premier Hirota, who continued to write his dead wife each week as his world moved nearer to hers. Generals Itagaki, Kimura, and Sato also turned to religion. The two foreign minis-ters in the dock, Togo and Shigemitsu, appeared more aloof than ever from the generals and admirals with whom they shared Su-gamo, the daily bus convoy, and Ichigaya. Marquis Kido also kept his own company. General Suzuki, the economic czar on the eve of December 7, remained as arrogant and defiant as ever. Ex-premier Koiso, armed with a walking stick, took brisker walks in the exercise yard. It was now December. The days grew shorter, and the pall that engulfed the three-mat cells of the accused deep-ened with the onset of winter.

22

POWs and Other Slave Labor

In mid-December 1946 the pivotal interest at the trial was on the cruelties the Japanese had meted out to prisoners of war and Asian slave laborers.* By all accounts the worst POW and forced-labor camps during World War II were located along a 258-mile strip of railroad track running through the almost impenetrable jungles of Thailand and Burma. The infamous Siam-Burma Death Railway was built by Allied prisoners of war and Asian slave laborers during 1942 and 1943 under conditions so vile that 27 percent of the POWs and more than half of the Asian press gangs perished. The Allied prisoners laboring on the death railway numbered around 50,000, a mix of Australians, Dutch, English, and Americans who had been taken prisoner in Malaya, Singapore, and Indonesia and shipped to the site like cattle. The number of "levies," largely Indonesians (Javanese), Burmese, Malays, Chinese, and Indians, will never be known but the figure may have been as high as 250,000 men, with a scattering of women and children. Using spades, baskets, and picks, the prisoners and coolies were forced to remove 3 million cubic yards of earth and 230,000 cubic yards of rock along the route. Unfortunately, the story of the Siam-Burma Death

*The IMTFE limited its inquiry into Asian forced labor to Chinese and Southeast Asians. Korean historians estimate that 5.4 million Koreans were forcibly conscripted by the Japanese between 1939 and 1945. Many Koreans were put into coal mines. Korea, a prewar Japanese colony, was not represented at the IMTFE, surely an Allied oversight.

Railway was romanticized and glamorized in a popular novel by Pierre Boulle and in a glossily packaged Hollywood film, *The Bridge on the River Kwai.*

The IPS established that Tokyo had ordered the construction of the railroad and that among those in the dock who had authorized the use of prisoners as laborers in violation of the Hague and Geneva Conventions were Generals Hideki Tojo and Heitaro Kimura. In addition, three Japanese major generals were identified as the commanders under whom the actual building of the railway had taken place. They had commanded two regiments of regular troops and several auxiliary units, including Korean guard units. With literally hundreds of thousands of troops, guards, prisoners, and slave laborers involved, and the movement of tens of thousands of tons of supplies to the construction site, the project could not be kept a secret, and the chain of command from Tokyo to the field commander was unobstructed. There were two strategic purposes for the railroad: the shipment of troops and supplies to the Burma front, where the Allies were counterattacking, and the exploitation of tungsten ore deposits along the route. Tungsten is used in the manufacture of munitions. There may have been another, ultrasecret motive for the railroad. Burma was thought to be a site of uranium deposits, necessary for Japan's atomic bomb project.

The Japanese atrocities in China and the Philippines paled by comparison with those at the railway construction sites. To observers in daily attendance at the tribunal, the prosecution's evidence always appeared to sink from bad to worse. Whenever I thought we had hit the bottom of Poe's indescribable pit, we descended, to our shock, to a lower level of depravity.

The Allied case was built on the testimony of survivors and on an official Japanese document, "Report by Japanese Government on Burma-Thailand Railway."

Dr. C.R.B. Richards, a British Army medical officer and survivor, testified about a camp where the Japanese commandant's policy had been "no work, no food." The commandant cured the sick by sending them to the nominal hospital to die. "I can imagine nothing more appalling than the conditions under which these men lived and died," Richards said. "It was in effect a living morgue." As for the camp itself, Richards said, "Troops were billeted in huts which had been evacuated the previous day on account of cholera deaths. . . . Coolies walked through the huts, spat, defecated and vomited everywhere. . . . At Upper Sonkurai Camp in August [1943] the latrines were flooded by incessant rain. One of them had broken its banks and a filthy stream oozed through the camp area and passed under the floors of the huts occupied by the hospital. . . . The men had nothing to wear except the clothing in which they were captured, and most of that had rotted or perished during the months of the monsoon.'' Protests by Allied officers to Japanese officers as high as the rank of general were met with vocal abuse and worse, including beatings with bamboo switches. If there was a shortage of men for a given job, Japanese guards would enter the ''hospital'' and drive the sick out with sticks. Those who could stand or walk, worked.

Another survivor testified that on one occasion 3,000 men had been shipped by rail from Singapore to Thailand in overcrowded trains with ''either nonexistent or revolting sanitary facilities.'' From the Thai railroad station the prisoners were marched by night through the jungle to the construction camps; as in the case of the Bataan Death March, they were beaten along the way. Work on the railroad varied from twelve to twenty hours a day, depending on the monsoon rains; there were no days off and no holidays; rations consisted of a ball of rice and a few pieces of fish; when a man took ill, his ration was cut by one third. Cholera, dysentery, beriberi, and malaria were rampant.

Irrespective of the number of lives lost, several witnesses testified, the prisoners were told that the railway had to be completed by 1943. One witness said that the Japanese told him there was ''no use quoting the articles of the Geneva Convention.'' He added, ''I gained the impression that everything was to be subordinated to the completion of the line by the end of August, and when this was not fulfilled they [the Japanese] became insane with rage.''

Another British Army physician, Major B.L.W. Clarke, testified that in seven months, at Chungkai Sick Camp, 1,400 prisoners out of 8,000 had died. At the hospital men were operated on without anesthetic and without surgical instruments. On one occasion five Japanese doctors visited the camp and observed an operation; one physician fainted, and another got sick to the stomach.

Sungkrai No. 2 Camp was known among the inmates as ''Death Valley.'' The prisoners were never afforded an opportunity to tidy up the camp, and during the monsoon the mud-floor huts turned into quagmires. When cholera broke out, those afflicted were sent to the "hospital," which was another hut with bare floor. There was no light in the hut, and patients who died at night remained among the living until daybreak. On one occasion thirty-eight cholera victims were left out in the monsoon rains for two days before burial.

Another camp survivor, Major R. J. Campbell, testified that in June 1945 a British officer who acted as interpreter at Tamarkan POW Camp had been beaten insensible and put for days in a slit trench that held six inches of rainwater and was infested with mosquitoes. "Later he was taken back to the guard room where he was threatened with torture," Campbell said, "as a result of which, he endeavored to commit suicide." He was emaciated and insane when rescued with the end of the war.

In another camp the testicles of a man who suffered from beri-beri swelled to such an enormous size—a form of elephantiasis—that he had to carry them around in his hands to walk. The Japanese made him the camp jester; he died in terrible agony.

The lowest level of depravity was seemingly attained at Kanburi Camp, astride the River Kwai. A tourist center today, the camp attracts both Allied survivors and former Japanese guards, all of whom still live with the horrors of the railway crowding their dreams. At one point 170 men, racked with malaria, dysentery, and cholera and covered with tropical ulcers, were compelled to crawl a two-mile stretch from a jungle camp to the new hospital at Kanburi. The hospital turned out to be an encampment recently evacuated by a Japanese cavalry unit. "There were twenty empty huts," a witness recalled, "in most of which there was animal dung and filth."

The tale of horrors sank ever lower. Several of the Western survivors testified that the Japanese treatment of the Asian slave workers was far worse than the treatment accorded European and American prisoners. Indonesian coolies who suffered from cholera, for example, were often forced into common pit graves and buried alive. Other coolies were regularly beaten and humiliated; women among them were insulted and violated; disinfectant was sprayed into the eyes of some laborers, ostensibly as a joke; one Japanese doctor viciously beat the coolies he examined for cholera, whether they had the disease or not (it made no sense that he struck them). The Western prisoners looked on in shock at this inhuman behavior, but a Japanese physician explained lightly to the Europeans that "coolies are subhuman and not worthy of consideration."

According to one affidavit, workers at one camp who could not walk were injected with "a red unknown fluid." All died within a few minutes. On another occasion sick coolies were offered a large tin of brown sugar. Those who ate the sugar, which turned out to be poisoned, died in agony later the same day.

When the clothes the Asian laborers had brought from home began to fall into rags, they were provided with gunny sacks for wearing apparel and as blankets. There was no change of clothing, so that in a short time "the cloth of almost all laborers was crawling with vermin, and most of them were suffering from a virulent type of skin disease," according to the evidence. When cholera broke out, the Japanese often sought to check the spread of the epidemic by cremating not only the dead but also persons whom they considered incurable. "There are many authentic cases of live cremations," one witness told the tribunal.

Burmese were pressed into labor gangs whenever a shortage of Indonesian and other imported Asian workers developed. Between April and July of 1943, 30,000 Burmese from the Rangoon area, some with their wives and children, were rounded up and marched to the railway site. One of the tragedies of the period is that the Japanese kept no complete records of their coolie laborers as they did of prisoners of war—although, of course, most of the latter records were burned at the Japanese surrender. Thus, the names of the tens of thousands of Asians who perished along the Siam-Burma track are not known, nor are their graves marked. Among them, for example, were many of the 200,000 Indonesians contracted as day laborers during the war who subsequently disappeared.

The testimony of Major Robert Crawford of the British Army was representative of the stack of sworn affidavits the prosecution introduced as evidence. The coolie camps, he said, had been heavily contaminated with feces, and the workers often slept on bare ground. The diet was inadequate, usually a bowl or two of rice daily, the water often contaminated, yet the Japanese were insensible to the workers' sicknesses and hardships. Crawford branded Japanese indifference "criminal neglect."

Crawford's affidavit, based on the reports of Allied survivors, gave these particulars on the treatment of the Asian slave laborers: Hintok Camp—cholera cases driven into the jungle and abandoned; Niki Bridge-Building Camp—high suicide rate; Wan Ye Hospital—4,000 patients dead in a twelve-month period; Kanburi No. 2 Coolie Hospital—about 5,000 patient deaths in an eighteen-month period.

Allied prisoners often reported on individual cases of mistreatment they had personally witnessed: Kanburi No. 2 Coolie Hospital, where "coolies were kept standing for hours with weights tied to the penis"—apparently for sport; Kinsayoke Checking Station, where coolies undergoing rectal swab examination for dysentery were, "one after the other, kicked violently by the Japanese medical officers"; Niki Camp, where members of a Japanese hygiene unit, during routine examinations, delighted in inserting glass rods into the vaginas of Chinese women patients; Upper Concuita Camp, where "sick coolies were used for the practice of judo and thrown over the shoulders of Japanese." At Concuita, too, fifty to sixty workers were killed with doses of morphia and potassium permanganate.

"These instances could be multiplied," Crawford said, "*ad nauseam.*"

Repeatedly, the Allies protested the mistreatment of prisoners of war and others in the Thai-Burmese camps. As in a game of badminton, the Japanese foreign minister of the day swatted back the diplomatic shuttlecock, dismissing the accusations as lies. On July 24, 1943, for example, the defendant Mamoru Shigemitsu, through the Swiss ambassador in Japan, replied to one protest by observing that "competent authorities . . . inform me that the prisoners of the Thailand Camp are equitably treated; furthermore, those who are sick have received the best medical treatment in the prisoners-of-war hospital." Shigemitsu's "competent authorities" were officials of the War Ministry. But repeated Swiss requests to visit the camps as a neutral power were denied. "So far as the matter of visiting the camp is concerned," Shigemitsu wrote, "authorization will not be given for the moment." It never was.

The crowning document of the Thai-Burmese phase was the "Report by Japanese Government on the Burma-Thailand Railway," an official document drawn up in Tokyo after the surrender and designed to give the Japanese point of view. The report divided "the so-called brutal treatment of Allied prisoners of war during the construction" into two parts: "(1) misconduct in the form of direct cruelty . . . (2) . . . deaths from illness among the prisoners during the work." In Tokyo's view, "There is a distinct difference in character between (1) and (2)."

The report consisted of ninety-one pages and eleven tables in Japanese and sixty-nine pages in English. However, at the outset, because there were "no data available in Tokyo . . . the cases under (1) are excluded from this report." The report also papered over the fate of the coolie slave laborers. "Many POWs fell victim of the work at last, much to our regret," the report said. "We should like to declare the Japanese troops [also] participated in the joys and sorrows of the POWs and native laborers in the construction work, and by no means completed or intended to complete the work only at the sacrifice of the POWs."

The report acknowledged, at a minimum, the deaths of 10,000 prisoners and 30,000 coolie laborers—both drastic underestimates when compared with eyewitness and documentary accounts of the death and disease prevalent during the year and a half that if took to build the railway. With pride, the report observed, "By special order of the director of construction, a monument was erected each in Thailand and Burma to console those departed spirits of the prisoners of war and ordinary laborers engaged in this construction work, a mass was held, and their souls deeply venerated in the fashion of [an] imperial Japanese ceremony."

In the dock, as before, whenever evidence of mass atrocities entered the testimony, Shigemitsu leaned forward and cupped his head in his hands. Toshio Shiratori's long face grew longer; he often bit his lip. General Muto's eyelids, no longer immobile, blinked rapidly as if he had developed a tic. Admiral Shimada, who sat behind Okinori Kaya, frequently leaned over the dock and ran his fingers nervously along the back of Kaya's seat. Several of the accused, Shigenori Togo among them, removed their headphones. General Itagaki, who had been alternately angry and cheerful since the beginning of the trial, looked downcast. He rarely looked, even out of curiosity, at a witness. Hideki Tojo continued his habit of taking copious notes and occasionally picking his nose; one suspected, after watching him for months, that the note taking was a theatrical device designed to impress the silent gallery while keeping himself occupied. Marquis Kido sat like a block of ice, cold and immovable. Would he, on behalf of his emperor, melt in tears with the coming of spring? General Suzuki alone maintained his constant scowl and arrogant posture, carrying his head high, although the dimple on his chin appeared to deepen.

Many in the dock appeared to await the fall of the other shoe. The IPS had promised linkage of atrocities to several of the accused, and so far only about a half dozen had been so connected. There was a feeling that there was more to come. Worse, from the defense's standpoint, the bench was privy to the prosecution's strategy and had permitted the IPS to proceed, satisfied that the tieback would be established before the end of the presentation of evidence.

More than a generation later, in Tokyo in 1976, Takashi Nagase, who had served as an English-language interpreter during the building of the railroad, saw Hollywood's glossy filmed version, *The Bridge on the River Kwai*. With understatement, and with candor, Nagase said solemnly, "I can tell you that the conditions for the prisoners of war who worked on the bridge were much worse than depicted in that movie." In looking back, one may ask, if there had been no IMTFE, where would the story of what happened be stored? The testimony of the Tokyo tribunal is the imperishable memorial to those Allied prisoners and Asian slave laborers who died along a stretch of track that, like their skeletons, the jungle has long since claimed.

The prisoners who labored on the Burma-Siam Railway were the "lucky ones"—at least they had survived the journey from their place of capture to the construction site. Except for a few war prisoners who were shipped by rail from Singapore and Malaya or who were captured in Burma, the POWs made the journey to the site by sea. A large percentage perished en route and are not counted among those who died building the railroad. With the exception of Burmese slave laborers, all the Asian coolies were also shipped to the site by sea. Nor were sea voyages limited to the Burma-Siam Railway. The hellships, for want of a better term, plied routes between points of capture and permanent prisoner-of-war camps in Formosa (Taiwan), Korea, Manchuria, and Japan. The conditions aboard these vessels were uniform: the prisoners and coolies were forced below decks, kept short on water and rations, provided with virtually no sanitary facilities, and beaten mercilessly.

This section of the prosecution's case was handled by Australia's Lieutenant Colonel Thomas F. Morname, a square-jawed, broad-shouldered officer. Morname produced twenty sworn affidavits of survivors and put several survivors of other hellship voyages in the witness box. The first affidavit set the tone: 1,900 American prisoners confined to the holds of the *Tottori Maru,* a freighter bound from Manila to Japan, the men packed so closely together that only two thirds of them could lie down at once. Although many of the prisoners had already contracted dysentery from rotting rations, they were provided with only six latrines. Many of the men slept in their own excreta.

The policy of harsh treatment, the Allied prosecution charged, was deliberate and was carried out on instructions of the navy general staff in Tokyo. The hellships bore no marks distinguishing them from regular transports, and they were armed with anti-aircraft and other weapons. They were attacked by Allied aircraft and submarines, and many of the POWs, civilian internees, and slave laborers drowned. One witness, the survivor of such an attack, painted a picture of the sea journey in terms that rivaled Dante's *Inferno.* His voyage had been aboard a 5,000-ton cargo ship carrying 1,750 European war prisoners (mainly Dutch), 600 Indonesian war prisoners (mainly Ambonese), and 5,500 Indonesian forced laborers (mainly Javanese) from Java on September 19, 1944. The prisoners were crowded into the ship's holds; "[we] were beaten into the hold . . . crammed together standing upright, since lying down or even sitting was impossible." Off Sumatra's west coast, in the Indian Ocean, the ship was torpedoed and sank in twenty minutes. Prisoners who survived the initial explosion and floundered in the water tried to grab the edge of a Japanese lifeboat, "but instead of taking them in, one of the Japanese chopped off their hands or split their skulls with a huge ax," the witness said. A Japanese corvette finally picked up survivors—276 Europeans, 312 Ambonese, and 300 Javanese. The survivors were confined to a Japanese prison camp on Sumatra. "When we came into this jail, the lavatories were full; thus, we had to relieve ourselves on the floor," the witness said. "The smell was penetrating and nauseating."

Regular Japanese Army troop transports, the IPS evidence showed, were also employed for moving war prisoners. On one voyage the *Nagao Maru* carried 1,650 prisoners and about 2,000 Japanese troops. Captain Edward N. Nell, a U.S. Army medical officer, testified that the prisoners were bottled up below decks. "The latrines were on deck, but the men with bowel disorder were unable to get to the deck. For three days there were no sanitary facilities below decks." At Moji, Japan, where the surviving prisoners disembarked, they were compelled to line up naked on the dock in full view of the public for a rectal examination.

On all these ships beatings were commonplace and prisoners died daily, with the corpses often thrown overboard like garbage. In several instances, as a matter of discipline, prisoners were beheaded on deck and their severed heads and torsos flipped overboard. In tropical waters particularly, these vessels were followed by scavengers—sharks. In port the bodies of dead prisoners were piled up to await burial at sea; on a hellship running from Ambon to Java, along the equator, the stench of corpses in Indonesian ports along the way was revolting.

Early in the war, on October 1, 1942, the *Lisbon Maru* steamed from Hong Kong with 1,816 prisoners and 2,000 Japanese troops. At sea two men who died of diphtheria were not removed from the hold in which prisoners were confined. The *Lisbon Maru* was torpedoed and settled with her stern caught on a sandbank. When the prisoners broke out of the holds, Japanese soldiers picked them off with rifles as they emerged from below. A handful of survivors reached a nearby island where "the Chinese treated [us] with great kindness, giving [us] food and clothing from their meagre supplies." Japanese landing parties soon appeared, however, and the men were recaptured and taken to Shanghai, where they were confined to Bridgehouse, one of the Kempeitai's notorious prisons.

Almost all the Japanese documents relating to the shipping phase of the trial had been successfully destroyed by the Japanese naval command at the time of Tokyo's surrender; in this instance the navy appeared more efficient then the army (a similar situation, coincidentally, had developed at the Nuremberg trial). But the IPS came up with one document, dated March 20, 1943, that told reams. The directive was stamped "*gunki*" ("secret") and marked "copy 24 of 70," like a numbered print. No other copy was ever found. The order read, "Do not stop with the sinking of enemy ships and cargoes; at the same time that you carry out the complete destruction of the crews of the enemy's ships, if possible, seize part of the crew and endeavor to secure information."

The extent to which the accused went to cover up such orders was demonstrated when the IPS introduced excerpts from the February 1, 1946, Sugamo interrogation of Hiroshi Oshima, in which the Japanese general and former envoy to the Third Reich admitted talking to Joachim von Ribbentrop about "naval activities" as part of the military collaboration between the Axis powers. At

Sugamo he was asked whether the Japanese navy had put out an order similar to Hitler's to murder the crews of torpedoed vessels. "The Japanese would not put out such an order," Oshima protested. When he was shown a copy of the March 20 directive, he said he had not known of its existence. Did Oshima recognize that the words in the Japanese naval order were in "the same order" as those of the Nazi order? "Yes," Oshima said lamely, "they are alike."

It would take literally thousands of pages to enumerate the other terrible moments relived at the IMTFE, the crimes committed by the Japanese at Shanghai's Bridgehouse, Manila's Santo Tomas, Singapore's Changi, and other lesser-known POW and civilian internee camps, among them Java's Tjideng,* North Borneo's Sandakan, Taiwan's Keelung, Manchuria's Harbin—site of Japanese bacteriological warfare experiments—and Japan's Fukuoka. They would nauseate the reader. Accordingly, I shall follow the lead of the Dutch associate prosecutor, who, recounting Japanese butchery in Indonesia, told the court, "I won't read any more of this," and Solis Horwitz, the American assistant prosecutor, who, while reading the affidavits of camp survivors, skipped over pages because "the material in there would be repetitious."

Even so, the final ten days of the prosecution's atrocity phase turned up staggering evidence linking Tokyo directly with conventional war crimes and crimes against humanity. Given the destruction of evidence at the end of the war, the IPS did an outstanding job of filling in the blanks in the chain of command between the cabinet in Tokyo and the commanders in the field. But there was more to come even after the prosecution ended its case. For strategic reasons, Joseph Keenan and his team deliberately held back much of the evidence with a view to ambushing the defense when it presented its case. Still, in the final days there was enough evidence presented to fill several history books.

The burly General Ryukichi Tanaka, for example, returned to the witness stand and promptly ran into heavy weather. As a former chief of the Military Affairs Bureau, he cited Generals Tojo, Kimura, and Sato in connection with atrocities; it was Tanaka

---

*Agnes de Keyzer, who later became my wife, landed in Java on September 17, 1945, after the surrender of Japan, as part of the Repatriation of Allied Prisoners of War group. She worked at the Tjideng Camp, Batavia (Jakarta), where about 10,000 women and children had been interned in what she described as "indescribable and unspeakable conditions." Earlier she had landed at Balikpapan, East Borneo, where the Dutch had to await British "permission" to land on Java.

who testified that Hideki Tojo had ordered "all prisoners of war to engage in forced labor," a decision made at a meeting of War Ministry officials in 1942 at Ichigaya—the very building where the IMTFE sat. Tanaka, however, absolved Foreign Ministers Shigemitsu and Togo of complicity in war crimes, describing the Gaimusho in this era as a "post office."

Tanaka posed a serious threat to the defense, and he underwent a searing cross examination. Defense attorney Logan wrung incriminating self-admissions from the general. Tanaka admitted he himself had direct links to the Kempeitai and, over the strenuous objections of the Allied prosecution, acknowledged that he was known "by the people in Japan as 'The Monster.' " A chill swept the tribunal. But the remorseful Tanaka defended himself. Why had he turned on his former comrades? "My expressions in this tribunal," he said, " are for the purpose of giving voice to the cause of why Japan has met her present fate. And that cause, I say, is the army's participation in politics and I should like to have—to let—the truth be known to the people in order to set this country aright, and also to let be known these truths to our posterity."

Several tidbits of information emerged that provided a fresh insight into Japan's mistreatment of POWs. The IPS tendered in evidence secret documents in which senior Japanese Army officers and civilian officials agreed on the need to parade Allied POWs in Korea publicly and to work POWs in Japan in degrading jobs to dampen pro-American and pro-British sympathies among the Korean and Japanese peoples. In one document General Itagaki, then the commander in Korea, asked imperial headquarters in Tokyo to ship him 2,000 Anglo-American POWs so that he could humiliate them and "make the Koreans realize positively the true weight of the might of our emperor," thereby stamping out pro-Anglo-American feeling. In Japan the governor of Kanagawa Prefecture secretly informed the War Ministry that the use of Allied prisoners as slave labor was necessary to weaken the "considerably pro-Anglo-American" attitude among the people in his region.

Evidence was also tendered suggesting that Tokyo planned to execute all POWs—more than 300,000—in the event of an Allied invasion of Japan. Repeatedly during the trial camp survivors testified that POW camp commandants had told them that they would be killed if Japan was invaded. No documents were introduced to support these charges; the supposition was that the secret directives relating to the disposal of POWs had been destroyed in the pyres ignited after Japan's surrender. However, as the prosecution's case drew to a close, after months of investigation, the IPS produced a War Ministry directive dated March 17, 1945, and stamped "Army Secret No. 2257" in which the vice minister of war, sitting in Tokyo, notified field commanders, "As the war situation has become very critical, I have been ordered to notify you not to make any blunders in the treatment of prisoners of war based upon the attached *Outline for the Disposal of Prisoners of War According to the Change of Situation* when the havocs of war make themselves felt in our imperial homeland and Manchuria [sic, not Manchukuo]." The outline appeared to be a brilliant exercise in double-entendre. The outline did not order the murder of prisoners, but it "recommended" that in the event of an Allied invasion of Japan, the prisoners "be set free." In the light of Japanese treatment of Allied prisoners during the war, it is fair to interpret this suggestion to mean "free from earthly concerns."

The prosecution also put in evidence the deposition of General Tadakazu Wakamatsu, a former member of the general staff, who disclosed that "during the summer of 1942 the decision to construct the Burma-Siam Railroad was made by the imperial general headquarters [in Tokyo]." And in another piece of damaging evidence, the prosecution tendered "Army Secret No. 2190" dated July 28, 1942, in which the accused General Kimura, then the vice minister of war, ordered that captured Allied airmen be treated as "war criminals." Occasionally the evidence touched on an unrelated subject and was left dangling without a follow-up. For example, on October 7, 1943, when ninety-six prisoners and internees were murdered on Wake Island in anticipation of a U.S. invasion of the island, the testimony of a Japanese admiral disclosed that "at that time we frequently received situation reports and orders from the fleet, one of them being that 'a new and powerful task force was organized and has departed from Hawaii' "—a confirmation that Japanese spies were still active at Pearl Harbor late in the war. But this admission was beyond the scope of the trial and was never amplified.

The wind-down phases of the prosecution's case included more excerpts from the interrogations of the accused at Sugamo, notably those of Generals Tojo and Muto.

Tojo explained that Japan's imperial general headquarters had been set up in Tokyo after the invasion of China in 1937, and that it met once or twice a week. Did the emperor attend every meeting? "No," Tojo replied. "Usually he was not there, only on special occasions." Where did the meetings take place? "In the palace," Tojo said. Did the meetings discuss the treatment of war prisoners? "I do not remember well . . ." Tojo demurred. Was, for example, the Bataan Death March ever discussed? "I do not remember." Well, as prime minister and war minister Tojo toured the Philippines—were there rumors? "There were rumors." Who was responsible for the march? "General Homma would naturally be responsible." Did Tojo or anyone in the government discuss the march with Homma? "I do not know if this matter was ever discussed." (Homma had been tried by the Americans as a war criminal shortly after the Japanese surrender; he was convicted and executed in the Philippines.) Were copies of Allied protest notes about the mistreatment of prisoners sent to the emperor, or was the emperor informed in any way about Allied complaints of Japanese inhumanity toward prisoners and others? "No, he was not," Tojo said firmly. Why not? Wasn't the emperor the commander in chief of the imperial Japanese armed forces? "The emperor was busy and had a great deal of work so I did this [handling of Allied protests] on my own," he replied. "Consequently, the emperor is not responsible in connection with this matter."

Was Tojo responsible as premier and war minister for the treatment of prisoners of war? "Yes," he said without hesitation. "I was responsible for their treatment." When was the Prisoners of War Bureau set up in the War Ministry? "Immediately after the outbreak of war," Tojo confirmed. Which war? "The Greater East Asia [Pacific] War," he said. Why was it set up? "This is according to international law." Then why was there no such bureau during the China War? "It was not necessary during the China Incident," he answered. What bureau was set up to handle Chinese prisoners? "There was no organization set up to deal with Chinese prisoners."

How did Tojo explain the atrocious behavior of the Japanese Army and Navy? "I am astounded at the truth regarding atrocities that is now being revealed in the newspapers," he said. "If the Japanese had followed the emperor's instructions, these atrocities would never have happened."

Tojo slept on these words, and the following day, March 26, 1946, told his Sugamo interrogators that he would like to amplify his remarks.

He returned to the subject of atrocities: "We did not suspect that such things had happened." Addressing himself to history, he added, "The emperor especially, because of his benevolence, would have had a contrary feeling. Such acts are not permissible in Japan. The character of the Japanese people is such that they believe that neither heaven nor earth would permit such things." His concern, he said, is that "the world [will] believe that these inhumane acts are the result of Japanese character."

Colonel Gilbert Woolworth, the American assistant prosecutor who read these excerpts into the IMTFE's record, paused and read the interrogator's note appended to them: "The preceeding portion of the answer was read back to the witness, who agreed as to its correctness."

Tojo also went on to claim that only the field commanders—the Hommas and Yamashitas—were responsible for the behavior of their troops, not the Japanese government. The ex-premier and war minister amended this statement, however, and led the trail back to Tokyo. "Of course, since I was the supervisor of the military administration," he conceded, "I am completely responsible." This admission brought Japanese crimes against humanity home to roost.

As for Japanese brutality generally toward Allied POWs and defenseless Asian civilian populations, Tojo retreated glibly behind the shallow defense that this reflected different traditions and customs between Japanese and others. "The Japanese idea about prisoners is different from that in Europe and America," Tojo said, assiduously avoiding the subject of Japan's mutilation of Chinese, Indian, Filipino, and other Asian prisoners of war. "In Japan," he continued smoothly, "it is regarded as a disgrace [to be captured]. Under Japanese criminal law, anyone who becomes a prisoner while still able to resist has committed a criminal offense, the maximum punishment for which is the death penalty. In Europe and America [again, no reference to Asia], it is different. A person who is taken prisoner is honored because he had discharged his duties, but in Japan, it is very different."

All the talk about different cultures and different concepts of evil was put to final rest, or should have been, by the comment of Tojo's co-defendant Akira Muto in the course of his interrogation at Sugamo. Bluntly, Muto was asked if Japan's last stand in Manila justified the raping of women and murdering of civilians. "Such is definitely not justifiable," Muto replied hotly. Then how could he explain the misbehavior of the Imperial Japanese Army? "I regret that you ask such a question," he said. "There is no army in the world or government in the world that will instruct its people to shoot or kill children or the civilian population." Thus, even Muto, a senior staff officer at the Rape of Nanking in 1937 and the Rape of Manila eight years later, recognized the existence of natural law. But wasn't his conscience troubled by his presence at both Nanking and Manila? Yes, he said. "After the atrocities in Nanking and Manila," Muto confided, ". . . I felt that something was lacking in the Japanese military education. . . . The troops that committed the atrocities in Nanking and Manila were men mobilized in a hurry, and they were not trained properly in military education." Was he ashamed of the behavior of the Japanese Army? "I felt that it was a shame," he replied. Did the senior officers of the army discuss the problem? Not formally, he said, "but among officers there were individual discussions." Were the officers worried because the atrocities reflected badly on the honor of the Japanese Army? "They were very much worried," he said.

Muto put atrocities in a new perspective. During the Sino-Japanese War in 1895 and the Russo-Japanese War of 1905, he pointed out, the Japanese army had committed no atrocities. The army's behavior was exemplary. After World War I, however, when Japanese troops were sent into Siberia to shore up anti-Bolshevik forces, "such tendencies toward atrocity came into the limelight, thereby proving that the quality and character of the Japanese was slowly deteriorating." The army's high-ranking officers, he continued, agreed that the situation could only be remedied by education in the home and school. What did he do personally to remedy the situation? He could do very little, Muto said, because "even after I became a lieutenant general I could not do anything as I was not a divisional commander," adding hastily, "In order to put anything into force, one has to be a divisional commander." If he had been a divisional commander, would he have remedied the situation?

"Yes," he said, with an inexplicable laugh.

During this chilling phase of the trial, the number of defendants dropped to twenty-five. The tribunal announced the death of Admiral Osami Nagano, the haughty, bull-necked former chief of the naval general staff, who had sat in the dock directly behind ex-premier Hirota and frequently waved to friends and spectators in the gallery. The sixty-eight-year-old admiral succumbed on Sunday, January 5, 1947, at the 361st U.S. Army Station Hospital from pulmonary tuberculosis, arteriosclerosis, and bronchial pneumonia. On his death Nagano's American counsel, John G.

Brannon, made public a letter from his client in which Nagano "regretted" that the United States had not been informed of the impending attack on Pearl Harbor at least "perhaps by two minutes." He termed the surprise attack on Hawaii "a mistake."

The previous year, following his indictment as a war criminal for the sneak attack on Pearl Harbor, the invasion of Indochina, and the murder of POWs, Nagano had assumed complete responsibility for the attack. "It was purely a strategic question," he said in a statement issued through his Japanese attorney, Hashiro Okuyama. "I assume entire responsibility for it." In the statement, which was published by the *Mainichi* newspaper on June 28, 1946, Nagano disclosed that he had opposed the alliance with Germany and war with the United States and that he believed Japan should withdraw from China, where it was engaged in "a war it could not win."

During the lunch break on the Monday following Nagano's death, I slipped a message to the defendants through the "chicken cage," asking for their reactions. Tojo expressed sorrow, "especially because the world could not hear from the admiral's own mouth of the true position of the Japanese Navy," and his foreign minister, Shigenori Togo, added, "I agree with Tojo"—cryptically, it turned out, because Togo's reason differed from Tojo's. Nagano had implied in a talk with Togo shortly before his death that he would reveal on the stand the true story of the attack on Pearl Harbor.

After the trial General Kenyro Sato, the youngest defendant in the dock, charged in his memoirs that Nagano had died at Sugamo of "maltreatment." According to Sato, when a window in Nagano's cell broke, Nagano covered it with a newspaper to block the winter winds. But a guard tore off the paper and—despite repeated requests—the window was not repaired. In this fashion, Sato claimed, Nagano contracted pneumonia. There is no evidence, however, to support Sato's charge.

Some three weeks after Nagano's death, at 4:12 P.M., Friday, January 24, 1947, Carlisle Higgins, an American assistant prosecutor, announced, "Mr. President, the prosecution will now rest." Technically, Higgins was correct. But in truth the IPS did anything but rest as the defense rushed in with a motion for a mistrial, an attack on the tribunal's jurisdiction, and a sheaf of motions for dismissal of the case.

From the defense standpoint the trial was now beginning.

23

Defense Parry, Prosecution Thrust

The defense motion for a mistrial puzzled Webb and the other Commonwealth judges. "If the court please, it is the plan of the defense to present a number of motions," David F. Smith announced. "For example, we have a motion for a mistrial on behalf of eleven defendants."

Webb raised his right hand to stop him. "I have never known of such a motion until now," he said. In British courts only on rare occasions will the defense move a motion for a new trial after a trial has been completed; in the United States a motion for mistrial is commonplace and is usually based on the assumption that the judges plan to review the proceedings at that point. But Webb said testily, "We are not prepared to do that." The bench refused to entertain the motion.

The stillborn motion charged that in "a thousand or more instances" the tribunal had admitted into evidence affidavits and other hearsay and thereby denied the accused the right to be confronted by the witnesses against them and to be afforded an opportunity to cross-examine such witnesses. The motion argued that the evidence covered fifteen different Japanese cabinets and "is so vast in quantity that no defendant can obtain a fair trial."

David Smith now presented another motion of dismissal on behalf of all defendants, arguing that Douglas MacArthur, as a U.S. citizen bound by the U.S. Constitution, had not been authorized by Congress to establish an international military tribunal or to appoint American and Filipino judges to the tribunal and had therefore "exceeded his lawful authority" in establishing the tribunal.

Webb was not impressed. He noted that the motion was based on the assumption that the court judicially noted the U.S. Constitution and the constitutions of the other ten countries on the bench without a request by the defense that it do so. "That is a wrong view in my opinion," Webb said petulantly. The only motion the court would tolerate was one based on the defense's contention that there was an absence of evidence or on some uncontested matter, he said. Smith explained that the defense sought to present the motion attacking MacArthur's jurisdiction because the defense ultimately intended to take its argument to the U.S. Supreme Court. "It is a matter of sheer indifference to us whether you go to the federal court in Washington," Webb said caustically, "or to the federal court in Sydney or to the federal court in Ottawa or to the federal court in Moscow or to any other court. One has as much right to review as the other."

Thereupon Smith produced a third motion, which he dubbed the "MacArthur Motion" and which Webb referred to as the "Supreme Commander Motion." This motion argued that "the tribunal is without jurisdiction or authority in law to hear and determine the indictment filed with the tribunal on 3 May 1946." This motion smacked strongly of the previous one, and Webb refused to listen to it on the ground that the attack was a "political harangue" and that the defense might raise it only in summing up its case. "It was not intended to be anything of the kind," Smith replied indignantly. Clearly there was little love lost between Sir William Webb and David F. Smith, who were destined to engage in fearful conflict in the months ahead.

Webb brought the legal fireworks to a close by recommending that the defense introduce individual motions for dismissal based solely on the grounds of insufficient evidence. The line formed on the right as lawyers for each defendant came forward with motions. The different counsel, reflecting the diverse interests of the accused, threw up a variety of arguments. Among the generals and admirals the common plea was "superior orders."

General Kimura, the former vice minister of war, claimed there was no evidence that he "did anything more than he was duty-bound to do as a soldier who was loyal to his country." General

Matsui's attorneys argued that "there is no evidence in the record establishing beyond a reasonable doubt that Matsui either ordered, caused, or permitted . . . or even had knowledge of the killings of thousands of civilians and disarmed soldiers in China." The attack on Nanking, which he commanded—they admitted—"was ordered by the headquarters of the Japanese army in Tokyo." Matsui "simply carried out such orders." Doihara's lawyers submitted that he was clearly "a member of the armed forces, and subject to the orders of his superior officers." General Muto, who was emerging as one of the archvillains in the dock, also fell back on "superior orders." As an army officer, his attorneys contended, Muto's duty was "to carry out the orders of his superiors"—a concept recognized by the military throughout the world. Tojo's counsel clearly had the most difficult argument of all. He could not plead superior orders for the period he was war minister; instead, he argued that "no positive legal evidence was offered to prove that this defendant participated as a leader, organizer, instigator, or accomplice" in any conspiracy to wage aggressive war; nor was there evidence that Tojo "issued a single positive order" to any subordinate to commit atrocities.

Suzuki, a lieutenant general and Japan's wartime economic czar, straddled the line between the civilian and military establishments and denied any and all responsibility for his acts.

On the civilian side Mamoru Shigemitsu's counsel submitted that "all the witnesses produced by the prosecution . . . have testified affirmatively to his efforts and his fruitful services toward peace between China and Japan." Ex-premier Hirota's motion for dismissal argued that his indictment was a "gross miscalculation" and a "grievous mistake," that Hirota had never served in the armed forces, and that when he became premier in 1936, "it was too late to set back the hands of the clock." Hirota's lawyers claimed that when the emperor ordered him to form a cabinet, the situation in Tokyo had been "strange and incredible," the capital thrown into "a state of terror" by an attempted coup of 1,400 army officers—the February Incident, as historians call it—and that the emperor had selected him to control "rebellious" army elements.

Hirota's motion was the first to refer to Hirohito. Marquis Kido, whose presence in the dock was a daily reminder of the emperor's absence, argued in his motion that "the mere fact that Japan did go to war after the failure of negotiations is no reason to say that

Kido or the elder statesmen are criminals." His lawyers claimed that Marquis Kido's position as lord keeper of the privy seal was "generally misunderstood. . . . Kido merely acted as a liaison officer between the emperor and the governmental officials." As for Kido's elated reaction to the success of the sneak attack on Pearl Harbor, his counsel asked, "Is the price of criminal immunity the corruption of patriotism?"

And, thus—to a man—each of the accused moved to dismiss the charges against himself. The prosecution relished the opportunity for rebuttal. "I now come to take the cases of the accused one by one," Arthur Comyns-Carr declared on January 30.

With obvious satisfaction the British associate prosecutor said he would go through the defendants alphabetically (although he did not keep to this order). "First of all, Araki," Comyns-Carr said zestfully. ". . . With so vast a story to tell any account must be incomplete." General Araki, he pointed out, had held a senior post in the War Ministry on the eve of the Mukden Incident and had assumed the portfolio of war minister while the Japanese invasion of Manchuria was in progess. "He must, therefore, have clearly understood what the Japanese forces were doing in Manchuria," Comyns-Carr said. And in an accusatory tone he ran down the list of defendants, arguing that the evidence had proved the following:

- Doihara was a "string-puller" at Mukden in 1931, had a hand in the army's opium trade, and had "a direct responsibility" for conditions in prisoner-of-war camps in eastern Japan before ending the war as commander of the notorious Imperial Japanese Seventh Army in Malaya, Sumatra, Java, and Borneo, where "thousands of murders and unnecessary deaths took place."
- Hashimoto, the racist and propagandist, participated in the Mukden plot and "in all associated plots of that period for the overthrow of the comparatively peaceful cabinets then in Japan."
- Hata, as inspector general of military education, held one of the three highest policy-making positions in the Japanese Army "and through [their] control of the war minister, could effectively control cabinet and other governmental policy and decision."
- Kaya, the financial overlord, claimed an ignorance of Japa-

nese outrages in China and elsewhere that was "incredible [and] could only have been by deliberate abstention from using the obvious sources of knowledge, which it was his duty to invoke." Comyns-Carr added, "It is impossible to conceive that such a large operation as the construction of the Burma-Siam Railway could have been carried out without consultation with and consent of the Minister of Finance."

- Hiranuma, as vice president or president of the Privy Council for more than a decade, and later premier, had "the opportunity of passing judgment upon all the principal decisions taken . . . and that this gave him the power to register his objections, if any, to the general policies pursued."

- Kido was "a strong and influential character, a cautious man [who] was not much concerned with the right and wrong of any policy as with the risks accompanying it." As the emperor's ultimate adviser "it was his duty to advise the emperor to insist on having these outrages investigated and put right, and in any case to insist on adequate steps being taken to prevent a recurrence of what had happened in China. From start to finish it does not appear that he ever drew the attention of the emperor, whose adviser he was, to the moral aspect either of the initiation of the Pacific War or of the manner in which it was conducted. His whole mind was on expediency."

- Hirota was the "godfather" of the Japanese conspiracy to plan, prepare, and initiate aggressive war. As premier, Hirota participated in the ministerial conference of 1936 at which the plans for an aggressive policy in China, East Asia, and Southeast Asia and toward the United States, Great Britain, and the Soviet Union were formulated. "This was the first time that these policies were formally adopted by a government, and show Hirota as their official godfather, if not their originator. In our submission he was an aggressor from start to finish, and the contrast between his public and private words and acts shows that he was a particularly clever one."

- Itagaki was an original member of the Mukden plot, and during the Pacific War he put Allied POWs on public exhibition. In addition, he shared responsibility for the "serious outrages against prisoners of war [in] Malaya, Java, Sumatra, and Borneo," where he served as field commander.

- Koiso was "one of the original leaders of the Manchurian

plot." As premier in 1944 and 1945 he "bears a very heavy responsibility with regard to outrages against prisoners of war and others [which] by the time he took office . . . had become notorious."

- Muto was a participant "in Japan's over-all aggression . . . (1) as an army officer in the field and (2) as an army officer in the War Ministry."
- Kimura, as vice minister of war in 1941, was "placed in a position not only to know but to take an active part in, and to assume responsibility for, the events of his period in office. . . . Above all, he must have been a party to the illegal decision to use prisoner-of-war labor on the rushed construction of the Burma-Siam Railway." And it was he who personally issued the directive ordering the death penalty for captured Allied airmen.
- Oshima was one of the chief architects of the Berlin-Tokyo-Rome Axis.
- Shigemitsu "cannot be permitted to hide behind such a defense as that submitted in his motion that the army 'misinformed him.' "
- Shimada, Tojo's navy minister, was "known to be an active supporter of the Tojo policy" and was privy to the surprise attacks of December 7.
- Shiratori, like Oshima, was a principal architect of the Tripartite Axis Pact with Hitler and Mussolini, an alliance that was engineered to promote aggressive war.
- Suzuki was linked to intelligence operations, the opium trade, thought control activities, and the Total War Research Institute; he was also president of the Planning Board, "a position of great authority because that board controlled economic planning in Japan." The prosecution noted that in a secret cable to Berlin, the German ambassador in Tokyo had reported that Suzuki "has created a position for himself that can be labeled as a kind of vice-chancellorship."
- Togo was the foreign minister directly in charge of Japanese-American negotiations in 1941, "even after the decision to open hostilities had been taken." He was a diplomat who made a "career of deception."
- Tojo, whose personal history was "one of steady and rapid advancement throughout the life of the conspiracy . . . [was] the effective leader of the conspiracy" to wage aggressive

war, and his responsibility for atrocities "has been so amply proved, and admitted, that it is needless to labor it by quotations."

- Umezu, the army chief of staff in 1944 and 1945, was conclusively proven to be connected "on all fronts and in Japan proper [with] the inhuman treatment of prisoners of war."
- Sato, Muto's successor as head of the omnipotent Military Affairs Bureau, "must have approved the Burma-Siam Railway decision" and other outrages.
- Oka, chief of the Bureau of Naval Affairs, was responsible for the hellships, and this "shows that it must have been navy policy."
- Hoshino, "the most powerful and influential man" in Manchukuo, trafficked in narcotics to finance the puppet state. His later career as president of the Planning Board and member of the Total War Research Institute paralleled Suzuki's.
- Matsui and Minami were dismissed as brutal militarists whose goal had been Japan's domination of Asia, regardless of the loss in human lives and freedom.

"Your Honor," Arthur Comyns-Carr concluded in his clipped British accent the next day, January 31, "unless the tribunal has any questions to put to the prosecutors, that concludes our reply to these motions."

Following a weekend conference of the judges, the legal maneuvering was concluded swiftly. On February 3 the bench denied the defense motions. "After due and mature consideration of all the motions for dismissal," Webb announced, ". . . the tribunal finds that the said motions are not well-founded and, therefore, they are overruled and denied." Hideki Tojo and the other accused listened attentively and unemotionally to the ruling.

Earlier, the bench had agreed to a two-week recess following the motions to provide the defense with more time to prepare its case. On behalf of the ninety-six Japanese and twenty-three American counsel who presently made up the defense roster, Colonel Franklin E. N. Warren, the late Matsuoka's former counsel who was now counsel for Doihara and was assisting in Hiranuma's defense, asked the court for additional time. The tribunal agreed. "A majority grant a recess of three weeks," Webb announced.

In the corridors, at this point, the talk was that the defense would take three months to complete the presentation of its case.

During this period I took a crude opinion poll about the outcome of the case. Among the prosecutors, the view was that there was enough evidence to send seven or eight defendants to the gallows and the remainder to prison, with the possibility that Mamoru Shigemitsu, the former foreign minister, would be acquitted. For example, Australian associate prosecutor Mansfield told me, "We have presented sufficient evidence to accord seven of the accused the death penalty and the remainder prison, with the possible exception of one acquittal." The defense attorneys surmised that between five and six defendants faced death, that between two and five would be acquitted, and that the remainder would be sentenced to prison terms. "Five may face the death penalty and five may be acquitted," William Logan, Marquis Kido's attorney, concluded. G. Carrington Williams, the defense counsel for Naoki Hoshino, also believed five defendants faced execution, but he saw little possibility for acquittals and expected the remainder to receive prison sentences. Alfred Brooks, who handled ex-premier Koiso's defense, thought six of the defendants would hang, two would be acquitted, and the remainder would be sentenced to prison terms. In the press corps, where fine points of the law tended to be disregarded, the consensus was that eleven defendants would face execution, two would be acquitted, and the remainder would be sent to prison. Among the Japanese I spoke to the feeling was that the prosecution had a strong enough case against eight accused to execute them but had no case against two defendants, and that the others faced prison sentences.

Among those who were thought to face a death penalty were Doihara, Hata, Itagaki, Kimura, Tojo, Matsui, Muto, and Sato—all generals except Hata, who was a field marshal—and Admirals Oka and, possibly, Shimada. Significantly, there were no civilians among them. Most observers thought Shigemitsu and Togo, the two foreign ministers of 1941–45, stood a good chance of acquittal, that they had been robots in Tojo's hands. Seven of the accused were thought by many to tread the line between a life or death sentence, Admirals Shimada and Oka, General Suzuki, and the civilians Marquis Kido, Baron Hiranuma, and Okinori Kaya. These views were based on the prosecution's evidence. The defense had not yet been heard from, and any mitigating circumstances for the behavior of the accused were still unknown.

The two most puzzling cases were those of ex-premier Hirota

and Marquis Kido, the emperor's close adviser. Hirota was linked indirectly to the Rape of Nanking, and some thought that he would receive a death sentence, while others felt he would be acquitted, and still others that he would receive a long prison term. Many thought that Kido, as the emperor's most intimate adviser, would pay the supreme penalty for his amoral, spineless advice. But on the basis of the Kido diaries, they also felt that Kido—and his emperor—had reluctantly mounted and then ridden the tiger and that this mitigating feature of his case would save him from the death penalty. Yet a number of IMTFE observers concluded that, for political reasons, Kido would be acquitted. The reason? Hirohito, who had acted on Kido's counsel, would have to be indicted if his principal adviser was found guilty.

The recess was a blessing to everyone at the tribunal. Bench, prosecution, and defense were all exhausted and welcomed the opportunity to catch up on the transcript, which now ran to 16,259 pages. During the three-week respite the custodial staff at Ichigaya worked feverishly to refurbish the complex, repainting the camouflaged exterior of the main building and putting in new plumbing. Japanese work crews dismantled the huge statue in front of the building of two Japanese soldiers carrying a bomb. Many of the journalists regularly attending the trial, now reduced to a hard core of news agency correspondents, drifted off to report on other aspects of the occupation. During an earlier recess, for example, I had spent six days as a member of Hirohito's entourage on his longest trip through Japan after the surrender, a memorable journey through Nagoya, Gifu, Ogaki, and Toyohashi. Large crowds, predominantly children who had the day off from school, greeted the emperor enthusiastically with cries of *"Banzai!"* Until then I had seen the emperor only once, at the Diet on the day he promulgated the new Constitution. Now I was with him day after day. Hirohito was surprisingly avuncular; dressed in a somber three-piece business suit, he exuded no aura of authority. As he passed the throngs, he raised his fedora and muttered constantly, in a reedy voice, *"Ah, so."* He sneezed frequently, perhaps because of some allergy. More surprisingly—something I had never read or heard about—he was mildly spastic; periodically and uncontrollably, his head jerked awkwardly. Surrounded by a mob of officials from the imperial household and others (including one British and two American correspondents and seventeen American MPs), the emperor gave the impression of a frightened bird. It was difficult to believe that in the name of this unobtrusive and bewildered-looking human being, who gave the impression that he would be more at ease in a library than on a white charger, Japan had been awash in blood for fourteen years—and that he had been revered by some as a god.

The February recess also gave me a new opportunity to look around Ichigaya. The hill, overlooking the B-29–devastated areas around it, was laced with air raid tunnels. Ichigaya complex itself had been spared in the raids as a possible future headquarters for the occupation forces; whether it would have been spared had the Allies known what was beneath it is debatable.

The tunnels intrigued me and, like one of the Hardy Boys, I occasionally wriggled into one with a flashlight to see what lay at the other end. Then I learned of the existence of a tunnel *inside* the War Ministry itself, below the courtroom, in the basement. Accordingly, one day, together with a couple of acquaintances, Lieutenants Jack Thompson and Robert Lee, I entered the rubble-cluttered tunnel. To our astonishment, we found ourselves standing on a wide, circular flight of stairs built of reinforced concrete. In the United Press story I later filed, I wrote, "It was like entering a mammoth tomb." Today, more than thirty-five years later, I still have an inkling of how Howard Carter must have felt when he descended the thirteen steps that led into the fabled tomb of the Egyptian pharaoh Tutankhamen. But the end of the stairwell in Tokyo did not lead to the mausoleum of a king—it led to the underground general headquarters of the former imperial Japanese armed forces. To reach the bottom we descended three tiers of steps to a long, dark passageway. The flashlight played on two immense open doors made of eight-inch steel plates and marked with the Japanese character for "west." Both steel panels were connected to a partially dismantled alarm system. We stepped through the doors.

The labyrinth was stripped clean, like the bones of a fish ravaged by crabs. We did not find a scrap of paper, not a desk or chair, not a filing cabinet, in two hours of wandering through this underground maze of anterooms, clerical offices, map rooms, conference halls, supply chambers, and the like. Some of the chambers were 200 feet long and 60 feet wide. The doors to some offices had built-in bulletproof-glass slits. Many rooms were equipped with fluorescent lighting, and others were covered with asbestos tile, apparently for soundproofing.

As we walked in awe through this hidden subterranean head-quarters I realized that it was from here that Tojo and his colleagues had directed the war. Now, literally, they sat directly above the site of their former power and glory, encased in the prisoners' dock like rare Japanese objets d'art in a vitrine.

Many of the rooms were connected by serpentine corridors that led from chamber to chamber and, sometimes, ran into blank walls. I lifted a manhole cover along the arteries and veins of a fantastic drainage system and found masses of pasty-white bacteriological life in the darkness. There were no rats. The only sound in this nightmare of construction was the occasional gurgle of water in the abandoned drainage system, probably rainwater that had seeped into this memory of Japan's dreams of conquest. The most intriguing door I found was ten feet high and covered with steel plates. It bore the Arabic numeral 3—and it was welded shut. What was behind it? I never found out.

As the recess drew to a close, I heard rumors that the Foreign Ministry had decided to finance the defense of the two career diplomats on trial, Togo and Shigemitsu. At a joint news conference shortly before the tribunal reconvened, Kiyose and Takayanagi sought to dispel these whispers. They admitted that the Gaimusho had assigned four legal advisers to the defense of Togo and Shigemitsu and former ambassador Shiratori, but Takayanagi branded as "entirely false" the rumor that the Foreign Ministry had contributed a yen to their defense. The Gaimusho, he said, maintained "strict neutrality," although he acknowledged that he himself was still on the ministry's payroll as a consultant.

I had maintained contact with Japanese and American defense lawyers during the recess, and the day before the defense was scheduled to open I acquired, through Japanese sources, a copy of the opening statements Kiyose and Takayanagi planned to read in court. It was, in the vernacular of the front page, a scoop, and I promptly wrote a "hold for release" story, slugged 9:30 A.M., February 24, the day the trial was to resume. The lead was based on Takayanagi's attack on the jurisdiction of the IMTFE, challenging MacArthur's authority to create the tribunal.

The United Press carried the story on its wires routinely, but that evening I had second thoughts, realizing that the court might throw out the opening statement. Other defense attacks on the tribunal's jurisdiction had been blocked, as in the case of the motions for dismissal. Sir William Webb and his colleagues had repeatedly ruled that they would hear these arguments only during the summation of the defense's case. Accordingly, I put out a "kill order," a device customarily used by news agencies to halt publication of a story. We decided to play it safe even if it meant losing a scoop.

At breakfast the next day I was astonished—and disturbed—to see the story, which had been killed overnight, played on the front page of *Stars & Stripes*. When the tribunal reconvened three hours later, all hell broke loose.

The courtroom was jammed. Every seat in the Allied and Japanese press sections and the public gallery was taken; the VIP section was crowded. This was the biggest turnout since the opening day of the tribunal the previous spring. Webb, his white hair streaming like a lion's mane, glowered from the bench. The marshal of the court no sooner announced, in a Jovian voice, that the tribunal "is now in session" than Webb roared, "Our attention has been drawn to an article that appears in *Stars & Stripes,* purporting to foreshadow the nature of the argument which would be presented by defense counsel. That article constitutes gross contempt of this court."

Webb disclosed that earlier in the morning a delegation from the defense had visited him and assured the bench that the defense had no responsibility in the affair. "I did not think for one moment they had," he said.

Webb demanded that the correspondent who had written the story appear at the lectern. As I rose from my seat, Itsuro Hayashi, who ran the Japanese defense's press relations, rushed to the podium, described the appearance of the story as "extremely regrettable," and demanded an inquiry. At the lectern, with all the judges arrayed in front of me and all the accused behind me, I explained that I had given an order to have the story killed. "Every newspaper followed those instructions except *Stars & Stripes*." And I concluded, "One point further, Mr. President: I have been covering the tribunal for a number of months and at no time have I ever attempted or tried in any way to embarrass the court or to in any way reflect on the security of the occupation."

Webb did not lower his voice. "Now we want to hear from the editor of the paper," he thundered.

After the midmorning break Captain Charles B. Taylor, the

editor, appeared. "The publication of that article was an error," he said, and he apologized.

"All you are entitled to publish is a fair report of the proceedings of this court," the wounded lion continued to roar. "You are not entitled to anticipate anything that will be said or done by the court or by any person appearing before the court. . . . Trusting such people with the custody of an article like that is like giving a high explosive to children. . . . In Britain, and I am sure in America, it is sufficient for a secretary of state to say that a document cannot be safely published without prejudice to the security of the country, and the *Stars & Stripes* management should remember that or should know it if they don't know it." Webb dismissed Taylor with a warning against a repetition of the incident.

Later that week Webb invited me to tea. "We could have sent you to prison," he said jocularly, "or ordered you hanged." This was vintage Webb. No matter how fierce the wind blew inside the courtroom, he was becalmed outside. At one point or another almost every member of the prosecution and defense had a run-in with him, only to discover that the mien of the Webb in black robes was 180 degrees apart from the Webb in mufti. "Webb was very autocratic and unfair in court," defense counsel George Furness recalled in an interview in Tokyo in 1981. "But he was very personable. One day, for example, at the Imperial [Hotel], where we were both staying, he came over to me and said, 'I was unfair and nasty to you today and Lady Webb [who had joined him in Tokyo] said I should apologize.' He was likable."

Many similar stories could be told. But there were exceptions. Defense attorney Aristides Lazarus disliked Webb both inside and outside court. "After a tough day in court, as he was leaving, I heard him say, 'Those bastard Americans,' referring to the defense," Lazarus said, "and all we were doing was our job." Lazarus never forgave Webb for that remark.

Likable or hateful, Webb dominated the trial. As we now passed into the defense phase, his acerbic exchanges with counsel would take an even more prominent place in the proceedings.

24

The Defense Opens, and the Generals Shout

The Japanese and American defense attorneys completed their strategy during the recess, dividing their case into five divisions—general, Manchurian, Chinese, Soviet, and Pacific—followed by a sixth phase in which each of the accused would take the stand on his own behalf (not all chose to do so). The defense's opening statement, a document of more than 100 pages, was divided into two parts—an outline of the case by Ichiro Kiyose and a challenge to the tribunal's jurisdiction, based on international law, by Kenzo Takayanagi.

Not all the defense counsel agreed with this strategy. All in the courtroom were shocked to hear attorney William Logan tell the tribunal that conflicting interests among the accused about the events since 1931 made a joint statement "impossible." Hirota, Hiranuma, Shigemitsu, Doihara, and Suzuki disagreed completely with the proposed opening statement; Oshima disagreed in part. Smith, on behalf of Hirota, announced that he would make his own individual opening statement because of Hirota's "special position in this case."

Ichiro Kiyose then settled down to reading the first half of the opening statement. In the judgment of most observers it was stale, recasting Japan's hollow prewar positions, though it did end eloquently.

"The defense," Kiyose declared at the outset, "will disprove each and every charge of criminality lodged against them." He then ticked off the defense's position on the issues raised by the IPS.

He dismissed the accusation that the Axis powers sought to dominate the world. "There is no greater misunderstanding than this," Kiyose said. No phrases were more subject to "misunderstanding," he continued, than the terms "New Order" and "Greater East Asia Co-prosperity Sphere," both of which, he said, were "in essence strangely similar to the 'Good Neighbor' Policy of the United States." The prosecution's charge that the defendants had engaged in a "conspiracy" was serious since the doctrine of conspiracy, "unique in the Anglo-American legal system . . . cannot be deemed to constitute international law." As for atrocities, the violation of human decency "as was alleged to have been committed against the Jews in Germany was never present in Japan, [and] we are prepared to produce evidence to explain the difference between the war crimes of Germany and the alleged acts of the accused." Interestingly, in the Japanese minds, the German crimes against humanity were now real, not alleged; this was post-Nuremberg.

Kiyose revived one old chestnut after another: "Japan possessed special rights and interests in Manchuria, and their legitimacy will be proved. . . . The responsibility for the Marco Polo Bridge Incident does not lie upon Japan. . . . The birth of Manchukuo was the result of a voluntary independence movement by the inhabitants of Manchuria. . . . China was responsible for the enlargement of the incident. . . . It was China that aggravated the incident and expanded its scope and magnitude."

As for narcotic trafficking, the use of opium was a tradition in China and, alluding to the Anglo-Chinese Opium War of the last century, had been spread, he said, "principally . . . by the Western Powers." The Japanese in several parts of China had committed atrocities, he admitted, and this was "most regrettable," but the Allied prosecution "unduly magnified and in some degree fabricated" this evidence. Japan's naval preparations prior to the autumn of 1941 "were defensive in nature and also not undertaken in anticipation of the Pacific War." As for criminal acts committed during the Pacific War, "much of the atrocities and cruelties alleged to have been committed by Japanese forces against prisoners of war did not come to the knowledge of many of these accused until they were disclosed in this tribunal." In developing a foreign policy, the Tokyo government had to be aware that "Japan was quite unable to keep its population alive by the products raised within the empire alone." As for the surprise attack on Pearl Harbor—no mention was made of the earlier assaults on Kota Bharu and other places—that was the result of "defective communications." Moreover, the fact that the U.S. Navy sank a Japanese midget submarine in Hawaiian waters between 6:33 and 6:55 A.M., December 7, showed that the Japanese attack on Pearl Harbor an hour later "did not come as a surprise attack."

It was only when he concluded his fifty-four-page opening statement that Kiyose rose to the historic occasion: "[The] truth we all here seek is not a matter of proving that one party is entirely right and the other absolutely wrong. Truth in the human sense often envelops itself with human frailties, but we must plumb, even though painfully, but with impartiality, the deeper causes that prompt modern global wars."

The accused in the dock sensed that this was their opportunity to set the record straight as they saw it. Only Hiranuma's long, equine face remained blank, his eyes half-closed. When the court rose for the lunch break and the judges filed out, Hiranuma remained seated. He was later helped from the dock by military police. After the recess, Warren, his American counsel, explained, "The Baron is getting elderly . . . and his health for some time has been delicate." Webb immediately granted permission for Hiranuma to leave the courtroom for medical attention, and the defendant was rushed to Sugamo's infirmary.

Kenzo Takayanagi now approached the lectern to deliver his attack on the charter and other points of law that had served as the basis of the United Press story. Webb stopped him short and threw it out. "In your concluding address we shall hear you fully on law," the president said. "[This] is the wrong stage of the case." But Takayanagi persisted that the tribunal's charter and jurisdiction were "fundamental legal questions" that should first be cleared up. It was now late afternoon, and Webb proposed that Takayanagi edit his statement overnight.

The following morning, February 25, Takayanagi announced that to his "great regret" he could not revise the document, then seized on the opportunity to declare, "The defendants on whose behalf I am speaking think that the law of the Charter is a momentous element in the present trial; their life and death, their confinement and liberty, depends in large measure upon its interpretation."

But Webb repeated his admonition. "We are not allowed to

permit you to put that argument at this stage," he said. Webb acted under Article 14C of the charter, which held that the prosecution and defense might each make "a concise opening statement." At the conclusion of the presentation of the evidence, Article 14F stipulated, the "accused . . . may address the tribunal."

The defense attorneys continued to do poorly. Not only did they have a weak case, but the demeanor of their principal witnesses, chiefly former Japanese Army officers, impaired their strategy. Today, almost forty years after the dissolution of the Imperial Japanese Army, it is difficult to appreciate the kind of roughhouse going it was. The army spoke a distinct language, not simply idiomatic. Both commissioned and noncommissioned officers always barked as if they were on a drill field. They rarely spoke civilly to one another or to anyone else. A friendly conversation between Japanese Army officers often sounded like a slanging match. Lieutenant Colonel Colin Sleeman, the assistant judge advocate general at Lord Louis Mountbatten's Southeast Asian headquarters, expressed it well in a book he edited, *Trial of Gozawa Sadaichi and Nine Others.* Japanese Army personnel, he said, engaged in "voice production." This, moreover, befitted the harsh life in the Japanese Army. "The average officer is arrogant and stupid," Sleeman recorded, "the average N.C.O. a bully, and the average soldier only too ready to abuse such authority as is left to him by a harsh discipline." Japanese officers frequently slapped around NCOs, who in turn batted around privates. Given the situation in presurrender Japan, in which the army was a state within a state, a law unto itself, the end result was the swashbuckling Japanese soldier—a holy terror both at home and abroad.

Among the first witnesses the defense put on the stand was Major General Kikusaburo Okada, the chief of the War Ministry's planning section, whose "voice production" shook the courtroom. He answered even the most innocuous question by shouting. Okada was not angry; he was simply back in familiar surroundings, Ichigaya. "Witness, you are giving your evidence in a way that we can hear, but there is no need to speak so loudly," said Webb, who was known to roar himself when the occasion demanded. "You have a microphone in front of you. It is rather distressing to have to listen to a loud voice in these circumstances."

Okada testified that the war plans he had drawn up ending in

1941 had no significance. But under cross-examination by New Zealand's Brigadier Ronald Quilliam, Okada was asked to explain why the plan preferred to "1942, and thereafter, [as] required wartime capacity, first year." Okada circled the question several times but never answered. "I think we have heard enough, Brigadier," Webb said.

But Okada, accustomed to command, tried to take charge. "I feel it is extremely regrettable that this most important question has been disallowed," Okada barked, his chin raised and his eyes focusing on Webb.

The president of the tribunal boiled. "I think we will have to deal with this Japanese major general," Webb flared. "He is not addressing the Japanese army now!"

Pandemonium broke out in the courtroom, and the marshal of the court shouted, "Order in the court!"

Webb instructed defense attorney Okamoto to "put the question you think you were wrongly prevented from putting." Okamoto asked the witness what the phrase "first wartime year" meant. But, even under friendly examination, the witness talked in circles, prompting Webb to ask the defense counsel, "Do you regard that as an answer?" Okamoto tried again and drew several more pointless replies. "The [defense] counsel is doing his best," Webb sighed. "The witness is utterly impossible."

With that comment the witness went off like a Roman candle on the Fourth of July. "I am not impossible!" Okada shouted. "I have not even said anything."

Again the court was thrown into uproar and confusion. "Order in the court!" the marshal demanded.

Sir William Webb announced curtly, "I do not think we should hear this witness any further." Okada was dismissed and he swaggered from the courtroom, the accused watching him with a mixture of admiration and horror.

The defense continued to have trouble with its generals. Major General Tadashi Katakura, who had been in Manchuria in 1931, no sooner entered the witness box than the court was provided with another demonstration of "voice production." But the defense counsel learned fast. "May I ask the witness to speak in a lower voice?" a Japanese attorney said politely. Yet, within a short time the decibels rose, and the embarrassed counsel pleaded with Katakura, "Will you speak in a low voice, please, Mr. Witness." Katakura tried, but it was hard to undo a lifetime's training. "Please reply in a softer voice," the attorney repeated later, "*please.*"

When General Torashiro Kawabe testified about the outrages at Nanking, Webb cautioned him, "General Kawabe, will you please speak close to the microphone and not speak so loudly."

These witnesses obviously did not help the defense's case. In their days of power, in uniform, wearing black boots and with a sword dangling from their belt, they must have presented an awesome spectacle. Suddenly, many of us in the courtroom realized that the seemingly meek, aging generals in the dock were of the same stock. Yet the "voice production" of witnesses was only a small part of the defense's overall problem. Frequently, under cross-examination, a witness's testimony crumpled like an *origami* flower underfoot.

Among the first to go down was Tsugo Fujita, the former legal counsel of the War Ministry. He testified that the Diet in presurrender Japan had exercised major influence in developing foreign policy. But during cross-examination, Fujita was confronted with the famed Ito *Commentaries on the Japanese Constitution,* as authoritative as Blackstone in Anglo-Saxon law. According to Ito, the emperor and his advisers handled foreign affairs, "allowing no interference by the Diet." What did Fujita think about that? "Legally," the chagrined witness said, "that is so."

Kumaichi Yamamoto, a career diplomat and former vice minister for Greater East Asia, painted an idyllic picture of Japan's Greater East Asia Co-prosperity Sphere as a vehicle for promoting goodwill, economic development, and independence among Asian countries. Did Japan try to promote that in the Philippines by looting the country? he was asked. "Maybe there were such incidents," the witness conceded. Is any of this looted property still in Tokyo? "I imagine that there are some things in Tokyo," he said. Was every important Filipino enterprise seized and turned over to Japanese commercial and financial interests? "They were taken only as a temporary measure," he said meekly. But he admitted that he could not recall a single instance in which an enterprise had been returned to Filipino ownership.

Juichi Yamaguchi, the former vice governor of a province in "independent" Manchukuo, testified that a Chinese warlord, General Tsang Shih-yi, had helped promote the Manchurian independence movement after the Mukden Incident, an indication that it was spontaneous and not a Japanese creation. Arthur Comyns-Carr, who was the defense's bugbear on cross-examination, asked the witness if it was not a fact that at first General Tsang had refused to participate and been arrested by the Japanese. After much yawing, like a vessel running in a heavy sea, Yamaguchi replied, "That is a fact."

General Soichi Amano, a staff officer during the Japanese invasion of central China, testified—as did a host of other defense witnesses—that Japan's advance into the core of China had been based upon three principles: "Don't burn. Don't violate. Don't loot." Another popular Japanese slogan was "Embrace the people with love." Comyns-Carr made short shrift of the general during the cross. How did the Japanese Army punish hostile Chinese? The witness did not know because he had not been stationed on the front lines, he said. From the bench Webb intervened: Could a Japanese soldier shoot any Chinese he regarded as hostile? Amano replied, "When a person is engaged in hostile acts, I believe he can be dealt with accordingly." Webb pressed the question again, and the witness obfuscated.

"Your Honor," Comyns-Carr said crisply, "I am content to leave it there."

General Katakura, one of the shouting generals, testified that during the Manchurian campaign in 1931 "there were no such things as prisoners of war." But under cross-examination he acknowledged that "many troops surrendered in groups." What happened to them? the British associate prosecutor asked. Chinese troops, the witness replied, generally fell into three categories: "Killed and wounded; those who surrendered in groups; and those who escaped or were missing." Well, what happened to those who surrendered in groups? "Those who resisted the Japanese troops and did not surrender, against such troops the fighting, of course, continued vigorously," he replied. But that still did not answer the question. Again Sir William Webb, in the British tradition, put a question from the bench. Was the witness referring to Chinese who showed a hostile attitude after capture? "No," the general said, "I am not referring to those who were hostile after capture." Comyns-Carr picked up the questioning:

Q: Well, what punishment was given to those who were hostile?

A: Those who showed a hostile attitude were still enemies, and therefore not under our control.

Q: In other words, you either absorbed them or put them to death, didn't you?

A: There were only three alternatives: to absorb them, to have them surrender, or to fight them to the end and repulse them; or else there were troops which dispersed and escaped.

During his cross-examination, Major General Yukihiro Hirata, who had been a field commander during the Mukden Incident, was asked if the Japanese attack on September 18, 1931, had taken the Chinese by surprise. "That I do not know," Hirata said. Well, he was in command, wasn't he? "I did not command directly," he said. "My subordinates took direct command." Well, asked the prosecutor, did General Hirata know that the Japanese attack took the Chinese by such surprise at Mukden that all the lights were on in their barracks when the Japanese opened fire? "I have not heard that for sure," he said uneasily. Did he know that the accused General Itagaki had arranged for heavy guns to be secretly set up in the Japanese compound at Mukden? He was not told about that, the witness said. When did he learn about it? "It was when these guns actually fired that night," he replied. Did he know a fake story was circulated by the Japanese that they were sinking a well in their compound when actually they were digging artillery emplacements? "I heard of that as a rumor only," Hirata said. Didn't he know that the big guns were secretly installed for action on the night of September 18? "I did not know that at all," he said.

Some of the defense witnesses were themselves being detained at Sugamo on war crimes charges. They rode to Ichigaya in the same bus that carried the accused. General Saburo Endo, for example, had been a staff officer in China and was suspected of having been involved in the commission of atrocities. He had not yet been indicted. Comyns-Carr subjected him to a devastating cross-examination. In his direct testimony Endo had repeatedly referred to the Chinese guerrillas as "bandits." What had he meant by that? the British associate prosecutor asked. "By bandits, I mean those who, as far as clothes go, wear civilian clothes, and in organization are under no responsible leader," General Endo explained. This reply gave rise to the following Q-and-A:

Q: Were they engaged in fighting on the Chinese side?

A: Yes.

Q: Then, really they are not bandits at all but what we call guerrillas, are they not?

A: No, there is a difference.

Q: What is that?

A: Guerrillas may wear civilian clothes but as far as their organization goes, they have a system of leadership and they are under responsible leaders. . . .

Q: How do you know that these people you speak of had no responsible leaders?

A: Although it is, indeed, difficult to distinguish guerrillas from these bandits . . . we were able to . . . generally.

Q: Isn't the truth that anybody who opposed you in Manchukuo or Jehol [part of China] you called a bandit?

A: We did not necessarily call them all bandits.

Q: Did you call most of them bandits?

A: Most of them were called bandits.

A parade of defense witnesses followed, mostly senior army officers, who testified that they never heard of the Japanese outrages committed in China until after the war. "I firmly believe that violence, plunder, and the like absolutely did not occur [in Nanking]," one officer averred. Another claimed that the Japanese entry into Hankow, China's industrial hub, had been "truly exemplary." Still another said of the Japanese Army in China, "We became very popular with the people."

The Joseph Keenan–Arthur Comyns-Carr strategy was to treat these witnesses with contempt. "May it please the tribunal," New Zealand's Quilliam said, "the prosecution does not desire to cross-examine." The IPS employed this put-down with increasing frequency as the defense's case progressed. Thus, when Lieutenant General Isau Yokohama testified that his instructions and those of his troops in China had been to "love the people," the prosecution waived its right to cross-examine him. "No cross," the prosecutor said dryly.

Clearly, the defense was destroying itself; it needed no assistance from the prosecution.

At times the gallery giggled out of either amusement or nervousness. They laughed when General Hisashi Takeda testified that when Japan's army in Korea crossed into Manchuria, in defiance of the emperor and the cabinet, Japan's army in Manchuria had been "grateful for their friendship."

Titters swept the courtroom during the testimony of Lieutenant General Shinichi Tanaka, chief of army operations from 1940 to 1942, who claimed that Japan had never plotted an aggressive war. The Russian prosecutor, Colonel Ivanov, handled the cross-examination. Several times he asked Tanaka if he had personally drafted plans for an attack on the Soviet Union in 1941–42 and for the 1941–42 invasions of Malaya, Java, Borneo, the Philippines, and so on. The general circled the questions warily and finally conceded, "It is a fact that I drew up operational plans by order of the chief of staff." But, Tanaka insisted, the plans had not been aggressive, only defensive in character. Ivanov asked the general if he did not think it was "very strange" that the Soviet Union had been threatening Japan when German armies were battering at the gates of Moscow and Leningrad. The witness said he did not think so. The IMTFE gallery laughed.

Ivanov asked the witness about the meaning of the statement by Colonel Hashimoto—the Russian pointed to the accused in the dock—who on January 5, 1942, had publicly declared that Japan's Greater East Asia Co-prosperity Sphere should include Manchukuo, China, the Soviet Far East, French Indochina, Burma, Malaya, the Netherlands East Indies, India, Afghanistan, Australia, New Zealand, Hawaii, the Philippines, and the islands of the Pacific and Indian oceans. The witness waved the question aside. Hashimoto had been a civilian at the time, Tanaka pointed out, and his views carried no weight with the War Ministry. Well, pressed Ivanov, had the witness drawn up plans for military operations against the Soviet Union, Burma, Australia, and other countries? "We were formulating operational plans for defense purposes," the general replied.

Before the new burst of laughter in the gallery could subside, Webb jumped in unrestrainedly. "What do you mean by that?" he asked incredulously. "Defensive [plans] against Australia, for instance?" The defense protested that the suggestion of such operations being planned came from the prosecution only. "The position is not so plain,'' Webb pointed out. "He was asked a question which included Australia, and he was satisfied to say that plans were defensive.'' Tanaka now backtracked and denied he had drawn up such plans.

The defense attorneys' strategy was misfiring. Unless they sought to prolong the trial in anticipation of a Communist conquest of China and a war in Europe between Russia and the Allies, a better strategy would have been simply to put the defendants in the witness box and let them present their own cases. As the makers of history they had a better knowledge of the origins of the war than anybody other than their opposite numbers on the Allied side. If they could not defend themselves in an open court, nobody else could do it for them.

During the defense's Manchurian phase General Minami, who would observe his seventy-second birthday on August 10, 1947, took the stand, the first of the Japanese defendants to do so. Jiro Minami had been war minister at the time of the Mukden Incident in 1931, a supreme war councillor between 1931 and 1934, and commander-in-chief of the Kwantung Army in the satellite state of Manchukuo from 1934 to 1936.

Minami's son-in-law, Major General Katakura, had been one of the shouting generals, but Minami appeared to have learned that "voice production" was detrimental to the defense. A new Minami took the stand, his voice carefully modulated. His appearance was new, too. When he was indicted, Minami's flowing white beard had earned him the nickname "Old Santa" among the MPs. He looked like he had stepped out of a classic Japanese woodcut. But on December 31, 1946, much to the bemusement of his co-defendants, the Minami who appeared in the dock was almost unrecognizable, his face sheared like a sheep's coat. "It is an old Japanese custom to clean house on the New Year,'' he explained to United Press through his chief counsel, Takeuchi Kintaro. "I have had a change of mind and decided to clean house also." He did not amplify the "change of mind," but the removal of his beard robbed him of his benign look. His new face acquired a hard, weathered cast with a tint of reddish coloring.

On April 10 Minami's American defense lawyer, Alfred Brooks, put him on the stand. For the occasion Minami wore a gray suit, white shirt, and black tie. He sat in the box, his head tilted back and his back upright. When he cupped a bad ear to pick up the first question put to him, Sato, Shiratori, Hashimoto, and Tojo smiled; Suzuki laughed aloud. (During the 1905 Russo-Japanese War, Minami's hearing had been impaired by artillery fire. After he testified, the U.S. Army provided him with a hearing aid.)

Seven days later Minami completed his testimony. Given the number of other defendants who were to follow, a quick calculation suggested that it would take a half year to get through them all if the length of Minami's performance was a benchmark. Like many of the defense witnesses who preceded him, Minami got himself trapped in problems of logic and semantics; sometimes he told an outright mistruth, and at other times he ducked behind the screen of "I don't remember."

In the event of a war with the Soviet Union, Minami testified, Japan needed Manchuria as a base of operations. But during his cross-examination, Arthur Comyns-Carr pointed out that Manchuria was part of China. "It was our intention not to have China become involved," Minami explained slyly. But, the British associate prosecutor persisted, if Manchuria was Chinese territory, how could the Chinese not be involved? "Manchuria was to undertake defense of that territory," the defendant said, warily circling the question and never answering it. Well, as war minister in 1931, could he have stopped the Kwantung Army's invasion of Manchuria? "Yes," Minami said. Why didn't he? "Because I could not," he replied evenly. "The military situation did not permit." But, Comyns-Carr pressed on, when the cabinet in Tokyo ordered the Kwantung Army to cease operations, what did he do as war minister? "Nothing," the defendant said ruefully. What was his reaction to the invasion of Manchuria by the Japanese Army in Korea? "As far as the government was concerned," Minami said, "there was nothing that it could do." Well, why didn't he simply order the army back to Korea? Minami went around in continually wider and wider circles, arousing the ire of Webb, who urged Comyns-Carr to persist in getting an answer. Finally, Minami acknowledged that he had advised the cabinet to approve the action of the army in Korea because "it could not be helped." Didn't the war minister control the army's finances? Comyns-Carr asked. Couldn't the war minister cut off funds to the Kwantung and Korean armies? "It had never been in my mind," the defendant said.

Minami engaged in so much artful dodging that an exasperated Webb practically accused him of evasion. "It is not in my mind whatsoever, Mr. President," Minami replied, "to evade any question on some matter with which I am well-acquainted."

Webb shot back, "You will convince us of that if you will answer questions."

Webb and defense counsel clashed repeatedly. Alfred Brooks objected often to Comyns-Carr's questions, prompting Webb to observe, "The cross-examination, the effectiveness of it is being largely impaired by these interruptions and by the halting translations at times." On one occasion, when Brooks cited Minami's right to a fair trial, Webb bristled. "We are not going to allow this court to be used for propaganda purposes. . . . American counsel as such have no terrors for us, nor have any other nation's counsel," Webb stated, still fuming at the implication. "We are here to conduct a fair trial, and we are not going to be browbeaten by American counsel or any other counsel."

Comyns-Carr's weakness, and that of the other European prosecutors, notably those of France and Holland, was turning a blind eye to European imperialism and colonialism in the Far East. The British prosecutor, trying to score a point, asked Minami if Japan's concept of a co-prosperity sphere embraced India, Burma, the Netherlands East Indies, and the Philippines. Minami said, "Yes." Ah, followed up Comyns-Carr, then the witness was never concerned with the rights of "proper sovereignties." Minami quickly closed the trap. "I believe," he snapped, "that Asiatics wished to be free of the yoke of foreign domination." When this exchange occurred in early 1947, Indonesia and Vietnam were embroiled in colonial wars, and India, Burma, and Ceylon strained for independence.

But Minami often damaged himself with the phrase "I don't remember." Asked whether or not he advised the cabinet to pull out of the League of Nations, the former war minister replied, "I do not remember," prompting Comyns-Carr to comment snidely, "Do you mean to say that you have forgotten whether you made such a remarkable proposal?"

During his week on the stand Minami faltered badly explaining his 1934–36 service as commander in chief of the Kwantung Army. Comyns-Carr probed the Japanese Army's trafficking in drugs in Manchuria and ensnared both the emaciated Minami and his flabby co-defendant General Doihara. Minami freely admitted that Doihara had been a Special Service Department intelligence agent, but when Comyns-Carr asked if Doihara had headed the department's opium trafficking, Minami denied it. "Doihara had nothing to do whatever with problems such as opium," Minami said vigorously. Well, did Special Service have anything to do with drugs? "I do not know," said the witness, who pointed out that as commander he had abolished the agency. An illuminating exchange followed:

Q: Wasn't the real object of abolishing the Special Service Department that you found that they were running the opium traffic for their personal benefit instead of for the benefit of the government of Manchukuo, and you wanted the latter to have the profits?

A: That may have been one of the reasons. . . .

Q: When the Manchurian government took over the opium traffic, was that not one of its principal sources of revenue?

A: I believe that was so.

When Minami left the stand, he was drained. However, he probably reasoned, as did many observers, that he had saved himself from the scaffold. The prosecution had failed conclusively to prove that Minami was privy to the original plot to seize Manchuria, although there was little doubt that he had been a sympathetic and enthusiastic supporter of Japanese expansionism after September 18, 1931, and that he had used his power and influence to thwart the cabinet's efforts to stop the war. Men like Minami, directly or indirectly, put Japan on the road that ended at Hiroshima and Nagasaki. As the Chinese are wont to say, under heaven all crows are black.

25

The Defense Stalls

After three months the defense had hardly gotten a quarter of the way through its case. Webb termed many of the defense witness's affidavits "all husk, little kernel." Many of the documents the defense tendered were barely more than prewar and wartime Japanese propaganda pieces. Webb termed these a "waste of time" and observed, "The tribunal has admitted many statements by the foreign minister and other Japanese ministers, including the accused, which might well appear to be propaganda," he said. "These had been admitted to enable the Japanese government's viewpoint to be revealed. But, obviously, it is unnecessary to tender many of these when, as a matter of fact, they are nearly all to the same effect."

The prolixity of the Japanese witnesses gave rise to anguish. "It is a Japanese weakness to express themselves in great length, and it is difficult to control it," Webb complained in his Anglo-Saxon way, "but the indulgence of this weakness has a devastating effect on the paper and ink supply. We have consumed one hundred tons of mimeograph paper and a vast quantity of ink. We are faced with an imminent shortage of both." The warning had no visible effect.

Examples of Webb's frustration over the length of the trial abound; so do the absurdities of extraneous material. In one instance Webb announced in open court, "The tribunal views with concern the waste of material and time due to the processing and tendering of, and argument upon, documents which the tribunal, in view of earlier decisions, is quite unlikely to admit as evidence." Earlier, Webb had asked the defense attorneys how much longer they estimated it would take to complete their case. The answer was "three to three-and-a-half months." But six months later the defense was still estimating that it would take another three months to complete their case.

Some of the judges felt that the defense was prolonging the trial unnecessarily. In a private memo to Webb, General Zarayanov complained bitterly that the trial was being "inadmissibly prolonged." The Russian judge added, "The tribunal does not always show the necessary criticism in appraising certain defense documents and admits these documents in evidence though many of them have either no probative value whatever or very little probative value, or are quite irrelevant or repetitious."

Webb disagreed. "Where the question is as to probative value, argument is desirable, if not necessary, as we have not the sure guidance of our national rules of evidence," Webb wrote back. ". . . The state of mind of an accused may afford him a defense, regardless of the actual facts. We have decided that in conference, and I have frequently stated it in court, again without a single dissent. This gives wide scope to the nature of evidence admissible in individual cases."

The Russians were not assuaged. "The major Japanese war criminals will die a natural death long before the International Military Tribunal passes its verdict," complained V. Berezhkov, writing in Moscow's *New Times*. "So the wisecrack goes in Tokyo, and there is no denying that it contains a good dose of truth." The Soviet commentator singled out both the defense and Webb as responsible for the trial's prolongation. "The defense has literally showered the tribunal with documents of all kinds with the idea of confusing and protracting the trial," he wrote. "Yet Sir William Webb, who does not miss an opportunity to complain of delays, is himself in a large measure responsible for the dilatoriness of the proceedings. Instead of ruling out statements of the defense counsel which are extraneous to the trial, he willingly allows them the floor."

Although many regulars at the trial would have heartily agreed with Berezhkov, the Russians were as guilty as anyone else in introducing extraneous material into the record. The Soviet Union tendered copies of telegrams between St. Petersburg and Tokyo in 1895. The defense went back further in history, trying to tender a copy of a Japanese imperial rescript promulgated in 622 B.C. But even more time was lost and confusion generated by the Westerners' utter ignorance of basic Far Eastern history. The Chinese, for example, refer to themselves as the Han race; in translation this emerged as Hun. The celebrated Sian Incident in the thirties, when the Nationalist and Communist Chinese forged a popular front against the Japanese, was misunderstood by Webb to refer to Siam. The Burmese leader Ba Maw was mistakenly called Bo Mo. Dr. Sun Yat-sen, the founder of the Chinese Republic, was wrongly identified repeatedly as Dr. Sen, including by Japanese counsel. Anyone with a rudimentary knowledge of Asian history was aghast at these malapropisms and anachronisms. The IMTFE not only lost face among Asian specialists but "precious minutes" correcting these gaffes.

One of the prosecution's weapons during cross-examinations was surprise. Comyns-Carr reveled in this tactic. Frequently, the IPS tendered a document that caught the defense off guard. "This document catches us by surprise," Franklin E. N. Warren acknowledged at one point, "and there are many defense counsel who should like to be informed on this matter to protect their own clients."

On another occasion, when a witness denied the existence of a clique in the Japanese Army, the prosecution produced an excerpt from the Kido diaries that used the term. The defense protested the tactic. There was no reason, Webb observed, why the prosecution should disclose everything it had in its arsenal before the cross-examination. "If you do that, as I have already said and as they indicated at Nuremberg, the advantage of surprise will be lost," Webb said. "And surprise frequently plays a big part in effective cross-examination."

Accordingly, the defense was put on guard against surprise.

Comyns-Carr, whom the defense considered villainous, employed surprise with abandon. For example, during the cross-examination of Kumaichi Yamamoto, the former vice minister for Greater East Asia, Comyns-Carr thrust into his hands a copy of a top-secret decision dated May 31, 1943, to incorporate the Netherlands East Indies into Japan. At the time the Japanese were publicly declaring that they had "liberated" Indonesia from Dutch rule and that the islands would become independent. Yamamoto shifted his weight restlessly in the box and reluctantly admitted that the document was genuine.

Then Comyns-Carr pulled another document from his hat, a cabinet decision on December 16, 1941, that Japan would govern the Greater East Asia Co-prosperity Sphere as a satrapy. Yamamoto grew increasingly restless and acknowledged that he vaguely recalled such a policy. Having thoroughly intimidated the witness, Comyns-Carr asked why the Japanese had closed down the school systems in occupied areas such as the Philippines. Yamamoto said he "regretted" that such a question was asked. Comyns-Carr repeated the question, and Yamamoto's answer gave an indication of how Japan was viewed at the time. "It was necessary from the standpoint of education to educate the people, to teach the people, to understand the true intentions of Japan and her army," Yamamoto said, "because of the fact that some of the native inhabitants in these occupied areas—not understanding Japan's intentions—were overwhelmed by a sense of fear."

Another problem faced by the defense was a witness altering testimony in the witness box to protect the accused. Goro Iwamatsu, the chief secretary to the defendant Araki when the general and ex-war minister filled in as minister of education, was confronted with a dilemma involving Araki and his predecessor in the education portfolio, co-defendant Marquis Kido. In his original affidavit Iwamatsu noted that compulsory military training in the Japanese public school system had been started in 1939 by Araki's predecessor, but on the stand he said he wanted to alter his affidavit. He claimed the decision to institute the training had been made four years earlier, thereby absolving both Kido and Araki.

"Are you being serious in answering these questions?" Comyns-Carr asked.

Iwamatsu feigned innocence. "What do you mean, sir?" the witness replied.

Another feature of the defense's strategy was to have witnesses testify to documents favorable to the accused and then declare that the documents had been destroyed at the surrender. One such incident involved Lieutenant General Fumio Oyama, chief of the army's Juridical Affairs Bureau from 1933 to 1945.

Oyama testified that Tokyo had repeatedly instructed its commanders to maintain discipline in the field and warned that soldiers who misbehaved in occupied territories would be punished

severely. Where, Comyns-Carr asked, were copies of these directives? "To our great regret," Oyama said, "entirely burnt at the
close of the war." But if the documents were harmless, why were
they burned? "I have made no investigation into the reason," the
witness said.

Admittedly, there had been potholes in the Allied prosecution's case because of the destruction of documents. That was to
be expected, and it surprised no one. But the destruction of documents favorable to the defendants was a new wrinkle. Comyns-
Carr was infuriated. "We are confronted with a situation in which
witness after witness comes forward to testify to the extremely
harmless and, indeed, meritorious character of the contents of
documents not produced and alleged to have been burned," the
British associate prosecutor said angrily.

After two months of this, Webb announced in court a new
ruling by the bench. "The court requires a convincing explanation
of the absence of any documents, the contents of which [the de-
fense] is endeavoring to prove," Webb said. "Why were these
documents burned at all, seeing they are in favor of the defense?
We assume the only documents burnt were those which would
compromise the accused, or, I should say, the Japanese government, including, of course, military secrets."

Logan offered an explanation. "It may very well be these were
burned in bombing raids," he said, but Webb brushed aside this
view: "Burnings and bombings are different processes," the president observed.

Getting back to Oyama's testimony, the chief legal officer in
the Japanese Army proved to be a fumbling witness. During cross-
examination he was asked if any cases involving Sandakan, the
POW death camp in North Borneo, had ever come before him. "I
have heard the name Sandakan," Oyama said feebly, "but I don't
know whose territory it is nor where it is located." Well, what
about the outrages at Nanking? "I am even unfamiliar with the
so-called Nanking case," the witness said. The prosecution, or so
it thought, had him. An earlier Japanese defense witness had confirmed that complaints about Nanking had been forwarded to the
War Ministry. "Such documents are not to be found in my department," Oyama contended. But wasn't this the business of the
army's Juridical Affairs Bureau? "No," he said emphatically,
burying himself deeper in a morass of incredulity.

In direct testimony Oyama cited as evidence of Tokyo's concern about the behavior of its troops a February 20, 1942, revised army law on rape. Why was the old law revised? he was asked during cross-examination. Because it was insufficient, Oyama explained. How did he know it was "insufficient"? Well, he testified, rape had been a complaint-based crime and without a complaint there was no case. Was the necessity for a revision of the law, making it a noncomplaint crime, the result of widespread rape that had not been dealt with? "Yes," Oyama said. In Nanking? "Not necessarily," he said. Then where? "In China," the general said.

And so it went, day after day, week after week, month after month. In a manner of speaking the defense was committing *hara kiri*.

Although the defense did not couch its position so crudely, it sought to equate Hiroshima and Nagasaki with the atrocities committed by Japan between 1931 and 1945. This posture had a great deal of support among the Japanese public. During the trial Webb received many letters, one from a seventy-year-old man who claimed that his wife and four children had been incinerated in a B-29 firestorm over Tokyo. "Have not the atomic bombing and the B-29 perpetrated the most inhumane acts, and were they not the most unpardonable events against humanity?" he asked. Japan's crime, he said, was that she had been "only misguided by the military clique."

The prosecution objected to the introduction of evidence about Hiroshima on the ground that the choice of weapons in the war had no bearing on the principal issues before the tribunal—aggressive war and premeditated mass-scale atrocities. Ben Bruce Blakeney, on behalf of the defense, countered with the "well-recognized right of retaliation" as an excuse for Japan's misbehavior. A confounded Webb, however, pointed out that retaliation follows, it does not precede, and he chided the defense for arguing that Japan's conduct of the war could be excused by the nuclear bomb. Well, Blakeney said, it could explain Japan's behavior between Potsdam and Hiroshima. "Those three weeks, of course, might be enough to convict one of the defendants," he said cryptically. At no point in the argument did the IPS refer to Japan's role in the nuclear arms race.

The bench also blocked the defense's argument that the spread of communism in China was relevant to the charge that Japan had waged aggressive war in China. Owen Cunningham, who presented the defense's argument, took the position that the Communists in China had issued Japan "a virtual declaration of war," that Japan had feared that the growth of communism in China posed a threat to Japan's security, and that the defense intended to show that "these fears were justifiable and that Japan took the action she did [in China] in good faith." The defense banked heavily on this strategy, and when the court ruled on its admissibility, the decision was, as one defense counsel put it privately, "far-reaching." In holding against the defense, Webb observed, "The tribunal is of the opinion that no evidence of the extent of the spread of communism or any other ideology in China or elsewhere is relevant." Significantly, however, he added, that when the accused took the stand, "they may tender their fear of communism in justification of their acts."

Twice in the defense's early going, startling evidence surfaced and then dissolved, like a bursting soap bubble.

Hisashi Takeda, who had been a staff officer in 1931, told how he had intercepted and decoded Chinese Army cables. "The code book of the Chinese army was obtained by us when we entered Mukden," he said. And Lieutenant Commander Tsunego Wachi, who in 1937 directed the Japanese Naval Radio Receiving Office at Owada, Japan, disclosed how he had intercepted an urgent coded transmission from the U.S. naval attaché in Peking to Washington. "As it was in a single cipher," Wachi said, "it could be easily decoded." The message reported to Washington that the 29th Chinese Army under General Sung Che-yuan would counterattack the Japanese at Marco Polo Bridge at 1700 on July 10. Wachi said he had notified the Navy Ministry, which in turn reported the information to the War Ministry, but "at first, the army did not believe it." The attack developed on schedule.

At this tantalizing point in the testimony, 4 P.M., April 23, 1947, Webb announced, "We will adjourn until half past nine tomorrow morning." But the next morning there was no follow-up as the prosecution waived cross-examination. The evidence that early in the game Japan had been breaking Chinese and U.S. codes was left dangling in court, perhaps for security reasons.

Additional intriguing evidence was introduced in what Owen Cunningham described as an effort to "save hours, perhaps days." He tendered in evidence a synopsis of "one of the greatest spy cases in history" to show how Moscow had infiltrated the power structure in Japan and Germany.

The evidence concerned the espionage ring operated by Dr.

Richard Sorge, a correspondent of the *Frankfurter Zeitung* and later press attaché at the German Embassy in Tokyo and confidant of Hitler's ambassador to Japan, Eugen Ott. Sorge's spies even penetrated Premier Konoye's council of advisers. At this time the German ambassador was "clearing his information through Sorge, who, in turn was relaying it to Moscow," Owen Cunningham stated, suggesting that Moscow was secretly manipulating Japanese-German relations. Cunningham apologized for offering only a synopsis of the case: "The burned German Embassy on the road to the War Ministry [Ichigaya] bears evidence that the confidential documents upon which this case is based are not available and other documents which verify these facts are not readily available to us." The reference to "other documents" was to evidence in MacArthur's possession. In 1947 the United States suppressed the Sorge spy-ring story, "since disclosure would reveal knowledge of espionage techniques," according to the chief of MacArthur's intelligence, Major General Charles A. Willoughby. This hardly seemed plausible, since the details were obviously known to Berlin, Tokyo, and Moscow. By a majority vote the IMTFE bench threw out the Sorge case as irrelevant and immaterial. Washington finally made the documents public in mid-1948. For the remainder of the trial at Tokyo, however, the Sorge ring flitted in and out of the testimony like a moth dancing around a candle.

In the background of the trial was the rapidly developing cold war, and this was mirrored in court in various ways. For example, the defense summoned as a witness Lieutenant Colonel Homer C. Blake, MacArthur's assistant chief of staff, G-2 (intelligence), to give estimates of Japanese military strength in Manchuria and Korea from 1943 to 1945. Blake arrived in court with an attaché case. His testimony was supposed to show that Japan had not possessed the strength to plan an aggressive war against the Soviet Union, as charged in the indictment. But the Russian prosecutor, General Vasiliev, shot that down by pointing out that the testimony did not cover the critical years 1941–42, when Russia's wartime fortunes had been at perigee and those of Japan at apogee. When Vasiliev asked Blake to produce the documents, Blake clutched his attaché case tightly and refused. "I am not at liberty to produce documents as they contain classified military information," he said. After much wrangling Webb interrupted and asked Blake who had the authority to disclose data for the years 1943–45. The witness replied humorlessly, "The assistant chief of staff,

G-2, Far East Command''—who, of course, was Blake himself.

The cold war emerged more openly in the clashes between the Soviet prosecutors and the defense. Early in the defense Vasiliev accused Aristides Lazarus, the American counsel for Field Marshal Hata, of "attempting to treat the U.S.S.R. as an accused at the trial," and Arthur Comyns-Carr rushed to back up his Russian colleague by branding the defense "needlessly offensive to one of the prosecuting nations." Lazarus, in turn, who was trying to introduce evidence to prove that Moscow had violated its neutrality pact with Tokyo by attacking Japan in the last hours of World War II, accused Comyns-Carr of being "vicious," adding that he never forgot that the bench represented "the Allies for whom I fought" but that he considered it his duty as a lawyer to "introduce all the evidence that will help our side."

The battle over maps that had plagued the prosecution's Soviet phase was refought when the defense introduced new maps to show that the Soviet-Japanese border wars in Mongolia in 1938 and 1939 had been fought on "indisputably Chinese" territory. The defense also accused the Russians of tearing Mongolia out of China and creating a puppet Mongolian People's Republic—in effect, a Soviet Manchukuo. The Soviet prosecutor, in rebuttal, expressed shock that anyone would question Mongolia's sovereignty or attempt to prove that Russia "is allegedly an aggressive party in her relations with China." Laughter swept the tribunal.

The fiercest clash between defense and Soviet prosecution ensued when Ben Bruce Blakeney protested to the bench the problems the defense encountered in trying to secure affidavits from Japanese witnesses, including nine generals, still held as war prisoners within the Soviet Union. He pointed out that the war had ended twenty-two months earlier and "this complex and elaborate trial has been in progress thirteen months," and yet during this period the defense had not been able to get one witness out of the Soviet Union. He added that there were many other witnesses the defense would like to summon from "behind the Iron Curtain," but it would be futile to expect favorable testimony "from a man with a gun in his back."

Vasiliev turned livid. He accused Blakeney of an "insolent attack on the Soviet Union" and broadened his assault on the defense generally. "[This] is not the first time that the defense insulted the country that I have the honor to represent here and is represented by one member of the tribunal," he charged. Looking at

Webb, he said, "I ask the tribunal to react."

Before Webb could open his mouth, however, Blakeney interjected that the Soviet prosecutor's remarks were "not only offensive but they are irrelevant," whereupon Webb appealed to both parties to desist.

On March 5, 1947, Webb came perilously close to losing control of the trail. The defense was taking direct testimony from a Japanese journalist on the downfall of prewar cabinets when David Smith, Hirota's counsel, objected: "I want to take an exception to the undue interference of the tribunal with the ordinary examination of the witness."

Webb was taking a note from a colleague—"I always give these notes priority"—and asked the court reporter to repeat what Smith had said. When he did, Webb flushed. "You will use respectful terms here, Mr. Smith," Webb stormed. "You will not speak of undue interference by the tribunal. You will withdraw that or you will leave this court as counsel, and you will apologize."

Smith started to say that for twenty years he had been using that language when Webb cut him off and again instructed him to withdraw the remark. "I will not listen to another word from you until you do," the Australian lion roared.

Smith replied that he had had no intention of offending the court "and I do not understand the nature of the impertinence to which Your Honor refers."

Webb for the third time asked that Smith withdraw the "offensive expression."

Now Smith glowered. "Well, I decline to do that, Your Honor," he said.

Webb called for a recess, and when court reconvened he announced that Smith was barred from court until he withdrew his remark. The Japanese defense lawyers were in tumult. Somei Uzawa, their chief, asked for a recess "in order that we may be permitted to confer among ourselves as to our future course," and explained that "it is difficult for we Japanese counsel to speak of such a thing, but, in our feeling, it seems as if there have been more restrictions placed upon the defense case than was in the case of the prosecution in presenting evidence."

Webb, sensing that the trial could collapse then and there, retreated. He held that Uzawa had missed the point, that Smith had insulted the tribunal, and that the "question for you to decide is whether you Japanese counsel desire this court to be insulted or whether you do not not. Do not try to confound the issue," Webb said sternly.

Uzawa was in a difficult situation, and he handled the crisis skillfully. He had made his point and was content to let it stand in the record. The defense, Uzawa said, held the "deepest respect" for the tribunal. Webb looked relieved, and the proceedings resumed—without Smith.

Immediately after court recessed for the day, a delegation of American defense attorneys—Yamaoka, Logan, Warren, Brooks, and Lazarus—visited Webb and told him that in U.S. courts Smith's language would not have been regarded as offensive. Webb accepted their statement and said that therefore Smith "in my opinion, had nothing for which to apologize." However, since the court considered the language offensive, Smith should withdraw it and express regret for having used it. A short time later Smith visited Webb and told him that he had objected to apologizing for something which he had not known to be offensive. Their meeting was inconclusive, however, and in a private memo to U.S. Judge Cramer, Webb observed, "Smith left without telling me what he proposed to do." Three months later, in June, not hearing from Smith, Sir William Webb circulated among his colleagues a paper, "Power of the Tribunal on Contempt Proceedings." Article 12 of the charter provided for expulsion from the trial, and Webb said he concluded that "counsel behaving as did Mr. Smith would be appropriately punished by refusing to hear them pending their repentance."

In July, Smith visited Webb in chambers, and the two strongly independent figures agreed that no apology was necessary but that Smith should regret using the phrase "undue interference." On Friday afternoon, September 8, Smith reappeared in court and expressed his "profound regret" for the language he employed earlier. But while he made his statement, Webb interrupted him three times and asked him to postpone the matter until Monday since the British, New Zealand, and Indian members of the bench were absent that afternoon. Smith got up his Irish. "[I have] no intention of coming back Monday," he said and announced his withdrawal as ex-premier Hirota's counsel. Outside the courtroom an irate Smith accused Webb of "sidetracking" on their agreement. "I have no intention of apologizing," he told the Allied and Japanese press. Smith also provided a touch of color about the inner working of the court. "I heard the Chinese judge tell

Webb, 'Make him apologize,' '' Smith said.

In the aftermath Webb summoned George Yamaoka and Hirota's three Japanese defense attorneys to chambers. According to Yamaoka, Webb related what had passed earlier between the American lawyers and himself, that Smith need not apologize but that he should regret the use of language that the court considered offensive, and withdraw it. "None of the American counsel questioned this account of what I said," Webb wrote Judge Cramer in a second confidential memorandum on the incident that was found in the Webb Papers in Canberra.

Smith was the first attorney expelled from the court.

Clearly, by this time the length of the trial was putting a strain on all parties. Among the defendants the tension was severe. General Matsui, for example, lost his military bearing; Nanking had closed in on him, and he knew it. A close friend and one of his divisional commanders at Nanking, Lieutenant General Hisao Tani, had recently been executed at Nanking, which once again was China's capital. Crowds had cheered and applauded as Tani was led to the firing squad. He almost collapsed en route but regained his composure and in a last statement declared that he had been wrongly condemned. At Yokohama that month the trials of Class B and C war criminal suspects continued apace, as did executions by hanging. In Saigon nine former members of the Kempeitai were hanged for beheading captured American airmen and abusing Vietnamese and French women prisoners.

In this same period, as the defense continued to present its case, Hideki Tojo received a chilling letter from Dr. Shichiro Ishikawa, a brain surgeon at Keio University. "I have been always inordinately interested in your brain," Ishikawa wrote, "and I have nourished a personal wish, if possible when the proper time arises, to secure your permission to have it submitted to scientific study."

Ichiro Kiyose, Tojo's chief counsel, politely turned down the request on the ground that it was "premature." But a few months later Tojo, himself a Shintoist, asked a cousin of his who was a Buddhist priest to provide him with a *kaimyo*, a posthumous Buddhist name. The name selected was questionable—Brilliant, Generous, Enlightened, Bright—but, significantly, the priest took it from a passage in Buddhist scripture which held that "all crimes" committed during one's lifetime are redeemable by virtue of the benevolent influence of Lord Buddha.

Of all the accused, Tojo appeared to be the most serene and secure. This was the conclusion of his co-defendants, his Japanese and American counsel, and U.S. prison personnel.

According to Yoshio Kodama in *Sugamo Diary,* it was a "miserable sight" to see former generals and cabinet ministers lose their composure. On June 13, 1947, when Kodama was summoned to Ichigaya as a defense witness, he discovered a "delicate situation" among the defendants. "Those on trial at Ichigaya have failed to gain true self-composure in those two years," he wrote. "Mr. Tojo seems to be the only one who has learned to go beyond the problem of death."

For all his baleful intrigues Kodama had engaging powers of observation. The windows of the buses that ran between Sugamo and Ichigaya were no longer papered over, and Kodama got his first glimpse of Tokyo since the surrender. Déjà vu overwhelmed him. "I looked out of the bus window and saw conglomerations of shops around Ikebukuro that reminded me of the thieves' markets in refugee towns in China during the war," Kodama wrote. "The children in the streets were in rags, and the faces of the mothers with children in their arms in front of the barracks were drawn and tired. The scene was the same as many I had witnessed in war-torn China.

"The misery of people in defeat is the same everywhere."

On March 20, a fortnight after the Smith incident, the IMTFE verged again on collapse. In Webb's chambers fourteen Japanese and American defense attorneys brought to his attention "a matter of greatest importance" they said they did not want to raise in open court. "I venture to bring it up, unheralded in chambers by reason of its urgency and in the hope of sparing us all embarrassment," said Ben Bruce Blakeney, their spokesman.

The issue was a blockbuster: "An imminent breakdown of the presentation of the defense case." This disclosure was not wholly unexpected. There had been talk since January that the defense was in trouble. "I have heard the rumors," Webb confessed, "and other judges may have heard rumors."

The defense's problem was multipronged. Until the prosecution neared a conclusion, the defense attorneys had not known what proof they had to meet. The defense could not plan a detailed counterstrategy. In addition, the defense was confused by a hodgepodge of procedures adopted by the tribunal, reflecting the different legal systems of the bench. The defense's mechanical equipment was overburdened; its staff, overwhelmed by a shortage of translators, typists, and clerks. Each American defense lawyer had the equivalent of two thirds a typist-secretary. Counsel often worked nights, over weekends, and on holidays. The bilingual Blakeney, who was preparing the defense of former foreign minister Togo and General Umezu, told Webb that he had worked the night before until 4 A.M. translating documents, "yet I am not ready with either my individual client's cases." Colonel Warren, who was handling Admiral Oka's and General Doihara's defense, interrupted, "It takes so much longer to carry on a conversation with our Japanese counsel through interpreters. . . . If we were working with lawyers who talked our language, we could accomplish more in five hours where we now spend twenty to fifteen."

The situation on the defense was grave. "We have the liveliest fear that the day will come, and come soon, when we shall have to announce in open court that we are unable to proceed," Blakeney said. His forecast was accurate; twice during April the defense required a week's recess to process documents. As a Japanese newspaper put it, "The wealth of evidence is such that the court is almost suffocated by it."

By June 10 the defense's collapse was complete. William Logan appealed to the bench in open court for a six-week recess. But Joseph Keenan's first lieutenant, Frank Tavenner, objected "strenuously." Tavenner said the IPS would agree to a lengthy recess if the defense immediately on its return presented the individual cases of the accused. Logan termed that "impossible." Webb warned the defense that "a majority of the tribunal are bitterly opposed to anything in the nature of a recess." Speaking for himself, Webb said he did not think the court needed a "vacation" and that the tribunal was prepared to carry on under the charter with a quorum of six judges. Logan was irked and insisted, "We are not asking for a vacation."

Behind the scenes the judges had wrestled for weeks with the question of a long recess. New Zealand's Judge Northcroft adamantly opposed a recess of any duration, and he was strongly backed by the Soviet, Filipino, and Chinese judges. In Webb's words, "a large majority" of the judges rejected outright the idea of a recess. But these judges were fooling themselves, for they had no choice in the matter. If the defense collapsed, so would the trial. Against their better judgment, then, a majority—including Webb—swung behind a recess.

In court the next day Webb announced that the tribunal had approved a six-week recess, starting June 23. He said the IMTFE had no option but to accept the "solemn assurances" of the defense that the recess was imperative. The recess touched off a nasty exchange between Webb and Jaranilla, the Filipino judge who was among the core opposed to recess. In a memorandum to Webb, Jaranilla set out his reasons. "It should be noticed that there is a prevailing desire to have the peace treaty concluded as soon as possible, and it would seem obvious that this case which attracted the world's attention ought to be finished before the peace treaty is entered into by the contracting nations."

Webb was furious. In a caustically worded memorandum the next day, he replied, "I am utterly indifferent as to what effect the doing of justice in this case has on the peace treaty. I am absolutely impervious to such political considerations."

On June 19 the defense wound up its Axis phase ahead of schedule, and the recess started immediately. The highlight of this phase was the macabre affidavit of Joachim von Ribbentrop, which Cunningham had elicited on his trip to Nuremberg the year before and which Hitler's foreign minister had signed shortly before he was hanged. It is historically fascinating that Ribbentrop spent his waning moments thinking about the Tokyo trial. In the affidavit he absolved Ambassador Oshima of responsibility for the course of German-Japanese relations and portrayed himself as a peacemaker who sought to resolve the differences between China and Japan after 1937. Ribbentrop admitted that he had pressed Japan to attack Singapore, but he claimed that Pearl Harbor had been a complete surprise. "For diplomatic reasons we had to express our pleasure about the event," he said. "This feeling was not genuine." Fittingly, the day ended with a reference to Pearl Harbor. When the tribunal reconvened on August 4, the defense plunged into the Pacific phase of the case.

26

Pearl Harbor Redux

"Should we ask the defense if they plan to show the United States attacked Japan at Pearl Harbor?"

This sarcastic remark, delivered in court by associate prosecutor Frank Tavenner, probably more than any other summed up the defense's main thrust during its Pacific War phase: The United States had forced Japan into war, luring Tokyo into striking first. This, of course, had been the recurrent theme of American isolationists, Axis sympathizers, and Roosevelt-haters in the forties.

Yoshitsugu Takahashi, the counsel for Admiral Shimada, delivered the defense's opening statement on the Pacific War and elaborated on the theme that "the attack on Pearl Harbor was not long in preparation, nor was it a premeditated act indicating aggressive war."

Takahashi summed up his view with the observation that "the powder keg of war with its many fuses was plainly visible for all to see. Who lit the first fuse is all-important—not which fuse set off the first blast." But the metaphor was faulty. The first blast had been along a stretch of South Manchurian Railway track on September 18, 1931, and the incontrovertible evidence was that the Japanese Army lit the fuse.

As for the mass murders and atrocities committed by the Japanese against war prisoners, civilian internees, and Asian slave laborers, Takahashi declared that "the Japanese government and leaders of the high command lived up to the benevolent and chiv-alrous spirit and that violences and mistreatments to prisoners of war and the civilian population were furthest from their wishes." During the Pacific War, he said, Japanese lines of communica-tions were cut and therefore food and medical supplies for pris-oners and internees were erratic and beyond the Japanese high command's control. This posture, of course, skirted the barbaric treatment of captives during the first year of the war, when Ja-pan's fortunes were riding high, and completely ignored Japan's behavior in China during the decade before Pearl Harbor.

The defense introduced witnesses who testified to Japan's lack of preparedness for war. Captain Tatsukichi Miyo, chief of oper-ations on the naval general staff from 1940 to 1942, declared that "to me, as one of the officers in charge of air operations, it ap-peared a sheer absurdity to try to fight against [Britain, the United States, and so on] when we were finding the single Chinese affair too much for us." Colonel Shinichi Tanaka, chief of the Opera-tional Planning Division of the general staff during the same pe-riod, testified that the planning of the invasion and occupation of the Philippines, Malaya, Singapore, Hong Kong, the Netherlands East Indies, Burma, and New Guinea were "not the result of a decision for war." And General Kikusaburo Okada, chief of war preparations in the War Ministry from 1940 to 1943, painted the bleakest scene of all: Japan, as a whole, had been woefully lack-ing in oil; shipping had been far short of what was necessary to maintain these far-flung operations; Japan had lacked resources for "protracted war"; and so on. Like a computer, Okada spit out figures on war production, shipbuilding capacity, and so forth.

Webb interrupted to ask, "How do all these details tend to exculpate the accused? They show nothing more than very careful preparation for war, and very soon. One would expect that kind of thing from the prosecution but not from the defense in such detail. This man might be a prosecution witness from all he says."

William Logan, who was directing the defense at this point, objected. "On the contrary," he fumed, "[the evidence] shows that there could be no war, based on the materials they had on hand."

Webb, however, persisted. "How does it help the accused to show that the man in the box advised against war and yet war was resorted to?" he asked. "A thousand Japanese may have weighed the situation and advised against war. Suppose they did?

Would they be called here to show their advice was disregarded?"

The defense made a big issue out of the American arms embargo against Japan as proof that the United States had intended to "choke" Japan. "And your case is," Webb interrupted, "because America would not supply you with arms, you were justified in attacking her, although you acquired them to attack some other nation."

Logan was unhappy: "That is not my point at all." The West's embargo had strangled Japan at a time when the United States was shipping arms to China, "who was engaged in war with Japan, and that strangulation of Japan led to the war." This line of reasoning drew a quick objection from the prosecution. Frank Tavenner pointed out that the Japanese could hardly plead as a justification for going to war the fact that America was shipping arms to countries that were victims of Japanese aggression.

During the testimony of Kumaichi Yamamoto, the suave director of the Gaimusho's East Asian Affairs and American Affairs bureaus during the years 1940 to 1942 and later a vice minister of foreign affairs, the IMTFE learned more about Japan's final note to Washington breaking off negotiations in 1941. Yamamoto testified that on December 2, 1941, a liaison conference had fixed 12:30 P.M., Washington time, December 7, for the delivery of this note. At a December 6 liaison conference, however, the delivery time was put off to 1 P.M. Why? Yamamoto waffled. "I was not informed of the reason at the time," he said. Well, what did he think the reason was? "Even today, to this day, I do not know anything more than the fact that the revision was made at the request of the high command." Was it connected with the attack on Pearl Harbor? "I never thought or knew whether or not it had anything to do with the attack on Pearl Harbor." Why was the hour first fixed for 12:30? "I have never heard of the reason."

Round and round Tavenner and Yamamoto went, until finally, on the afternoon of August 18, Tavenner asked Yamamoto if he denied that the delivery of the note had been shifted "for the purpose of enabling the foreign minister and the high command to more nearly synchronize the time between the delivery of the note and the bombing of Pearl Harbor."

"I deny that it was made for such a purpose," the witness said triumphantly. But he had dropped into a trap.

"Then why did you state this morning that you did not know the purpose?" the Allied prosecutor asked.

Yamamoto now volunteered the information that on December 2, the day after the imperial conference formally decided to go to war, the vice chief of the navy general staff, Rear Admiral Seiichi Ito, who had helped plan the Pearl Harbor attack the previous April and was killed during the war, had made "a very strong request that in view of the necessity of conducting a surprise attack and inflicting heavy damage upon the enemy at the outset of the opening hostilities, the high command would like to have Japanese-American negotiations left alone and unruptured up to the time of the opening of hostilities." But, the witness continued, the foreign minister—the accused Shigenori Togo—had "insisted" that the break in negotiations "must be handled with utmost propriety and care and that at least a notification giving notice of the severance of the negotiations was absolutely necessary."

As for the famous fourteen-part "final" note, Yamamoto acknowledged that the first thirteen parts had been dispatched promptly and that the fourteenth part was held up in Tokyo for more than fifteen hours. "I have no knowledge whatsoever as to whether this, the filing of these notes, had anything to do with actual hostilities," he said.

To this day many Japanese and the revisionists in the West claim that the note to Washington was scheduled to be delivered before the attack on Pearl Harbor. The delay in presentation is ascribed to "typing problems" within the Japanese Embassy. However, on the witness stand, Yamamoto admitted that Japanese Ambassador Kurusu in Washington had been instructed not to trust his confidential typist with the note but to give the job to embassy officers. They were inexperienced.

Despite the evidence that the Japanese had traditionally employed "delay" in the transmission of messages as a diplomatic ploy, the prosecution failed to follow up the reason for the high command's request. Thus, for example, when Roosevelt sent the emperor a personal message on December 6, 1941, Hirohito did not receive it until after the attack on Pearl Harbor because it was "inadvertently" delayed by the army. During the Mukden crisis, as previously noted, the courier sent from Tokyo to Manchuria the night before the incident, with instructions to the Kwantung Army not to take overt action, was "inadvertently" delayed until after the incident to deliver his message; the same was true of Hirohito's order to the Japanese Army in Korea not to cross into Manchuria—it was "inadvertently" delayed until after the army crossed the border. The militarists' technique of delay was as transparent as cellophane.

The prosecution's reason for not pressing the defense about the "typing problem," Tavenner told the court, was that "in this instance, it was impossible for the prosecution to know what occurred within the confines of the Japanese embassy at Washington." In any case, as had been brought out in previous testimony, the note was not a declaration of war. With or without the note, Washington was at a complete loss as to when, where, and how the Japanese would strike. For that matter, Japan's twin ambassadors in Washington were also in the dark.

Yamamoto left the stand with an air of satisfaction. Other than the slip about the high command wanting a surprise attack, he had done well. But the next day, much to the surprise of the defense, the prosecution asked that he be recalled to the stand. Had the prosecution discovered some new evidence overnight? Webb asked mockingly.

"That is precisely correct, Your Honor," Tavenner said. "The information came to us for the first time after the closing of court yesterday." The prosecution did not reveal the source. When Yamamoto returned to the stand in late afternoon, Tavenner launched into his questions. In light of the high command's request, he asked the witness, at what conference was it decided that Japan would continue the talks as a cover for the surprise attack on Pearl Harbor? Yamamoto was indignant. "No decision that Japan was to continue the negotiations until the surprise attack was ever arrived at *in any conference held at any time*" (italics added).

Lifting a page out of Perry Mason, Tavenner thrust a document into Yamamoto's hands. "I . . . ask you if you can identify it," he said.

Yamamoto studied it and paled. "This was never adopted in the foreign office," he said in a low, stumbling voice. "This is a mere research draft proposal."

The "mere" draft rocked the IMTFE. The document, marked "*kimitsu*" ("state secret," the highest security classification in the Foreign Ministry), was entitled "Outline of Future Diplomatic Measures Vis-à-vis the United States." The original typescript read, "For the time being we should continue the negotiations . . . to facilitate the execution of our own plans." The last sentence in the document was handwritten and interposed into the typescript. It read, "Such being the case, although it will be necessary to break off the negotiations at a proper time, we should make it our main object for the time being to strictly guard lest the real intentions of the Empire be perceived.''

Whose handwriting was that? Mine, Yamamoto confirmed. Tavenner went for the jugular: ''In other words, what you are speaking of here are negotiations that were to be falsely conducted, is that true?''

Yamamoto answered weakly, ''We had no intention of deceiving anyone.'' At this high point court adjourned until the following day, August 20.

In the morning Tavenner again went for the kill. Had this document been prepared on November 27? Yamamoto was not sure, but it had been around then. The significance, of course, was that the Japanese fleet had sailed for Pearl Harbor on November 26.

The interest of the bench was piqued. On behalf of a colleague whom he did not identify, Webb put several questions to Yamamoto. Had a copy of the document ever been presented to Foreign Minister Togo? No, the witness said. Was the document ''printed'' (retyped)? No, there was only the original. Was it circulated? No, it was not circulated. Webb leaned over the bench, his robe resembling a large black cloud. ''I have another question on behalf of a member of the tribunal,'' he said. ''You testified that the hostilities were accorded only December first. If so, why is it that in your affidavit you stated that your fleet was dispatched to Hawaii on November twenty-sixth?''

Yamamoto was steadfast. ''I had no knowledge whatsoever of the dispatch of the Japanese fleet, or anything pertaining to military operations,'' he said. Webb went round and round trying to pry the lid off Yamamoto's reply. Repeatedly, in effect, Webb asked whether Yamamoto's ''mere'' draft of November 27 was linked to the Japanese fleet's departure for Pearl Harbor the day before. But the witness repeatedly denied knowledge about naval affairs.

That ended the bench's cross-examination. But the IPS was not yet done. Tavenner continued his cross-examination and got Yamamoto to reiterate his statement that the ''mere'' draft had been neither retyped nor circulated.

Did the witness recognize this? Tavenner asked as he thrust another document at Yamamoto. Almost inaudibly, the witness said, ''This is a typed copy of a draft on which I made penciled notes.''

"So the draft was typed, with the interlineations that you had made, as shown by the document itself?" Tavenner asked.

"Yes," Yamamoto replied, "that is so." Who received it? There was no fixed practice of distribution, the witness said, whereupon Tavenner produced several copies of the same document bearing a legend that seven copies had been made. The IPS possessed all the copies except numbers one, two, and four. Who got them? The witness did not know. Tavenner suggested the accused Shigenori Togo, as foreign minister, must have gotten the first copy.

This inference produced a strenuous defense objection. "The whole suggestion that any inference [is] to be drawn from these documents is one calculated only to prejudice these defendants, not to constitute legal proof against them," said Ben Bruce Blakeney, Togo's defense counsel.

In this taut atmosphere Yamamoto left the stand. As the trial continued in its examination of the Pearl Harbor attack, he became one of many who had a bad time. According to the defense's evidence, corroborated by the prosecution's Kido diaries, Prince Takamatsu reportedly told Hirohito on November 30, four days after the Japanese imperial fleet put to sea for Hawaii, that the navy thought it had no chance of success in a war against the twin naval powers, Britain and the United States. The emperor then consulted with the chief of the naval general staff—the accused late Admiral Nagano—and Prime Minister Tojo. At this meeting Tojo expressed confidence in the result. Against this evidentiary background Sir William Webb blurted from the bench, "The emperor then directed that the program be carried out."

The defense, across the board, appeared stunned by the offhand remark. "If the tribunal please," William Logan, rushing to the lectern, said, "as far as the emperor is concerned, he was following constitutional government." This prompted Webb to express his view of Hirohito publicly for the first time. The exchange between Webb and Logan was intellectually vigorous:

WEBB: But I don't share your view of the constitutional position of the emperor. If a cabinet advises a king to commit a crime, and the king directs that it be committed, there is no constitutional protection.

LOGAN: But if the cabinet advised the emperor—

WEBB: The king can do no wrong under the constitution.

LOGAN: If the cabinet advises the emperor that it is necessary for the country to go to war for self-preservation and self-defense, self-defense is a good defense to any crime. They didn't want to go to war, Your Honor. All the evidence points against it. They knew that they couldn't win the war, and the prosecution evidence so shows it and so does ours. They were driven to it.

WEBB: When you raise self-defense, you change the constitutional ground. That is a different matter. It will remain that the men who advised the commission of a crime, if it be one, are in no worse position than the man who directs the crime be committed.

LOGAN: Of course, that is based on the assumption that a crime has been committed.

The exchange made headlines and overshadowed the collapse in the next few days of the defense's contention that Japan's militarists had not engaged in deception on December 7 and that Japan's war preparations had not been long-standing. Under cross-examination several defense witnesses conceded that Japan had attacked the British settlement in Shanghai and the British territories of Malaya, Singapore, and Hong Kong on December 7 (December 8, Pacific time) without warning of any kind, not even a "final note," much less a declaration of war. And one witness, Captain Tatsukichi Miyo, practically single-handedly wrecked the defense's argument that the December 7 surprise attacks were "not long in preparation."

Miyo testified that Japan had adopted "peacetime defensive plans" against British Asia as early as November 1940, and that Japanese aircraft had conducted a clandestine aerial reconnaissance of Kota Bharu on January 31, 1941, almost a year before the sneak attack. Arthur Comyns-Carr asked the naval captain, "Do you call an invasion of another country so many miles away a 'defensive plan'?" Well, Miyo said, "if" the British established a base close to Japan and "if" the British fleet approached Japan,

Tokyo would have to possess "defensive plans." This prompted the British associate prosecutor to ask, in his most sarcastic manner, whether it was "a coincidence that that place of which you made the reconnaissance in January was the precise spot on which the Japanese invasion force landed on eighth December, 1941?"

Miyo's reply is a classic in the annals of the IMTFE: "No. What I am stating is just the contrary. The purpose of the aerial reconnaissance was to find out whether there were any appropriate places for landing operations . . . and it so happened that it was in that particular area over which an aerial reconnaissance was conducted that an appropriate landing place was found."

Other defense witnesses did no better.

27

Defendants Take the Stand

It is axiomatic among many criminal lawyers that if a case is going against the defendant, the accused should take the stand. Not so for many of those at Ichigaya. The axiom held in the cases of Generals Matsui, Muto, and Itagaki, among others, but some of the accused took the stand for reasons beyond their own defense: Togo to settle old scores, Tojo to justify to his countrymen and history a war that had ended in disaster and three million Japanese dead, Kido to protect his emperor. All told, fifteen of the accused took the stand. Prominent among those defendants who avoided the witness box were Generals Doihara, Kimura, and Sato, and Field Marshal Hata. There was nothing they could say on the stand that might not intertwine them with conventional war crimes and crimes against humanity. Some avoided taking the stand because their position was too complicated to explain; a good example was Baron Hiranuma, the firebrand premier before the war and now a victim of political burnout. Others felt the Allied case against them to be weak and the less said the better, among them Shigemitsu and Hirota.

The accused adopted different strategies for defending themselves. Several defense attorneys delivered opening statements—for example, those of Admirals Oka and Shimada. Others skipped an opening statement and plunged into the presentation of defense witnesses and documents with either their client taking the stand

(Togo) or avoiding it (Minami). Hata's American attorney offered no opening statement and no documents and did not put his client on the stand, but he did rely on witnesses. Many of the individual defenses were dull and short-lived, particularly those of Hashimoto, Hoshino, Kaya, and Umezu. Others produced dramatic confrontations between the accused and the prosecution, as in the case of Tojo, or between the accused and other defendants, as in the case of Togo. Some defendants' cases were wrapped up in a day (Hashimoto); others took as long as a week (Tojo).

The individual phases ran roughly alphabetically from Araki in September 1947 to Umezu in January 1948, and consumed 4,443 pages of the record. The galleries were packed during this period, and even VIPs had difficulty obtaining tickets to the performances.

General Araki's defense was handled by Lawrence J. McManus, a former New York assistant district attorney who had specialized in the prosecution of international cartels. "The prosecution has mistaken General Araki as a leader of the military clique," McManus said. On the stand Araki claimed, "I did everything in my power to avoid war, and the tragic consequences in which Japan finds herself today."

The prosecution made short shrift of him, however. Araki claimed that he had opposed the occupation of Nanking, prompting Arthur Comyns-Carr, who had handled the cross-examination, to ask him if he had read accounts of atrocities at Nanking. "No," Araki said. Why not? "Because even at that time I did not hear of it as even a rumor." But he admitted that as war minister he had sent Japanese troops into China's eastern provinces to "pacify the bandits." How do you pacify bandits? Comyns-Carr asked innocently. ". . . It is difficult for me to answer," Araki said. Kill them? "I do not believe that was so," the defendant said. Well, what is a "bandit"? One who acts lawlessly, Araki said righteously. And how did he define "act lawlessly"? Violating peace and order, Araki said. And what was the Japanese mission in China? "It was the duty of the Japanese army to maintain peace and order," Araki said.

General Doihara's defense was next, directed by Kinjiro Ohata, a fifty-year-old Berlin-trained criminal lawyer, who claimed that his client had "had nothing whatever to do" with atrocities in Singapore and Sumatra, where he had ended the war as field commander. Doihara did not take the stand, but a witness on his behalf testified that Doihara's Special Service Department, which the prosecution had linked with espionage, terrorism, and drug trafficking, had been simply a press information office. During the cross-examination a Chinese assistant prosecutor, Judson T. Y. Nyi, produced a secret department report that observed with satisfaction, "In South China, to hear the names of Generals Doihara and Itagaki is something like 'mention a tiger and the people turn pale.'" The witness admitted that the document was genuine.

Colonel Hashimoto avoided the witness stand, as did the next defendant, Field Marshal Hata. One of Hata's chief witnesses was General Masatoshi Miyano, who had served under Hata in China and who went to great lengths to explain that Hata had opposed the execution of the captured Doolittle flyers in 1942. But this testimony led him onto a reef. David Sutton, a prosecutor who had fared poorly in previous cross-examinations, asked the witness whether Hata had exercised jurisdiction over the Kempeitai in China. "Yes," Miyano confirmed, "he did." Were the captured Doolittle airmen given the "water torture," hung on a peg on a wall, stretched on the rack, bound in leg-irons, not permitted to wash or shave, and beaten regularly and viciously? "I do not know," the witness said, but he conceded that Hata had ordered the Doolittle group tried by a military tribunal as war criminals on August 13, 1942. The prisoners were not given the opportunity to plead and were not provided with defense attorneys, nor were the proceedings translated for their benefit. The nominal trial lasted less then two hours.

Another witness on Hata's behalf was former premier Yonai, in whose cabinet he had served as war minister. During Yonai's cross-examination he repeatedly answered "I do not know anything about it" when asked a string of questions about Hata's activities. The bench was annoyed, and Sir William Webb observed that "he must know what went on in his own cabinet." Yonai's dilemma was personally painful; although he hated the generals, he had been Hata's close friend. Ten times, in one instance, Yonai was asked to read a paragraph from a news story about a note Hata had sent him, and ten times Yonai said he did not recall the note. Webb exploded, "The prime minister is the most stupid witness I have ever listened to."

Hoshino was another accused who did not take the stand. Carrington Williams, his defense counsel, observed that Hoshino's great crime appeared to be that he had served as chief secretary in the Tojo cabinet, but in that position he "could neither voice his opinion nor vote in the cabinet meeting but was concerned primarily with work of an administrative character."

Joseph Keenan's return to prominence at the tribunal coincided with the Hiranuma defense. Keenan never managed to shed his crimebuster outlook. At one point during the cross-examination of a defense witness Keenan made the point that under Tojo "the gangster element—I dislike using that term but I know of no other word that more neatly expresses it"—had gotten control of Japan. But Keenan may not have been wide of the mark. Hiranuma's grandniece, Setsuko Hiranuma, who appeared in the witness box in kimono and *obi*, recounted an incident that had occurred in the final hours of the war and that was a frightening reminder of the Japanese Army's reign of terror in Japan since the early thirties. Hiranuma was her mother's uncle, and she always called him *Oji-san* or "Grandfather." At about 5:30 A.M. on August 15, 1945, the day of the emperor's surrender broadcast, Setsuko testified, she heard a din and loud shouting outside her home.

> I looked through my window and saw a gang of men coming through the front gate. . . . Just the day before one of the [police] guards, Tanaka Hiroshi, told me he did not like the way army planes—that is, Japanese army planes—had been flying low over our house and that we had better be prepared in the event they should drop bombs on us.
>
> I knew the mob entering our front gate had come up after *Oji-san* because they had the police guards—about fifteen in all—lined up in a single row with their hands over their heads, and I heard the leader of the gang [shout]: 'Don't you know what sort of a [expletive deleted] Hiranuma is? You don't know, eh? He is a notorious leader of the pro-Anglo-American group. He is a traitor. Don't you realize that our country is going to collapse and be destroyed? Guarding such an arch-traitor, you should be ashamed of yourselves.'
>
> . . . By this time a number of soldiers in uniform had come into the house and were throwing gasoline all over the house and setting fire to all the rooms one after another. Paper doors, screens, and mats caught fire. . . . Some of the gang who raided our house that morning appeared to have been students, and one of them threatened *amah* and my

children with a drawn sword in an attempt to force her to tell him where the old man was. He looked extremely vicious holding his drawn sword over his head, and *amah* thought sure he was going to kill her. . . . By the time I had located the children and learned *Oji-san* was in hiding, the house was a full blaze, and it was completely destroyed.

Thus, even the defense witnesses could not avoid unmasking the criminal mentality that had held Japan hostage during the painful years covered by the Allied indictment.

The prize witness in the Hiranuma defense was Admiral Keisuke Okada, the former premier and prosecution witness. Okada testified that Hiranuma had not supported the Pacific War and that in 1943 he had joined the peace faction, which wanted the war "brought to an end by whatever means possible." But Okada's most interesting testimony came when he told of the meeting among the elder statesmen, Premier Tojo, and the emperor on November 29, 1941, three days *after* the imperial Japanese fleet had sailed for Pearl Harbor. "We were not told that the government had decided on war," Okada said. Did Okada know the Japanese fleet had sailed? "I did not know at all," the admiral replied. Did the emperor know that the fleet was en route to attack Pearl Harbor? "I do not believe—most likely the emperor knew nothing about this fact," Okada said. If the elder statesmen knew, would they have counseled the emperor against war? "Yes," the witness said, "that is so." Was, therefore, the summoning of the elder statesmen "a mere gesture and a fraud"? The witness replied, "Depending on one's views, perhaps, it might be described that way."

At this point Keenan went to conspicuous pains to clear the emperor of the suspicion that he should have been indicted, apparently in reply to Webb's biting remark earlier that if the cabinet advised Hirohito to commit a crime and the emperor ordered its commission, the emperor was culpable. Keenan asked Okada if the emperor "was unable, with all of his power, to avoid it [the Pacific War]."

The former premier was emphatic: "Yes," but Webb intervened. "I fail to see the relevancy of that in this trial," he said.

Well, Keenan argued, a criminal element had taken control of Japan and "defrauded the people of Japan into believing that the emperor was behind the war."

Webb replied, "This is the first time in this lengthy trial that that has been suggested, and it is contrary to the prosecution's evidence."

Keenan flushed. "Mr. President . . . the accused in the dock are the people we believe are really responsible for this war," Keenan declared. "If there had been anyone else, they would have been in the dock, too."

Kiyose, the deputy head of the Japanese defense, quickly moved to protect the militarists in the dock, especially his client, Tojo. The result further damaged Tojo, however, as Kiyose pursued the November 29 meeting in the emperor's presence. This testimony developed:

KIYOSE: On just what point did the government refuse to give information, saying that they were state secrets?

OKADA: All.

KIYOSE: Do you mean to say that the government did not reply to any one of your questions?

OKADA: Yes, that is so.

KIYOSE: . . . Is it not true that what you were after was not the future course of action the government was planning to take, but the actual situation as it then existed and as it had been developing up to that time?

OKADA: What I wanted to know concerned not only the present but also concerned the future.

KIYOSE: What did you want to know about the present and future?

OKADA: I wanted to ask what the government intended to do.

Okada took advantage of the questioning to testify that during the elder statesmen's audience with the emperor, "I told the emperor that . . . the more I asked of the government, the more concerned and worried I became."

What did the emperor reply? Kiyose asked. According to Okada, the emperor was silent during the conference except to say at the start, "This has become an impossible situation." Well, how did Okada respond to the emperor's remark? "I knew the emperor's feelings very well," the admiral said. "He was not concerned with the winning or losing of a war as much as his hatred for war . . . and I agree with this sentiment of the emperor."

The next day, outside the courtroom, Joseph Keenan felt constrained again to defend the Allied decision not to indict Hirohito. "A thorough investigation," he told Allied newsmen, "convinced the prosecution that there was no evidence available to support a charge that the emperor participated in the conspiracy." This prompted the *North China Daily News,* on September 27, 1947, to take Keenan to task. If the doctrine was to be maintained that the head of a state was responsible for the actions of his ministers, the paper said, then it would appear that at the very least Hirohito should have stood trial. The doctrine had doubtlessly been discarded for political reasons, the writer added. "But, whatever the motive, Hirohito was not indicted before the International Tribunal, and the question of his innocence or guilt in the matter has never been at issue before it," the editorial continued. "Yet at a late stage of the trial the prosecution, for motives best known to itself, sought to elicit from one of the defendants in cross-examination testimony calculated to prove the innocence of the emperor."

This incident, the *North China Daily News* said, "was indicative of the manner in which both prosecution and defense have exercised a roving commission in the performance of their duties and explains why the trial is dragging out to such an intolerable length. Compared with the Nuremberg trial . . . this trial at Tokyo has nothing to commend it; it appears to be just about as amateurish as any body of apparently learned men could possibly make it. If in the circumstances Sir William Webb has displayed irritation, he deserves sympathy rather than criticism. More than that, he is to be credited with an attempt to keep the trial within manageable limits [although] he is not succeeding as well as he might."

Koki Hirota, the former foreign minister and premier, was another prominent defendant who chose not to take the stand. He was too vulnerable. George Yamaoka, who had stepped in as Hirota's American counsel following David Smith's expulsion, told the court, "Upon the advice of his present counsel, the accused Hirota will not testify in his own behalf."

The defense witnesses on Hirota's behalf testified that he had not had "the slightest inkling" of the Marco Polo Bridge Incident that touched off the Sino-Japanese War and that he had done "everything in his power" to seek a local settlement of it. As proof, Yamaoka introduced the texts of Hirota's speeches, news conferences, statements in the Diet, and so forth. But the prosecution ambushed Yamaoka by tendering in evidence secret Gaimusho cables and reports showing that within the inner councils of Japan Hirota had been known as a hard-liner who pressed for a bigger war in China. Incredibly, even the Japanese general staff regarded Hirota as "aggressive."

Under cross-examination, Hirota's witnesses testified that Japanese diplomats in Nanking had reported the mass-scale atrocities to Hirota and that "we considered most of them to be facts." The most prejudicial admission in this round came from Itaro Ishii, one of Hirota's aides who had run the Gaimusho's East Asia bureau in 1937 and 1938. On the stand he acknowledged the Rape of Nanking.

> Q: Mr. Witness, in your affidavit you mention that immediately after the fall of Nanking you received a telegram from the acting [Japanese] consul-general at Nanking concerning atrocities committed by the Japanese army. Now, that telegram—I take it that it was in Japanese?
>
> A: Yes, it was written in Japanese.
>
> Q: How was the term "atrocities" rendered in Japanese?
>
> A: At that time there was no general term or special term used for the acts that had been committed.
>
> Q: I wish to ask, what was referred to by the term "atrocities"?
>
> A: . . . rape, incendiarism, and looting.

In spite of—or perhaps because of—this damaging testimony George Yamaoka continued introducing any and all documents he could find to help his client. Privately, the Soviet judge sharply criticized Webb for acting like a "spectator" during this phase of the case and for admitting documents on his behalf that had no or little probative value. As a result, General Zarayanov wrote in a private memo to Webb, the trial was "inadmissibly prolonged [although Hirota] is tried because he was one of the outstanding leaders of the Japanese ruling clique and was actively carrying out aggression and imperialistic policy of Japan for a period of more than ten years." Zarayanov was especially critical that Hirota's "trivial" speeches and declarations were admitted in evidence when "it is a matter of common knowledge that [his] words are at variance with deeds."

In a reply, Webb said he felt that Yamaoka was trying to establish Hirota's state of mind and reminded Zarayanov that in conference the judges, "without a single dissent," had agreed that such material might afford a defense. But Webb ruefully conceded that "reading the record carefully, one may see only now, in the light of events, how the cross-examination might have been shortened."

Next, General Itagaki, Doihara's companion in terror, took the stand, probably because he had nothing to lose; the evidence of his complicity in the Mukden Incident and other terrible deeds was conclusive. In the background of Itagaki's appearance on the stand, a squabble broke out between Joseph Keenan and the Filipino associate prosecutor, Pedro Lopez, who had assembled the evidence against Itagaki and protested Keenan's decision to have Chinese assistant prosecutor Nyi handle the cross-examination. "My decision remains unaltered," Keenan informed Lopez in a bluntly worded memorandum. "I must, of course assure you that there is not the slightest ground for complaint that the decision is 'unfair to the country' that you represent. Itagaki, as far as that goes, particularly affected the Chinese people with what we believe to be a long series of crimes. . . . I am not aware that he ever appeared in the Philippine Islands."

General Masataka Yamawaki, who had served as Itagaki's vice minister of war, was a typical witness. The prosecution presented him with a collection of statements by Japanese soldiers returning from China. Itagaki had taken these statements and then imposed absolute silence on the returning soldiers for reasons of "military discipline and public morale." Yamawaki acknowledged the collection's authenticity, and for the first time the Japanese public was able to read excerpts of it.

- "At XX we captured a family of four. We played with the daughter as we would with a harlot . . . and then killed her."
- "One commander unofficially gave instructions for raping as follows: 'In order that we won't have problems, either pay them money or kill them in some obscure place after you have finished.' "
- "In a half a year of battle about the only things I learned are rape and burglary."
- "The prisoners of the Chinese army were sometimes lined up in one line and killed to test the efficiency of the machine gun."

On October 7, 1947, the beetle-browed Itagaki took the stand in his own defense. He placed the blame for the Sino-Japanese war on "anti-Japanese sentiments" among the Chinese, and he glided over the atrocities there and in Sumatra and Singapore, where he had also commanded. His roughest time during cross-examination was when Nyi, holding a paper in his hand and shielding it from the accused, asked Itagaki whether or not it was true that during a conference with the emperor in July 1938 Hirohito had "severely reprimanded" him, describing "the actions of the army in the past [as] abominable" and accusing the army of "arbitrary and sneaky" behavior with "absolutely no obedience to central orders."

"That is not so . . ." Itagaki protested. "Where did you get such a report? What is your ground for asking me such a question? Tell me very definitely where you got that fact [sic]!"

The Chinese prosecutor remained insouciant. "This is not the occasion for you to ask me," Nyi said coolly. It was only months later, during the summation of its case, that the prosecution produced the secret Saionji-Harada diaries from which this and other inside information was taken. The late Prince Saionji, a revered elder statesman and confidant of Hirohito, had kept a personal diary that was transcribed by Baron Kumao Harada, his private secretary. The prosecution kept the existence of the diaries a secret, introducing excerpts from them with increasing frequency. Later, when the defendants found themselves trapped between the Kido and Saionji-Harada diaries, the defense went to great effort to impugn them as "misrepresentations."

In 1952, four years after the IMTFE ended, the relatives and friends of Itagaki gathered his private papers, including the letters and the diary entries he had written at Sugamo, and published them as his *Secret Memoirs*. In a 1947 entry Itagaki indicated that he was preparing himself for the dark journey that lay ahead. "Since early last year I have been on trial at Ichigaya by the Allied powers . . . a proper fate for me. It is not a question of what my sentence will be. I have tried to purify the mental state of mind I had at the start of the trial. My quiet life in Sugamo was a heaven-sent opportunity for me to study—which I could not in the past because of my hurried life—and of late I have begun to read books on Buddhism and have attained serenity of mind."

Itagaki, the fire-eater, was followed to the stand by a milquetoast, Okinori Kaya, a faceless bureaucrat, a man who stamped reports, circulated red tape, prided himself as an administrator, and—like Nuremberg's Albert Speer and Hjalmar Schacht—enjoyed mixing with the Beautiful People of the New Order. Kaya was defended by Michael Levin, a labor lawyer and former dean of the Milwaukee College of Law, whose opening statement stressed Kaya's banality. "He held conventional administrative offices . . . and performed his duties in a conventional and routine manner." As finance minister in 1937–38 and 1941–44, of course, he had worked out the financing of the China and Pacific wars and such projects as the Burma-Siam Death Railway; he was also a member of the cabinet's opium committee, since opium was a source of revenue.

On the stand the fifty-eight-year-old bureaucrat described his role in the government. "I had no connection whatsoever with the so-called rightist or leftist or military clique," Kaya said, "nor was I a member of a political party." He had nothing to do with Japan's aggressive wars. "We civilian members of the cabinet were not consulted," he continued. He never heard of atrocities. He had toured Europe's battlefields in 1919, and "the wide devastation and the horrors of war sank into my bones."

To Kaya's embarrassment the prosecution produced his public addresses made during the previous decade. Unlike Hirota, he had openly celebrated war. "All the world is marveling at the glorious results our forces have been achieving in the present China Incident," Kaya boasted in a representative speech. In the year of the Rape of Nanking and other horrors he described China as "something like a cancer, and since surgical removal is necessary, Japan has been performing that role." Kaya was especially pleased with this speech and was convinced, he said after its delivery, that it was a speech "which history will not forget." He delivered it in 1938 at his birthplace—Hiroshima.

If Okinori Kaya was an ambitious paper-pusher who got trapped in the Great Game, the defendant who followed him to the stand was the linchpin of the dock, the true power broker, the *only* man among the accused who knew the extent of the emperor's complicity in the terrifying years covered by the indictment. Almost everything associated with Marquis Kido was an amalgam of court intrigue, calculated detachment, and devious complexity. Nothing about him was simple: His diaries contained 5,920 entries; his interrogations at Sugamo filled 775 pages. William Logan, Kido's American counsel, offered a no-frills defense. He put his client directly on the stand. Kido's week-long odyssey opened with his reading a 297-page deposition. He dissociated himself—and his emperor—from the militarists. The army's grandiose war plans had "terrified" him; Japan's alliance with the Nazis had "tormented" him because it divided the world and would lead Japan into war against the United States. Hirohito complained to him that the army was strangling the emperor with floss silk, a Japanese metaphor for killing a person with kindness.

In an extraordinary statement, lost in the avalanche of IMTFE testimony, Kido implied that the atomic bombing of Japan had been a blessing because it ended the war swiftly. "It is my inward satisfaction," the emperor's agent said, "that I was instrumental in saving another twenty million of my innocent compatriots from war ravages and also the Americans tens of thousands of casualties, which would have been caused had Japan gone on fighting to the bitter end . . . engaging the invading Americans in a decisive battle of the Japanese mainland."

The militarists in the dock were stunned by Kido's performance. "The testimony of senior statesmen Koichi Kido has definitely placed him in opposition to the defendants who were formerly in the navy or army," Yoshio Kodama wrote in his *Sugamo Diary*. "On the bus back to Sugamo the opposing parties literally glared at each other with shooting sparks." Generals Sato and Muto were especially bitter. "The army is blamed for everything," they said. Threatening, the hotheaded Colonel Hashimoto said, "Ordinarily, a scoundrel like this would be choked to death. But we can't do a thing like that now."

Associate prosecutor Comyns-Carr planned to conduct the cross-examination, and it had the makings of a great matchup between two sophisticated, cunning, and wily adversaries. But Joseph Keenan could not resist the spotlight and shunted Comyns-Carr aside. A Keenan-Kido confrontation also held great promise but of a different character. Keenan was coarse, offensive, hard-nosed, the prosecutorial bully; Kido was overly sophisticated, innately polite, subtle, and discursive, sensitive to the nuances of each word. The confrontation produced splendid theater. Frequently, Keenan admonished the defendant to "indulge me a moment so we can . . . talk in the plainest language possible."

The tone of the cross-examination is caught in this exchange: "Mr. Kido," Keenan asked, "you were dealing with a crowd of assassins and murderers, weren't you, by your own recitation?"

Keenan's language shocked Kido, and he tapped his toes on the floor in agitation. "I was not dealing with them directly," Kido demurred.

"But," said Keenan, who knew that Kido's predecessor had been assassinated by the militarists, "they were coming around the fringes of the Lord Keeper and the nobility, weren't they?"

Kido's toes tapped faster. "Yes, that happened from time to time."

With the marquis in the box it was impossible to avoid mention of Hirohito's place in the scheme of things—even for Joseph Keenan, the emperor's Allied legal shield. Kido insisted that the emperor was constitutionally impotent. Well, asked Keenan, "if the cabinet agreed upon war, the emperor of Japan would have no actual power to prevent it?"

Kido's face lit up like a Japanese lantern, and his toes were still. "Yes," he said, aglow, "the emperor had no power to prevent it."

But Keenan blew out the light. "So his signing of the rescript [declaring war] was a mere gesture, is that so?" Keenan asked.

Kido's toes began tapping again. "I don't understand the meaning of the word 'gesture,' " he said. "What do you mean?"

In this instance, Keenan explained, fraud—"fraud upon the people of Japan to make them believe that it was the act of their emperor when in truth and in fact he couldn't do anything else regardless of his real wishes and desires and his feelings for the best interests of Japan."

Webb broke in. "Mr. Chief of Counsel," the president of the tribunal said, "we are not trying the emperor."

Keenan drifted off in another direction, only to return to the subject. If the emperor did not want war, Keenan persisted, why didn't Kido recommend that Hirohito refuse to sign the imperial rescript declaring war? "A decision made by the cabinet and high command cannot be vetoed by His Majesty the emperor," Kido said. What was there to stop it? "The emperor was in no position to reject such advice," Kido said. But Keenan hammered away: Why not? What was there to stop him? Custom, the defendant replied, adding hastily that Hirohito had tried to block the war when he instructed Tojo as premier and war minister to start new negotiations with the United States with "a clean slate."

This explanation prompted Webb to ask, "Where did he [the emperor] get that authority?" Kido backed up slightly, describing this maneuver by Hirohito as "a rather advanced step."

Given the testimony during the Itagaki and Kido phases of the trial, it was becoming increasingly apparent that the emperor was not quite the docile, apolitical figurehead he was made out to be.

Keenan turned to the Saionji-Harada diaries, but Kido—their rival for the emperor's affection—doubted Baron Harada's credibility. The baron, Kido said, was "one of my greatest friends . . . but I cannot place my utmost confidence" in his transcription of Prince Saionji's diaries.

Even so, Keenan asked, did Kido tell Harada on April 20, 1939, that "if the emperor's ideas are not changed, there will exist quite a gap between His Majesty and the army and rightist groupings?" Kido denied making the statement. Did Kido tell Harada on September 22 of the same year that "the present emperor has too much of the scientist in him and has no sympathy for the ideas of the right wing. It is very troubling because he is too orthodox [conservative]?" Again Kido denied making such a statement.

Keenan shifted laterally in his attempt to prove that Kido had exercised a baleful influence on the emperor. Under questioning, Kido admitted that in 1941 the navy had opposed the war and that if the navy had voted against war, the army would not have been able to start it, although as a result the army might have assassinated "a few people." Keenan asked, why hadn't Kido encouraged the navy to hold out for peace? "Well," Kido dodged, "I couldn't say anything about that." But the defendant conceded that on October 15, 1941, three days *before* Tojo was installed as premier, he had known Tojo wanted war. If this was so, Keenan asked, why did he plump for Tojo as premier? In the hope Hirohito could change Tojo's mind? "Yes," Kido said meekly. Well, did the emperor have anything to do with the decision to go to war against the United States? "The emperor thought it was a very bad thing," Kido averred. Then, Keenan observed, the emperor's approval was "merely a formal acquiescence on his part to something that had been decided by others?"

Kido's reply was evasive, but with a bulldog's tenacity Keenan pressed the question, and Kido finally acquiesced. "In plain language, yes." Kido now exposed his true concern: Without Tojo as premier and war minister, the army would have run amok. In the last analysis, as viewed by the emperor's foremost adviser, the issue of war or peace was transcended by fear of the army.

But Keenan would not let the subject rest. Why didn't Hirohito summon the generals and simply tell them, "I do not want war under any circumstances and I want you to control the army to see that there is no outbreak on that account"? After 31,000 pages of testimony the IMTFE had gotten down to the gut issue. The tribunal strained to hear Kido's answer, but it was anticlimactic. He could not reply, Kido said, because the question was hypothetical. Kido's innermost fear was now on display: If the army had not gotten its way, Japan would have been plunged into bloody civil war. The Allied chief of counsel turned to the bench and said, "We contend that that wouldn't be a sufficient excuse if the choice were between a rebellion here in Japan or loosing war upon the world."

Kido had protected himself and his emperor ably, but as the fencing continued, Keenan undermined Kido's credibility by zeroing in on events at the palace in the early hours of the day Pearl Harbor was attacked. When Kido heard that Roosevelt had sent Hirohito a cable, at 2:40 A.M. Kido proceeded to the palace, where he met Foreign Minister Togo. Did Kido learn the contents of the Roosevelt cable? "No," Kido said. Did he attempt to find out what was in the telegram? Yes, he said, but as Togo was about to tell him, the emperor summoned the foreign minister into audience. Did Togo have the telegram on him? Kido thought so. Why didn't Kido accompany Togo to the audience? Kido said he felt the matter should be handled only between foreign minister and emperor, although he confessed that a conference with the emperor at that hour was "very unusual." Did Kido think that Roosevelt's message was a desperate American attempt to keep the peace? "I felt it was something very important," Kido said.

But after Togo left the palace and the emperor retired, Kido said, he simply went home and "failed to grasp the opportunity" to speak to the emperor. He didn't even telephone Togo's home to find out what had happened; the thought, he claimed, did not occur to him.

Keenan erupted like a Celtic volcano. "Is not your whole story absurd and a deliberate falsehood, and didn't you know all the contents of the telegram even before you went to the imperial palace?" Kido stuck to his story. Well, Keenan asked, did Kido know that at almost that exact moment Pearl Harbor was being bombed? "I did not know." Then was it sheer coincidence that he, the emperor's chief adviser, was in the palace at that very unusual hour as Pearl Harbor was attacked? "I know nothing at all about that," the defendant said.

Day after day the duel between Keenan and Kido proceeded in this fashion—parry, thrust, and lunge. In his diary Kodama expressed a view that was widely held among Kido's co-defendants. "This fox is . . . [blaming] everything on militarists and nationalists," he wrote. "He is trying to lead the judges and prosecutors of eleven countries astray by laying down a smokescreen. He has said, 'Half my life has been spent in fighting the military caste.' It is really scandalous. A senior statesman is a man who thinks other people are fools. Will this fox succeed in fooling the world, or will he end up as fox soup?"

After Kido's dramatic testimony, the courtroom proceedings settled into a comparatively dull routine. The defenses offered by Generals Kimura and Koiso were unspectacular and brief. Kimura, who had served as Tojo's vice minister of war and later field commander in Burma, did not take the stand. The evidence against him was overwhelming, from his directives concerning POWs to the Burma-Siam Death Railway to a sheaf of grisly atrocities by forces under his command, including the machine-gunning of ninety-seven Burmese civilians for refusing to reveal information about Allied paratroopers and the butchering of 630 Burmese at Kalagon a month before the war ended.

Koiso's involvement in the plots surrounding the Mukden Incident and other conspiracies was also proven. Nevertheless, he took the stand and earned the distinction of being the first general among the defendants to express remorse for the behavior of the Imperial Japanese Army. "Such cases as described in this court of cruel and inhuman acts were beyond my imagination," he said contritely.

28

Sir William Webb Leaves the Bench

While to all outward appearances the tribunal was proceeding on its slow, rather predictable way, in the judges' chambers there was pandemonium. In early October, just before the Kido testimony, J. B. Chifley, Australia's prime minister, had ordered Sir William Webb home to take up his seat on the Supreme Court as it completed its 1947 term, a five-week period covering November and December. Without Webb, the high court consisted of six judges, leaving the possibility of an equal division of opinion should a constitutional issue emerge. The Australian Constitution does not provide for the appointment of an acting judge; accordingly, Chifley proposed either that the Tokyo trial adjourn or that the IMTFE arrange for the defense to submit only documentary evidence during Webb's absence.

A shaken Webb rushed off to see MacArthur and the Allied commander was livid. In a cable to Chifley on October 7, 1947, MacArthur warned, "In my opinion it would amount to an international calamity to have the presiding magistrate relieved at this late date from his seat on the tribunal. Sir William's relief at this decisive stage would tend to demoralize the entire proceedings." MacArthur said there was "little doubt" that the trial would end by February 24, in time for Webb to rejoin the Court at the start of its 1948 session.

Australia's wartime foreign minister, who had been an inti-

mate associate of MacArthur, Herbert V. Evatt, now intervened
with his own cable to MacArthur in which he told the supreme
commander that Webb's absence from the High Court "is prejudicial to the administration of justice in Australia" and pleaded
for MacArthur's "intervention" with the IMTFE to resolve the
crisis.

Webb's colleagues on the bench were as outraged as Mac-
Arthur; several judges maintained that they had put off urgent
work at home to see the trial through and that Webb should do
the same. As Webb admitted privately later, his colleagues opposed an adjournment that "discharged purely Australian business." A majority of the justices also rejected the idea that the
tribunal order the defense to rearrange their case to accommodate
Canberra.

On October 20 Webb wrote Sir John Latham, the chief justice
of the High Court at Melbourne, a private letter explaining the
critical nature of the Tokyo situation. "I was hoping that I would
not miss a second of the trial and still entertain that hope." The
Latham letter, which is in the Australian War Memorial archives
at Canberra, is of historical interest because it reveals Webb's
state of mind about the accused. "Kido and Tojo," he wrote,
"are in my opinion the two most important accused." Webb did
not want to miss their defense. As it turned out, the wrangle over
his departure got him through the Kido phase and as far as Koiso.

But Chifley was insistent, and both Webb and MacArthur ultimately bowed to the wishes of Australia's premier. At the end
of October Webb cabled the news that he would leave for Australia as soon as his wife—another complication—was discharged
from a Tokyo hospital, but he added that by returning home "[I]
will miss the defense of Togo, Tojo and Umezu." (In point of
fact, Webb missed the defense of ten accused and returned to
Tokyo on December 15 in time to catch Togo, Tojo, and Umezu.)
This was, indeed, a sorry spectacle, the more so since Australia's
High Court heard no case of significance while Webb sat.

On November 7 Webb finally went public, shocking the courtroom with the announcement "I am returning to Australia." A
gasp swept the big room. Owen Cunningham, Oshima's defense
counsel, who had engaged already in bruising encounters with
Webb, objected with disbelief. "It is the basis of my objection
that it is the duty of a justice to attend the trial at all times, unless
sickness intervenes," Cunningham bristled. "The privilege of ab-

sence has been so abused during this trial that it is necessary at this time that the record show a protest.''* Cunningham proposed that in Webb's absence the court adjourn, or that Webb disqualify himself from further participation in the trial and MacArthur designate a new president, or that "the case be dismissed and that we all go back to our own countries.''

At this point two defense attorneys, Lawrence McManus and Michael Levin, jumped to their feet and dissociated themselves from Cunningham's assault. Cunningham, nevertheless, was only warming up. "It is an imposition upon the accused and their counsel, is a reflection upon the dignity of the court, the importance of this proceeding, and the loyalty of the Supreme Commander," Cunningham said of Webb's action. "It is the duty of Australia to accede to the Allied powers and make their sacrifice."

Webb cut him off. "That is purely political," he roared, "and I do not think we should listen to you." Webb then observed that the absence of the president of a court had precedence in law, and he cited a case arising out of the Boer War that was "covered by a decision of the highest court in the British Empire, and there is no higher court in the world."

The latter remark seared Cunningham. "Well, being an Irish-American, Your Honor," Cunningham snapped back, "that doesn't bind me." He then cited the U.S. Judicial Code, Section 217, and the battle went on from there, leaving the accused baffled and the spectators bemused. The charter covered the crisis; Article 3 provided that the trial might be conducted when only six of the eleven judges were present.

On Monday, November 10, the tribunal reconvened without Webb. Many observers thought New Zealand's Judge Northcroft would fill in for Webb as acting judge, a role he had played before. As the first order of business the clerk of the court read an order from MacArthur, dated three days earlier, appointing General Cramer, the U.S. judge, acting president of the IMTFE.

In Webb's absence Matsui, Minami, Muto, Oka, Oshima, Sato, Shigemitsu, Shimada, Shiratori, and Suzuki made individual defenses; Matsui, who was confined to the U.S. Army's 361st Station Hospital, put in a brief appearance out of turn and returned

*Among other absences, Judge Pal, now at the side of his ailing wife in Calcutta, had missed half of the individual defenses, and was not expected to return until November 12.

to his bed. All of them, except Generals Minami and Sato and ex–foreign minister Shigemitsu, took the stand in their own defense.

Minami, who had held the post of war minister in 1931 and been a member of the Supreme War Council from 1931 to 1934, offered a perfunctory defense, claiming that the evidence that would have exonerated him of plotting aggressive war had been "burned at Ichigaya at the surrender." Muto's defense was also weak, but he took the stand; like General Itagaki, he had nothing to lose. Although he had been present at the mass-scale atrocities at Nanking and Manila and held the rank of lieutenant general, the second highest rank in the Japanese Army, on December 7, 1941, he claimed that his work had been "clerical" and that he was also "utterly ignorant" of atrocities.

Admiral Oka drew unusual attention when he took the stand because he was the first naval officer to do so. The former chief of the Bureau of Naval Affairs and later vice minister of the navy denied that the navy had ordered a sneak attack on Pearl Harbor, pinning failure for the delivery of advance warning on the accused Shigenori Togo and his Foreign Ministry. Oka also expressed remorse. "With reference to the alleged atrocities of the naval units," he said, "as an officer in the Japanese navy, I cannot help but feel sincere regret. In view of the history and education of the Japanese, it is incredible, and I cannot understand how such acts ever occurred."

The next defendant, Tojo's navy minister, echoed Oka's line on atrocities and Pearl Harbor. "As I sat in this courtroom and heard for the first time the recounting of many instances where Japanese naval personnel mistreated prisoners of war, I was both shocked and ashamed," Admiral Shimada told the tribunal. "Under no conceivable interpretation of Japanese naval regulations and teachings could such conduct have been tolerated." His remorse notwithstanding, during his cross-examination the Allied prosecution tied him directly to the hellships and the misuse of POWs as forced laborers. The IPS produced a directive from Shimada ordering the transfer by sea of POWs from Indonesia to Japan and another order assigning POWs as slave laborers in factories at Hiroshima and Osaka. "I have no recollection . . ." he mumbled. "I have absolutely no recollection of that."

Shimada proved to be one of the great dissemblers on the stand. Asked if, on November 30, 1941, as the Japanese fleet steamed for Hawaii, he had met the emperor to give him naval intelligence, Shimada said, "No. There was no such occasion." U.S. Navy Captain Robinson, an assistant prosecutor, cited evidence that he in fact had done so. "You suggest in your inquiry that we went to the imperial palace to advise His Majesty, the emperor," Shimada said in a Gallagher-to-Sheehan exchange. "That was not so. We went to the imperial palace in response to a summons for advice."

Robinson, with cynicism, said, "Now, do I understand the answer is 'yes'?"

"Yes," Shimada nodded, "we had an audience."

Robinson asked him if it was true that the navy had provided the emperor with a general outline of the forthcoming operations and that Hirohito had insisted that the United States be notified prior to the attack. "I don't know anything about it," Shimada said smoothly. Was it his duty to know? "That sounds to me like a very queer question," the sea lord said, "a very difficult question to answer."

Acting President Cramer made a rare intervention: "Answer the question, witness," he ordered sternly.

". . . I cannot say 'yes' or 'no,' " Shimada struggled. Well, did Shimada deny that the emperor had expressly requested that the United States be notified before the bombing? "I do not deny it," the defendant said.

As the fates planned it, Shimada's second day on the stand was December 8, 1947, six years to the day after Hirohito issued his rescript proclaiming, "We hereby declare war on the United States and the British Empire." Was the emperor's rescript, which was delivered at 11:30 A.M., the Japanese declaration of war? "I think the way you state it might invite misunderstanding," Shimada said. But hadn't the attack on Pearl Harbor started almost seven hours earlier? "Seven hours before what?" Shimada asked gallingly. And so it went, but the parochial-minded American prosecutor missed the point, and Judge Cramer, apparently at the behest of Britain's Lord Patrick, who fed him a series of notes, questioned the witness from the bench.

Did Shimada know about the Japanese attacks on Kota Bharu and other British areas *before* Pearl Harbor? "Yes," Shimada said, "I did." Did he know that no notification had been given to Britain in advance? "Yes," he admitted. Why was there no notice? Because at the staff meeting at which the timing of the attacks was arranged, "due to some accident," no staff officers attended from the unit that was scheduled to attack Malaya, "and so, from that, the result was that the unit attacked shortly prior to the delivery, the time of delivery of the notification," the ex–naval minister said. He added, "And this is a matter concerning which I feel only the profoundest regret."

The truth was that the Japanese had to time their landing in Malaya with high tide, which was close to midnight, while the attack on Pearl Harbor—in another time zone far to the east—was set for daybreak.

After Shimada was dismissed, Ambassador Oshima, immaculately attired in bow tie and tailored suit, strutted to the stand and played down his personal relationship with Hitler, Göring, Himmler, Ribbentrop, and the rest of the Nazi mob. "I knew of the concentration camps but I have never seen them," Oshima said. "And also I heard rumors of maltreatment but I have never investigated the facts." Oshima's worst moment came when he admitted that he personally had shown Hitler a military map of Singapore. But he denied that they had discussed attack plans "or anything of that nature." Well, didn't Hitler at least ask Oshima how long it would take the Japanese to reduce Singapore? "Yes," Japan's envoy to Berlin confessed. "He did."

Oshima's Axis partner in the dock, Toshio Shiratori, the bombastic anti-Semitic Japanese envoy to Mussolini, also minimized his dealings with Il Duce, Count Ciano, and other Italian Fascist leaders. "Mussolini did all the talking and would scarcely allow me to say anything beyond climbing in occasionally," he testified from the stand.

During cross-examination the prosecution produced evidence to show that on his recall to Tokyo, Shiratori had developed close relations with General Ott, the German ambassador to Japan, and that Shiratori had furnished him with "important secrets of the Japanese government."

"I deny that most emphatically," Shiratori declared shrilly from the stand. But, significantly, he added, "Much of Ambassador Ott's information, such as it was and false as it was, I am informed, came from the confidential secretary of Prince Konoye, one Hidemi Ozaki, who was later tried and executed. Ozaki was a Communist and associate of [Richard] Sorge, a German by birth, but, I am further informed, a Russian spy who had worked his way as a newspaperman into the confidence of General Ott. It seems my name was sometimes used merely to give credit to this sort of information without my knowledge.''

The tribunal seemed to lean forward to catch the cross-examination. How did Shiratori know? Who informed him? But there were no questions; the Allied prosecution dropped the matter summarily. The Sorge spy ring, like bacteriological warfare, Japan's quest for an atomic bomb, and other sensitive matters, was on Joseph Keenan's—read: Washington's—list of taboos.

General Suzuki, whom the prosecution had identified earlier as wielding enormous power behind the scenes, followed Shiratori to the stand. As head of the cabinet planning board, Suzuki had mobilized the economy for total war, yet in the witness box he proclaimed his ignorance of any war plans. He even claimed he had learned that the Japanese fleet had sailed "one or two weeks before the commencement of hostilities" only from his fellow inmates at Sugamo. Like Admirals Oka and Shimada, he accused the Foreign Ministry under Shigenori Togo of failing to deliver an advance warning of attack. "This [was] left up to the foreign minister," he said accusingly.

Among the men in the dock Suzuki had a consistently distinctive air—disdainful, lordly, overbearing, and insolent.* He lost none of his arrogance when he acknowledged, under cross-examination, that his planning board had exercised control over POWs employed as laborers in Japan. Did he ever see POWs at work in Japan? "Yes," Suzuki said, "once, at a coal mine."

Matsui's turn came next. The aged general looked wan, his eyes were dull, and his gaunt cheekbones rode high on his lined face. The consensus was that he would not live to the end of the trial. Matsui was the second general—the first had been Koiso—to express remorse. "I had no desire to turn Nanking into a field of carnage, and I was most sorry when that happened," he said. ". . . I cannot help but feel profound regret for this sad event." From the stand he recounted how, after his return from Nanking, he had built a shrine at his home and placed it in a clump of blood-soaked earth that he had brought back from China. There, he said, he "prayed for the repose" of the souls of the Chinese and Japanese war dead.

The most clipped defense was presented by General Sato, who

---

*General Teiichi Suzuki, today ninety-two, lives in reasonably good health in obscurity in the interior of Japan. He and the Nazi deputy Führer, Rudolf Hess, are the sole survivors among the defendants at the Tokyo and Nuremberg trials.

had held the all-powerful position of chief of the Military Affairs Bureau in the War Ministry in 1942–44, where directives for the handling of POWs, civilian internees, and Asian slave laborers were approved. Sato's counsel, James N. Freeman, a former U.S. Navy Department lawyer, did not put his client on the stand but produced several witnesses to testify that Sato's role in the War Ministry had been minor. Their assertions were contradicted by statements during his interrogations at Sugamo, when he had described his post as "the policymaking bureau of the ministry."

Sato was an astute observer at the IMTFE. In his memoirs, bearing the heavy-handed title *Prospect and Retrospect of the Greater East Asia Wars,* he described Sir William Webb as "an imposing figure with a brilliant mind, a man of strong will who did not want to be a loser," while Joseph Keenan was "very vulgar and arrogant." Sato surmised that there was "ill-feeling" between the Australian president and the American chief prosecutor. "We [defendants] were spectators of this friction between Webb and Keenan, and it sometimes worried us," he wrote. "It was an emotional problem between the two, and we generally sympathized with Webb." But during one legal skirmish the accused were "very grateful to Keenan," Sato continued. "It concerned the emperor's war responsibility." Like others at the IMTFE, Sato felt Webb did not hide his belief that the emperor should be tried or at least subpoenaed as a witness. Keenan strongly fought Webb on this point. "Had the emperor been tried as a war criminal or been summoned as a witness," Sato said, "we would not have felt we were alive."

Like most of the other defendants, Sato was wary of the Chinese judge, Mei Ju-ao, whom he considered a "hanging judge." But he viewed India's Pal, who had returned from Calcutta in time to catch Sato's defense, as a "special person." The Indian judge unfailingly bowed to the defendants before he took his seat on the bench each day. This daily action puzzled the accused and many others at the IMTFE. In his memoirs Sato made a shocking disclosure. He revealed that Pal had paid him a visit at Sugamo after the trial ended and told him, "You were the leaders of Japan. Through that leadership Asia was liberated. With that in mind, I express my respect [to the accused]."

Unknown to anyone at the tribunal during the trial, the war criminals had a ringer on the bench.

29

Togo, Tojo, and Umezu

On December 15, 1947, the marshal of the court intoned, "For the tribunal, all members sitting." Webb was back—in time to hear the individual defenses of Togo, Tojo, and Umezu. Shigenori Togo's case was spectacular, producing headlines; Hideki Tojo's was anticlimactic, although it attracted the biggest house; and Yoshijiro Umezu's was torpid.

Umezu did not even take the stand, nor did his attorneys deliver an opening statement. His witnesses portrayed him as a glorified bureaucrat. This was the only defense offered by a general who had once commanded the imperial Japanese armies in China, served his co-defendant ex-premier Hirota as vice minister of war, and ended the war as chief of the army general staff. He had suffered the ultimate humiliation by virtue of this latter position, being the officer who formally surrendered the imperial Japanese armed forces aboard the *Missouri*.

By comparison, the Togo defense was not only striking but illuminating. Ben Bruce Blakeney, his American counsel, presented a lengthy opening statement, including a prologue by Kenzo Takayanagi, who was still legal adviser to the Gaimusho. The Foreign Ministry was not going to abandon its own to the militarists in the dock.

Togo was on the stand from December 17 to December 26, 1947 (the court recessed on Christmas Day). His German wife—

he had done three tours of diplomatic duty in Germany between 1919 and 1939—and their daughter attended each session. At the outset, in a puzzling maneuver, Joseph Keenan announced that to speed up the trial, the IPS had dropped all counts in the indictment against Togo before his appointment on October 18, 1941, as Tojo's foreign minister. The court was surprised. The most astonishing aspect of the "deal," as Blakeney later referred to it, was the willingness of the Soviet Union to agree to the bargain. Why should Stalin be so magnanimous—especially when the Russians took a hard line against the other defendants, in particular Mamoru Shigemitsu, who had been Togo's predecessor as ambassador in Moscow and whom none of the Allies except Russia had wanted to indict?

Given this odd development, there were rumors that Togo's case was "special," although precisely why was left in the air. There was speculation—never proven—that the "deal" had something to do with the Sorge spy ring, but how this was a factor remained a mystery. During Togo's cross-examination, the mystery heightened when, to the puzzlement of the bench, Keenan asked Togo about his relations with the German assistant military attaché in Tokyo between 1940 and 1942, Lieutenant Colonel Fritz von Petersdorff, who later turned out to have been a Nazi spymaster. Togo denied that he even knew Petersdorff, and Keenan promptly dropped the matter (he raised it again when Tojo was on the stand, but Tojo did not recall knowing him either).

In a lengthy deposition Togo charged that since 1931 the militarists had increasingly dictated Japanese foreign policy. "The foreign minister . . . was quite powerless," he said. He accused the army of repeatedly deceiving the Foreign Ministry. As an example, he cited the army's secret collaboration with the Finance Ministry in printing foreign occupation currency about a year before Pearl Harbor; "I learned this for the first time in this tribunal," he said. The navy also deceived him. "I did not dream that the Japanese navy would ever attack the American fleet at Pearl Harbor," he claimed. But he freely confesses that he had been privy to the conspiracy to deceive the emperor. Thus, when the two Japanese ambassadors in Washington proposed to Tokyo that Roosevelt and Hirohito exchange messages to defuse the crisis, Togo said, "the plan was not reported to the emperor."

Togo was perhaps the most sophisticated defendant in the dock, including Kido. But Togo, as suave and shrewd as he was, also possessed what Americans call street-smarts. He recognized that the generals and admirals had set him up as the villain in the sneak attack on Pearl Harbor, and he fought back. His late co-defendant, Admiral Nagano, then chief of naval operations, and Vice Admiral Ito, the vice chief, had both told him, Togo testified, that "the navy wishes to carry out a surprise attack," and they demanded that "the negotiations [with the U.S.] be left undetermined in order that the war be started with maximum possible effectiveness." This was a stunning disclosure, and the tribunal tingled. Togo added that he had been "disgusted" with their request and told them that "we should think of our national honor." The request was debated at an imperial liaison conference, he said, attended by six of the accused in the dock—Tojo, Kaya, Suzuki, Hoshino, Oka, and Muto. All of them supported the navy and inveighed against him; Colonel Hashimoto was the hardest hard-liner of all. Since none of them backed him, he said icily, "that is perhaps the best explanation for the fact that none of them now remembers this altercation."

The Japanese and American defense attorneys for Admirals Shimada and Oka were visibly agitated. John Brannon, Shimada's counsel, asked whether Shimada, as navy minister, had ever told Togo, as foreign minister, that he wanted to attack the United States without a declaration of war. "Shimada sat in complete silence and did not utter a single word," Togo said, referring to the liaison meeting.

The navy now opened its own bomb bay. Admirals Shimada and Nagano, Brannon announced, had jointly questioned their fellow defendants at Sugamo prison on this point, and not one of them could recall the navy's requesting a surprise attack. Brannon asked Togo pointedly, "Are you prepared to say that these men are actually lying now?" Excitement in the courtroom heightened.

"Well," Togo replied, "I do not have much confidence in the memory of these men." Brannon repeated his question, and this time Togo said that since the American defense counsel asked him, "I am not hesitant about talking about what took place within the walls of Sugamo Prison."

In the middle of May 1946, Togo testified, after lunch at Ichigaya, Shimada approached him and suggested that he join Admiral Nagano and himself for "a talk" later. "Shimada expressed the desire that I would not say anything about the fact that the navy desired to carry out the surprise attack," Togo told a stunned tribunal. "He also said something, in the nature of a threat, saying that if I said so, it would not be worth my while." There was commotion in the courtroom. The previous January, Togo continued, ten days before Nagano died, the late admiral confided to him at Sugamo that Togo was going "to bear the full responsibility for the attack on Pearl Harbor." Togo said he had asked Nagano, did this include responsibility for the element of surprise? "Bear all the responsibility," Nagano said.

The bench was open-mouthed. "Well," Brannon said, "I want to understand this point perfectly. Admiral Shimada and Admiral Nagano confessed to you that they did want to attack Pearl Harbor without any notice being given but that they didn't want you to talk about it . . . is that true?"

"Yes," the defendant said. "Generally, as you say."

Togo, it should be pointed out, could not understand why the issue of whether or not there had been a surprise attack on Pearl Harbor created such a storm at the tribunal. The Japanese press, he noted from the stand, "widely publicized the fact that the surprise attack on Pearl Harbor met with great success, and I think elsewhere the phrase 'Surprise attack on Hawaii' was used."

Now it was Keenan's turn to cross-examine. Did Admirals Shimada and Nagano themselves threaten Togo with bodily harm when they uttered their threat?

"No," Togo said.

"Well," Keenan asked, "what kind of threat was it?"

Togo replied, "I didn't feel any necessity for asking at that time."

Turning to another area, Keenan asked him whether, when he visited the emperor at 3 A.M. on Pearl Harbor Day, he had read Roosevelt's message to Hirohito proposing that "Japan and the United States should agree to eliminate any form of military threat?"

"I read the message word for word to His Majesty," Togo said. (In his opening remarks the ex–foreign minister had said that the first he had heard that the army delayed delivery of the Roosevelt message was at the IMTFE.)

Did Togo discuss Roosevelt's message with Hideki Tojo, the premier and war minister? Yes. Did he and Tojo decide on the emperor's reply? Yes. "Are you indicating that the emperor of Japan was a mere figurehead and obtaining his consent was noth-

ing more than a rubber stamp to be put on by you?'' Togo replied
so evasively that even Keenan could not pin him down. Keenan
shifted his ground: Was Hirohito dressed in full naval uniform at
that meeting? Yes. Did Togo think there was significance in the
fact that Hirohito wore a naval uniform ''at or about the time
when naval hostilities were being opened against the United States
at Pearl Harbor?''

''I don't think,'' Togo said with a straight face, ''there was
any special significance at all.''

When it came to exposing the generals and admirals in the
dock, Shigenori Togo did not hesitate; but when it came to the
emperor, he was no Judas. He left the stand with his loyalty to
Hirohito unquestioned.

On December 26 Tojo's Philadelphia lawyer, George F. Blewett, announced, ''We are now ready to open the individual defense of former Premier Tojo.'' Tojo paused dramatically in the
box and blew his nose before taking the stand; among Japanese,
the gesture reflected his contempt for the IMTFE. Ichiro Kiyose,
who masterminded the Tojo defense, read an opening statement
that was a caricature of the evidence. ''Japan had neither planned
nor prepared beforehand for the war against the United States,
Britain, and The Netherlands''; in China, Japan had entertained
''neither territorial ambition nor the idea of economic monopoly'';
the Axis had been designed to ''avoid war''; Japan's attack on
the Anglo-American powers had been ''provoked by the Allied
nations''; Tokyo ''had scrupulously prepared to deliver the lawful
notification of war to the United States of America prior to the
commencement of hostilities''; the purpose of Japan's Greater East
Asia Co-prosperity Sphere had been to ''secure political freedom
for all peoples of Greater East Asia''; the charge that Japan had
been ruled by ''militaristic cliques'' was ''groundless . . . sheer
imagination''; finally, Tojo ''neither gave orders for, tolerated, nor
connived at any inhuman acts.''

The opening statement contained not a scintilla of remorse.
''No witness will be called other than Tojo himself,'' Kiyose announced.

Attired in the same khaki army uniform, shorn of insignia and
badges of rank, that he had worn through the trial, Hideki Tojo
was a media event, and he knew it. He basked appreciatively once
again at stage center. About 500 spectators lined up beginning at

6 A.M. at Ichigaya for tickets, although only 200 seats for the Japanese public were available. Scalpers peddled tickets at 500 yen apiece, the same rate as for an afternoon of Kabuki theater. By comparison, tickets to the most popular film in Tokyo, Bob Hope's *Road to Morocco,* cost 100 yen. The VIP gallery at the IMTFE was packed. Mrs. Douglas MacArthur and her nine-year-old son sat in the front row. "Arthur wanted to see Tojo," Mrs. MacArthur explained.

On the stand Tojo produced a 60,000-word, 250-page deposition. The affidavit was his appeal to history and sought to justify his actions. But it also served a very different purpose. It testified to the Japanese Army's warped worldview. Tojo cited Anglo-American aid to China as "the chief obstacle to the conclusion of the China Incident." Japan had moved into Indochina after the fall of France for reasons of "self-defense." It was "absolutely untrue" that the Japanese Army had delayed Roosevelt's message to the emperor. By cracking Japan's diplomatic code, the United States had "full knowledge of our attack prior to its actual launching." Tojo accepted "administrative responsibility" for the treatment of POWs and civilian internees—but he made no reference to Asian forced laborers. Tojo charged that the Doolittle fliers had "invaded the Tokyo area" and committed "war crimes" in violation of established international law—this after ten years of Japan's bombing the Chinese mainland. Tojo admitted that he had approved the use of POWs as laborers on the Burma-Siam Railway but claimed that "there was not even the faintest thought in our minds" that this was inhumane. He termed "an utter absurdity" the charge that Japan had been an aggressor power between 1931 and 1945. He reiterated that "I believe firmly and contend to the last that it was a war of self-defense and in no manner a violation of presently acknowledged international law." He absolved Emperor Hirohito of responsibility, declaring that "the full responsibility" for the Pacific War rested on the cabinet and high command and was "absolutely not the responsibility of the emperor."

Not once did he express remorse for the millions of dead and maimed—only that he had lost the war. "As to the other question, the responsibility for defeat," he said, "I feel that it devolves on me myself as premier."

His co-defendants, judging by their expressions and private remarks later to their counsel, applauded Tojo's performance, particularly his action in absolving the emperor of responsibility. "In the trial, Tojo tried in his testimony to help every one of the defendants," the defendant Naoki Hoshino, his fire-eating cabinet secretary, wrote in his memoirs. "Tojo's conduct was magnificent." By restating Japan's propaganda line of the thirties and forties, Tojo also recaptured public support. Tokyo's front-page headlines ran: EMPEROR NOT RESPONSIBLE (*Asahi*); ADMITS RESPONSIBILITY FOR DEFEAT, STRESSES "EMPEROR FOR PEACE" (*Mainichi*); EMPEROR NOT RESPONSIBLE FOR WAR OPENING, I TAKE BLAME FOR DEFEAT (*Yomiuri*).

However, it was not so much the Japanese rallying around Tojo as around Hirohito. The *Nippon Times* remarked trenchantly, "None of the papers mentioned one significant point which the foreign news agencies stressed, namely, that Togo's affidavit was reminiscent of prewar Japanese military propaganda." But one major Japanese daily, the *Mainichi*, observed in an editorial, "No matter how vigorously Tojo may insist that Japan resorted to hostilities in self-defense, the series of wars Japan waged cannot be described as wars for self-defense."

On Christmas Day, 1945, when the IPS was organized, Joseph Keenan had handpicked John W. Fihelly, former chief of the criminal division of the U.S. attorney general's office, to take charge of Tojo's case. Early in the trial, it will be recalled, the tribunal ruled that only one Allied prosecutor might examine a witness. When the IPS launched its cross-examination of Tojo, Keenan surprised the court—and his colleagues—by asking permission to cross-examine Tojo in collaboration with Fihelly. A majority of the judges ruled against him. Instead of stepping aside in favor of Fihelly, however, Keenan announced that he would handle the cross alone. Fihelly, visibly upset, stalked out of the courtroom—and never returned.

Robert Donihi, Keenan's youthful assistant and admirer, acknowledged that "Keenan was very jealous and for this reason Fihelly never got to try the case." And defense attorney George Furness, recalling the incident, said, "Keenan was not up to it, but we on the defense did not object." To be charitable, the cross-examination was less than a success. But it was good theater. Keenan and Tojo were a study in similarities. Both were coarse, provincial-minded, brusque, sarcastic, and self-righteous. Even the village idiot, however, could have scored debating points against Tojo, who viewed the world from the bottom of a well. Tojo's affidavit had more holes in it than a colander. But instead of prob-ing Tojo with a stiletto, Keenan used a meat cleaver. The IPS was embarrassed; the bench dismayed; the defense contemptuous. "Accused Tojo," Keenan said gratuitously, "I shall not address you as a general because, of course, you know there is no longer any Japanese army."

The cross examination went downhill from there. For exam-ple, completely oblivious to the European colonialism and impe-rialism in the Far East, Keenan asked Tojo if he believed that all people have the right to self-determination. "Of course," Tojo replied. Keenan followed up: Who had given Tojo the right to determine what way of life should be imposed on the people of East Asia? "You mean me?" Tojo replied as laughter flooded the tribunal. "No, I got such rights from nowhere." Well, was Tojo ashamed of Japan's alliance with Hitler? "No," Tojo snapped, "I do not entertain any such cowardly views."

In one absurd exchange Keenan and Tojo debated the respec-tive political systems of the United States and Japan. Tojo felt the president and emperor were the highest authority in their respec-tive countries. "Well, there is this difference," Keenan said pompously, "the people of the United States choose their presi-dent every four years by direct vote. This is not true in Japan."

What this had to do with the great issue of war criminality before the tribunal was beyond the court's grasp. "What is the relevance of this, Mr. Chief Counsel?" an irked Webb asked. This dialogue ensued:

KEENAN: But, Mr. President, if it is offensive in any way to take a few moments in this courtroom in this historic trial to let the people here know the authority of the president of the United States government, I shall not press the point. I shall go immediately to something else on a further indication from the court.

WEBB: Go immediately to something else.

KEENAN: I believe the court means that it would like to have me so do, it is not a command.

WEBB: It is the acceptance of any invitation by you. We don't want to hear any more questions of that type.

The cross-examination broke down when Keenan inquired, "Would you agree with me, Mr. Tojo, that aggressive wars are crimes?"

Tojo's pained defense attorney objected. "That certainly is a question for this tribunal to determine," George Blewett said, and an exasperated Sir William Webb crackled, "We are getting no help from this type of cross-examination!"

Tojo sat comfortably in the witness box and smirked as the Allied chief prosecutor told Webb that he, Keenan, was "not so stupid" as to assume Tojo's reply would settle the issue, but did Webb seek to preclude the prosecution from getting the defendant to admit he was guilty of the crime of aggression?

Webb gulped. "He was not invited to make an admission of guilt," Webb corrected. "Now the position is this: His honest and reasonable, though mistaken belief in the existence of a state of facts is a defense. His opinion or belief as to the law is not a defense and is irrelevant except on the question perhaps of mitigation, if he is found guilty. The only man found guilty of aggressive war, and of aggressive war alone, at Nuremberg, was not sentenced to death;* so Nuremberg may have thought that belief as to the law, mistaken belief, may be a circumstance of mitigation, but they did not say so. I am only stating the fact. If I am asked whether I think aggressive war is a crime and I say that I think it is not a crime, am I guilty of anything?"

Webb sustained the objection.

Despite Keenan's unpreparedness Tojo made a fool of himself. One example will suffice: Under oath, the former premier and war minister declared that he "really didn't know" that the Japanese fleet had sailed for Hawaii in November and that although he met Hirohito "several times" during the first week of December, they did not discuss the impending strike at Pearl Harbor. "I spoke with him on greater matters than that," Tojo said silkily, "on war itself, as a whole, which included that matter."

Only once on the stand did Tojo lose his composure and smugness. Did he deny all responsibility as war minister for the death of POWs? "I don't recall what kind of orders were issued at the time," Tojo said hesitantly, "so I am unable to give an exact reply."

Historically, the highlight of the cross-examination came when, under relentless questioning by Keenan, Tojo confessed that the

*Rudolf Hess.

emperor had "consented, though reluctantly, to the war," and, worse, that "none of us [Japanese] would dare act against the emperor's will," a remark suggesting that Hirohito had the power to stop Japan's slide into war.

For the defendants in the dock this was the gravest moment of the trial. Their worst nightmare, that Hirohito would be dragged into the case, bordered on realization. In the September 5, 1959, *Nihon Shuho,* Keenan's Japanese confidential secretary, Seiichi Yamazaki, wrote cryptically that the men in the dock "at this moment . . . were ready to die for the emperor." Yamazaki went on, "I would like to unburden myself by disclosing a great secret about the trial." The secret was how Keenan, through an intermediary, had appealed to Marquis Kido to persuade Tojo to correct his remark "at any risk to himself." MacArthur was determined not to jeopardize the security of the occupation or the future of Japanese-American relations by involving the emperor in the IMTFE under any circumstances whatsoever. Thus, on January 6, 1948, more than a week after Tojo's slip, in the course of questioning Tojo on Henry P'u Yi, the puppet emperor of Manchukuo ("He betrayed our confidence before this tribunal," Tojo said bitterly), Keenan suddenly switched to Hirohito.

KEENAN: While we are discussing the subject matter of emperors, it might be an appropriate moment to ask you a few questions on the relative positions of yourself and the emperor of Japan on the matter of waging war in December of 1941. You have told us that the emperor on repeated occasions made known to you that he was a man of peace and did not want war, is that correct?

TOJO: I was then speaking to you of my feeling toward the emperor as a subject, and that is quite a different matter from the problem of responsibility, that is, the responsibility of the emperor.

KEENAN: Well, you did make war against the United States, Great Britain, and the Netherlands, did you not?

TOJO: War was decided on in my cabinet.

KEENAN: Was that the will of Emperor Hirohito, that war should be instituted?

TOJO: It may not have been according to his will, but it is a fact that because of my advice and because of the advice given by the high command, the emperor consented—though reluctantly—to the war.

INTERPRETER: The first part should be corrected: It might have been against the emperor's will.

TOJO: The emperor's love and desire for peace remained the same right up to the very moment when hostilities commenced, and even during the war his feelings remained the same. The emperor's feeling in this regard can be clearly ascertained from the imperial rescript given on the 8th of December, 1941, declaring war. . . . That is to say, the imperial rescript contains words to this effect: This war is indeed unavoidable and is against my own desires.

Tension ran high during this colloquy, but according to Seiichi Yamazaki "what people saw there was just a fake play . . . conducted by the mutual agreement of Keenan and Tojo." Thus, the most volatile crisis during the trial was contained as a result of a secret agreement between the Allied chief of counsel and the most-wanted war criminal in the dock.

Clearly, Tojo's defense was anticlimactic. Reviews in the Japanese press were mixed. The *Nippon Times* wrote, "There can be no doubt that Tojo's stock has risen considerably because he exonerated the emperor from responsibility for the war and accepted the blame himself, but the vast majority of Japanese have never held and still do not hold any high respect for him." However, many Japanese, especially those under forty, the newspaper continued, "still believe that the war, as Tojo declares in his affidavit, was forced on the country."

When Tojo's cross-examination was concluded, Keenan drove to Atami, the resort city south of Tokyo, to unwind or, as Frank White of the Associated Press delicately put it, "to recuperate from his cross-examination bout with Japan's wartime leader."

30

Rebuttals
and Summaries

The trial was now moving toward summations. Admiral Shimada
retook the stand to refute Togo's charge that the admirals had
threatened him at Ichigaya and Sugamo if he revealed that the
navy had planned a sneak attack on Pearl Harbor. According to
Shimada's testimony, in 1946 he and the late Admiral Nagano had
heard "rumors" that Togo was going to scatter the navy's beans.
He and Nagano confronted Togo about the rumors, Shimada confirmed, but there were no threats. They simply told Togo that he
"should be more careful about the truth." Shimada then branded
Togo's charge "absurd and unthinkable" and accused Togo of
"running away behind a smokescreen" to cover his bungling as
foreign minister of the delivery of the December 7 declaration of
war. "The honor of the navy has been impugned by Togo's testimony," Shimada said hotly.

When Shimada returned to the dock on Monday, January 12,
1948, George Yamaoka announced, "Mr. President, and members
of the tribunal, I wish to state that the defense has no further
evidence at this time." The defense rested.

Departing from Anglo-American law the IMTFE ruled to admit all rebuttal evidence that "has probative value and is important." The defense was dismayed. "The prosecution has closed
its case," George Furness objected, "and the court should move
on to the next phase, summations." The defense reserved the right

of surrebuttal or reply, prompting one attorney in the courtroom to groan, "This trial will go on *ad infinitum*."

For the next three months the courtroom was in turmoil as each party sought to score points against the other. Classic tomes such as *Wigmore on Evidence* and *Winthrop's Military Law and Precedents* became as commonly cited as the funnies in a newspaper on Sunday morning. It was a banquet for lawyers.

Legal technicalities aside, the prosecution's new evidence exploded like firecrackers. Some highlights:

- At a secret imperial conference in 1938, in the midst of the China War, the militarists talked of bigger and better wars, prompting Hirohito to ask sarcastically, "[Can] Japan simultaneously carry out preparations against the Soviet Union, Great Britain, and America?"
- Two weeks before the Mukden Incident, the Foreign Ministry reported that the Japanese Army in Manchuria planned an "incident" and warned that the army would "ruin the position of the empire by behaving rashly."
- A top-secret minute confirmed the plans of the Japanese Army to finance military operations and the occupation of China by trafficking in opium.
- At an *in camera* meeting of the Japanese House of Peers, a baron expressed alarm at the atrocious behavior of Japanese troops in Nanking and elsewhere and demanded to know what the government planned to do about it, compelling Marquis Kido, the emperor's adviser, to admit the army's "shortcomings" and to announce secretly plans for "remedial measures."
- In 1939 Ambassador Oshima directly negotiated Axis arrangements with Adolf Hitler and reported to the War Ministry, not the Foreign Ministry.
- In 1942 Oshima and Hitler agreed that the Axis must slaughter the crews of torpedoed Allied ships. "We . . . cannot let any humanitarian point of view govern," Hitler said, and Oshima replied, "[The] Japanese, too, are forced to follow these methods."
- A surprise prosecution witness who served aboard the Japanese submarine *J-8* testified that the "naval general staff had ordered all survivors of sunken ships to be killed."

The biggest legal flaps were set in motion by the introduction of excerpts from the now fully revealed Saionji-Harada diaries and by references to the Sorge spy ring. It developed that there were five different sets of diaries, covering the period between 1929 and 1940, the year Prince Saionji died at age ninety-one. The notebooks filled 10,000 pages and had been hidden in a vault at the Sumitomo Bank for fear the militarists would seize and destroy them. In his foreword Saionji explained that he had started a diary because the militarists were perverting the emperor's position on political matters "almost beyond imagination." The diaries revealed step by step how the militarists strangled Hirohito with floss silk.

The defense argued strenuously that the diaries were clouded by unreliability, that they were based on rumors, hearsay, and gossip. A representative entry, dated July 28, 1937, reported that Hirohito was shocked by the army's staging of the Marco Polo Bridge Incident and had described the army as "abominable" and "sneaky." The emperor had ordered, "Hereafter you must not move one soldier without my command!" The militarists ignored him.*

The other courtroom hassle revolved around the mysterious Lieutenant Colonel von Petersdorff, the assistant German military attaché in Tokyo who was a Nazi spy. He turned up in the witness box as a Soviet prisoner of war, Moscow's surprise witness. The Russians used him to prove that Tokyo had plotted war against the Soviet Union. Petersdorff, however, also testified that he knew Hideki Tojo—he was never asked if he knew Shigenori Togo—and that he had transmitted military intelligence to Berlin two or three times weekly, gathering the material from the Japanese high command and other contacts, including Richard Sorge, the German journalist and embassy official in Tokyo. Under cross-examination, defense lawyer Owen Cunningham desperately tried to get into the record Sorge's identification as a KGB mole, but he was blocked by Soviet objections that this was irrelevant, a position sustained by the tribunal. The imbroglio over the Sorge spy

*In *Japan's Imperial Conspiracy* (New York: Morrow, 1971), David Bergamini dismisses the Saionji-Harada diaries as stage-managed to protect Hirohito "in the event that the emperor ever needed whitewashing." This commentary mirrors Bergamini's thesis that Hirohito was not a puppet but *the* puppeteer. The difficulty with this interpretation is that the accused Kido, whose loyalty to the emperor was never questioned, even by his enemies in the dock, fought to block the diaries' admission at the trial because they were severely critical of him as the emperor's adviser. Between 1952 and 1956 the diaries were published in Tokyo in nine volumes.

ring led to this triangular byplay among Cunningham, Webb, and the Soviet prosecutor, General Vasiliev:

VASILIEV: . . . The defense counsel has no right to state that this man was a Russian spy or a spy of some other country.

CUNNINGHAM: Well, Your Honor, I wish to assure the tribunal that this is no gratuitous insult to the Russian spy or any other government. The fate of three nations rested to a great extent upon the information which Richard Sorge was sending out of the German embassy.

WEBB: This is a statement you have no right to make unless you can establish it or have a right to establish it.

CUNNINGHAM: That is no idle statement, Your Honor.

WEBB: It is a statement of fact which you have no right to make, and it is difficult to see how you can ever hope to prove it.

CUNNINGHAM: . . . I can give you three factors which went into that statement very simply.

WEBB: You cannot hope to justify making such a statement before this court.

CUNNINGHAM: Well, now, I certainly can't hope to justify it unless I have an opportunity. . . .

WEBB: We consider evidence, and evidence alone; the law, and the law alone. We are not going to be affected by prejudice such as you like to create. Proceed with your cross-examination, please.

CUNNINGHAM   (to Petersdorff): When did you discover, if you did discover, that Richard Sorge was a Russian spy?

WEBB: General Vasiliev.

VASILIEV: I object to this question on the same ground.

CUNNINGHAM: I think the question is justified.

WEBB: By a majority, the objection is sustained
               and the question disallowed.

CUNNINGHAM: Do you know, Mr. Witness, that Ambas-
               sador Ott was relieved of his post as am-
               bassador to Japan on account of the
               developments in the Richard Sorge case?

VASILIEV: Objection on the same grounds.

And so it went, until an exasperated Webb declared, "This
Sorge issue is purely a collateral side issue, introduced probably
for the purpose of wasting our time. We know in criminal jurisdic-
tions we do not subject our police to any examination as to the
sources of their information. . . . What bearing has it on any issue, even on the question of the credibility of this witness?" Webb
admitted, however, that he did not know if any of his colleagues
agreed with him, so he declared a recess. After the judges debated
among themselves for almost an hour, the majority agreed that
the accuracy or inaccuracy of the information Petersdorff had received from Sorge was a collateral issue that the IMTFE had no
authority to investigate; thereafter, all questions on the Sorge spy
ring were disallowed.

At the end of January the defense launched its surrebuttal.
Having lost the fight on the Saionji-Harada diaries, the defense
did an about-face and tendered its own excerpts from the controversial notebooks, this time—lawyers being lawyers—over the
strong objections of the prosecution.

A fortnight later, on February 10, the court moved onto a new
legal plane—mitigation. The IMTFE ruled that evidence in mitigation should be offered upon completion of all other evidence
and *before* the summations, an unusual position in Anglo-American law, where proceedings in mitigation are customarily conducted after the verdict and before sentencing. Stranger still, the
tribunal, which was badly split on the issue, made the ruling even
though Frank Tavenner and Silis Horwitz for the prosecution and
William Logan and Bruce Ben Blakeney for the defense met with
Webb in Chambers and jointly opposed presenting evidence in
mitigation before verdicts.

The prosecution's summation was pure Keenan, a disconcert-
ing medley of logic, eloquence, and bombast. Assisted by a relay

team of Allied prosecutors, Keenan took two weeks to recapitulate the Allied case.

The chief prosecutor appealed to the tribunal not to forget the background to Japan's surrender. "It literally required atomic bombs to jolt them from their seats of authority," Keenan recalled. "To terminate their criminal careers even this terrific force was insufficient until reinforced by an unprecedented act on the part of their emperor. We must not ignore these facts."

Keenan also indirectly noted that among the stumbling blocks to the acceptance of the Potsdam terms had been the Allied demand for the trial of Japanese war criminals. If the IMTFE had not been created, he said, the Allied war aim would have been "vain and useless."

In his inimitable style Keenan harped on the criminal nature of the accused, who "like most criminals," pleaded innocence. Their defense was that no one among them wanted to bring about this war, Keenan said, yet under their stewardship Japan had pursued an unbroken course of aggression from Mukden to Hiroshima that led to the "revolting slaughter of millions of their neighbors."

Keenan emphasized the criminal nature of the defendants' rule in Japan, citing the prewar murder of two Japanese premiers and the attempts made on the lives of two others. When "the leader of these irresponsible militarists," Hideki Tojo, was selected as premier in 1941, the advisers of the emperor had been in mortal fear of assassination if they did not go along. "Truly," Keenan said, "this was a reign of terror." As for Hirohito, Keenan charged that the defendants had made him a "divinity or figurehead" as their interests demanded. The surprise attack on Pearl Harbor was symbolic of their "fraud, guile, and duplicity."

It seems never to have occurred to the men in the dock, Keenan went on, that their first obligation was to Japan, to set their own house in order. Japan's problem was not that she had to defend herself from without—nobody intended to invade Japan—but, Keenan said, she had to defend herself from "evil, malignant, and ruthless elements" within. Keenan suggested snidely that the accused should have pleaded insanity as a defense.

The basis of the prosecution's legal argument was that Japan had been a signatory to the Kellogg-Briand Pact, which outlawed war as an instrument of national policy. Keenan failed to observe that the pact provided for no criminal sanctions in the event the treaty was breeched, but argued that the men in the dock had violated the treaty and therefore had committed a crime. Using the language of Nuremberg, Keenan branded aggressive war "not only an international crime but the supreme international crime." He demanded that the accused receive the "maximum punishment known to mankind" and the "sternest punishment known to law." Keenan later told correspondents that he meant "the death penalty."

The last relay team completed its recital on March 12 when Colonel Ivanov, the assistant Soviet prosecutor, announced, "Your Honor, this concludes the prosecution's case."

Somei Uzawa, chief of the Japanese defense section, who followed, sounded the clarion call of the Social Darwinians. War, he contended, is to human history what storms, floods, and earthquakes are to natural history. "The defendants," Uzawa said, ". . . are innocent men who act and live under reason," adding, "It is inconceivable that they conspired to commit the wrongs alleged in the indictment, or that if set free they would conspire aggressions again and again."

Kenzo Takayanagi followed Uzawa with the argument that the Allies had overreached themselves in trying the accused and were guilty of applying *ex post facto* law, "sheer lynch law in the guise of justice." In support of this charge he cited the action of Thailand's high court in releasing a dozen major war criminal suspects on the ground that a new law punishing war criminality could not be enforced retroactively without charges of applying *ex post facto* law. In this subtle fashion Takayanagi drew attention to Thailand's absence from the bench, although Siam, as it was then called, had been the only independent country in Southeast Asia at the outbreak of the Pacific War.*

Takayanagi also argued that crimes against peace and against humanity were unheard of in international law and that the term "aggressive war" was suspect because the phrase was amorphous, elusive, and indefinable. Then, striking at the West's Achilles' heel, Uzawa put the trial within a historical context. Mindful of the ongoing colonial wars racking Indonesia and Vietnam in 1948 and of other nationalist movements pressing for independence in the Far East, Takayanagi observed that Western conquerors had never been penalized during the preceding three centuries for their aggression in Asia. He weakened this thrust,

---

*The Allies were divided on Thailand: Britain and France considered Thailand in the Japanese camp during the war; China and the United States, an ally.

however, by alleging that "cultural differences" between Occident and Orient accounted for the mistreatment of Allied POWs and civilian internees, omitting any reference to Asian slave laborers and to the brutal character of the Japanese occupation in China, the Philippines, and elsewhere—not to mention Japan's behavior in harshly governing earlier Asian acquisitions such as Korea and Formosa.

It took the defense more than a month to complete its summation. The sum total could be reduced to one line: Rightly or wrongly, the accused were not criminals but patriots; if their actions had been based on love of fatherland, "then we submit [they] cannot be held to be criminal by this tribunal."

On a rainy Friday, April 6, 1948—almost two years after the IMTFE had convened—the participants repressed a sigh. "The tribunal reserves its judgment," Sir William Webb intoned, "and adjourns to a time to be fixed and announced."

A week earlier the cherry tree in a corner of the execution yard of Block 5C at Sugamo Prison, which had failed to blossom the previous year, burst into bloom.

31

Decision
at Tokyo

On March 24, 1948, during the summation phase of the trial, Sir William Webb wrote Alan Mansfield, the Australian associate prosecutor, who had returned home, "We expect to be a month on our deliberations—the same as Nuremberg; but we have twice as much evidence." On June 4 Joseph Keenan returned to Tokyo from a lengthy absence in the United States, and five days later, before taking off for Washington again, announced he would be back "by August 1, when the judgment is ready."

"The difficulty is not so much in coming to a conclusion as in expressing the reasons within a short compass," Webb complained on June 30 in a letter to John Higgins, the former U.S. judge who had resigned earlier from the IMTFE but with whom Webb had maintained a correspondence. "Compared with the volume of evidence, even a long judgment would be relatively short."

By mid-July, however, Webb felt constrained to write Mansfield that "even you must wonder why we are so long." Webb ascribed the delay in reaching a judgment to "the number of accused and counts, the amount of evidence, and the composition of the tribunal." The last point cried out for a fuller treatment, but Webb tactfully did not amplify his remark. From afar, it looked as if the trial was suspended by a hung bench.

Ichigaya had become a ghost of its former self. The security force was reduced to a skeleton crew; the prosecution's staff shrunk from 509 to 12; and among the allied prosecutors only 2 were left, Frank Tavenner and Solis Horwitz. Most of the U.S. defense counsel had also departed, but a baker's dozen remained in Tokyo and formally petitioned the IMTFE for permission to visit the accused weekly until judgment day. "We feel out of justice to both attorneys and accused that we should be granted some consideration in visiting them," the petition said.

Webb and his Chinese colleague thought the request should be refused outright. New Zealand's Northcroft felt the decision belonged to SCAP, not the tribunal, and in an aside added, "This may be as good an excuse as any other for their continuing to stay on here at the expense of the USA taxpayer." The Soviet, British, Filipino, Indian, and U.S. judges all signed a note that read, "I agree with Justice Northcroft." Only the judges of the Netherlands, Canada, and France reacted favorably to the petition. Henri Bernard wrote a note to Webb in impeccable English stating that he did not understand what the fuss was all about: In France such a request was "elementary," and the court would automatically approve it in "the interests of humanity."

The attorneys' petition was handed over to SCAP, and General MacArthur, subscribing to the French viewpoint, promptly approved the visits.

Almost nothing is known about the deliberations that led to the tribunal's final judgment. But from the Webb Papers at Canberra it is plain that the power to preside over the drafting was shifted from the president of the tribunal to the U.S. justice, General Cramer, who emerged as chairman of the seven-member Majority Drafting Committee. The Majority, as it was called, consisted of the Big Four—Great Britain, the United States, the Soviet Union, and China—and the Philippines, Canada, and New Zealand. Exactly what happened? "It does not seem proper to give judgments about my colleagues," Röling wrote me. "We agreed, at the time, not to disclose what happened in chambers. From the dissenting opinion of Bernard it appears that many things were not in the proper way. *Especially the formulation of the judgment, which was written down by the majority without preceding discussion by the whole bench*" (italics added). The only explanation is that the Majority over the preceding two years had found themselves more often than not in harmony. As Röling's reference to Bernard indicated, the French justice, a member of the minority, was so disturbed by the drafting procedure that he filed a dissenting judgment in which he publicly charged that in reaching a judgment at Tokyo "the eleven judges were never called to discuss [it] orally." Bernard considered the judgment invalid.

Under Cramer, the former chief legal officer of the U.S. Army, the Majority divided its workload into subcommittees dealing with the charter, Hirohito, the China War, the Pacific War, and so forth, and free rein was given to argument in chambers.

The British and Canadian judges, for example, wrestled with the law of the case, holding that under the Kellogg-Briand Pact of 1929, to which Japan was a signatory, "a war of aggression was not merely illegal but was criminal." Employing the Nuremberg judgment as a kind of crib sheet, Patrick and McDougall also concluded that the Tokyo charter, like the Nuremberg charter, was decisive and binding on the tribunal, a point questioned in particular by the French and Indian justices. Webb, incidentally, was in complete agreement with the Majority. "What I should have done had I concluded otherwise—whether I should have resigned or continued in office and disregarded the terms I considered *ultra vires* [in excess of legal authority]—I need not indicate," he said in a memo to his colleagues. "But if I had to decide, I should not lose sight of the fact that the Tokyo Charter, unlike the Nuremberg Charter, is not the creation of the Allied Powers themselves. It is not part of the Instrument of Surrender but is made in performance of it by the Supreme Commander. The controlling document is the Instrument of Surrender. The Charter must conform to it; and, in my opinion, it does."

Other areas covered by the judgment produced broad divisions even within the Majority, however. For example, New Zealand argued that if an accused was found guilty of waging aggressive war, the conspiracy count against him should be dropped because it merged with the more serious offense of waging war. But Lord Patrick disagreed strongly and contended that the charge of conspiring was more serious than waging because "those who conceive and develop the purpose of waging an aggressive war are much more blatantly blameworthy than those who later participate in the waging." Patrick threatened to "write a dissenting judgment" if the conspiracy charges against the accused were dropped and by that threat won over New Zealand. Northcroft retreated as he had retreated earlier in his clash with Webb. "I have difficulty in escaping Lord Patrick's conclusion," he wrote in an August 18 minute.

In another retreat, on September 13, Northcroft pointed out that Australia, New Zealand, and the Netherlands had declared war on Japan *before* they were attacked. If Japan's attacks against Singapore and the Philippines had failed, he argued, Japan might not have ventured farther south. Webb was astonished by that reasoning. "It is a revelation for me to learn that any member of the tribunal thinks the Netherlands and Australia attacked Japan and were the aggressors," he said. He pointed out that the evidence showed that Japan's war councils had decided to attack all three countries, and added that "the formal declaration of war did not render the Japanese innocent; nor the Allied powers guilty of the aggressive war which eventuated." Northcroft agreed that "it would be absurd to say that the Netherlands or Australia were aggressors," but he added, "At the same time, I see difficulty in holding that Japan unlawfully attacked them. I suggest that Japan's crime was conspiracy to wage aggressive war against the Netherlands and Australia, not the waging of such a war."

When the Majority circulated their Pacific War draft, Webb wrote General Cramer with satisfaction on October 4 that "I note that the Majority agree with me that the Netherlands, Australia, and New Zealand were the victims of Japan's aggression."

Obviously, Hirohito was going to be a difficult subject, and some observers of the IMTFE speculated that Webb had been excluded from the Majority because of Australia's hard-line position on the emperor. Webb, in a memo to the Majority, for example, protested their failure to incorporate a Kido diary entry of November 30, 1941, "showing the part played by the emperor in starting the war."

As it developed, the death penalty issue split Webb and the Majority badly. On June 8 Webb presented the Majority with "my views of the whole case." Although he had been excluded from the Majority, Webb held that "as President I think it is my duty to take the lead in suggesting what we should do with the accused." Webb argued that the lightest sentence that should be imposed on an accused was life in prison and that the maximum penalty should be the same, except that they should be confined to "some isolated place outside of Japan." Webb said he opposed the death penalty as "purely vindictive."

Cramer was outraged: ". . . Some years ago another war criminal, Napoleon, was exiled. He escaped, and history tells us what further harm he did." In a memorandum to Webb on June 15, Cramer accused him of "practically saying that you do not believe in capital punishment. . . . Do you mean to say . . . that they should not be executed when the result of their acts has been not one murder but many thousands of murders? Or do you mean to say that no murderer should be sentenced to death?''

As for vindictiveness, the American major general fired back, "It is a strange view to me that sentencing a criminal to death *in accordance with the law* for the crimes he has committed could be termed 'vindictive.' It is a matter of *justice,* plain and simple." But in the next breath Cramer conceded that "there is no specific statute in international law saying that those responsible for planning or waging aggressive war shall be sentenced to death."

Cramer apparently had misgivings about the tone of his memorandum and sought to mollify Webb the following day in another note: "No matter what the Majority may think of the rest of the case, there is no question but that the President should take the lead when we come to considering what we shall do with the accused."

Webb seemed relieved. On June 17 he wrote Cramer a memo. "I greatly appreciate your note. . . . I am inclined to think that the accused would prefer swift, spectacular death to banishment to some remote part of the earth. However, we can discuss that later. I am satisfied merely to raise the question so that the matter receives early and full consideration. After all, the sentence is the most important act in a criminal trial and one upon which judges frequently differ."

The idea of exile as a punishment was not novel. A month before, Tsunego Wachi, the Japanese naval captain who broke the U.S. embassy code in China, had ruffled several of the judges with a similar proposition. Wachi, who became a Buddhist priest after the surrender, proposed in letters to Webb and Keenan that Tojo should be exiled to Iwo Jima. Wachi had commanded the island before its fall and described exile as the "worst" punishment the IMTFE could impose on the guilty. His proposal appeared in *Stars & Stripes* and upset Judge Jaranilla, who considered the story contempt of court. On May 14 Webb passed the Filipino judge's complaint on to SCAP with the observation that under the Tokyo charter "we really have no authority" in the matter. SCAP conveniently lost it.

Wachi's proposal was one of many on the disposition of the Class A war criminals. In Shanghai the Russian-language newspaper *Novosti Danya* held that the Soviet people and the world "await impatiently to hear the sentence passed upon the major

Japanese war criminals," adding, "The world is expecting a just and severe verdict." The article lambasted the IMTFE defense for prolonging the trial, accused the American defense attorneys of "insolence" during the trial, and blamed Webb for tolerating their conduct.

But a more serious incident provoked the tribunal on September 7. Owen Cunningham, the controversial defense counsel who had brawled with Webb repeatedly, delivered a paper at the American Bar Association meeting in Seattle. His title was provocative: "The Major Evils of the Tokyo Trial."* His single-spaced, six-page fulmination was topped by the amazing revelation that Judge Pal, who had been absent in India during most of the drafting of the judgment, "has already completed his dissension judgment, recommending dismissal of *all* counts and acquittal of *all* defendants" (italics added). Cunningham made these charges, among others:

- The object of the trial was vengeance, vindication, and propaganda.
- The prosecuting nations, including Russia, had failed to show themselves free from the crimes charged against the Japanese.
- The very existence on the court of a Russian judge and prosecutor reduced the proceedings to a paradox.
- The Tokyo charter was definitely *ex post facto.*
- The accused had not been afforded a fair trial.
- Cross-examination had been so limited as to amount to suppression of evidence.
- The prosecution witnesses had been favored, the defense witnesses abused.
- The judges had been absent for months at a time during the trial.
- Aggressive war had never been adequately defined nor understood nor made punishable. If aggressive war was a crime, then why did nations make nonaggression pacts?

The defendants at Sugamo greeted this broadside with both elation and despondency. In his enthusiasm, and apparently without consulting his client, Oshima, Cunningham had widened his

*On the same program a circumspect H. A. Hauxhurst, one of Keenan's assistant prosecutors, spoke for the IPS. Hauxhurst pointed out that the judgment was not "an accomplished fact by this time" and therefore limited his remarks.

attack on the tribunal to include Hirohito. "The role of the emperor and the application of the novel principle of individual responsibility for acts of state are irreconcilable," Cunningham declared. "If the prosecution wanted the truth as to individual responsibilities, why did they not call the emperor of Japan to the witness stand? Did they not have the courage to do so? They have asked the tribunal and the world to believe that the Emperor didn't know what was going on and, if he did, that he did not have the power to prevent it. I do not think the tribunal will be carried away with such legal acrobatics.

"No one can accept the prosecution's theory that the emperor of Japan was a puppet of Tojo," he said. "It will be very interesting to see how the judgment juggles this question."

Two days later, in a memo to his colleagues, the contents of which probably would have surprised Cunningham, Webb wrote, "If the American Bar Association thought Mr. Cunningham was guilty of contempt of court I feel sure they would not have listened to him," the president said. ". . . I intend to take no action beyond writing this memo to all members." But in a private letter to Judge Mansfield Webb expressed his annoyance. "It looks like the beginning of proceedings of some kind," he said. "I hate these things. They take up time and engender a lot of ill feeling. . . . I suppose you remember Cunningham quite well; so I need not describe him."

Several of the justices did not take the matter lightly. On October 13 the IMTFE announced that Cunningham was barred "from further proceedings before the tribunal." Cunningham was furious. But he declared that he would not fight his ouster since it was not necessary for him to make a further appearance in court. He also got in a parting shot, sending the tribunal a three-page letter in which he accused "some" members of the court of conducting a Star Chamber. "The right to be heard fully before punishment is inalienable," he declared. "The action of the court further sustains what I charged in my address before the Bar."

The French judge was appalled by the tribunal's action. In a note to Webb, Henri Bernard dissociated himself from the court's behavior and held that "the procedure against Mr. Cunningham did not sufficiently allow the latter means of defending himself."

Perhaps the most troubling aspect of the Cunningham incident was the disclosure of the way the Indian judge tilted. Cunningham did not give his source for this information. However, as early as

September 23 a United Press dispatch reported that Judge Pal, who had returned from India on September 10 and left again for India that day, "had submitted to his government and other quarters a lengthy dissenting opinion taking exception to the views of some of the eleven-nation judges on the criminality of the Japanese defendants on trial." Nonetheless, in a letter to a friend a fortnight later, Webb wrote, "He [Pal] is reported to have revealed his judgment. Actually, he did not. In fact, he never told anybody outside tribunal circles that he had written a judgment. That is what he told me, and I have no reason to disbelieve him." Webb had been gulled.

For months the question of how to handle dissenting judgments roiled the tribunal. The Majority opposed reading such a judgment in court even though it necessarily would be part of the trial record. On July 9 the Majority, with Webb's concurrence, agreed that "differences of opinion in individual cases will not be the subject of dissenting judgments." But by November 1 the Majority judgment was ready and Pal had returned from India. In a memo to Webb that day, the Indian justice declared, "I desire to read out my judgment in open court." In India dissenting judgments were always read in court, he continued, and "I desire to follow that procedure here." Pal asked Webb to come to an early decision because, he wrote, "in informal conversation with some of my colleagues I felt the possibility of some difference amongst us even in this respect."

When Pal and Webb met informally to discuss the situation, Pal learned that in his absence the Majority had voted that no dissenting judgment would be read in court. At Nuremberg the dissenting judgment had not been read either, but that was because it was not ready at the time the tribunal delivered the judgment. Even so, there is no record that the dissenting judge in Germany desired to read his judgment in open court.* Pal pressed Webb, however, at a minimum to announce in court the existence of a dissenting judgment. The Majority agreed.

As the judges drafted the judgment in 1948, the world appeared to be sliding toward another world global conflict.

In Europe Czechoslovakia yielded to an ultimatum and was

---

*The sole dissent at Nuremberg was lodged by the Soviet judge, Major General I. T. Nikitchenko, who felt the sentences were too light. The Russian opposed the acquittal of three defendants and held that Rudolf Hess, Hitler's deputy, who received life, should have been hanged.

absorbed into the Soviet bloc; the Soviet Union blockaded West Berlin; the Communists intensified the civil war in Greece; the French and Italian Communists organized general strikes. In Asia the Communists captured the Vietnamese nationalist movement and took over direction of the struggle against French colonialism; a similar maneuver in Indonesia, where nationalists engaged the Dutch, was crushed by the Indonesians; Communist-inspired insurgencies flared in Burma, the Philippines, and Malaya; and the great civil war in China moved to a climax.

The gods mocked the IMTFE. Manchuria, the seedbed of war in 1931, was again on the front pages. The day before the tribunal reconvened on November 4 to read the judgment, Mukden fell to the Communists. Webb, in a letter to a friend, summed up the anxiety of the period. "The Japanese are putting the place together again," the Australian judge wrote. "I hope they won't be burned out in another raid. It isn't a very bright world."

On November 4 queues of Japanese and Allied spectators formed outside Ichigaya. Among the spectators was Owen Cunningham, who announced that he had filed an application with the tribunal for a review of his expulsion (the tribunal ignored it). Three of the accused were missing—Ambassador Shiratori, who was suffering from tuberculosis; General Umezu, who was hospitalized with cancer; and Baron Hiranuma, who had celebrated his eighty-first birthday in September with a respiratory infection. It took eight days to read the tribunal's judgment, and during that time Hiranuma was the only one of the trio strong enough to attend court. At one point Okinori Kaya, the financial overlord, fell ill and was confined to his cell at Sugamo.

Joseph Keenan was also absent. Overseas air travel in 1948 was still uncertain, and Keenan did not reach Tokyo until three days after the reading had begun.

Inside and outside the courtroom the question was: Who would be sentenced to die? General Itagaki was among those who expected the worst. "After my death," he wrote his wife, Kikuko, "I want no funeral service, and no grave." Generals Muto and Kimura were surprisingly optimistic. They confided in General Sato that they expected to slip the death penalty. Hideki Tojo expected it. Admiral Shimada and Ambassador Oshima were braced for it. "I spent all day trying to figure out who will be sentenced to death," Yoshio Kodama, who remained at Sugamo, still awaiting trial, wrote in his diary. "A few persons said, 'Mr. Tojo and Mr. Shimada are absolutely doomed but the others would have their life spared.' " Chaplain Hanayama reported that while awaiting judgment at Sugamo, several of the accused had turned toward Buddhism, notably Generals Doihara, Itagaki, Kimura, Matsui, and Tojo, and civilians Kaya, Kido, and Hirota. Hanayama conducted special services for them. In his sermons he preached to them of the need to prepare in their limited earthbound life for the unlimited life to come, to achieve inner peace by standing aloof from life and death, and to die with honor and dignity since each man must die once. Outside the courtroom, George Francis Blewett, Tojo's American attorney, reported, "They all prepared themselves a long time ago for the worst."

Webb, and Webb alone, read the verdict. His performance was bravura. The first 82 pages of the judgment dealt with the law of the case and the conduct of the trial. The next 919 pages contained a recital of facts that had emerged from the almost 50,000 pages of testimony, and the conclusions to be drawn from them. The last 81 pages included the section of greatest interest to press and public—and accused: the individual verdicts and sentences.

The public was jarred at the outset of the reading. The tribunal threw out forty-five of the fifty-five charges in the indictment on grounds of redundancy, lack of jurisdiction, the merging of one count into another—or because a charge was "stated obscurely." The ten counts retained covered crimes against peace (conspiracy to make and wage war) and atrocities.

The judgment ascribed the length of the trial to the penchant of prosecution and defense to scrap over "every event, important and unimportant." The tribunal took the defense witnesses to task for their "prolix equivocation" and said that their evasiveness "only aroused distrust." The judgment also observed that there were gaps in the evidence and attributed this partly to the burning of evidence. The bench said it had relied heavily on the Kido diaries, which the judgment described as "a document of importance," and the Saionji-Harada diaries, which it called "helpful and reliable."

On points of law, the IMTFE held, in the Nuremberg mold, that the Tokyo charter was not *ex post facto* law but an expression of international law then in existence. The tribunal argued that it was not unjust to punish an aggressor but that it would be unjust not to do so. As for "aggression," the judgment conceded that there was "difficulty" in defining the word but added that Japan's unprovoked attacks on her neighbors "cannot but be characterized as wars of aggression. . . . For many years prior to the year 1930, Japan had claimed a place among the civilized communities of the world and had voluntarily incurred [treaty] obligations designed to further the course of peace, to outlaw aggressive war, and to mitigate the horror of war," the tribunal held. "It is against that background of obligation that the actions of the accused must be viewed and judged."

In the years after 1928, the first year of the indictment, Japan had launched a succession of expansionist wars. The critical questions, the judgment said, were: Why did these things happen? Who were those responsible for their occurrence?

The judgment put the responsibility primarily on the Japanese Army, which it accused of usurping power in Japan by intimidating or assassinating anyone who opposed its policies. Ultimately the militarists had made themselves the masters of Japan's destiny.

The judgment found that Japan had instigated the Mukden Incident and had waged aggressive war against China from 1931 to 1945; also that to finance her operations in China and to weaken Chinese resistance, "Japan sanctioned and developed the traffic in opium and narcotics"; also that Japan's use of slave labor had its origins in the China War, where "Chinese laborers were kept in concentration camps . . . fed short rations and furnished no medical attention whatever." The judgment held that Japan had initiated the aerial bombing of civilians on October 8, 1931, in China and that the bombing of the most populous nation on earth had continued for the next fourteen years.

The overall judgment could be reduced to a sentence on page 986: "We have come to the conclusion that the charge of conspiracy to wage aggressive wars has been made out [and] that these acts are . . . criminal in the highest degree."

The tribunal dismissed outright the accused's defense, that the Allies had imposed an economic embargo and that Japan's acts of war were justifiable measures of self-defense. "The argument is indeed merely a repetition of Japanese propaganda issued at the time she was preparing for her wars of aggression," the judgment declared. "It is not easy to have patience with its lengthy repetition at this date when documents are at length available which demonstrate that Japan's decision to expand to the North, to the

West, and to the South at the expense of her neighbors was taken long before any economic measures were directed against her, and was never departed from.''

In the areas of conventional war crimes and crimes against humanity the judgment was equally stern. It held that Japan between 1931 and 1945 had freely practiced torture, murder, rape, and other cruelties of the most inhumane and barbarous character as state policy to make her aggression so brutal and savage that the will of people to resist Japan would be broken. The finding was set forth in these historic words: "During a period of several months the tribunal heard evidence, orally or by affidavit, from witnesses who testified in detail to atrocities committed in all theaters of war on a scale so vast, yet following so common a pattern in all theaters, that *only one conclusion is possible—the atrocities were either secretly ordered or willfully permitted by the Japanese government or individual members thereof and by the leaders of the armed forces*" (italics added).

Who of those in the dock were responsible? The judgment placed responsibility on the army and navy ministers, the army and navy chiefs of staff, the chiefs of the Military and Naval Affairs bureaus, the inspector general of military education, the members of the Supreme War Council, and the field commanders. Among the accused thirteen had occupied these positions between 1931 and 1945: Doihara, Hata, Itagaki, Kimura, Koiso, Matsui, Minami, Muto, Oka, Sato, Shimada, Tojo, and Umezu.

The judgment was laced with details about the commission of conventional war crimes and crimes against humanity. The massacres and death marches that were cited made Lidice, Czechoslovakia, and Malmédy, Belgium, pale by comparison, although other than the Rape of Nanking, the Burmese-Siam Death Railway, and Bataan Death March, most of the world has long since forgotten Japan's atrocities in Asia. The tribunal listed the locations and dates of more than seventy-two large-scale massacres carried out by the Japanese Army outside of China alone as evidence that these events were the result of policy-making decisions and were an integral part of Japan's war strategy. "Massacres were freely committed as a means of terrorizing the civilian population and subjecting them to the domination of the Japanese," the judgment held. Most of the massacres had been ordered by commissioned officers, including high-ranking generals and admirals. The judgment added dryly that at no stage in the trial had the accused done more than "plead complete ignorance of the happenings deposed to."

The judgment made occasional references to subjects that had been thought of as taboo during the trial. In usurping power in Japan, the judgment held, the army "in a measure succeeded in diverting to their own ends the patriotic sentiment of loyalty to the emperor." As for the *zaibatsu,* the judgment observed that Chinese captives who refused to serve in Japan's puppet armies in China had been transported to Japan "to relieve the labor shortage in the munitions industries." This labor force was supplemented by recruiting Asian laborers "by false promises, and by force. . . . Little or no distinction appears to have been made between these conscripted laborers on the one hand and prisoners of war and civilian internees on the other hand. They were all regarded as slave laborers and to be used to the limit of their endurance." For this reason the judgment "included these conscripted laborers in the term 'civilian internees.' " The lot of the Asian slave laborers was found to have been worse than that of Allied POWs.

The Japanese as a people were not blamed for the reprehensible and criminal behavior of the imperial Japanese armed forces. The judgment observed that Japan's young people had been indoctrinated with the belief that the greatest honor for a Japanese was to die in the service of the emperor and that the greatest dishonor for a Japanese was to surrender to the enemy. As a result the typical Japanese soldier viewed the surrendered enemy as "being disgraced and entitled to live only by the tolerance of their captors."

The tribunal emphasized, however, that the Japanese military alone was not responsible for conventional war crimes and crimes against humanity. "The Japanese Government condoned ill-treatment of prisoners of war and civilian internees [including Asian conscripted laborers] by failing and neglecting to punish those guilty of ill-treating them or by prescribing trifling and inadequate penalties for the offense," the judgment held. "That Government also attempted to conceal the mistreatment and murder of prisoners and internees." In conclusion, the judgment summarized the core view of the majority of the IMTFE as follows:

> These far-reaching plans for waging wars of aggression, and the prolonged and intricate preparation for and waging

of these wars of aggression were not the work of one man. They were the work of many leaders acting in pursuance of a common plan for the achievement of a common object. That common object, that they should secure Japan's domination by preparing and waging wars of aggression, was a criminal object. Indeed, no more grave crime can be conceived of than a conspiracy to wage a war of aggression or the waging of a war of aggression, for the conspiracy threatens the security of the peoples of the world, and the waging disrupts it. . . . The tribunal finds that the existence of the criminal conspiracy to wage wars of aggression . . . has been proved.

32

The Verdict
Is Read

□

"The tribunal will now proceed to render its verdict in the case of each of the accused," Webb announced on November 12, 1948, as the IMTFE emerged at the end of the tunnel. The night before, the defendants who were keeping diaries had been informed that if they were sentenced to death they would not be permitted to continue their writing. "Had dinner after the close of the trial today," the beetle-browed Itagaki wrote matter-of-factly in his last entry. "There was a thorough medical examination at the hospital. Returned to my cell about 7 P.M. There was a complete change of bedding and sleeping garments, and of other articles." But he revealed a restless atmosphere within the prison that night. "It seems there are those who are happy and those who are worried," the former war minister said. "As for myself, I am, as always, immovable as a mountain."

At Ichigaya, Sir William Webb read the verdict as he had read the judgment, in a clear, firm voice. No one was acquitted.

All of the accused except Matsui and Shigemitsu were found guilty under Count 1 as "leaders, organizers, instigators, or accomplices in the formulation or execution of a common plan or conspiracy . . . [to] wage wars of aggression, and war or wars in violation of international law." All except Matsui, Oshima, and Shiratori were found guilty under County 27 of waging unprovoked war against China. All except Araki, Hashimoto, Hirota,

JUDGMENT AT ICHIGAYA

Count	1	27	29	31	32	33	35	36	54	55
ARAKI	G	G	X	X	X	X	X	X	X	X
DOIHARA	G	G	G	G	G	X	G	G	G	O
HASHIMOTO	G	G	X	X	X				X	X
HATA	G	G	G	G	G		X	X	X	G
HIRANUMA	G	G	G	G	G	X	X	G	X	X
HIROTA	G	G	X	X	X	X	X		X	G
HOSHINO	G	G	G	G	G	X	X		X	X
ITAGAKI	G	G	G	G	G	X	G	G	G	O
KAYA	G	G	G	G	G				X	X
KIDO	G	G	G	G	G	X	X	X	X	X
KIMURA	G	G	G	G	G				G	G
KOISO	G	G	G	G	G			X	X	G
MATSUI	X	X	X	X	X		X	X	X	G
MINAMI	G	G	X	X	X				X	X
MUTO	G	G	G	G	G	X		X	G	G
OKA	G	G	G	G	G				X	X
OSHIMA	G	X	X	X	X				X	X
SATO	G	G	G	G	G				X	X
SHIGEMITSU	X	G	G	G	G	G	X		X	G
SHIMADA	G	G	G	G	G				X	X
SHIRATORI	G	X	X	X	X					
SUZUKI	G	G	G	G	G		X	X	X	X
TOGO	G	G	G	G	G			X	X	X
TOJO	G	G	G	G	G	G		X	G	O
UMEZU	G	G	G	G	G			X	X	X

The results of the IMTFE trial, defendant by defendant. Blank: No Indictment; G: Guilty; X: Not Guilty; O: No Finding.

Matsui, Minami, Oshima, and Shiratori were found guilty under Counts 29, 31, and 32 of waging aggressive war against the United States, the British Commonwealth, and the Netherlands. Only Shigemitsu and Tojo were found guilty under Count 33 of waging war against France (in Indochina). And only Doihara, Hiranuma, and Itagaki were found guilty under counts 35 and 36 of waging war against the USSR.

Counts 54 and 55, the only other charges that had not been thrown out by the tribunal, dealt with atrocities. Under Count 54 the tribunal found Doihara, Itagaki, Kimura, Muto, and Tojo guilty of having "ordered, authorized, and permitted" inhumane treatment of POWs and others. Under Count 55 the tribunal found Hata, Hirota, Kimura, Koiso, Matsui, Muto, and Shigemitsu guilty of having "deliberately and recklessly disregarded their duty" to take adequate steps to prevent atrocities.

There were 207 verdicts.

As the above table shows, only three of the accused were found guilty of a single charge, Oshima and Shiratori, the two Axis ambassadors, and Matsui, who had commanded Japan's armies in China during the Rape of Nanking.

Before sentencing, Webb revealed publicly for the first time the existence of separate opinions. "Under the Charter," the president announced, "the judgment I have read is the judgment of the tribunal." But, he disclosed, the Indian judge dissented wholly from the majority, and the French and Dutch members of the tribunal dissented in part. The Filipino judge had filed a separate concurring opinion. As for himself, Webb said cryptically, "I share the view of the majority as to the facts, but without recording any dissent, I have filed a brief statement . . . of some general considerations. . . ." There was a murmur in the courtroom.

These documents, he continued, would form part of the transcript but they would not be read in court. The defense had been provided with the texts of the separate opinions in advance and had applied for a reading of them in open court. But the tribunal held firm to its earlier decision in rejecting Judge Pal's request to do so. "The tribunal adheres to this decision," Webb said with finality.

Webb ordered the defendants removed from the dock and returned singly for sentencing. The defendants filed out of the courtroom under guard and were placed in the customary "chicken cage" that was their holding area. They bowed to each other and shook hands. Some shed tears. Hoshino, Tojo's cabinet secretary, now a banked spirit, had a premonition that this was the last time he would see Tojo. "I grasped Tojo's hand firmly," he wrote' in his diary. "I shed tears and said farewell. . . . Tojo said, 'Pardon me for having brought even you to such a situation.' "

After recess, at 3:35 P.M., the marshal of the court summoned the tribunal into session for the last time.

The door to the dock opened, and Araki, accompanied by MPs in white helmets and white gloves, entered. The former war minister had been a familiar figure during the trial, sitting stiffly on the edge of his chair and periodically running a hand over his Bismarckian mustache. Now his frame sagged, and he rocked back and forth like a punch-drunk boxer. "Accused Araki, Sadao," Webb intoned, "on the counts of the indictment on which you have been convicted, the International Military Tribunal for the Far East sentences you to imprisonment for life." Araki immediately regained his composure, stood erect, and, shoulders thrown back, marched out of the dock accompanied by his guards. Webb repeated the formula fifteen more times in the course of the seventeen minutes it took to read out the sentences, sending the following convicted war criminals to prison for life: Hashimoto, Hata, Hiranuma, Hoshino, Kaya, Kido, Koiso, Minami, Oka, Oshima, Sato, Shimada, Shiratori, Suzuki, and Umezu.

Only two of the accused, both foreign ministers, received lesser prison terms. Mamoru Shigemitsu was sentenced to seven years and Shigenori Togo to twenty years, each from the date of his arraignment.

For the menacing Doihara and six others—Itagaki, Kimura, Matsui, Muto, Hirota, and Tojo—the formula changed ominously. "Defendant Doihara, Kenji," Webb said solemnly, "on the counts of the indictment on which you have been convicted, the International Military Tribunal for the Far East sentences you to death by hanging." In twenty-three years on the bench this was the first time Sir William Webb had ever handed down a death sentence.

The sentences were inconsistent. Koki Hirota, the former premier and foreign minister, was the only civilian sentenced to death; he took the fall for Japan's civilian leaders. But he was not the most important civilian in the dock. That position was held by the emperor's adviser, Marquis Kido. All the others sent to death were generals. With the exception of Matsui, all had entertained intimate links with the fanatical, expansionist, and conspiratorial Kwantung Army clique in Manchuria. Although the United States had been the catalyst in setting up the IMTFE, and although the Americans were accused by some of thirsting for revenge against the men who had executed the attack on Pearl Harbor, no naval officer in the dock received the death penalty. Moreover, those condemned for war crimes had been more deeply involved in the China than the Pacific phase of the war.

One salient feature of the verdict was that everyone convicted under Count 54, which dealt with atrocities, was sentenced to the gallows. Matsui was acquitted of every charge except Count 55, dereliction of duty in preventing atrocities, and nevertheless was sentenced to death. Of the six others who were also found guilty under Count 55, three joined Matsui on the gallows, two were sentenced to life imprisonment, and a third received a seven-year prison sentence. In the laymen's view this and other sentences made no sense.

"It is difficult to explain judgments: the question why one gets a death sentence, and the other only imprisonment," Judge Röling commented in a written interview in 1982. "The behavior in court may have played a role and the tactics of defense-counsel. . . . Even the question at what moment the court had to make up its mind may have been significant. If accused A, a not so notorious person, is dealt with just after the deliberations and sentence concerning a notoriously cruel accused, he will benefit from the fact that the Court will be inclined to give expression to the difference between the two." And in a significant disclosure, Röling continued, "In Tokyo it took an unexpected short time to determine the penalties. Sir William Webb used as president tactics which were perhaps usual in labour-conferences, but very unusual in Court deliberations. He refused to acknowledge the seriousness of the opinion of those who took the standpoint that a judge, convinced that an accused deserved the death penalty, might not be willing to have that accused sentenced to death if there was only a majority of six to five for the death penalty."

Under the Tokyo charter sentences were to be arrived at by "a majority vote." No judge after the trial revealed the vote on specific death sentences. Among prosecutors, however, the consensus was that the IMTFE had voted seven to four for the death penalty for the generals and six to five on Hirota. Some defense sources claimed that all the death sentences had resulted from a six-to-five vote, but this is extremely unlikely. The constant majority for the death penalty is believed to have consisted of China, the Philippines, Great Britain, Canada, and the United States, and at different times the Soviet Union, New Zealand, and the Netherlands. Australia, India, and France consistently opposed the death sentences. Since the trial there has been speculation that General Zarayanov opted against the death penalty on the grounds that such extreme punishment had been abolished in the Soviet Union; yet nobody doubted the Marxist-Leninist regime's penchant for imposing death in Soviet kangaroo courts, and at Nuremberg the Soviet justice filed the only dissent on grounds that the sentences were insufficiently harsh. Moreover, among the Webb Papers at Canberra there is a memorandum from Zarayanov, dated February 4, 1948, in which the Soviet judge wrote, "It is quite obvious that if the accused are found guilty this gives ground to believe that in some cases this would entail the severest sentence provided in the Charter."

Whatever the case, at 4:12 P.M. on November 12, 1948, two years and ninety-eight days after it had convened, the IMTFE adjourned.

As in the case of Araki, each accused had stood alone in the dock to hear the world's judgment (the tribunal represented the majority of mankind). Each had put the translator's earphones on his head to hear the sentence. An MP helped Minami remove his headset after the former war minister heard the tribunal sentence him to prison for life. Minami simply stood there, fumbling nervously with his earphones. Hirota, the agnostic who believed life ended in "blankness," smiled wanly at his two daughters seated in the press section after he heard his death sentence. Each of the defendants, except Oshima, had bowed either to the court or to the gallery on entering the dock. Oshima, the general and ambassador who had consorted with Hitler and Himmler and who was considered more Nazi than the Nazis, stood defiantly at attention in the Prussian mold. Tojo bowed to the tribunal before he heard his sentence and again before leaving the dock. Among those who had been sentenced to hang, Doihara alone looked relieved. "The moment the sentence was pronounced," Doihara said afterward, "all my worries left me, and almost at once I began to feel better." Itagaki had a different reaction. "I am overwhelmed by remorse," he mumbled. But little remorse was expressed by the others. "My conscience is as clear as sun and moon," Kaya, the financial bureaucrat, said after being sentenced to life.

In the courtroom there was pandemonium. Correspondents rushed to the telephones. Mrs. Shiratori wept openly in a corridor. Togo's wife collapsed in his attorney's office. Mrs. Tojo, who had declined to speak of her feelings during the trial "because I felt that my husband would prefer it that way," said she would not organize a petition for the commutation of his death sentence. "Our nation is filled with people whose families died in the war," she said. "It is natural that it is now our turn."

Embittered, Hirota's son said it was better that his father die on the gallows than languish the rest of his years in prison. But both the prosecution and defense attorneys felt otherwise. As Robert Donihi, Keenan's young assistant, put it, "I was shocked by Hirota's death sentence." And George Furness, for the defense, observed in 1981, "I don't think Hirota should have hanged." When Furness visited Sugamo to confer with Shigemitsu, his client, the former foreign minister, told him, "Don't worry about me. Hirota's sentence is the most unjust of all. Help him, not me." For his part Joseph Keenan later told Furness and Shigemitsu, on a visit to Japan after the 1952 peace treaty, that he thought Shigemitsu should have been acquitted. And in his postwar memoirs, Shigemitsu said he himself was convinced that he had done all that was possible to alleviate the suffering of war prisoners, civilian internees, and Asian slave laborers, but that "since everything was under the control of the army, no one else could interfere," adding, "The Tokyo Tribunal adjudged me guilty on the point. It is not for me to question their verdict."

The lawyers on both sides gave the other sentences mixed reviews. Tojo's conviction hardly caused a stir. "I guess he had it coming," G. Osmond Hyde said. And a defense attorney admitted privately, "I certainly can understand the conviction and sentencing of Doihara and Itagaki." Another American defense attorney, George Yamaoka, felt Kido's conviction to be tenuous. "For political reasons I can understand why they indicted the emperor's adviser, but for legal reasons I don't see it," he said. Yamaoka thought that Shigemitsu, Togo, Hirota, and possibly Hiranuma should have been acquitted. "How could these civilians control an army which ruled by assassination and was filled with fanatical junior officers?" he asked. Surrendering Japan's army on the deck of the *Missouri* had been the ultimate humiliation and punishment for Umezu, he mused.

The witnesses for the prosecution and defense also had mixed reactions to the verdicts. One example here will suffice. The controversial General Ryukichi Tanaka, who had testified as a witness for both sides and whom the judgment branded "a witness of no credit," felt at peace with himself. "I feel that I have done my duty to avenge the crimes committed by the Japanese army," he told the Japanese press. ". . . I have done my best to prove the innocence of the emperor, who was helpless in the face of the pressure of the militarists." For that matter Tojo was also satisfied with the outcome of the trial because he had, Tojo said, succeeded in absolving the emperor of guilt. Perhaps this is the reason he bowed deeply to the court on judgment day.

As the defendants left the dock one by one, those who had received the death penalty were taken to a separate room.

"I received life imprisonment," Sato, the former head of the Military Affairs Bureau and, at fifty-four, the youngest of the defendants, wrote in his memoirs, "and after retiring to the waiting room, I stationed myself at a point where Tojo, flanked by MPs, appeared." Sato told him, "I want to say farewell." Then tears filled Sato's eyes, and his voice choked. "Tojo cast a warm look toward me," he recalled, "and quietly disappeared into the next room."

Sato added with candor that he had entertained "a strange feeling" when he escaped the death penalty, noting, "I must honestly admit that I was happy to live." The samurai warrior did not really know how happy he should have felt. Röling, the Dutch judge, in his separate opinion, believed Sato should have hanged as a former chief of the murderous Military Affairs Bureau, which had issued many of the directives for handling POWs, civilian internees, and Asian forced laborers.

At Sugamo several of the Class A prisoners who had not yet been indicted were also "surprised" by the leniency. In an authorized biography published in 1960 Nobusuke Kishi, a member of Tojo's cabinet and a Class A suspect who was never indicted, expressed "astonishment" that "only" seven of the accused had been condemned to death. He felt that if the tables had been reversed, no Japanese court would have accorded Allied defendants the opportunity of defending themselves. Kishi served as prime minister of Japan from 1957 to 1960.

But the focus within the prison was on the Sugamo Seven. In his memoirs and in press interviews the Buddhist chaplain Hanayama gave a capsule report on the last days of the condemned prisoners. Matsui, he said, was worried that after his execution his wife would follow him by committing *hara kiri,* and he promised to abandon his Shintoism for her Buddhism if she promised to live. Matsui also confessed to Hanayama that the Rape of Nanking was a "national disgrace" and implied that the real culprit was one of his junior officers, a member of the imperial family, Prince Asaka, who had commanded troops on the scene. Kimura's family was Christian, and pleaded with him to be baptized before his execution. He refused. Muto's daughter wrote of her regret that she could not accompany him on his last journey and that she looked forward to their reunion on "the other shore." Hirota wiled away the time in solitude, playing solitaire. And Tojo penned a *haiku,* or classical seventeen-syllable poem: "Oh, look/see how/the cherry blossoms/fall mutely."

Throughout Japan people gathered at radio sets to hear the sentences. A shop on the bomb-shattered Ginza set up a loudspeaker, and several hundred persons formed a crescent. "A solemn atmosphere prevailed," a Japanese newspaper reported. And when Webb started to pronounce each sentence, there was "a strange, voiceless commotion among the people." At a home for destitute soldiers within the compound of Kaneiji Temple, another circle formed around a radio. After the verdicts were read, one man in tattered shirt and trousers said, "I believe there may be other responsible persons who were overlooked."

At the Imperial Palace, behind the gray moat and the gray walls, Hirohito and Empress Nagako listened uneasily to the verdicts. For the occasion the emperor wore neither an admiral's nor a general's uniform nor ceremonial court dress. He was attired in a Western suit. Hirohito's aides described him as "somewhat shocked" that Kido, his intimate adviser, was sentenced to life and that Hirota was sentenced to death. He received the other sentences impassively.

Many people at the tribunal shared the experience of the prisoner at Sugamo who wrote in his diary, "I stayed awake until late last night, thinking quietly about today's judgment."

33

Opinions,
Dissent,
and Appeal

People also thought about the separate opinions that were released to prosecution, defense, and press but were not read in court. The words of the judges provided a kaleidoscopic glimpse into the arguments surrounding the drafting of the judgment.

For example, the judgment was silent on Hirohito, but in his concurring opinion Sir William Webb was not. Webb observed that the prosecution's evidence had proved "beyond question" the authority of the emperor when he had done what atomic bombs could not do: stop the war. Webb also believed the emperor had had a hand in starting the war. "The immunity of the Emperor, as contrasted with the part he played in launching the war in the Pacific, is I think a matter which the Tribunal should take into consideration in imposing sentences," Webb said. In strong language Webb likened Hirohito to "the leader in the crime" who was granted immunity from prosecution. The Australian jurist did not go so far as to suggest that the emperor should have been prosecuted. "That is beyond my province," he said. "His immunity was, no doubt, decided upon in the best interests of all the Allied Powers." Nonetheless, Webb felt there was no escape from the fact that Hirohito's authority had been required to sanction the war, and if he did not want war—and, Webb noted, "the evidence indicates that he was always in favor of peace"—Hirohito should have withheld his authority. "It is no answer to say that he might have been assassinated," Webb said sternly. "That risk is taken by all rulers who must still do their duty. No ruler can commit the crime of launching aggressive war and then validly claim to be excused for so doing because his life would otherwise have been in danger."

Webb now challenged the death penalties imposed on seven accused, but he did so by tilting at windmills. Death would appear to be the minimum punishment for a crime so great as initiating war, with its accumulated evil, Webb observed, as he pointed out that no defendant at Nuremberg had been sentenced to death for waging aggressive war, although Nuremberg had branded aggressive war the supreme international crime. But nobody at Tokyo had been sentenced to death for that crime, either. At both Nuremberg and Tokyo the gallows were reserved for defendants who had incited or been otherwise implicated in mass-scale atrocities. "Unless the Japanese accused are to be treated with less consideration than the German accused, no Japanese accused should be sentenced to death for conspiring to wage . . . aggressive war," Webb said. Finally emerging from behind his scarecrow, Webb recommended that those found guilty of atrocities should be exiled abroad in the Napoleonic tradition. He held this punishment to be "a greater deterrent to such men than the scaffold or firing squad." Another consideration, he felt, mitigated against their execution—the advanced age of the condemned. "It may prove revolting to hang or shoot such old men."

Webb's rough prickly exterior concealed a soft custard interior. Webb's views were hardly a surprise to those close to him. In this respect the popular Tokyo caricature of Webb as a hanging judge was one of complete misrepresentation.

In his concurring opinion the Filipino judge took sharp issue with his Australian colleague, attesting to the integrity of the judges in following their own consciences and not that of either SCAP or the Allied prosecution. "I am constrained to differ on a few only of the penalties to be imposed by the tribunal—they are, in my judgment, too lenient, not exemplary and deterrent, and not commensurate with the gravity of the offense or offenses committed," Delfin Jaranilla wrote. Jaranilla, whose land had been ravaged by the Japanese like no other except China, was with Judge Mei of China among the bench's strictest hard-liners.

Jaranilla characterized the crimes of the accused as "monstrous." He also attacked the defense's contention that the use of the atomic bomb against Japan had been inhuman and unwarranted. "The purpose of the arguments, as far as I can see, was to minimize the responsibility of the defendants in this case for the atrocities and inhuman acts committed during the war," Jaranilla said. He went on to remind the tribunal that when the atomic bomb was dropped, Tokyo had not yet surrendered. Japan was weakened by reverses but still occupied extensive areas of China, the Philippines, and other countries. "If a means is justified by an end, the use of the atomic bomb was justified," Jaranilla declared, "for it brought Japan to her knees and ended the horrible war. If the war had gone on longer, without the use of the atomic bomb, how many more thousands and thousands of helpless men, women, and children would have needlessly died and suffered, and how much more destruction and devastation . . . would have been wrought?" Jaranilla did not comment on Hirohito's role in terminating the war.

In his concurring opinion Jaranilla called for stiffer sentences but shied away from particulars. Not so the Dutch judge, B.V.A. Röling, who agreed with Webb and the Nuremberg tribunal that as international law then stood, no one should be sentenced to death for having committed a crime against peace. Internment for life he deemed "appropriate punishment." Accordingly, in his separate opinion, Röling approved the life sentences handed out to the sixteen accused except in the cases of Admirals Shimada and Oka, Generals Hata and Sato, and Marquis Kido, the emperor's confidant. "As for the accused Oka, Sato, and Shimada . . . they should have been found guilty of conventional war crimes and should have been punished with the supreme penalty." Röling was the only judge to come out openly for stiffer penalties for the naval officers in the dock; by implication he, alone, called attention to the hellships and the behavior of Japanese forces on islands under naval control, notably in the southwest Pacific and the Malay Archipelago.

In proposing the death penalty for Admirals Oka and Shimada and General Sato, Röling also approved the death sentences meted out by the tribunal except in the case of Hirota. Here he not only balked but held that Hirota should have been acquitted. "A tribunal should be very careful in holding civil government officials responsible for the behavior of the army in the field," he observed.

Röling also called for the acquittal of Kido, taking issue with the tribunal and even sharper issue with Webb's separate opinion. Röling held that the evidence showed that the emperor had disapproved of Japan's aggressive policies without being able to alter their course. "The evidence in this trial does not warrant the statement of the prosecution [and Webb] that the emperor would have been able to prevent the war by simply forbidding it and that men such as Kido should have advised him to do so. . . . From the limited power of the emperor follows the limited power of his adviser."

In addition to calling for the acquittal of Hirota and Kido, the Dutch judge held that Hata, Shigemitsu, and Togo should also be acquitted. Mixing in Field Marshal Hata, the man who had commanded Japan's armies in China, with the two former foreign ministers appeared incongruous. But Röling claimed that the IPS had failed to link Hata to atrocities. It seems that Röling was influenced by evidence that Hata had opposed the Pacific War and favored the withdrawal of Japanese forces from China.

The Dutch jurist felt that Shigemitsu and Togo were statesmen and diplomats who had worked for peace rather than war, that Togo had entered the Tojo cabinet in 1941 to prevent the Pacific War and "if he failed, he would be compelled to remain in that cabinet lest he betray his country and its government," and that Shigemitsu had done likewise when he entered Tojo's cabinet in 1943. "To enter a cabinet, and to assume an office through which one obtains the power necessary to be able to work for peace, is a duty rather than a crime," Röling said emphatically, upbraiding the Majority for its findings on both defendants.

The dissenting judgment of Henri Bernard was at odds with Röling's and revealed how confused the bench was over Hirohito's culpability, or lack of it. "It cannot be denied," the French judge wrote, "[the case] had a principal author who escaped all prosecution and of whom in any case the present defendants could only be considered accomplices." Bernard accused the Allied prosecutors of making the defendants responsible for the acts of "the principal author" when they were really his accomplices.

Bernard, without going into detail, also cited "defects of procedure" in the case, such as the failure of the bench to meet even once to discuss the judgment. "A verdict reached by a tribunal after a defective procedure cannot be a valid one," Bernard wrote, bristling at the Majority's cavalier treatment of the minority.

Much of the French member's dissent was written in convoluted prose, but it was evident that he disapproved of the atomic bombing of Japan. Although he did not clarify his remarks, he held that in the Majority's view a Japanese scholar who worked on the atomic bomb would not be criminally responsible for the annihilation of a population in one blow "if it were effectuated by soldiers acting upon the order of a general" even if it meant the destruction of a whole city. And there he left it hanging.

If Bernard's dissenting opinion was couched in obscurantist language, Radhabinod Pal's 1,000-page-plus dissenting judgment was virtually unreadable. Pal's trains of thought often ended up on remote sidings, and he flip-flopped so frequently that some of his conclusions strained credulity. Thus, in one paragraph, on Nanking, he held that "I might mention in this connection that even the published accounts of Nanking 'rape' could not be accepted by the world without some suspicion of exaggeration." But in another paragraph he acknowledged that "there is no doubt that the conduct of Japanese at Nanking was atrocious and that such atrocities were intense for nearly three weeks." In another statement he held that "in my opinion, Japanese commanders were legally bound to maintain their army's discipline and to restrain the soldiers under their command from perpetrating these atrocities." In regard to the Rape of Manila, however, "we cannot attach much importance to what happened there . . . [because] it became impossible for the Japanese commanders to control their troops effectively." Elsewhere he cited the "Bataan Death March [as] an atrocious brutality" but later dismissed it "as an isolated instance of cruelty."

The Bengali judge's dissent is peppered with curiosities. Pal described Manchukuo as "the *alleged* puppet government of Manchuria" (italics added). Public opinion in Japan, he held, "even during the war . . . truly vigorously functioned." Then on the Hague and Geneva Conventions: "A war in violation of treaties, agreements, or assurances without anything more may only mean a breach of contract. In my opinion, such a breach would not amount to any crime." In addressing himself to the Siam-Burma Death Railway, Pal held, "I do not hesitate to say that the accused Tojo was fully responsible for it; but this violation of the rules regarding the labour of prisoners of war is a mere act of state." Pal concluded, "It is not criminal *per se* and I would not make him criminally liable for it." By the same token, the Japanese who tortured and executed Allied fliers "in my opinion . . .

did not commit any crimes." Japan's alliance with Hitler was made to avoid diplomatic isolation and not to prepare for war, "and I do not think there is anything in the prosecution's evidence which would lead us to reject this explanation [by the defense]." In considering the attack on Pearl Harbor he concluded, "Everything, at least on the Japanese side, seems to have been done with sincerity, and I do not find any trace of treachery anywhere in it." Pal did not comment on the Japanese sneak attack on Malaya and other places *before* the attack on Pearl Harbor.

Pal whitewashed virtually *all* the acts of the accused. "Whatever they did," he contended, "they did it out of pure patriotic motives." The Chinese and Filipino judges were appalled, as were some of the European judges, who felt Pal's judgment, with the same logic, would have freed the accused at Nuremberg.

Pal's dissent was crowned by his extreme verdict: "For reasons given in the foregoing pages, I would hold that each and every one of the accused must be found not guilty of each and every one of the charges in the indictment and should be acquitted on all those charges."

Charitably, Pal's judgment may be ascribed to the Hindu penchant to be all things to all men. But this is too exotic an interpretation. Two subterranean themes ran constantly through his judgment. One was that the West was sitting in judgment of Japan and applying a double standard, since the Japanese had done in Asia only what the West had done before. The other was an antiracism refrain, that Japan had sought to demolish the myth in Asia of the white man's superiority. It is not easy for either Occidental or Oriental to take issue with these twin historical perspectives. But Pal lived in the past, certainly not in the age of the Hague and Geneva Conventions or Pact of Paris. Worse, he ignored the racism of the Japanese. The evidence at the IMTFE conclusively proved that the Japanese had been more inhumane toward Chinese, Filipinos, and other Asians than toward Europeans and Americans. Unintentionally, in his judgment, Pal himself revealed his sense of superiority over the "coolies" of East Asia; repeatedly, for example, he referred to Indonesians as "natives," the white man's pejorative for colonized peoples.

Perhaps Pal's outlook is understandable. Of the three Asian countries on the tribunal in 1948, India was the only one governed by white rulers.

In recent years, with the revival in Japan of nationalist sentiments, Pal has become a hero of sorts among the neo-ultras. Saburo Ienaga, the Japanese author of *The Pacific War* and other books and essays, put it this way: "Justice Pal's dissent at the Tokyo war crimes trial, at least in Japan, has been a valuable source of support for those who seek to justify the 'Greater East Asia War.' Although many who favor this position have probably never read through Justice Pal's opinion, they see it as an important document which provides ammunition for their views." Ienaga, incidentally, encountered the same problem faced by others in trying to read Pal. "I was painfully aware of the difficulties in following Pal's train of thought," he said politely.

Given Pal's hostility toward the West, especially toward the United States, whose use of the atomic bomb to help end the war Pal likened to "the only near approach to the directives . . . of the Nazi leaders during the second world war," it may seem odd that his views have not gained popularity among Marxists-Leninists and other Americophobes. But the leftists and the "useful idiots," as Lenin called his assorted camp followers, have had a genuine problem with Pal. In his judgment Pal contended that Japan had been justified in going to war in China because it was fighting "the spread of communism" and that Tokyo had had a legitimate fear of the Soviet Union.

In India, Pal has been revered for his "unique" contribution to international law. Commentator T. S. Raman Rao, a fellow Bengali, praised Pal as the only judge at either Tokyo or Nuremberg "who refused to be bound" by the attempt to break new ground in international law. The defense at the IMTFE was delighted by Pal's performance. In one of the great understatements of the trial, Ichiro Kiyose told the press, "I appreciate Pal's worthy reasoning."

In the end all the IMTFE judges except Pal signed the tribunal's judgment. Röling and Bernard did so with the proviso that their separate opinions form part of the record. Copies of the transcript, judgment, and separate opinions were delivered to each member state of the Allied Council for Japan, the UN, the National Diet Library in Tokyo, and nineteen other libraries across Japan. Additional copies were shipped to Allied national archives. Sets were also spirited off by judges, defense and prosecuting attorneys, journalists, and others.

Just as the trial and verdict at Nuremberg had generated dissatisfaction among Western commentators, particularly lawyers and academics, many criticisms were also directed at the Tokyo trial.

In an undated ten-page brief in Joseph Keenan's papers at the U.S. National Archives, the Allied chief prosecutor took on the commentators point by point. Keenan divided Tokyo's critics into three groups. "The first one would let all [war criminal suspects] go scot free . . . to begin the whole business over again since they have already in this trial declared that they have done no wrong," Keenan wrote. "The second group complain that many more should be tried than those presently accused"—apparently a reference to the failure to prosecute the emperor—"[and] the third group complain that the prosecution does not know what it is doing . . . its personnel was and is too green to understand the . . . complexities of the Japanese. . . . These complaints include a general charge of 'lack of stature' [among the judges and lawyers].

"In answer to the criticism of those opposing these trials on the ground that they have no law to support them, we do have a right to ask, do not treaties make law?" Keenan asked. ". . . What should be done with those who were really responsible for [breaking] these treaties, whose chief aim was to provide for peace instead of war? . . . The hope of world peace lies in agreements embodied in treaties. No thinking person would deny this."

As for the argument that the IMTFE failed to prosecute Hirohito, Keenan argued that "we have attempted to get the chairman of the board and the president and executive vice-president and we have left out the clerks and the tellers and the secretaries." The emperor, he averred, "was only nominally the head," adding, "He was in truth and in fact a constitutional monarch." But Keenan hedged. "Where notable omissions have been made, in most instances it is now felt that such was justifiable for the real purpose of this prosecution, namely, to get at the right ringleaders, the real responsible individuals."

As for the charge of incompetency, Keenan readily acknowledged that "it is regrettable that there were not enough American or other Allied lawyers of 'stature' present in Japan who could have gathered all this evidence and who could have had many years of experience needed to thoroughly understand the Japanese government and the Japanese mind and its complexities." He said the IPS did not claim "to know a great deal about these so-called complexities. But they do believe their intensive study and experience over a year has given a sufficient insight into the operation of the Japanese government and its method of operation to [draw] conclusions.''

Japanese opinions on the trial and verdict were many and varied. *Nihon Keizai,* the economic journal, observed that if the trial had been solely "victor's justice," as Hideki Tojo alleged, there would have been no need for the "stupendous efforts and labor" involved in mounting the trial. The *Nippon Times* pointed out that the trial had had many defects, deficiencies, and limitations but that the tribunal's judgment was profound because it provided a version of modern Japan's history unfamiliar to the Japanese. "The Japanese people must ponder over why it is that there has been such a discrepancy between what they thought and what the rest of the world accepted almost as common knowledge," the paper said. "This is at the root of the tragedy which Japan brought upon herself." Attorney General Shunkichi Ueda, who had opposed the China War and been briefly incarcerated during the Pacific War, said dryly, "The judgment was expected." And for the voiceless, faceless millions of Japanese who had been killed, maimed, and wounded during the war, a widow lamented, "I cannot recover my lost happiness even if I read the judgment. . . . Ah! if there had been no war." To others the trial was unnecessary: The accused should have committed *hara kiri* at Japan's surrender. "It would have been better," a twenty-nine-year-old wounded veteran said, "if they had died soon after the end of the war." Another remarked, "When I think of the dead, the penalties meted out to the defendants are too light."

Hirota's death sentence caused widespread surprise and indignation. A hastily circulated petition on Hirota's behalf garnered more than 300,000 signatures. Momentarily, too, Webb's judgment thrust Hirohito before the footlights. Some hypersensitive members of the emperor's entourage thought Webb's commentary was an indirect signal from MacArthur for the emperor to resign, and rumors swept Japan that Hirohito might abdicate.

"What are the feelings of the emperor?" the *Kokusai Times* asked in a typical commentary on Webb's judgment. "The emperor . . . cannot continue to conceal his responsibility for war crimes." Several provincial papers called for the emperor's abdication as an apology to the Japanese people. "It is indisputable that the emperor himself is also responsible for the war," one daily said. The war "was launched in the name of the emperor," Jiichiro Matsumoto said. "From this point of view, it is a wonder that the emperor was excluded from the trial." In disgust, Matsumoto derided the emperor as "weak-minded." But the harshest attacks on the emperor stemmed from the Communist press, which SCAP had naïvely fostered in the early days of the occupation as part of the "democratization" of Japan. *Akahata* (*Red Flag*) demanded the emperor's removal.

In his memoirs, *With MacArthur in Japan,* William J. Sebald, MacArthur's political adviser, revealed the depth of MacArthur's anger with Webb. The general accused the president of the tribunal of "playing cheap politics" on the Hirohito issue with a view to ingratiating himself at home, since Australian public opinion toward Hirohito was on a par with the "Hang the Kaiser" sentiment of World War I. Sebald spelled out the potential political fallout if the emperor, in the aftermath of Webb's opinion, resigned. ". . . The whole system of authority and control, symbolized by Hirohito's relationship with MacArthur, might have been destroyed suddenly, creating chaos or, at least, great opportunities for chaos," Sebald wrote. "Among other considerations, this situation would have given the Communists their most favorable moment to ignite turmoil at a period when they were approaching the peak of their postwar strength in Japan."

A few days after the Tokyo judgment Hirohito wrote MacArthur in a secret letter that he would not abdicate. The emperor reiterated that decision in the course of a courtesy call paid upon him by Joseph Keenan before the chief Allied prosecutor returned to Washington. It is also likely that Keenan acted as SCAP's courier on that visit—a role he had played periodically during the trial—and relayed a message of support from MacArthur to the emperor. And on November 20 the *Mainichi* quoted palace circles to the effect that the emperor felt it was his "highest responsibility" to remain on the throne during Japan's rehabilitation and reconstruction.

In the midst of this turmoil the defense at the tribunal established a fifteen-member committee to prepare an appeal to MacArthur, who was empowered under Article 17 of the Tokyo charter to review and "at any time reduce" the court's sentences. The appeal reached MacArthur on November 21 and was signed on behalf of all defense counsel by Shigenori Togo's American attorney, Ben Bruce Blakeney, who would shortly be killed in an air crash.

The principal themes of the appeal were that the defendants had not received a fair trial and that the verdict was not that of the tribunal "but of a clique of it." the appeal called upon MacArthur for "a fearless act of statesmanship."

MacArthur as Supreme Commander was an agent of the eleven-nation Far Eastern Commission, which in turn was represented collectively in Tokyo by the Allied Council for Japan. Both bodies were composed of the same countries represented at the IMTFE and on April 3, 1946, more than three weeks before the trial opened, the FEC had approved a policy paper that instructed MacArthur to consult with the allied diplomatic representatives before acting under Article 17. Accordingly, on November 24, 1948, the council met with MacArthur in Tokyo.

An outstanding account of this critical session is contained in Sebald's memoirs. Like many other diplomats, Sebald had opposed the idea of a trial of political and military leaders. "Although I was familiar with many of the sordid events covered in the indictment, my instinct told me that, on the whole, it was a mistake to hold the trial," he wrote. But he conceded, "No one can read the judgment of the IMTFE and not be impressed, indeed shocked, by the story of Japan's spiritual and moral deterioration during the decade prior to Pearl Harbor."

As for the council meeting with SCAP, Sebald, with MacArthur's agreement, wanted to seize the moment to answer Webb's gratuitous and politically damaging opinion of the emperor, but the U.S. State Department constrained him from doing so.

Sebald recorded the council's recommendations during its review of the sentences. The United States, China, New Zealand, the Philippines, the Soviet Union, and Great Britain had no changes to recommend. Canada, which was also a member of the Majority, in a subtle maneuver announced that it would not oppose a reduction in sentences, reinforcing the belief that in the six-to-five vote that had sentenced former premier Hirota to death, Canada had held out for a prison sentence. Australia, in contrast to Webb's opinion, opted for no change with the qualification that Canberra, like Ottawa, would not oppose a reduction of sentences. India favored the commutation of all death sentences to life imprisonment. Once again, the Netherlands offered the most specific recommendation, this time a reduction of sentences: Hata's and Umezu's from life to twenty years in prison; Togo's from twenty to ten years; Shigemitsu's from seven to two and a half years (this would have freed him immediately); and Hirota's from death to life imprisonment.

The American *shogun* had had many bitter and lonely decisions to make during the war, but in his own memoirs MacArthur described his duty to review the sentences as "utterly repugnant." Sebald observed, "I had not seen him display such deep emotion before." For a general to hang six other generals and a civilian head of government must have been painful, indeed. In a statement to the council, which was released publicly, MacArthur concluded that he could conceive of "no juridical process where greater safeguard was made to evolve justice . . . [that] it is inevitable that many will disagree with the verdict; even the learned justices who composed the tribunal were not in agreement . . . [and] if we cannot trust such processes and such men, we can trust nothing." He upheld the sentences.

Typically, MacArthur exploited the moment to advance his own thinking on larger issues. He called for the global renunciation of war—"the most malignant scourge and greatest sin of mankind"—and in a grand gesture to bind the wounds between Japan and the Allies, he declared, "To this end, on the day of execution, I request the members of all the congregations throughout Japan of whatever creed or faith in the privacy of their homes or at their altars of public worship to seek divine help and guidance that the world will keep the peace, lest the human race perish." Little did he suspect that he would be at war in little more than a year—in Korea.

Seven of the defendants now carried their appeal not to the International Court of Justice at The Hague, but to the U.S. Supreme Court. Two of the accused were on death row, Hirota and Doihara; the others were Kido, Togo, Sato, Shimada, and Oka. The essence of their appeal was that MacArthur had exceeded his authority in setting up the tribunal, the same argument the defense had made during the trial.

As legal situations are wont to do, the issue shifted its focus at Washington. The fate of the war criminals turned into a test of whether the Supreme Court had the power to review the White House's conduct of foreign affairs and exercise of military power abroad. "The issues are truly great ones," said Supreme Court Justice Robert Jackson, the former chief American prosecutor at Nuremberg. The nucleus of the problem was that the Nuremberg tribunal had been set up under a four-power agreement while the Tokyo tribunal had been created by MacArthur, under the surrender terms, as an agent of the Far Eastern Commission.

On December 7, 1948, coincidentally the seventh anniversary of the attack on Pearl Harbor, the Supreme Court voted five to four to hear the case. The Court said it would first decide whether it had jurisdiction before reviewing the verdicts. Justice Jackson cast the deciding vote.

In Japan the vote caused a "sensation," as one Japanese newspaper put it. The average Japanese expressed astonishment, admiration, and puzzlement over the American legal process. At SCAP, however, there was consternation. The head of Mac-Arthur's legal section, Colonel Alva C. Carpenter, conceded that the court's action had "come as a surprise." For once Joseph Keenan, now in Washington, had no comment. A few days earlier he had conferred with Truman and quoted the president as expressing gratification over the manner in which the trial had been conducted.

Some of America's allies were irritated. Here was another example of U.S. egocentrism. The world was expected to dance to the Supreme Court's tune. On December 15 the Far Eastern Commission acted. It declared that the tribunal "is an international court appointed and acting under international authority"—the commission's. The implication was plain: The U.S. courts had no jurisdiction in the matter.

The next day the case was argued before the Court. In his brief U.S. Solicitor General Philip B. Perlman held that irreparable damage would be done if the Supreme Court arrogated to itself the power to review the executive branch's execution of foreign policy. Perlman insisted that MacArthur, in his position of Supreme Commander, "is taking orders only from the Far Eastern Commission."

Justice William O. Douglas, a controversial leader of the court's liberal wing, was startled. "Do you mean an American general who acts for another government as well as this one would be beyond the reach of the Court?"

Perlman replied, "It does in this case."

On December 20, after two days of arguments in public and three days of deliberation in chambers, the Court by a six-to-one vote held that "the courts of the United States have no power or authority to review, to affirm, set aside or annul the judgments and sentences." Jackson did not participate in the vote on the ground that his role at Nuremberg was a conflict of interest, and another justice, who ultimately went along with the majority, did not announce his vote immediately. The defense had arrived at a dead end.

* * *

For seven weeks the Sugamo Seven had awaited the outcome of the legal skirmishing, writing *haiku,* reading Buddhist scripture, playing solitaire. After their sentencing on November 12, they had been returned to Sugamo and transferred to Block 5C, one to a cell. No other prisoners were held in the block, which contained more than fifty cells. The prisoners were kept under twenty-four-hour surveillance by a detail of eight security personnel who were rotated every six hours. Each prisoner was observed every fifteen minutes for respiration and arterial bleeding. The Americans were determined to avoid another Göring episode.

The cells, eight by five and a half feet, each contained a desk, washbasin, and toilet. A *futon* mattress was placed on the floor, and each prisoner was provided with blankets. The cell block was heated, as the days were now growing darker and colder. Double-mesh screens covered the cell windows. The condemned men were provided with Japanese cigarettes one at a time, and they had to be lit by a guard. The electric bulb in each cell was never extinguished.

The defendants sentenced to prison terms were also confined at Sugamo. They were incarcerated in the Blue Block, which had been used for women inmates before the war. A high wall separated the Blue and 5C blocks, but from the second story of the Blue Block the electric lights in the cells of the condemned were readily visible. "Each morning I got up," General Sato confided in his diary; "I would gaze at the Block and say to myself, 'Nothing has happened.' . . . Morning after morning passed like this for more than a month." On the evening of December 22, the day after the defense lost the legal battle in Washington, Sato had a premonition that he would not see the electric lights aglow the following morning.

He was right.

34

Justice on the Gallows

Hanging is a practice of great antiquity and has been inflicted as a signal indignity on a condemned prisoner in a uniquely conspicuous fashion. It is akin to hanging an animal's carcass in a butcher shop. "Thus," concluded a British royal commission of inquiry into capital punishment—coincidentally launched a year after the hangings in Tokyo—"hanging comes to be regarded as a peculiarly grim and derogatory form of execution, suitable for sordid criminals and crimes." Given the fascination of the Japanese with beheading victims, if not bayoneting them, as the trial testimony revealed, it is morbidly interesting that the diary of Master Franz Schmidt, the public executioneer at Nuremberg in the sixteenth century, observed that beheading was a dignified form of execution while hanging was disgraceful, and that the substitution of the sword for the noose at the last minute was viewed as an "act of favor" or clemency.

General Sato, whom the IMTFE sent to prison for life, wrote in his diary of his bitterness over the manner in which the convicted Japanese war criminals were executed. "Aside from the question of whether it was right or wrong to sentence six generals and one premier to death, why were they not sentenced to be shot to death?" Sato inquired. "Even if the tribunal sentenced them to be hanged, MacArthur was empowered to review the sentences. . . . MacArthur did not have even a scintilla of the so-called compassion of the warrior."

Since the executions were being conducted by the U.S. Army, the army's manual of procedures for military executions applied. "The person will be notified of the time of execution no less than twenty-four hours prior thereto," the manual, a restricted document, read. Accordingly, at 9 P.M., December 21, 1948, in alphabetical order, each of the condemned men was led from his cell to a tiny makeshift chapel on the ground floor of Block 5C. Before the Americans took over Sugamo, there had been no chapel. Each prisoner wore formless army work clothes, the letter P for prisoner stamped on the back. With Chaplain Hanayama at his side, the prison commandant, Colonel Morris C. Handwerk, announced, "The execution will take place at 00:01 hours 23 December 1948 at Sugamo Prison." The war criminals took the news quietly, looking ashen and grim; Hirota was glassy-eyed.

As each prisoner left chapel, he was weighed—a portent of things to come. Weights were needed to calculate the "drop." Mercifully, the drop had been developed by trial and error in the last century for the purpose of speeding up the death of the victim—snapping his spinal cord and bringing death almost instantly, instead of permitting him to dangle at the rope's end, slowly suffocating to death or even more slowly dying of apoplexy. There was another problem: If the drop was too long, the convicted person's head might be torn from the body. Hideki Tojo, for example, weighed 130 pounds (he had neither gained nor lost weight in prison); thus, according to the U.S. Army manual of procedure, when the trap was sprung, Tojo would be dropped 7 feet, 7 inches.

At the meeting with Colonel Handwerk, Tojo acted as spokesman. The condemned men's last request was for a simple, Japanese-style meal, perhaps chopped pickles wrapped in cold rice and a cup of saké. Handwerk made no commitment. But the next day, their last day, they dined on rice, *miso* soup, and broiled fish. When Hanayama administered the last rites, each gulped down a cup of rice wine except Kimura, who was not a drinking man and sipped only a little.

December 22 was a cold day, and the dead leaves of the paulownia tree blew across the empty courtyard separating the prison block from the death house. From afar, the other prisoners could see the Sugamo Seven shuffle slowly over the frozen earth of the exercise yard for the last time, each handcuffed to a guard. "Without intending to do so," Yoshio Kodama noted in his diary, "I found my eyes turned away from them." Like other prisoners gazing on the former power brokers of Japan, he could not help wondering whether what he saw was reality or a nightmare. It was a bit of both.

The condemned men spent their final day and evening writing farewell letters and in prayer as Hanayama prepared them for their journey. Muto alone admitted that he had "surges of fear" and confided to Hanayama that "the others have them, too."

At 11:30 P.M. four of the prisoners—Doihara, Matsui, Tojo, and Muto, in that order—each handcuffed to two guards, entered the makeshift chapel, lit candles, burned incense, and, almost inaudibly, chanted Buddhist scripture. They shook hands with one another, softly uttered the word *sayonara,* and accompanied by Hanayama wended their way across the courtyard to their appointment. Matsui, at seventy the oldest of the quartet, now reconciled to his fate, raised a cry of resignation and defiance: "*Banzai! Banzai! Banzai!*" The others joined him. Hanayama left them at the door to the death chamber, which was ablaze with light. Along one wall were two men in dark suits and two generals in uniform—the Australian, American, Chinese, and Russian members of the Far Eastern Commission, whom MacArthur had summoned as witnesses. No Japanese was present other than the condemned men. Unlike the authorities at Nuremberg, MacArthur had barred all photographers and even banned official photographs as documentary evidence that the executions had been carried out. With the compassion of the warrior, MacArthur had spared them the ultimate indignity of having their pictures in death splashed across the world's front pages.

In the center of the room was the elevated platform reached by thirteen steps; four ropes hung from the gallows. Each line was fashioned of one-inch manila hemp. The day before, the ropes had been cut into eighty-foot sections, boiled, and stretched to eliminate springiness, stiffness, or tendency to coil. The hangman's knot, known among ancient mariners as "the knot that stops the wind," had been greased with wax to ensure smooth sliding.

At the foot of the steps the handcuffs were removed from the prisoners, and their arms were pinioned to their sides with two-inch-wide body straps. Slowly they climbed the steps. On the platform, each standing by a rope's bight, their ankles were bound together by a one-inch-wide strap. The noose was now placed snugly around each prisoner's neck, with the knot directly behind the left ear. Placing the knot on the left ensured that it would end up in front when the trap was sprung, throwing the prisoner's neck back violently and snapping his cervical column while rupturing the spinal cord. Misplaced, the knot would travel behind the neck and throw the neck forward. If that happened, the condemned could dangle for a quarter of an hour or more before suffocating to death.

The only known eyewitness account of the executions is Sebald's memoirs. "They seemed to shuffle as they walked, and each face was a vacant stare as it passed me," he wrote. A single word from the officer of the guard crackled: "Proceed!" The traps were sprung. The execution moved so swiftly from life to death—it took one and a half minutes—that as Hanayama recrossed the courtyard to return to his chapel cell and to administer the last rites to the second group, consisting of Itagaki, Hirota, and Kimura, he heard "a loud crash" and involuntarily looked behind him. To Sebald the traps "sounded like a rifle volley."

A medical officer, stethoscope in hand, attended each of the suspended men, whose pants were now discolored by the relaxation of the sphincters and escape of urine and feces. There were also semen stains due to the turgescence of the genital organs as a result of hypostasis, a by-product of violent death. When the officer was satisfied that the men were dead, he summoned the senior medical officer, who confirmed the report and announced, "I declare this man dead." The senior officer delivered these pronouncements as follows: for Doihara at 12:08½ A.M.; for Tojo, 12:10½ A.M.; for Muto, 12:11½ A.M.; and for Matsui, 12:13 A.M. A U.S. Army Graves Registration team cut the bodies down, took fingerprints, and placed the bodies in wooden coffins.

At nineteen minutes after midnight the second group entered the death house. "As they passed me, Hirota turned his head and looked straight into my eyes," Sebald said. "It was an exchange of glances in which he seemed to appeal to me for sympathy and understanding."

Itagaki was pronounced dead at 12:32½ A.M., Hirota at 12:34½ A.M., and Kimura at 12:35 A.M.

The death certificates, signed by the two medical officers and now stored at a U.S. National Archives building in Maryland, simply certified that "we were in attendance at the execution by hanging of . . ." The certificates did not spell out whether death had been instantaneous—whether the cervical vertabrae were fractured—or whether the condemned man had died of asphyxia as a result of the blocking of the air passages. Whatever the case, the Sugamo Seven did not die slowly.

The wooden coffins were now loaded onto an army truck and convoyed in a light rain to the Yokohama Municipal Crematorium, an ugly, squat stucco building perched in a bombed-out ravine and distinguished by a 200-foot smokestack rising above it. Seven iron fireboxes, fueled by wood and coal, consumed the remains of the war criminals. The ashes of the Sugamo Seven were put in four-by-five-inch black boxes that resembled traditional Japanese lunchboxes, taken away, and scattered to the winds. The crematorium was heavily guarded by American sentries with fixed bayonets. "It reminded me of the way Japanese police lined up when Tojo made his wartime tours," Hiroshi Tobita, the head of the facility, said. A Japanese staffer in the United Press Tokyo bureau saw it differently. The unceremonious procedure at the crematorium, he wrote, offered no more dignity than a common garbage incinerator.

The next day, Christmas Eve, MacArthur announced the release of all Class A war-criminal suspects. With an air of finality, his announcement read, "This release completes the disposition of all former major war crimes suspects held in Japan."

With the executions the last international military tribunal in history to sit in judgment of major war criminals concluded its business. In history? Well, Nuremberg was the first, and Tokyo was the last. In the event of a third world war there surely will be nobody left to judge—or to sit in judgment.

The Indicted
Class A
War Criminals

ARAKI, GENERAL SADAO (1877–1966). Minister of war, 1931–34; Supreme War Council, 1934–36; minister of education, 1938–39; senior adviser to the cabinet, 1939–40. An early advocate of Japanese military expansionism. Arrogant and swashbuckling, he depicted the war with China as a "gift of the gods." While education minister, he restructured the Japanese school system along military lines. During the early stages of the Pacific War, he was an important influence on Premier Tojo. Convicted on Counts 1 and 27. Sentenced to life imprisonment. Paroled in 1955.

DOIHARA, GENERAL KENJI (1883–1948). Commander, Kwantung Army, 1938–40; Supreme War Council, 1940–43; army commander in Singapore, 1944–45. From his early days as a military officer, he was a master of intrigue, terrorism, and clandestine operations. Doihara was also deeply involved in the army's drug trafficking in Manchuria. Later, he ran brutal POW and internee camps in Malaya, Sumatra, Java, and Borneo. Convicted on Counts 1, 27, 29, 31, 32, 35, 36, 54. Sentenced to death.

HASHIMOTO, COLONEL KINGORO (1890–1957). Held various commands, including that of an artillery regiment during the Rape of Nanking in 1937. A consummate insider, he was a leader of the fanatical junior officers who were the force behind the assassinations and coups d'état in the 1930s. Hashimoto also played a major role in staging the Mukden Incident, which eventually led to war with China. The author of political books and tracts and of racist propaganda, he was important in mobilizing Japanese public opinion behind the Pacific War. Convicted on Counts 1 and 27. Sentenced to life imprisonment. Paroled in 1954.

HATA, FIELD MARSHAL SHUNROKU (1879–1962). Supreme War Council, 1937; commander, China Expeditionary Force, 1938, 1941–44; minister of war, 1939–40. In the 1930s Hata was one of the warhawks who planned Japan's invasion of China and other foreign adventures. As a field commander, he personally directed the conquest of the city of Hankow and was in overall command of troops who perpetrated countless atrocities against Chinese civilians. Convicted on Counts 1, 27, 29, 31, 32, 55. Sentenced to life imprisonment. Paroled in 1954.

HIRANUMA, BARON KIICHIRO (1867–1952). Privy Council, 1924–39; founder and president, Kokuhonsha (right-wing patriotic society), 1926–28; premier, 1938; minister of home affairs, 1940; minister without portfolio, 1940–41; president, Privy Council, 1945. An autocratic nobleman who was a major political figure in Tokyo, Hiranuma was an early proponent of war who changed his mind in 1943, when he participated in a secret scheme to sue for peace. Convicted on Counts 1, 27, 29, 31, 32, 36. Sentenced to life imprisonment. Paroled in 1955.

HIROTA, BARON KOKI (1878–1948). Ambassador to the Soviet Union, 1928–31; foreign minister, 1933–36; premier, 1936–37. A protégé of Mitsuru Toyama, founder of the powerful Black Dragon secret society, Hirota became the "godfather" of Japanese politics in the early thirties. He was foreign minister during the Rape of Nanking and other atrocities perpetrated by the army. As premier, he led his cabinet in planning the invasions of Southeast Asia and the Pacific islands, in addition to continuing the undeclared war against China. Convicted on Counts 1, 27, 55. Sentenced to death.

HOSHINO, NAOKI (1892–1978). Chief of financial affairs, Manchukuo (Manchuria), 1932–34; director of general affairs (chief civilian officer), Manchukuo, 1936; minister without portfolio, 1940–41; chief cabinet secretary, 1941–44. He directed financing of Japan's occupation of Manchuria through the army's trafficking in drugs there. A fanatical hard-liner, Hoshino drafted the declarations of war against Britain and the United States and was the war's most enthusiastic supporter in the cabinet. Convicted on Counts 1, 27, 29, 31, 32. Sentenced to life imprisonment. Paroled in 1955.

ITAGAKI, GENERAL SEISHIRO (1885–1948). Chief of staff, Kwantung Army, 1936–37; minister of war, 1938–39; chief, army general staff, 1939; commander in Korea, 1941; Supreme War Council, 1943; commander in Singapore, 1945. Another arrogant, ruthless militarist who plotted war in the 1920s and 1930s. Later, troops under his command in China and elsewhere terrorized prisoners and civilians. Itagaki was responsible for prison camps in Java, Sumatra, Malaya, Borneo, and elsewhere. Convicted on Counts 1, 27, 29, 31, 32, 35, 36, 54. Sentenced to death.

KAYA, OKINORI (1889–1977). Minister of finance, 1937–38, 1941–44; president, North China Development Company, 1939–41. An early advocate of selling narcotics to the Chinese to finance the expenses of the occupation forces. At North China Development, Kaya plundered China's industry and exploited her natural resources for Japan's benefit. Later in the war he arranged financing for the Siam-Burma Death Railway, with the knowledge that POWs and civilian slave laborers were building it, often at the cost of their own lives. Convicted on Counts 1, 27, 29, 31, 32. Sentenced to life imprisonment. Paroled in 1955.

KIDO, MARQUIS KOICHI (1889–1977). Chief secretary to the lord keeper of the privy seal, 1930–37; minister of education, 1937; minister of welfare, 1938; minister of home affairs, 1939; lord keeper of the privy seal, 1940–45. A high-ranking imperial chamberlain and practical politician who was Emperor Hirohito's closest adviser during the most critical periods of the wars with China and the Allies. His secret diary, which he kept during all of his time at or near the seat of power, was the prosecution's bible during much of the Tokyo trial. Convicted on Counts 1, 27, 29, 31, 32. Sentenced to life imprisonment. Paroled in 1955.

KIMURA, GENERAL HEITARO (1888–1948). Chief of staff, Kwantung Army, 1940–41; vice minister of war, 1941–43; Supreme War Council, 1943; army commander in Burma, 1944–45. In the War Ministry he helped plan the China and Pacific wars, including surprise attacks. Later, Kimura approved the brutalization of Allied POWs and was the field commander in Burma when civilian and POW slave labor built and died on the Siam-Burma Railway. He was also linked to atrocities against the Burmese civilian population. Convicted on Counts 1, 27, 29, 31, 32, 54, 55. Sentenced to death.

KOISO, GENERAL KUNIAKI (1880–1950). Vice minister of war, 1932; chief of staff, Kwantung Army, 1932–34; army commander in Korea, 1935–38; minister of overseas affairs, 1939; governor-general, Korea, 1942–44; premier 1944–45. A ruthless proponent of Japanese expansionism, Koiso was an important member of the military clique that ran Japan in the 1930s and 1940s. He was known among the Korean population as "the Tiger of Korea" because of his brutality. As premier, he was aware of POW death camps. Convicted on Counts 1, 27, 29, 31, 32, 55. Sentenced to life imprisonment.

MATSUI, GENERAL IWANE (1878–1948). Personal appointee of the emperor to the Geneva Disarmament Conference, 1932–37; commander, China Expeditionary Force, 1937–38. A leader in several of the ultrapatriotic secret societies that flourished in Japan during the 1920s and 1930s. At the disarmament conferences he was in fact a representative of the militarists, who wanted war. Troops under his overall command were responsible for the Rape of Nanking in 1937 and other atrocities. He retired in 1938 and then ceased to play an active role in military affairs. Convicted on Count 55. Sentenced to death.

MATSUOKA, YOSUKE (1880–1946). Japan's chief delegate, League of Nations, 1933; president, South Manchurian Railway, 1935–39; foreign minister, 1939–40. In addition to holding these high positions, Matsuoka was the author of jingoistic books and pamphlets and a fiery public speaker in favor of the military's expansionist policies. An admirer of both Hitler and Stalin, Matsuoka orchestrated the Axis alliance with Germany and Italy and a nonaggression pact with the Soviet Union. Died of tuberculosis early in the trial.

MINAMI, GENERAL JIRO (1874–1955). Minister of war, 1931; Supreme War Council, 1931–34; commander, Kwantung Army, 1934–36; governor-general, Korea, 1936–42; Privy Council, 1942–45. Bullnecked and domineering, Minami was an early leader of the warmongering army clique that controlled Japan in the 1930s and 1940s. After conquering and brutalizing Manchuria and planning the "holy war" against China, he ruled Japan's Korean colony with an iron fist. Convicted on Counts 1 and 27. Sentenced to life imprisonment. Paroled in 1954.

MUTO, GENERAL AKIRA (1892–1948). Vice chief of staff, China Expeditionary Force, 1937; director, Military Affairs Bureau, 1939–42; army commander in Sumatra, 1942–43; army chief of staff in the Philippines, 1944–45. Troops under his command participated in both the Rape of Nanking and the Rape of Manila. Muto also had overall direction of POW camps in Sumatra, where he recruited Indonesians as slave laborers. Convicted on Counts 1, 27, 29, 31, 32, 54, 55. Sentenced to death.

NAGANO, ADMIRAL OSAMI (1880–1947). Delegate to naval disarmament conferences, 1931–33; navy minister, 1936–37; fleet commander, 1937; navy chief of staff, 1941; naval adviser to the emperor, 1944. Early in his career, Nagano was naval attaché to the Japanese Embassy in Washington. In 1941 he was the key planner of the surprise attacks on Pearl Harbor, Hong Kong, Manila, and other areas in the South Pacific. Died of natural causes during the trial.

OKA, ADMIRAL TAKASUMI (1890–1973). Chief, Naval Affairs Bureau, 1940–44; vice minister of the navy, 1944. He was another important participant in planning the surprise attacks perpetrated by Japanese naval forces during the second week in December 1941. Later in the war his bureau issued directives for the transport of Allied POWs and civilian slave laborers aboard the infamous "hellships," on which thousands died. Oka also administered some POW and civilian internee camps on Pacific islands and promulgated orders to shoot survivors of torpedoed Allied ships. Convicted on Counts 1, 27, 29, 31, 32. Sentenced to life imprisonment. Paroled in 1954.

OKAWA, SHUMEI (1886–1957). He held no formal government positions, but Okawa was the major intellectual force behind the rise of the Japanese militarists in the 1930s. He plotted the assassination of two premiers and played a key role in the Mukden Incident. In his writings and his speeches Okawa was an early and outspoken advocate of war with China, the United States, and the European Allies. Afflicted with syphilis and addicted to drugs, he broke down in the courtroom on the first day of the trial. Okawa was sent to a psychiatric ward, from which he was released in 1948, a free man.

OSHIMA, GENERAL HIROSHI (1886–1975). Military attaché in Germany, 1934–38; ambassador to Germany, 1938–39, 1941–45. As a diplomat, he operated more as a representative of the War Ministry than of the Foreign Ministry. A vain, arrogant *bon vivant,* Oshima was considered by many Japanese to be "more Nazi than the Nazis." He helped forge the Axis Pact with Germany and Italy and was an intimate of Hitler, Himmler, Göring, and Ribbentrop. At one point he organized an abortive plot to assassinate Stalin. Convicted on Count 1. Sentenced to life imprisonment. Paroled in 1955.

SATO, GENERAL KENRYO (1895–1975). Section head, then chief, Military Affairs Bureau, 1942–44; assistant chief of staff, China Expeditionary Force, 1944; army commander in Indochina, 1945. An unyielding, remorseless militarist, he boasted after Pearl Harbor that Japan would dictate peace terms in the "enemy capital"—Washington, D.C. As commander in Indochina he approved directives on the transportation and treatment of prisoners of war and civilian internees, many of whom worked as slave labor on the Siam-Burma Railway. Convicted on Counts 1, 27, 29, 31, 32. Sentenced to life imprisonment. Paroled in 1956.

SHIGEMITSU, MAMORU (1887–1957). Ambassador to China, 1931–32; vice minister of foreign affairs, 1933–36; ambassador to the Soviet Union, 1936–38; ambassador to Great Britain, 1938–41; foreign minister, 1943–45. A career diplomat who held important posts in the militarist-dominated governments of the 1930s and 1940s, Shigemitsu nevertheless favored peace with China and an end to the Pacific War. He and General Umezu signed the instrument of surrender in 1945. The Soviets insisted on his indictment. Convicted on Counts 27, 29, 31, 32, 33, 55. Sentenced to seven years in prison. Paroled in 1950, he reentered the political arena and was appointed foreign minister in 1954.

SHIMADA, ADMIRAL SHIGETARO (1883–1976). Vice chief of naval

staff, 1935–37; commander, China Fleet, 1940; navy minister, 1941–44; Supreme War Council, 1944. Suave, unctuous, and weak-minded, he was an uncritical supporter of the militarists. Shimada authorized the naval surprise attacks in December 1941. Later in the war naval units under his overall command massacred Allied POWs, transported prisoners and civilian internees aboard hellships, and killed any surviving crew members of torpedoed Allied ships. Convicted on Counts 1, 27, 29, 31, 32. Sentenced to life imprisonment. Paroled in 1955.

SHIRATORI, TOSHIO (1887–1949). Director, Information Bureau, Foreign Ministry, 1929–33; ambassador to Italy, 1938–40; adviser to the foreign minister, 1940, A career diplomat who was a rabid supporter of military expansionism, he favored an alliance among Germany, Italy, the Soviet Union, and Japan to dominate the world. As ambassador, Shiratori became a confidant of Mussolini and Foreign Minister Ciano and was a key man with Oshima in forging the Axis Pact. Convicted on Count 1. Sentenced to life imprisonment.

SUZUKI, GENERAL TEIICHI (1888–   ). Chief, China Affairs Bureau, 1938–41; president, Cabinet Planning Board, and minister without portfolio, 1941–43; adviser to the cabinet, 1943–44. An early and active supporter of militarism, Suzuki masterminded the mobilization of the Japanese economy during the war. He was also involved in Japan's drug trafficking in China and approved the use of POWs and civilians as slave laborers. Convicted on Counts 1, 27, 29, 31, 32. Sentenced to life imprisonment. Paroled in 1955.

TOGO, SHIGENORI (1884–1948). Ambassador to Germany, 1937; ambassador to the Soviet Union, 1938; foreign minister, 1941–42, 1945. A career diplomat who was removed from his post in Germany because of hostility toward the Nazis, Togo conducted peace negotiations with the United States prior to Pearl Harbor attack. (During the trial he charged that these negotiations had been prolonged on orders from the militarists, who wanted a cover for their surprise attacks.) Convicted on Counts 1, 27, 29, 31, 32. Sentenced to twenty years in prison.

TOJO, GENERAL HIDEKI (1884–1938). Chief, Manchurian secret police, 1935; councillor, Manchurian Affairs Bureau, 1936; chief of staff, Kwantung Army, 1937–38; vice minister of war, 1938; minister of war 1940–44; premier, 1941–44. As wartime premier, Tojo was a virtual dictator, for he also headed the Ministries of Foreign Affairs, Home Affairs, and Education. A stubborn, narrow-minded militarist, he was known as a brilliant tactician and an appalling strategist. The Allies considered the ruthless Tojo to be the arch-criminal of the Pacific War. Conscious of his guilt and ashamed of his defeats, Tojo assumed full responsibility for all the actions of his government and the military during the war. Convicted on Counts 1, 27, 29, 31, 32, 33, 54. Sentenced to death.

UMEZU, GENERAL YOSHIJIRO (1882–1949). Section chief, general staff, 1931–34; commander, China Expeditionary Force, 1934; vice minister of war, 1936–38; commander, Kwantung Army, 1939–44; army chief of staff, 1944–45. Another member of the militarist clique in the army, he emerged as a power broker in the 1930s. Umezu was known in Japan as "the Ivory Mask," a tough, enigmatic leader who was respected and feared by all. With Foreign Minister Shigemitsu he signed the instrument of surrender in 1945. Convicted on Counts 1, 27, 29, 31, 32. Sentenced to life imprisonment.

B

The IMTFE's Findings on the Indictment

In Count 1 of the Indictment it is charged that all the defendants together with other persons participated in the formulation or execution of a common plan or conspiracy. The object of that common plan is alleged to have been that Japan should secure the military, naval, political and economic domination of East Asia and of the Pacific and Indian Oceans, and of all countries and islands therein or bordering thereon, and for that purpose should, alone or in combination with other countries having similar objects, wage a war or wars of aggression against any country or countries which might oppose that purpose.

There are undoubtedly declarations by some of those who are alleged to have participated in the conspiracy which coincide with the above grandiose statement, but in our opinion it has not been proved that these were ever more than declarations of the aspirations of individuals. Thus, for example, we do not think the conspirators ever seriously resolved to attempt to secure the domination of North and South America. So far as the wishes of the conspirators crystallised into a concrete common plan we are of opinion that the territory they had resolved that Japan should dominate was confined to East Asia, the Western and South Western Pacific Ocean and the Indian Ocean, and certain of the islands in these oceans. We shall accordingly treat Count 1 as if the charge had been limited to the above object.

We shall consider in the first place whether a conspiracy with the above object has been proved to have existed.

Already prior to 1928 Okawa, one of the original defendants, who has been discharged from this trial on account of his present mental state, was publicly advocating that Japan should extend her territory on the Continent of Asia by the threat or, if necessary, by use of military force. He also advocated that Japan should seek to dominate Eastern Siberia and the South Sea Islands. He predicted that the course he advocated must result in a war between the East and the West, in which Japan would be the champion of the East. He was encouraged and aided in his advocacy of this plan by the Japanese General Staff. The object of this plan as stated was substantially the object of the conspiracy, as we have defined it. In our review of the facts we have noticed many subsequent declarations of the conspirators as to the object of the conspiracy. These do not vary in any material respect from this early declaration by Okawa.

Already when Tanaka was premier, from 1927 to 1929, a party of military men, with Okawa and other civilian supporters, was advocating this policy of Okawa's that Japan should expand by the use of force. The conspiracy was now in being. It remained in being until Japan's defeat in 1945. The immediate question when Tanaka was premier was whether Japan should attempt to expand her influence on the continent—beginning with Manchuria—by peaceful penetration, as Tanaka and the members of his Cabinet wished, or whether that expansion should be accomplished by the use of force if necessary, as the conspirators advocated. It was essential that the conspirators should have the support and control of the nation. This was the beginning of the long struggle between the conspirators, who advocated the attainment of their object by force, and those politicians and latterly those bureaucrats who advocated Japan's expansion by peaceful measures or at least by a more discreet choice of the occasions on which force should be employed. This struggle culminated in the conspirators obtaining control of the organs of government of Japan and preparing and regimenting the nation's mind and material resources for wars of aggression designed to achieve the object of the conspiracy. In overcoming the opposition the conspirators employed methods which were entirely unconstitutional and at times wholly ruthless. Propaganda and persuasion won many to their side, but military action abroad without Cabinet sanction or in defiance of

Cabinet veto, assassination of opposing leaders, plots to overthrow by force of arms Cabinets which refused to cooperate with them, and even a military revolt which seized the capital and attempted to overthrow the government were part of the tactics whereby the conspirators came ultimately to dominate the Japanese polity.

As and when they felt strong enough to overcome opposition at home and latterly when they had finally overcome all such opposition, the conspirators carried out in succession the attacks necessary to effect their ultimate object, that Japan should dominate the Far East. In 1931 they launched a war of aggression against China and conquered Manchuria and Jehol. By 1934 they had commenced to infiltrate into North China, garrisoning the land and setting up puppet governments designed to serve their purposes. From 1937 onwards they continued their aggressive war against China on a vast scale, overrunning and occupying much of the country, setting up puppet governments on the above model, and exploiting China's economy and natural resources to feed the Japanese military and civilian needs.

In the meantime they had long been planning and preparing a war of aggression which they proposed to launch against the U.S.S.R. The intention was to seize that country's Eastern territories when a favorable opportunity occurred. They had also long recognized that their exploitation of East Asia and their designs on the islands in the Western and South Western Pacific would bring them into conflict with the United States of America, Britain, France and the Netherlands, who would defend their threatened interests and territories. They planned and prepared for war against these countries also.

The conspirators brought about Japan's alliance with Germany and Italy, whose policies were as aggressive as their own, and whose support they desired both in the diplomatic and military fields, for their aggressive actions in China had drawn on Japan the condemnation of the League of Nations and left her friendless in the councils of the world.

Their proposed attack on the U.S.S.R. was postponed from time to time for various reasons, among which were (1) Japan's preoccupation with the war in China, which was absorbing unexpectedly large military resources, and (2) Germany's pact of non-aggression with the U.S.S.R., in 1939, which for the time freed the U.S.S.R. from threat of attack on her Western frontier, and might have allowed her to devote the bulk of her strength to the defence of her Eastern territories if Japan had attacked her.

Then in the year 1940 came Germany's great military successes on the continent of Europe. For the time being Great Britain, France and the Netherlands were powerless to afford adequate protection to their interests and territories in the Far East. The military preparations of the United States were in the initial stages. It seemed to the conspirators that no such favorable opportunity could readily recur of realizing that part of their objective which sought Japan's domination of South-West Asia and the islands in the Western and South Western Pacific and Indian Oceans. After prolonged negotiations with the United States of America, in which they refused to disgorge any substantial part of the fruits they had seized as the result of their war of aggression against China, on 7th December 1941 the conspirators launched a war of aggression against the United States and the British Commonwealth. They had already issued orders declaring that a state of war existed between Japan and the Netherlands as from 00.00 hours on 7th December 1941. They had previously secured a jumping-off place for their attacks on the Philippines, Malaya and the Netherlands East Indies by forcing their troops into French Indo-China under threat of military action if this facility was refused to them. Recognizing the existence of a state of war and faced by the imminent threat of invasion of her Far Eastern territories, which the conspirators had long planned and were now about to execute, the Netherlands in self-defence declared war on Japan.

These far-reaching plans for waging wars of aggression, and the prolonged and intricate preparation for and waging of these wars of aggression were not the work of one man. They were the work of many leaders acting in pursuance of a common plan for the achievement of a common object. That common object, that they should secure Japan's domination by preparing and waging wars of aggression, was a criminal object. Indeed no more grave crimes can be conceived of than a conspiracy to wage a war of aggression or the waging of a war of aggression, for the conspiracy threatens the security of the peoples of the world, and the waging disrupts it. The probable result of such a conspiracy, and the inevitable result of its execution, is that death and suffering will be inflicted on countless human beings.

The Tribunal does not find it necessary to consider whether there was a conspiracy to wage wars in violation of the treaties, agreements and assurances specified in the particulars annexed to Count 1. The conspiracy to wage wars of aggression was already criminal in the highest degree.

The Tribunal finds that the existence of the criminal conspiracy to wage wars of aggression as alleged in Count 1, with the limitation as to object already mentioned, has been proved.

The question whether the defendants or any of them participated in that conspiracy will be considered when we deal with the individual cases.

The conspiracy existed for, and its execution occupied, a period of many years. Not all of the conspirators were parties to it at the beginning, and some of those who were parties to it had ceased to be active in its execution before the end. All of those who at any time were parties to the criminal conspiracy or who at any time with guilty knowledge played a part in its execution are guilty of the charge contained in Count 1.

In view of our findings on Count 1 it is unnecessary to deal with Counts 2 and 3, which charge the formulation or execution of conspiracies with objects more limited than that which we have found proved under Count 1, or with Count 4, which charges the same conspiracy as Count 1 but with more specification.

Count 5 charges a conspiracy wider in extent and with even more grandiose objects than that charged in Count 1. We are of opinion that although some of the conspirators clearly desired the achievement of these grandiose objects, nevertheless there is not sufficient evidence to justify a finding that the conspiracy charged in Count 5 has been proved.

For the reasons given in an earlier part of this judgment we consider it unnecessary to make any pronouncement on Counts 6 to 26 and 37 to 53. There remain therefore only Counts 27 to 36 and 54 and 55, in respect of which we now give our findings.

Counts 27 to 36 charge the crime of waging wars of aggression and wars in violation of international law, treaties, agreements and assurances against the countries named in those counts.

In the statement of facts just concluded we have found that wars of aggression were waged against all those countries with the exception of the Commonwealth of the Philippines (Count 30) and the Kingdoms of Thailand (Count 34). With reference to the Philippines, as we have heretofore stated, that Commonwealth during the period of the war was not a completely sovereign State and so far as international relations were concerned it was a part

of the United States of America. We further stated that it is beyond doubt that a war of aggression was waged in the Philippines,
but for the sake of technical accuracy we consider the aggressive
war in the Philippines as being a part of the war of aggression
waged against the United States of America.

Count 28 charges the waging of a war of aggression against the
Republic of China over a lesser period of time than that charged
in Count 27. Since we hold that the fuller charge contained in
Count 27 has been proved, we shall make no pronouncement on
Count 28.

Wars of aggression having been proved, it is unnecessary to
consider whether they were also wars otherwise in violation of
international law or in violation of treaties, agreements and assurances. The Tribunal finds therefore that it has been proved that
wars of aggression were waged as alleged in Counts 27, 29, 31,
32, 33, 35 and 36.

Count 54 charges ordering, authorizing and permitting the
commission of Conventional War Crimes. Count 55 charges failure to take adequate steps to secure the observance and prevent
breeches of conventions and laws of war in respect of prisoners
of war and civilian internees. We find that there have been cases
in which crimes under both those Counts have been proved.

Consequent upon the foregoing findings, we proposed to consider the charges against individual defendants in respect only of
the following Counts: Numbers 1, 27, 29, 31, 32, 33, 35, 36, 54
and 55.

Selected Bibliography

Brines, Russell. *MacArthur's Japan*. Philadelphia: J. B. Lippin-cott, 1948.

Brooks, Lester. *Behind Japan's Surrender*. New York: McGraw-Hill, 1948.

Browne, Courtney. *Tojo: The Last Banzai*. London: Angus and Robertson, 1967.

Butow, Robert. *Japan's Decision to Surrender*. Palo Alto, Calif.: Stanford University Press, 1954.

———. *Tojo and the Coming of the War*. Princeton, N.J.: Princeton University Press, 1961.

Coughlin, William J. *Conquered Press: The MacArthur Era in Journalism*. Palo Alto, Calif.: Pacific Books, 1952.

Feis, Herbert. *Japan Subdued*. Princeton, N.J.: Princeton University Press, 1961.

Fleisher, Wilfred. *What to Do with Japan*. New York: Doubleday, 1945.

Gimenez, Pedro M. *Under the Shadow of the Kempi*. Manila: A. Narvaez, 1946.

Glueck, Sheldon. *War Criminals*. New York: Kraus Reprint Corp., 1966.

Grew, Joseph C. *Ten Years in Japan*. New York: Simon & Schuster, 1944.

Hanayama, Shinso. *The Way of Deliverance: Three Years with the Condemned Japanese War Criminals*. New York: Charles Scribner's Sons, 1950.

Ike, Nobutaka, ed. and trans. *Japan's Decision for War: Records of the 1941 Policy Conference*. Palo Alto, Calif.: Stanford University Press, 1967.

Kato, Masuo. *The Lost War*. New York: Alfred A. Knopf, 1946.

Keenan, Joseph, and Brendan Brown. *Crimes Against International Law*. Washington, D.C.: Public Affairs Press, 1950.

Kido, Koichi. *Diary of Koichi Kido,* Tokyo: Tokyo University Press, 1966.

Kodama, Yoshio. *Sugamo Diary*. Japan: Radiopress, 1960.

Konoye, Fumimaro. *The Memoirs of Prince Fumimaro Konoye*. Tokyo: Okuyama, 1946.

Layton, Edwin T., with Roger Pineau and John Costello. *"And I Was There": Pearl Harbor and Midway—Breaking the Secrets*. New York: William Morrow, 1985.

Lewe Van Aduard, E. J. *Japan from Surrender to Peace*. The Hague: M. Nijhoff, 1953.

Lewis, John R. *Uncertain Judgment: A Bibliography of War Crimes Trials*. Santa Barbara, Calif.: Clio Books, 1979.

Lu, David J. *From the Marco Polo Bridge to Pearl Harbor*. Washington, D.C.: Public Affairs Press, 1961.

Meskill, Johanna Menzel. *Hitler and Japan: The Hollow Alliance*. New York: Atherton Press, 1966.

Minear, Richard. *Victor's Justice*. Princeton, N.J.: Princeton University Press, 1971.

Mosley, Leonard. *Hirohito: Emperor of Japan*. Englewood Cliffs, N.J.: Prentice-Hall, 1966.

Neumann, William L. *The Genesis of Pearl Harbor*. Philadelphia: Pacifist Research Bureau, 1945.

Oya, Soichi, ed. *Japan's Longest Day*. London: Souvenir Press, 1963.

Piccigallo, Philip. *The Japanese on Trial*. Austin, Tex.: University of Texas Press, 1979.

Russell, E.F.L. *The Knights of Bushido*. New York: E. P. Dutton, 1958.

Sato, Kenryo. *Greater East Asia War Memoirs*. Tokyo: Tokuma Shoten, 1966.

Shigemitsu, Mamoru. *Japan and her Destiny,* ed. by F.S.G. Piggott. New York: E. P. Dutton, 1958.

Shimomura, Kainan. *A Secret History of the War's End*. Tokyo: Kamakura Bunko, 1948.

Tiltman, Nessell. *Nightmares Must End*. London: Mayflower Press, 1940.

Togo, Shigenori. *The Cause of Japan*. New York: Simon & Schuster, 1956.

Toland, John. *The Rising Sun*. New York: Random House, 1970.

Tolischus, Otto D. *Tokyo Record*. New York: Reynal & Hitchcock, 1943.

UN War Crimes Commission. *History of the United Nations War Crimes Commission and the Development of the Laws of War*. London: His Majesty's Stationery Office, 1948.

van der Post, Laurens. *The Prisoner and the Bomb*. New York: William Morrow, 1971.

Ward, Robert E., and Frank J. Shulman. *The Allied Occupation of Japan*. Chicago: American Library Association, 1972.

Warner, Denis A. *The Sacred Warriors: Japan's Suicide Legions*. New York: Van Nostrand Reinhold, 1982.

Wheeler, Keith. *The Fall of Japan*. Alexandria, Va.: Time-Life Books, 1983.

Willoughby, Charles. *Shanghai Conspiracy*. New York: E. P. Dutton, 1952.

Wolfinger, Jarritus. *Preliminary Inventory of the Record of the International Military Tribunal for the Far East*. Washington, D.C.: National Archives and Records Service, PI 180/RG 238, General Services Administration.

Index

2885 019